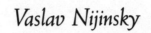

Vaslav Nijinsky

VASLAV NIJINSKY
A Leap into Madness

by Peter Ostwald

A LYLE STUART BOOK
Published by Carol Publishing Group

Copyright © 1991 by Peter Ostwald

A Lyle Stuart Book
Published by Carol Publishing Group

Editorial Offices
600 Madison Avenue
New York, NY 10022

Sales & Distribution Offices
120 Enterprise Avenue
Secaucus, NJ 07094

In Canada: Musson Book Company
A division of General Publishing Co. Limited
Don Mills, Ontario

Manufactured in the United States of America

10 9 8 7 6 5 4 3 2 1

Carol Publishing Group books are available at special discounts
for bulk purchases, for sales promotions, fund raising, or
educational purposes. Special editions can also be created to
specifications. For details contact: Special Sales Department,
Carol Publishing Group, 120 Enterprise Ave., Secaucus, NJ 07094

Library of Congress Cataloging-in-Publication Data

Ostwald, Peter F.
    Vaslav Nijinsky : a leap into madness / by Peter Ostwald.
        p.   cm.
    "A Lyle Stuart book."
    Includes bibliographical references and index.
    ISBN 0–8184–0535–X (cloth) :
    1. Nijinsky, Vaslav, 1890–1950.   2. Ballet dancers—Russian
S.F.S.R.—Biography.   I.   Title.
    GV1785.N6088   1991
792.8'092—dc20   90-20646
    [B]   CIP

To
Chantal and David

Contents

Nijinsky's art ranks so high in the
history of human achievement that
the slightest detail is both important
and essential, provided it throws some
light on his unusual gifts.
                    Prince Peter Lieven[1]

Preface

This book explores the origins, manifestations, and treatment of Vaslav Nijinsky's madness. The successful first half of his life has become legendary, but his breakdowns and terrible decline have never been fully described. "What really happened to our father?" I was asked by Nijinsky's daughters when we first met. No one seemed to know. There were many myths, to be sure, and lots of gossip: he went mad because Diaghilev rejected him; he wasn't really mad; his wife drove him crazy; he never danced again; he died in an insane asylum; he was cured with insulin treatment—all untrue. So I decided to reconstruct his career, giving equal weight to the early years, when he was one of the world's most glamorous performers, and to the later years, when he was a tragic invalid.

The life of Vaslav Nijinsky has intrigued me since medical school when, as an usher in the San Francisco War Memorial Opera House, I saw many ballets, including *Petrushka,* starring Léonide Massine in what had been one of Nijinsky's favorite roles. We often heard concerts conducted by Pierre Monteux, who had also been with the Diaghilev company. Igor Stravinsky himself frequently appeared in San Francisco as guest conductor for the ballet and the symphony. What was said about Nijinsky—the glitter as well as the gloom—not only seemed fascinating, but disturbing. After reading his purported "Diary," and Romola Nijinsky's two books, I felt confused and sensed there must be much more to this case than meets the eye.[2]

It was very helpful to see what dance critics like Geoffrey Whitworth, Cyril Beaumont, and Edwin Denby had to say. And the books by Paul Magriel, Françoise Reiss, Vera Krasovskaya, and Derek Parker; the remarkable biography and other contributions of Richard Buckle; Valentine Gross's delightful sketches; and Lincoln Kirstein's epic *Nijinsky Dancing*—all gave valuable insights into this man's career.[3] Also very important were the observations about Nijinsky by Anatole Bourman, Alexandre Benois, Tamara Karsavina, Misia Sert, Serge Lifar, Anton Dolin, Lydia Sokolova, and others who had known him personally (Lydia Lopokova's letters appeared just as my book went to press; thus it was too late to review them). But nowhere could I find information about Nijinsky's psychiatric problems beyond what his wife Romola had told (or made up) in her books and interviews. As Richard Buckle points out, Nijinsky's life consisted of "ten years growing; ten years learning; ten years dancing; thirty years in eclipse."[4] The first twenty years have been beautifully described by Bronislava Nijinska, his sister and companion in growing and learning.[5] His ten years of dancing are known to everyone who is familiar with the Diaghilev era.[6] But what about those "thirty years in eclipse"?

My decision to do the necessary research was not free of conflict. From the beginning I realized that a book about his madness would probably be upsetting to those who prefer to remember Nijinsky as "the most prodigiously adulated virtuoso in ballet history."[7] It was not my wish to detract from this image in any way. And yet, to show a genius as a madman might, I felt, be interpreted as criticism of Nijinsky. Surely there has been enough of that. I hope that what I have discovered will make people more appreciative of his contribution to the ballet and more tolerant not only of Nijinsky as a person, but also of Diaghilev and Romola, who have often been unfairly blamed for his downfall. I also had ethical reservations about disclosing the private agonies and sometimes horribly psychotic behavior of Vaslav Nijinsky. As a practicing psychiatrist, I know that many of the shocking things we see in hospitals cannot be made public. Therefore, I consulted with colleagues and with an expert in medical ethics before completing this book. Their feeling was that the facts, if honestly reported, can do no harm. More than anyone else, it was Nijinsky himself who helped me to resolve this dilemma. In a notebook written at the beginning of his leap into madness, the great dancer stated: "I want to tell the truth. . . . I do not want to offend people. . . . I cannot keep silent. . . . I must speak." He said that he wanted to write a book about his "life, death, and feelings," and that this book ought to be "published in many thousands of copies."[8]

Without the approval and cooperation given me by Tamara and Kyra Nijinsky, the research for this book could not have been done. There was understandable reluctance at first. "Don't the dead have the right to rest in peace?" Tamara asked during our initial interview in Phoenix, Arizona. Only after agreeing to show the Nijinskys all my findings and to publish nothing of which they disapproved did I contact the various hospitals and medical offices involved in this case. After that, when we realized how much valuable information about Nijinsky had never been used by his previous biographers, the daughters became more and more interested in the research and contributed all kinds of additional documents as well as extremely valuable insights. I am deeply grateful for access to the family archives.

What about Nijinsky's medical records, doctors' reports, and nurses' notes? I knew that these would not wait indefinitely for a historian. Many hospitals have a policy of destroying old records after a certain number of years. Files also get lost during wars, revolutions, and other social upheavals. When I arrived in Kreuzlingen, Switzerland, where Nijinsky had spent many years as a patient, I found the famous Bellevue Sanatorium unoccupied, the beautiful park where he often went walking overgrown with weeds, the buildings dilapidated and ready to be demolished. Miraculously, his medical file had been stored for safekeeping in the library of Tübingen University, along with 6,000 other case records. I was equally lucky with Nijinsky's medical records from the Cantonal Hospital in Münsingen, and the substantial documentation by doctors in St. Moritz, Zürich, Budapest, Vienna, and London. In Leningrad, thanks to *glasnost*, it was possible to locate Nijinsky's personnel and medical files in the State Historical Archives of the USSR. They revealed, to everyone's surprise, that as early as 1910, when Nijinsky was only twenty-one years old and not yet dancing full time for Diaghilev, he had received a psychiatric diagnosis from one of the St. Petersburg physicians who was asked to evaluate his pattern of recurring disability.

Questions about Nijinsky's diagnosis will concern us from time to time in this book, and because no autopsy was performed, some of these will always remain unanswerable. Many people today think that Nijinsky was schizophrenic. In reviewing the documentation, we find that he was given a variety of diagnoses, including neurasthenia, depression, mania, epileptic-twilight states, catatonia, and paranoia, not to mention conditions such as obesity, dancer's heart, hypertension, arteriosclerosis, and uremia. In presenting his case to colleagues, I was impressed with the fact that almost no one today would consider him to have been afflicted with schizophrenia. Romola Nijinsky, too, was thought to be mentally ill at times, and diagnosed to be "hysterical," "paranoid," and "psychopathic." This kind of technical jargon is meaningless unless it is put into a historical perspective, and I will try to do that throughout the book.

It could not have been written without the help and advice of numerous people. I would like to acknowledge and thank them.

To members of the Nijinsky family, his daughters Kyra and Tamara, his granddaughter Kinga Gaspers, and his niece Irina Nijinska Raetz (Bronislava's daughter, who graciously received me into her home in Los Angeles), I owe the greatest debt. Another family that was extremely helpful is that of Dr. Ludwig Binswanger, the psychoanalyst who accepted Nijinsky as a patient in 1918. Thanks to his son, Dieter Binswanger, M.D., I was able to gain access to the confidential material in the Tübingen Archives, and obtain assistance in interpreting it. Wolfgang Binswanger, M.D., also helped substantially by giving me first-hand information about the personnel and everyday happenings in his father's sanatorium when Nijinsky was a patient there. Dr. Norman Elrod and Mrs. Dorothy Taylor gave me additional insights into the atmosphere of the Bellevue Sanatorium.

Professors Manfred Bleuler and Klaus Ernst helped to locate case records at the Burghölzli Institute, including Eugen Bleuler's evaluation of Nijinsky. Heinz Balmer, M.D., Professor of the History of Medicine at the University of Zürich, gave invaluable assistance in identifying the doctor who had treated Nijinsky in St. Moritz. Jean-Pierre Panchard, M.D., Director of the Psychiatric Hospital in Münsingen, Switzerland, allowed me to review all of Nijinsky's medical records in that institution. Ms. Tina Tesfai gave me access to material in the city archives of St. Moritz, and there were others in Switzerland who shared invaluable information.

In Germany I was greatly aided by Dr. Volker Shäfer, Archivist of the

Tübingen University Library, and Professor Fichtner of the Department of Medical History at Tübingen University. Professors Walter Bräutigam and Helm Stierlin of Heidelberg University reviewed the Nijinsky case for me and helped me to understand the status of European psychiatry in the first half of the twentieth century. In England, Mr. David Leonard let me have copies of medical documents sold to Dance Books Ltd. by Romola Nijinsky. Mr. Richard Buckle took time to tell me about his biographical research on Diaghilev and Nijinsky. Ms. Asya Chorley helped me with documents pertaining to the Diaghilev era that have passed through Sotheby's in London. Dr. Martin Bax found information for me about Nijinsky's physicians in London and the hospital where he died.

In Leningrad, Professor August Shereshevsky not only opened doors and provided me with an excellent Russian translator, Mrs. Svetlana Melenevskya, but together with other colleagues at the Bekhterev Psychoneurological Research Institute shed light on the practice of czarist and soviet psychiatry.

In Paris, Mme Nicole Wild provided access to documents in the Bibliothèque de l'Opéra, Mme Françoise Stanciu-Reiss cordially discussed the results of her own research, and M. Jean-Michel Pourvoyeur gave valuable information and pictorial documents.

In Budapest, Mr. Michael Cenner has been of continuing help in obtaining medical as well as family documents on Nijinsky. (Tamara Nijinsky translated these from Hungarian into English. Lise Deschamps Ostwald helped to translate documents from French into English. I am personally responsible, unless noted otherwise, for the translation of all documents originally in German.) Thanks also to psychiatric colleagues at Lipótmezö Hospital for showing me the ward where Nijinsky was confined, and to Mr. Nicholas Paszty for helping me locate records there.

In the United States I received advice from Professor Paul Robinson of Stanford University and Mr. Faubian Bowers in New York about studies of European and Russian history of the late nineteenth and early twentieth centuries. Professor Simon Karlinsky of the University of California in Berkeley translated parts of the Nijinsky "Diary" and gave insights into Russian culture during the Diaghilev period. Mrs. Nancy Van Norman Baer of the De Young Museum in San Francisco, and Professor Alessandra Comini of Southern Methodist University in Dallas provided important information about the art of that era. Mrs.

Millicent Hodson-Archer, during a visit of the Joffrey Ballet, discussed with me certain aspects of Nijinsky's choreographic work. Professor Paul Ekman of the University of California consulted with me on facial expressions in various Nijinsky photographs. Hugo Taussig, M.D., of New Bedford, Massachusetts, gave me information about Dr. Clare Haas, one of Nijinsky's physicians. Mr. Daniel Gesmer of Rockford, Illinois, gave me access to his very comprehensive bibliography on Nijinsky. Mr. Richard Stootz of San Francisco lent me books from his fine collection. Librarians at the University of California, the Performing Arts Archives in San Francisco, and the Dance Collection of The New York Public Library were extremely helpful in obtaining resource material. At the School of Medicine of the University of California in San Francisco, where I work, I have received exceptional support from Drs. Leon Epstein, Carroll Brodsky, Frank Johnson, and Jurgen Ruesch of the Department of Psychiatry, and from professional colleagues in the Health Program for Performing Artists, an organization we have formed in order to better understand, evaluate, and treat talented people who have undergone a long period of training, have entered an extremely competitive work environment, and are exceptionally vulnerable to a variety of physical and psychological stresses.[9]

It has been greatly advantageous to receive criticism and guidance from readers of the preliminary manuscript, including Carol Weed, M.D., Joseph Stephens, M.D., members of the Nijinsky family, Mr. Glenn Allen, Ms. Renee Renouf, Lillian Bennett, M.D., Alexandra Botwin, Ph.D., and Wolfgang Lederer, M.D. Dr. Emilio Romero of San Antonio, Texas, and Mr. Brett Kahr of London discussed with me aspects of Nijinsky's psychodynamics. Other colleagues who have given technical and diagnostic help with the Nijinsky case include Alan Lockwood, M.D., Raphael Reider, M.D., Jonathan Mueller, M.D., Richard Norris, M.D., Alan Stone, M.D., Ph.D., James Morrison, M.D., Eric Heydt, M.D., and Edward Green, D.D.S. In terms of learning about aspects of ballet technique, I am indebted to teachers at the San Francisco Ballet Company, and to Joanna Harris, Ph.D., Carla Guggenheim, D.O., and other friends in the dance community.

I am grateful to Professors Dianne Middlebrook and Barbara Babcock of Stanford University for inviting me to participate on a regular basis in their seminar on biography at the Institute for Research on Women and Gender; also to Professor Eric T. Carlson for letting me present preliminary findings on Nijinsky to the History of Psychiatry seminar at Payne Whitney Clinic in New York; and for opportunities to speak about Nijinsky to the Bay Area History of Medicine Club, the American Psychoanalytic Association, the American Medical Writers Association, and the Department of Psychiatry of Herrick Hospital.

My friend Mario Sartori, who helped at the beginning with matters of publication, died before the book went to press, and I mourn his loss. Patrick O'Connor has given me very valuable editorial advice. Carole Stuart has been a marvelously supportive person to work with. Above all, the love, encouragement, and artistic influence of my wife Lise Deschamps Ostwald made it possible for *Vaslav Nijinsky* to see the light of day.

Peter Ostwald
San Francisco
July 14, 1990

NOTES

1. Prince Peter Lieven, *The Birth of Ballets-Russes*, 316.
2. Romola Nijinsky, *Nijinsky*; Romola Nijinsky, *The Last Years of Nijinsky*; Romola Nijinsky (editor), *The Diary of Vaslav Nijinsky*.
3. Geoffrey Whitworth, *The Art of Nijinsky*; Cyril W. Beaumont, *Vaslav Nijinsky*; Edwin Denby, *Dance Writings*; Paul Magriel, *Nijinsky, an Illustrated Monograph*; Françoise Reiss, *Nijinsky, A Biography*; Vera Krasovskaya, *Nijinsky*; Derek Parker, *Nijinsky, God of the Dance*; Richard Buckle, *Nijinsky*; Valentine Gross, *Nijinsky on Stage*; Lincoln Kirstein, *Nijinsky Dancing*.
4. Richard Buckle, *Nijinsky*, 443 in the hardcover edition, 538 in the revised edition; (Hereafter, the revised edition will be cited as RBN.)
5. Bronislava Nijinska, *Early Memoirs*.
6. Lynn Garafola, *Diaghilev's Ballets Russes*.
7. Alan M. Kingman, in Judith, Lynne Hanna, *Dance, Sex and Gender*, 129.
8. Vaslav Nijinsky, unpublished notebook on "Death," 91. (Hereafter, cited as Notebook on "Death.")
9. Robert Sataloff, Alice Brandfonbrener, and Richard Lederman (editors), *Textbook of Performing-Arts Medicine*.

*There is no great genius without a
touch of dementia.*
                    Seneca[1]

Introduction

Genius and Some of Its Hazards

Dancing is the most natural and instinctive of all the arts. It consists of motion organized in space—of patterned movement—an innate property of life. The spermatozoon twists and flagellates, propelling itself into the undulating ovum to produce a zygote, which explodes into embryonic action. Only a few weeks later, the human embryo, less than two centimeters long, is a dancing organism, flexing and extending its limbs, twisting the neck and trunk, swallowing, and moving the chest. Soon the mother begins to feel such activities within her abdomen, and if she wishes, they can be shown to her by means of sonography, a safe technique for visualizing the fetus before it is born. Once the baby arrives, its innate movement patterns are of course quite obvious. They are symmetrical and seem much looser and floppier than those of an older child. The newborn's thighs, for example, can be rotated, so that the knees and toes point sideways rather than straight ahead. This natural movement is exactly the same as what dancers call "turnout," a standard position for the legs in classical ballet. And if you hold an infant up and let its feet touch a surface, it will make steplike movements resembling a dance. Gradually, more complex actions are organized into the child's behavior. Crying gives way to articulated expressions of pain and distress. Babbling turns into speech, and cooing becomes laughter and joy. The infantile flapping of arms and legs resembles swimming and dancing movements. These evolve into "mature" forms of locomotion—crawling and walking—and a large repertoire of postures and gestures used for communication.

If we listen to what dancers tell us about their childhood it will become apparent that an interest in movement and learning how to control it develops very early. "I started off toddling, at first fairly straight," recalls Tamara Karsavina. "Then my feet carried me faster and faster till I could not follow them. Father caught me up just in time." Anton Dolin remembers his early fascination with heights. "I always seemed to be climbing something." And when he fell, it was comforting to be picked up in his brother's "strong arms" and be carried home. Anna Pavlova remembers being entranced by the fairyland of ballet at age eight, when she was taken to the theater for the first time. "I could not withhold a shout of delight." She told her mother that she wanted to dance like "the pretty lady who plays the part of the Princess." Strong emotions are obviously associated with these early experiences, and persons older and more powerful than the child play an important role in guiding his or her first adventures in dancing. But exactly how and why certain children are especially gifted and become prodigies is not clear.[2]

The nineteenth-century French neurologist Jean Charcot proposed that some human brains may be innately designed to favor vision, others to excel in the realm of sound, and still others in "kinesthesia," or the art of movement. More recently, the Harvard psychologist Howard Gardner has expanded this idea to include at least seven different "domains" of behavior for which certain children seem to be "pretuned" or have "special intelligence." These include the ability to excel in mathematics, abstract reasoning, music, athletics, verbalization, spatial relationships, and dealing with people.[3] Some examples come to mind: pianist Glenn Gould sensed long before he was able to talk that within him resided a special capacity for making music; physicist Albert Einstein was attracted so powerfully to abstract and mathematical modes of thinking that speaking often proved to be impossible when he was a child and people assumed he was mentally retarded; the Brontë sisters did miraculous things with words on tiny slips of paper when they were very young; and sculptor Michelangelo, long before completing his adolescence, impressed the Medicis with his immense artistic genius.

But having a pretuned or specially intelligent brain does not ensure success in the prospering of great talent. A suitable environment is needed for the extraordinary child. Again, we do not know exactly what it has to be. In some cases, one finds adversity. Charles Chaplin had an alcoholic father, who abandoned the family, and a psychotic mother who could not take care of him properly. As a small child, he had to pinch-hit for his sick mother in vaudeville, the beginning of a spectacular career as comedian, actor, and filmmaker. In other instances there was affluence. Felix Mendelssohn received steady guidance from his parents and a very fine education. Often, although not invariably, there seems to be a match between what a parent wants the child to accomplish and the child's exceptional ability. Wolfgang Amadeus Mozart's father, for example, was himself an outstanding musician and a teacher who knew how to foster the boy's amazing virtuosity. Pablo Picasso had a father with great facility as a painter, and this too seems to have evoked genius in the child. Yehudi Menuhin's mother dedicated herself fiercely to the production of prodigies. She found the best teachers for her gifted son and two daughters and made sure they would practice and succeed.

Family support is not enough, however. The social structure has to be receptive to a prodigy's strivings, and the time must be right for a particular form of excellence to be appreciated. Thus, one observes clusters of genius—during the Italian Renaissance, for example, with its crop of magnificent painters, or in Central Europe, where an abundance of great composers was generated during the eighteenth and nineteenth centuries. Russia for the past one hundred years or so has been producing extraordinary dancers, and the United States has recently amassed a cohort of computer geniuses. This "co-incidence" between prodigy and environment has been studied by the psychologist David Henry Feldman. It is a fascinating process, with the child's exceptional talent forcing the environment to respond or to resist, while the parents and other social influences exert pressure in molding the child's personality and in determining the direction "genius" will take.[4]

We have no idea how many prodigies actually survive this process of selection and molding. Compared to the large number of children with vitality, talent, and "creativity," the cohort of geniuses seems small. Is there something in the environment that works against a very brilliant, supremely gifted child—a sort of social inertia tending to inhibit originality and genius, or possibly to destroy it? (Oscar Wilde once quipped that "the public is wonderfully tolerant; it forgives everything except genius.") Or does exceptional talent carry with it the seeds of its own destruction? This was one of the debates among nineteenth-century eugenicists. Some scientists even regarded genius as unhealthy, invariably connected to "madness," like opposite sides of the same coin. Many greatly talented people seemed to die young in those days, or to go crazy. We now know that these tragedies often were a result of poor diet or physical injuries that can disable people when they are young, or infectious diseases like tuberculosis and syphilis, which are treatable today. Yet the idea that genius and poor health go together persists. The German psychiatrist Wilhelm Lange-Eichbaum compiled hundreds of such cases for his classic treatise about "Genius, Madness, and Fame."[5]

Vaslav Nijinsky is a good example of someone with exceptional talent who was nurtured by his environment, became a child prodigy, was catapulted to fame, fell ill, and went mad. It may be somewhat strange to think of him as a genius. (Goethe observed that in Germany all geniuses were once thought to be "short, weak, or hunchbacked. But commend me to a genius who has a well-proportioned body!") Nijinsky made his mark on the world with his phenomenal body, which could dance, leap, and create extraordinary roles on stage. He was the greatest male dancer of his generation, perhaps of the twentieth century. It is often said that he "invented" the male dancer of our time. Not only that, but Nijinsky also created a completely new style of ballet, with choreography that used movements and expressions never before seen in the theater. He also tried, but less successfully, to be a painter and a composer. Finally, he wrote one of the most moving pieces of self-analysis in the history of the performing arts, a series of notebooks about what it felt like to be a genius turning into a "lunatic." There can be little doubt that Vaslav Nijinsky, like other great artists of his time (Schönberg in music, Joyce in literature, Picasso in painting), expanded the boundaries of human consciousness.[6]

Unfortunately, Nijinsky was also someone who suffered greatly because of certain handicaps that he carried with him from childhood. As Feldman points out, "prodigies are specialists in the extreme, pretuned and preorganized to seek expression for a set of highly specific capabilities; [thus] they may find themselves without some of the more general skills needed to negotiate a place in the existing culture."[7] While Nijinsky excelled in body movement and dramatic communication, he lacked verbal ability—he could never speak or write very fluently or coherently and thus remained handicapped in organizing his life, taking care of practical matters, negotiating contracts, and getting along with people. He also had a tendency to be depressed, to isolate himself, and to withdraw from social contacts. These are serious handicaps for someone in the performing arts who must excel in public, less so perhaps for writers, painters, or composers, who can work leisurely in private. Nijinsky needed an audience, and as his emotional problems worsened over the years, he engaged more and more in odd posturing, stubborn silence, and violent temper tantrums. Many people felt then, and still do today, that these were symptoms of madness.

The life of a dancer is hazardous. Enormous demands are made on the body, and the incidence of physical injury is very high (eighty percent, according to a recent study).[8] In addition, there are the constant stresses and strains of having to do one's best in front of an audience and the fear of failure (not to mention the fear of success, which brings added responsibility and even more stress). To be a superstar—Nijinsky was one of the first in our century—also exposes a performer to exploitation from those who seek to bask in his fame, share the heat of the spotlight, and make money. This adds to the hazards of being hugely successful, as Nijinsky was for half of his life. But then he succumbed to crippling mental disease and agonizing physical decay. This is a tragedy worth pondering. It may also teach us how to better understand and appreciate the struggles of great artists and, we hope, to keep them in good health. For these are the pioneers of human culture, the men and women who make life worth living for all of us.

NOTES

1. Seneca, *De tranquillitate animi*, vol. 15, c. 62.
2. Tamara Karsavina, *Theatre Street*, 16; Anton Dolin, *Last Words*, 3; Keith Money, *Anna Pavlova*, 3.
3. Howard Gardner, *Frames of Mind*.
4. David Henry Feldman, with Lynn T. Goldman, *Nature's Gambit*.
5. Wilhelm Lange-Eichbaum, *Genie, Irrsinn, und Ruhm*. For further discussion of the "genius-madness" problem, see Ray Porter, *A Social History of Madness*.
6. H. Stuart Hughes, *Consciousness and Society*.
7. Feldman, 10.
8. Ann P. McNeal, Andrea Watkins, Priscilla M. Clarkson, and Isabel Tremblay, "Lower Extremity Alignment and Injury ..."

Vaslav Nijinsky

Russia is love, Russia is my mother.
I love my mother.
Vaslav Nijinsky[1]

Chapter 1

The Eighth Wonder of the World

Vaslav Nijinsky was born in Russia at a time when the art of ballet was in a state of rapid development. His parents were professional dancers, which further optimized the chance that his exceptional talent for movement, jumping, and mimicry would be recognized early. As a teen-ager he was already so spectacular that people called him "the eighth wonder of the world." He is one of the few dancers in history to be considered a genius.

The boy's parents, Eleonora Bereda and Thomas Nijinsky, had come from Poland. They made a living as ballet dancers in theaters and opera houses as well as circuses and carnivals throughout the Slavic countries. It was a precarious existence, entailing an irregular income and frequent moves from towns to villages. It also involved their three young children in numerous public performances, the sort of existence formative for many artists then and now. These parents understood, from their own training, that unless ballet lessons commence early, the body's innate capacity for turnout will be lost owing to the demand for walking, which forces the feet to point forward, in the same direction as the eyes. They also knew that dancing can be a very enjoyable emotional experience for children, akin to the pleasure of music and sports. Such so-called "nonverbal" activities do not require language, hence can readily be practiced long before children speak correctly or go to school. The Nijinskys' oldest child Stanislav, his brother Vaslav, and the baby Bronislava thus were encouraged to become "natural" dancers, and they took to the ballet the way ducks take to water.

With so intensive an early introduction to the performing arts, it may happen that other skills having to do with intellectual and social development are relatively neglected, and this seems to have been true of the Nijinsky children. All three were handicapped to some extent by growing up in a family for whom being on stage and pleasing the public always came first. To establish a nurturant environment and close emotional ties was a secondary consideration at best, one for which neither parent had been well prepared.

Eleonora Nicolaevna Bereda, Vaslav Nijinsky's mother, was born in Warsaw, Poland. She was the last child in a family headed by a cabinetmaker who was addicted to gambling, which produced mortifying anger in his wife. He gradually lost his money and the family savings in card games, became increasingly depressed, and died, presumably of a "heart attack," when Eleonora was only seven years old. (Her memory of losing her father at so early an age may have been a factor in sensitizing her son Vaslav to the fear of heart disease.) Soon after the death of her father, Eleonora also lost her mother, who in a state of pathological mourning had refused to eat and died miserably. These childhood disasters were catastrophic. Eleonora grew up without parents. She was raised by her four orphaned siblings and a housekeeper. She became fearful and transmitted many anxieties to her own children. (One of Vaslav's recurring fears was that Eleonora might "starve to death" unless he took proper care of her.) She developed a tendency to react to frustrating circumstances with explosive rage or helpless depression (another trait she shared with her children). Unhappy at home and very restless, Eleonora and her sister Stephanie, against the wishes of their brothers, enrolled in Warsaw's excellent ballet school. From there they were recruited to dance in Russia, Poland's large neighbor, which at that time had control over the country. They were the youngest girls in the troupe, and they spoke only Polish. They made a living—thirty-five rubles a month when Eleonora was twelve, later increased to sixty—but life was hazardous. "Friends were lost, new friends were made, there was no time for deep attachments." Eleonora's motto, which she passed on to her own children, was "one for another through fire and water."[2]

At age nineteen, after seven years of dancing and traveling, Eleonora wanted to settle down, marry a Russian artillery officer who had fallen in love with her, and leave the theater. But a few days before the wedding, while driving through Warsaw, her Russian fiancé made some disparaging remarks about the Poles and bragged how his country had subjugated hers. "Eleonora did not say anything [bearing one's pain in silence was a family trait], but she realized that now she could not marry a Russian officer."[3] She broke the engagement and rejoined the ballet company. It was only eight years later, when Eleonora was twenty-seven years old, that she established a firm attachment to a man, another dancer, and married him.

Thomas Lavrentievitch Nijinsky, then twenty-two years old, was also Polish. Born in Warsaw, he came from a family of revolutionaries. Both his grandfather (a landowner who had lost his property) and his father (a railroad employee) had been active in anti-Russian uprisings. Thomas himself was something of a rebel, breaking with family traditions at the age of eight by insisting that he wanted to work in the theater and become a dancer. After his graduation from the Wielki Theater School, the leading state school for performing artists in Poland, he began working in Russia, where Polish-trained dancers were much in demand.* Thomas was a tall, virile, and handsome young man, much admired for his strength and athletic ability. He was capable of unusually high leaps and had great talent as an actor. He had proposed marriage to Eleonora (perhaps as a way of seducing her) when they first met in one of the theaters where both of them were dancing. Thomas was twenty years old at the time, and she apparently resisted his advances for a while, citing his extreme youthfulness as a reason not to get involved. He seemed emotionally immature and had a reputation for impetuous, violent behavior. Eleonora liked but also feared him. One day he pulled out a revolver and said this was the last time he would

---

*Almost all of the great "character" dancers in the company Sergei Diaghilev later founded, the Ballets Russes, were Polish. They were considered the most fiery and persuasive actors, including of course Vaslav Nijinsky.

propose to her. Afraid he might harm her or himself, she agreed to get married. The ceremony took place in Baku (the Caucasus), in May 1884.

Their first child, Stanislav, was born three years later. "Stassik" was accident-prone. One day he ran headlong into the cook, who was carrying a tureen of hot soup, and a shower of scalding liquid came pouring down over his head. Another time he tripped and fell underneath a heavy platform with sharp spikes that injured him. It is not clear to what extent this dangerous tendency to get hurt was a product of the little boy's impulsivity and poor judgment or of his parents' inability to supervise him properly, since both of them were working full time. Stassik was a little more than two years old when his brother Vaslav came along.

The precise circumstances of Nijinsky's birth remain uncertain. It is said that his parents were on tour and in Kiev when he arrived; there are stories of Eleonora having danced until her labor began. ("He was born in a shirt," she told his sister Bronislava, meaning that the fetal membranes were attached to his head, which was considered a sign of good luck.[4]) Documents on file in Warsaw record Nijinsky's date of birth as 17 December 1889, but all of his psychiatric records as well as most of his travel documents and identity cards say it was 28 February 1889, which would have been 12 March 1889, according to the new Russian calendar. His sister used that date, and the biographer Vera Krasovskaya as well as researchers at The New York Public Library Dance Collection give 12 March 1889 as the date of his birth. Richard Buckle and Lincoln Kirstein put the year back to 1888, while Nijinsky himself often said he was born in 1890. (For example, a notebook written in 1919 says, "I am now twenty-nine years old. I know that I was nineteen when I made the acquaintance of Diaghilev [in 1909]."[5] Nijinsky's marriage certificate, 10 September 1913, records his age as twenty-three. His wife gave his birthday as 28 February 1900 in her first book, and 28 December 1890 in her second. Ian Ferguson, who has studied the question extensively, thinks that Nijinsky was probably born on 12 March 1890 and had a horoscope drawn up accordingly.[6]*

---

*There are several ways to explain the confusion, but no way to be sure on what date Nijinsky was born. Often mentioned is his mother's anxiety about his eligibility for military service in Russia, and that she may have lied about the date to the Polish authorities. Another possibility is the change in the Russian calendar system in 1923, which advanced all dates. Transcription errors may have been made. (Nijinsky's death certificate, in London, says he was fifty-nine years old when he died on 11 April 1950.)

Soon after his birth, his mother found herself pregnant again. She was thirty-three years old, had engaged a wet nurse for Vaslav, and was trying to pursue her career as a dancer. Another pregnancy so soon was "distressing," and she did not want her husband to know about it. "For married artists without a permanent home, it was a hardship to have a large family," wrote Bronislava Nijinska. "The managements in the private theaters were reluctant to offer engagements to artists encumbered with many children."[7] So Eleonora took matters into her own hands and tried to reverse the situation by jumping from a high table. She attempted to abort herself a number of times, but did not succeed. When Bronislava ("Bronia") Nijinska was born, on 8 January 1891, Vaslav was less than two years old.[8]

Although a two-year-old child still needs a mother or nurse to feed and protect him, he is no longer completely dependent on a care-giver and has begun to feel like a separate entity. The stage of personality development has been reached at which a child is able to recognize emotion in social relationships, to empathize with other people, and to recognize how they feel about him and he feels about them. He has learned that some people are his friends while others are not and to respond with the corresponding signs of acceptance or rejection. In contrast to an infant's screams and grimaces, which are physiological signals for self-preservation, a two-year-old makes socially meaningful gestures and produces words. (Girls tend to do this earlier than boys.) Indeed, the second year of life witnesses the development of symbolic communication. Children learn to play, to speak with sentences, to express their wants and wishes, and to use their imagination creatively. Such skills are needed to establish a sense of self, to become independent, and to master the environment. They enable a child to cope effectively with separation from his caretakers, and to grow up.[9]

With the appearance of a baby sister before he was two years old, Vaslav's sense of himself as a person in the world became closely linked to the presence of Bronislava. Coming into the family while her brother was still learning how to distinguish between pain and pleasure, love and hate, attention and avoidance, reality and fantasy, she soon was part of his way of organizing his behavior in human relationships. They felt very close to each other, and often played together. Bronia, a very bright and precocious child, became part of "Vatsa's" inner life, a sort of constant companion, as he was for her. They were soulmates as well as playmates. Later they danced and made ballets together. And Bronislava, who was more verbal than Vaslav, became the chronicler of their growing up. It was, like the love-bond between Mozart and his cousin or Mendelssohn and his sister, an artistically productive sibling relationship.

Unfortunately, something terribly destructive happened while Vaslav was still a baby and Bronislava an infant. It was the cruel maiming of their older brother, a disaster that affected all three children for the rest of their lives. Apparently their parents were busy, and the nurse was not sufficiently watchful. Stanislav climbed up on a windowsill, pushed open the panes, and plunged headlong down to the cobbled street, four floors below. He was found there unconscious, with blood running out of his ears, nose, and mouth. The hospital records are no longer available, but one can assume that there was some brain damage. Stanislav remained in a coma for several days and later had a severe learning disability. This tragic accident not only destroyed his future as a dancer—all three children were expected to excel in the art of ballet—and left the field wider open to his younger siblings (then, as now, ballet was a highly competitive enterprise), but it also brought the specter of mental illness to the Nijinsky family. At first Stassik was very "quiet and gentle," perhaps somewhat retarded. After puberty he became unruly and disorganized. He would scream violently and disrupt what his brother and sister were doing. Finally it became necessary to hospitalize him, an event that deeply affected the entire family and may have set the stage for Vaslav's anxieties about mental disease as well as his tendency to mimic disturbed people.[10]

Vaslav made rapid progress with his dancing. He loved taking lessons from his parents and by age four already stood out on account of the complex movements he could execute so deftly. He could dance the mazurka and the waltz much better than the other children. "He felt himself to be quite a hero," Bronislava comments, perhaps a little jealously. She was observing a bit of his arrogance, part of the façade the little boy would adopt while exhibiting his specialness. Child prodigies not infrequently see themselves as idiosyncratic, odd, and "out of context" with the society they are born into. Society in turn regards them with awe, which can add to their sense of alienation. Nijinsky, as one of his admirers later commented, "seemed to have been born for dancing and for nothing else."[11]

His first public success occurred when he was four years old and danced the hopak during an Easter performance. Vaslav played the role of a girl.

With his slightly dark skin, big brown eyes, and long fluffy eyelashes, it was impossible to tell that he was a boy. He looked like a little Ukrainian girl in his white cross-stitch embroidered shirt with wide sleeves, and a Ukrainian dress, decorated with spangles. On his head was a garland of artificial cornflowers, poppies, and long blue and yellow ribbons, and around his neck he wore many multicolored beads.[12]

One can imagine what this meant to a boy of four who was close to his sister. "How exciting to be applauded. And what an attractive costume. It makes me look like a girl, like Bronia. She admires me." On the other hand, he may have felt embarrassed. His brother Stassik had been dressed to look like a Cossack; perhaps he or one of the other boys teased Vaslav. How would one expect him to react? "I am not a girl. I can prove it. I will be wild and aggressive, like my father." To identify with Thomas Nijinsky could not have been too difficult for Vaslav. They often danced together. They shared a talent for mimicry, and both had great power for leaping. Thomas supervised his son's training and encouraged him to imitate his own difficult dance steps. One is reminded of the role Leopold Mozart played in directing his son's genius and pushing him to the front of the stage whenever possible. Mozart's father was stern and controlling, however; Nijinsky's seems to have been more tempestuous and incautious. In that respect, too, the boy may have wanted to be like him, for we know that as a child Vaslav had the makings of a daredevil.

He loved to climb the highest trees, to swing wildly from the branches, and then drop down. Recklessly, he scampered all over the equipment in circuses where his parents were employed. (Even today the Russian circus uses ballet dancers in some of the acts. It was work the Nijinsky family had to accept. His mother later was ashamed to admit it.) Vaslav would rush out of attic windows onto an adjacent building, balance precariously on the edge of the roof, chase the pigeons nesting there, and practice other hair-raising stunts. His hyperactivity seems to have satisfied a hunger for movement. Bronislava says it gave him "rapturous delight."[13] Surely it also helped to improve his physical coordination and gave him opportunities for asserting his independence. The memory of Stassik's disastrous fall and self-injury may have been in his mind, along with the wish to avoid such a calamity. It seemed to thrill Vaslav to tempt fate, to beat the odds. One of his most famous adult roles was in the ballet *Le Spectre de la Rose,* in which at the end he made a spectacular flying leap out a window. This astonishing performance regularly thrilled the audience and may also have demonstrated to Nijinsky that he could safely do something that had nearly destroyed his brother.

His mother was disturbed by Vaslav's rambunctious behavior. She sensed in him something dangerous, like the bravado and gambling spirit of her father. And having seen her older son suffer a crippling injury made Eleonora feel more protective toward the younger one. The family lived at that time in Novaya Derevnia (New Village) on an island near St. Petersburg in the Neva River delta. Vaslav often disappeared from the house, which made his mother more anxious than ever. He wanted to run about on his own, explore the neighboring fields and villages, play with animals along the way, wander into gypsy camps to join in the music and dancing, and roam around with strangers at the theater. She feared he might get lost or be kidnapped by gypsies. The police were called several times to return him to the house, whereupon he would be severely punished, beaten with birch sticks.

Vaslav remembered the fear of these beatings more than the pain, but they did not change his behavior, which is typical of hyperkinetic children. This clinical syndrome, also called "attention-deficit disorder," is characterized by constant overactivity, unpredictable behavior, irritability, explosiveness, sleep disturbances, a short attention span, difficulty concentrating, and poor school performance.[14] Nijinsky described every one of these symptoms in his autobiographical notebooks. In addition, he may have been dyslexic, handicapped with reading and writing, which would have contributed to the problems he had in school. His speech was never very fluent either. There were times when he seemed unduly silent, very pensive, and "immersed" in his thoughts. Perhaps he already experienced some feelings of depression as a child. His sister recalls him kneeling in prayer: "I never asked him whether ... he found himself, as I did, in his thoughts, far from earth and on the very brink of heaven."[15]

When he was six or seven years old, his father took him to the Neva River and tried to teach him how to swim. The way Nijinsky described it later, his father threw him into the water; he "sank to the bottom" and nearly drowned.

> I could not swim, but I felt I had no air, then I closed my mouth. I had little air, but I kept it, thinking that if God willed I should be saved. I

walked straight on, I knew not where. I walked on and on and suddenly felt a light under the water. I realized that it was shallow in the place I was going to, and went quickly. I reached a wall. The wall went straight up. I did not see the sky. I saw the water above me. Suddenly I had a feeling of physical strength and jumped. When I jumped I saw a rope. I clung on to the rope and was saved.[16]

His memory of this event may have served as a screen for other, less conscious, early stresses. At the time when Vaslav nearly drowned, his parents were involved in a serious marital crisis. Eleonora, because of her domestic responsibilities, could not always accompany her husband on the long trips that were part of a dancer's life. During one of their separations, when Thomas Nijinsky was in Finland, he had gotten involved with another dancer named Rumiantseva. After returning to his family, he continued to spend time with her, and she became pregnant. (This led to an illegitimate child named Marina. We do not know what became of her.) Bronislava sensed that "some sad changes were happening within our family," and presumably Vaslav did too. The children were seeing less and less of their father, and during "long agonizing nights" they overheard Eleonora's "trembling, tormented voice" and Thomas's "agitated tones."[17] He wanted to leave his family and live with Rumiantseva. Both of Vaslav's parents were inclined to temper tantrums, and his father could become violent. ("He sometimes had attacks of rage that bordered on insanity."[18]) Vaslav barely understood what was happening, but he recalled later seeing his mother "in a humble room" and feeling frightened. "Why do you cry?" he asked her. "Father has left us," she answered.[19]

Bronislava describes her brother's reactions as very "stormy," an escalation of "reckless escapades and disobedience." It was probably his way of trying to deal with the grief of losing his father, to mask his inner suffering, as his sister says, and externalize his anger. In doing so, he often took his mother's side in arguments, which made the situation even worse. "Mother told him not to interfere," Bronislava writes. "Vaslav would simply avoid Father and try not to look in his direction. It was as if he were throwing Father out of his heart."[20]

This was the first time his heart had been broken, and his fear of it breaking again as well as the masking of feelings and avoidance of confrontation became character traits as he grew up. By the time Vaslav was eight years old, his mother, now a single parent, had moved to St.

Petersburg, then the capital of Russia, and was doing her best to raise the children by herself. It was a mixed blessing for the boy. On one hand, he was now the primary object of his mother's concern and affection and master of the house, a kind of Oedipal victory that made him feel more confident and triumphant. On the other hand, he no longer had a male dancer to emulate or a father to love. That brought confusion, sadness, and a yearning for masculine influence. To his mother's everlasting credit, she took steps to remedy the situation by enrolling him for further training at the Imperial School of Ballet in St. Petersburg.

The coming together of a highly gifted child who needed artistic refinement and a cultural institution that required raw talent could not have been more timely. During the nineteenth century, classical dancing had fallen on bad times throughout Europe, but in Russia the ballet was prospering. Outstanding dancers, including Virginia Zucchi and Enrico Cecchetti from Italy and Marius Petipa from France, had come to work in St. Petersburg and teach at the Imperial Theater. Generous funds for the performing arts were available from the czar's private purse. Tchaikovsky and other major composers were writing music for the ballet. Elegant, aristocratic audiences would fill the theater twice a week for performances of *The Sleeping Beauty, Pharaoh's Daughter,* and other popular full-length classical ballets. A cadre of distinguished soloists was emerging, including the brothers Nicolas and Sergei Legat, the popular Matilda Kchessinska (mistress of Czarevitch Nicholas II), the brilliant Michel Fokine, and the charismatic Anna Pavlova. Each year a new crop of young dancers graduated from the Imperial Ballet School to fill the ranks of the corps de ballet. Those who were truly outstanding might become soloists.

Formal studies usually began at age nine or ten, a desirable time for developing a child's strength, mobility, and coordination. Gaining admission to the Imperial School was no easy matter, however, and applicants were rigorously screened in terms of their physical and mental aptitudes. Nijinsky nearly failed the medical examination—"he appeared awkward in manner and delicate in health"—perhaps owing to a deficient diet within the prior year when his mother had to struggle against extreme poverty. However, she was on good terms with Enrico Cecchetti, and some of the other teachers at the school also knew of her husband's reputation as a great dancer. So they took a closer look at the boy. He had exceptionally well-developed thigh muscles. Dancer Nicolas Legat recalls telling him "to move a few paces away and jump.... His leap was phenomenal.... I had him put first into the Junior boys' class under my brother Sergei, but he made such rapid progress that I had him removed very soon to the Senior class and then to the class of Perfection."[21]

The training was rigorous and demanding. Classes began at nine in the morning and lasted until late in the afternoon. The boys wore a special uniform that consisted of a woolen shirt and trousers, all in gray, a wide black belt with copper buckle, a blue cap with visor, and high-topped boots. At first Vaslav wore it "like a theatrical costume," his sister reports. (She also mentions his immense appetite, and how he would anxiously watch his brother's plate at dinner, to make sure the older boy did not receive a larger portion.[22]) At school Vaslav stood out not only because of his physical superiority—he danced harder and better than any of the other boys—but also because of his problems in verbal communication. One of his peers, the dancer Anatole Bourman, says that he had "one of the worst Polish accents I had ever heard! That alone would bar him, for every student accepted by the Imperial Russian Ballet School was required to speak perfect Russian, and to be alert mentally. The boy, Nijinsky, had spoken with hesitation, distraught at the unexpected reaction he had evoked. He seemed almost stupid ... a slow thinker."[23] He had little contact with girls. Talking to them was not permitted during classes and extracurricular mingling of the sexes was strictly forbidden. Further social isolation resulted from Vaslav's unusual appearance, his high cheekbones and slanted eyes, common Tartar features for which he was often teased. His classmates called him "the little Japanese." Envious no doubt of his success with the teachers, they made taunting remarks: "Are you a girl, to dance so well?" He was quick to anger and frequently got into fights.[24]

Vaslav's insecurity may have been compounded by his mother's protectiveness. Despite his protests, she insisted on taking him to school every day and picking him up after classes. "Only girls walk to school accompanied by their mothers," he told her. "They will laugh at me and call me a girl if they see me walking with you, Mama."[25]

But her concerns for Vaslav's safety were well taken, for on 13 March 1901, during his third year, a gang of boys played a terrible trick on him, which led to a life-threatening injury and set him back one semester in school. Using a heavy wooden music stand, they erected a barrier and dared him to jump over it. As he approached it running, one of the boys rubbed soap on the floor to make it slippery, while someone else raised the barrier to an unexpected height. Vaslav hit it full force. He crashed to the floor, severely injuring his abdomen. Excruciating pain developed in the area of the liver. He was examined by Dr. V. Yakobovitch, sent by ambulance to the St. Petersburg Imperial Hospital, and quickly lost consciousness. The impact had produced severe internal bleeding, an abdominal hemorrhage due to laceration of the liver. Vaslav was in a coma for four or five days, after which "he looked up with enormous eyes and smiled [but] did not say a word to us . . . [and] towards the end of the school year he was allowed to leave the hospital, though he had to remain at home on a special diet for a long time."[26] Clearly there had been severe trauma, both physical and psychological. Massive bleeding into the abdominal cavity probably had occurred, producing a drop in blood pressure, with concomitant effects on the general circulation. Marked reduction of blood pressure can lead to the coagulation of blood within the main arteries of the brain, a serious complication. "Water-shed infarcts," as these are called, tend to form in the frontal lobes and spread sideways. If that happens, there may be loss of speech (aphasia) and other behavioral symptoms. (Nijinsky's fall might also have pro-duced a head injury, which could have damaged his brain directly.) Children tend to be much less susceptible to the long-term effects of brain damage and recover more completely than do adults, but the psychological consequences can be very serious. Nijinsky's mother feared there had been an injury to his "spine" and that he might not be able to dance again. Her anxiety was probably transmitted to the children, especially since Stanislav had already been brain-damaged.

Nijinsky dates his fear of death to this traumatic event when he was severely injured, lost consciousness for several days, and had to stay in the hospital until the end of the school year: "I know what death is. Death is a terrible thing. I have felt death many a time. I was dying in a clinic when I was fifteen years old. [In fact, he was only twelve.] I was a brave kid. I jumped and fell. I was taken to the hospital. In the hospital I saw death with my own eyes. I saw foam coming out of the mouth of a sick man. . . . "[27] Bronislava also explains that this patient was a young "groom from the Royal Stables, who had been kicked in the stomach by a horse. . . . " He lay in the next bed to Vaslav's, talked to him, and suddenly expired, which would have been another terrifying experience for the Nijinsky children.[28]

Vaslav's subsequent years at the ballet school were marked by serious problems in both academic performance and social behavior, possibly a complication of his childhood "accident." (It is worth noting that several other boys in his class were also injured during those years, and that the mortality rate among his peers was surprisingly high, reflecting the rough fate of dancers then, as today.) Although Vaslav consistently did well in music, gymnastics, drawing, and other subjects that do not depend on verbal skills, his performance in reading, writing, mathematics, history, and science remained deficient. This, plus his generally asocial manner and belligerent conduct, led to frequent reprimands. "I was ring-leader in many pranks," he wrote later. "I did a lot of pranks and all the boys liked me for that." One of these pranks, after a rehearsal of the ballet *Corsair* on 19 September 1901, consisted of shooting wads of paper out of a carriage window with a slingshot. A bystander was apparently hit in the eye. The teacher who witnessed this incident reports that Vaslav and two other students had been caught "misbehaving themselves" in the back of the carriage (read "masturbating," advises my Russian consultant). "Especially Nijinsky and Lukianov very often misbehaved themselves in this way." He was punished by "abolition of the school stipend for three months," which produced severe economic hardship for Vaslav's mother. Even before he had completed his third year of school, Eleonora was warned that he might be expelled.[29]

Despite these setbacks, Vaslav went on to become a boarder at the school. There are several photographs of him in a school uniform, with silver insignia (crown, wreath, and lyre) on his round collar. He slept in the spartan, whitewashed dormitory for boys, with its rows of institutional beds (not very different from a hospital ward). Contact with his mother and sister was curtailed, but he still saw them during holidays. He also went to church, and there met the boy he later remembered as "Isayev, my friend in masturbation." With him, Vaslav seems to have established a pattern of retreating to bed whenever he felt overwhelmed by conflicting demands. He blamed Isayev for teaching him "bad things" that interfered with his dancing.

> I liked him, but felt that what he had taught me to do was a bad thing. I suffered when I wanted to do it. I wanted to do it every time I went to bed.... I noticed that no one in school knew about my habits and therefore went on with them. I continued until I noticed that my dancing was beginning to deteriorate.... I started combating my lust. I said to

myself "I mustn't." I learned well. I gave up masturbation. I was about fifteen years old. [30]

Guilt stemming from sexual activity was to be the source of major conflicts for many years, related in part to the protective attitude of his mother, who disapproved of what Bourman (glossing over Vaslav's obvious escapades with boys) called his "perfectly healthy concern over girls,"[31] and also reflecting the prejudices of his time. That "self-abuse" could weaken the body was a belief many dancers (and other young men) shared at the time. Whether Vaslav ever counseled with an adult about his teen-age anxieties is not known; even if he did, that might not have been helpful, since many teachers and even medical doctors around the turn of the century considered masturbation to be harmful and homosexuality a sin if not a crime. The atmosphere in Russia was generally repressive. During an attempted uprising against the czar in 1905 (the so-called "Bloody Sunday" massacre), Vaslav saw corpses littering the streets and was struck in the face by a whip-wielding Cossack, which probably further intensified his fear of physical injury (and may explain why he remembered himself as being "fifteen" years old when he was first hospitalized).

Of great benefit to the stabilization in adolescence of Nijinsky's personality as well as his artistic development was the influence of his teacher Sergei Legat. Only twelve years older than Vaslav, Legat took the boy under his wing from the beginning and treated him as his favorite pupil. He was a handsome and very athletic dancer, whom Vaslav probably loved and emulated as he had his father. But this relationship, too, ended in a traumatic separation when Legat, who was involved in a complicated love affair with the dancer Marie Petipa, committed suicide. The circumstances are not altogether clear. Apparently Legat had chosen the wrong side during the 1905 revolution. According to Tamara Karsavina's highly informative book, Legat felt he was a "traitor," began to "rave" to his mistress, and slashed his throat with a razor.[32] The suicide of this man, a great dancer and Vaslav's teacher, may have affected Nijinsky's attitude toward emotional disorder in later years.

Following the loss of Legat, Vaslav's training was supervised by Pavel Gerdt, an outstanding premier danseur and character actor who helped the young dancer perfect his tremendous talent for mimicry. "I have sat in Gerdt's class," writes Bourman, "and watched Vaslav playing with such power and conviction in his gestures that the goose flesh crept eerily over my whole body, and fear itself invaded me."[33] This ability to shock, astonish, and frighten people was to become one of Nijinsky's greatest assets, part of his charisma on stage, and also a highly disturbing feature of his psychotic behavior in later years.* Another formative influence was the stern, demanding teacher Mikhail Obukhov. But Nijinsky's greatest asset, his ability for high leaps, he seems to have developed on his own by doing special exercises to strengthen the muscles of his calves and feet, and his Achilles tendons. He also learned to empower his toes in such a way as to give additional lift to his feet as they rose from the floor.

A certain mystique has always been attached to his extraordinary leaps. "Suddenly a tremendous jump straight up, *grand échappé,* his legs firmly locked together," writes his sister, "he remains thus poised in midair."

> "Nijinsky flies across the whole width of the stage with *grand assemblé entrechat-dix* . . . he seems to linger two or three seconds in the air before coming down . . . he flies diagonally across the whole stage . . . he soars high in a *sissonne soubresaut,* the body arched back, suspended in midair."[35]

Whether we would find this as impressive today as it was then is debatable. The teaching of ballet technique has improved greatly and there have been other dancers with enormous jumping skills since Nijinsky—Eglevsky, Nureyev, Baryshnikov, to mention only three. Yet those who saw him always found Nijinsky's elevation most remarkable. Karsavina thought it was "all unreal and could not have been; the boy looked quite unconscious of his achievement, prosy, and even backward."[36] Nijinsky was short, only five feet, four inches, which probably added to the illusion of height when he was up in the air. He also trained himself to breathe in a special way, imperceptibly expanding and contracting the chest sideways to give the impression of soaring. It never failed to amaze people. (There has been speculation that Nijinsky's feet were unusual, with the bones resembling those of a bird.

---

*Children who have been traumatized often relive their pain and express it unconsciously in symptoms as well as creative activity. Psychoanalyst Lenore Terr writes that "if trauma infects a very talented youngster, that child may hone his talents down to the purpose of lancing his ever-purulent abscess."[34]

None of his medical records support this assumption, nor can I detect anything abnormal in photographs of his feet. X-rays were taken in New York in 1916, but I have been unable to locate them.)

Even before graduating from the Imperial Ballet School, the better students were allowed to participate in performances of opera and ballet at the Maryinsky Theater. Thus, Nijinsky was immediately recognized to be a dancer of great distinction, remarkably agile, and extremely energetic. Because of his great strength, reliability, and sensitivity to the needs of the other dancers, he was sought out as a partner. (Partnering requires a fine sense for music, maximal nonverbal communication, and great discipline.[37]) Before his eighteenth birthday Nijinsky was allowed to join the great Anna Pavlova for a pas de deux in Mozart's opera *Don Giovanni,* and he was selected to dance the slave in *Le Pavillon d'Armide,* a new ballet by Michel Fokine, who created this role especially for him. His graduation on 29 April 1907 was a major event. He appeared in many numbers, including a pas de deux called "The Prince Gardener," with the leading ballerina Ludmilla Schollar.

> Her costume was sewn with spangles, so that in the supported *pirouettes* Vaslav's hands were cut between thumb and forefinger and her dress was covered in blood*—which was considered a bad omen.[38]

The audience was enthralled with his performance. The critics gave superlative reviews. His family were enormously pleased, including his father, who had arrived from some distance just in time to see him graduate. There was never any question of Nijinsky's dancing in the corps de ballet, as most graduates had to do. He was so exceptional that within seven weeks he was appointed a full-fledged "Artist of the Imperial Theaters," at a monthly salary of sixty-five rubles. Soon he was also sought out as a teacher for the children of wealthy families, which provided additional income. Nijinsky lacked the ability to communicate in words and was never considered a capable teacher. Nevertheless, because of his great reputation he was able to command very high fees, up to 100 rubles, for private lessons in the great mansions of St. Petersburg.

---

*I cite this "ominous" event here, in the context of an otherwise successful graduation exercise, because many years later, when Nijinsky was mentally ill and no longer dancing, he would repeatedly and compulsively pick his thumb with his forefinger until blood flowed.

At the invitation of Matilda Kchessinska, who had powerful connections at court, Nijinsky spent the summer following his graduation dancing at the summer resort of Krasnoe Selo, in an exclusive theater reserved for the families of government officials. Although this job provided an income of only 250 rubles, it was a great honor to be selected by this famous ballerina (eighteen years his senior) as her partner. To show his appreciation, the czar gave him a gold watch, embossed with the imperial eagle. Most of his earnings Vaslav turned over to his mother, who thus was able to move into a better apartment. His father, who was then working in the large city of Nijni Novgorod (now called Gorky) east of Moscow, also sought to benefit from Vaslav's success. He invited Vaslav for a visit that summer, hoping to introduce the boy to his mistress, have him dance for his friends, and entice him into joining his own ballet troupe. Vaslav was reluctant to go. It would be a long trip, nearly a thousand miles, and his sister advised him not to take it; better just to write "Father a good long letter." His mother, however, insisted that Vaslav should go. (She was still depending on her husband for occasional child-support payments.) The meeting turned out to be unpleasant, fraught with tension and rivalry. Thomas Nijinsky, once a famous dancer but now past his prime, seemed oversolicitous and condescending toward his now more famous son. He had reserved a room in his hotel for Vaslav, but the boy refused to stay there. A bitter argument broke out when Vaslav invited his father for dinner and then angrily refused to meet Rumiantseva, the woman who had replaced his mother and given birth to his illegitimate half-sister. Thomas felt insulted. "A son should not speak this way to his father." Vaslav was adamant. "If I sat at the same table with her, how could I ever look my mother in the face again?" Abruptly he walked out of the restaurant, and what was to be a one-week visit ended after twenty-four hours. It was the last time Nijinsky would ever see his father, who from then on stopped writing and sent no more money to his family.[39]

On returning to St. Petersburg, Vaslav felt emotionally upset. "I was no longer cheerful because I felt death," he recalled some ten years later. "I was afraid of people and used to lock myself in my room. My room was narrow with a high ceiling. I liked looking at the walls and at the ceiling because all this spoke to me of death."[40] This seems to have been Nijinsky's first clinically significant episode of depression, and the reasons for it, as far as we can tell, were multiple. Most immediate was the acute rupture of his relationship with his father, reawakening all the earlier pain of childhood separation from this dancer and role-model. Second was the loss of predictable routines to which Vaslav had become accustomed as a student. Without environmental structure and support he felt helpless. "I finished school at the age of eighteen," he wrote later. "I graduated and was let out. I did not know what to do because I did not know how to dress. I was used to uniforms. I did not like civilian dress and therefore did not know how to wear it.... I felt free but the freedom terrified me.... I did not know life."[41]

Such reactions are not unusual among graduates of highly regimented institutions, but for Nijinsky, already somewhat handicapped by difficulties in verbal communication, it was particularly stressful to have to make the transition from "student" to "artist" status so quickly. He now had far more freedom and independence than ever before. This he could use to good effect in his dancing, which became more original and creative, but in matters of ordinary daily life— decisions on where to eat, what clothes to wear, or with whom to spend his spare time—he was often at a loss. He waited for others to make these decisions for him. In this respect, one could say that Nijinsky had a dependent personality. At the same time he was perfectionistic, with extremely high standards, so that it was difficult for him to accept praise from anyone but himself. Nijinsky often seemed to be his own worst critic, and he distrusted compliments, especially if he felt they were undeserved. He enjoyed admiration and felt proud of his accomplishments, but he did not like to be "praised" because it made him feel uncomfortably boastful: "I read that I was being called 'child prodigy.'... I did not like what was being written about me because I felt it was all praise."[42]

Paradoxically, Nijinsky's public performances, which so greatly delighted his audiences, made him feel vaguely dissatisfied. Where other solo dancers acknowledged their applause ostentatiously, he was usually reticent, bowing in a noticeably modest, self-effacing manner. Even his great leaps he tended to disparage, telling people, when they praised him, "I'm not a jumper; I'm an artist!"[43] Nijinsky recognized that applause was no substitute for love. Yet love was what he knew he needed and always craved. It was terrifying for him to have to admit that there was little love to be gotten from those who shared his competitive work environment: "I wanted love not only from the Corps de Ballet, but from the first and second men and women dancers too, and ballet masters and ballerinas. I sought love and realized that there was no love. That it was all filth. That everyone looked for praise and praise again or compliments." During a performance of *Swan Lake* on 25 November 1907, he became so flustered that he stopped dancing his variation of the pas de trois in the first act and began taking his bows while the orchestra was still playing. For this he was "verbally rebuked" by the director of the theater.[44]

One of the most effective ways to overcome feelings of depression is through physical activity. Nijinsky always felt at his best when he was doing his exercises, practicing and preparing new roles, organizing and rehearsing his ballets, or performing. Moving and showing his body was essential to his well-being; inactivity was always a source of stress. Here again, his new status as an "artist" seemed paradoxically dissatisfying. Although it allowed him to star in the solo roles of great classical ballets, these assignments were rotated among all the principal dancers, which meant that Nijinsky was now dancing less frequently than he had as a student or if he were a member of the corps de ballet. (He later recalled having "danced only four times" during his first year at the Maryinsky Theater, in a season that lasted eight months. This loss of opportunity to dance in public he attributed to "the intrigues of artists, men and women. I was no longer cheerful because I felt death.")[45]

Into this quagmire of depressiveness there now stepped a man who both helped and hindered Nijinsky's career. He was Prince Pavel Lvov, a member of the aristocracy, extremely wealthy, unmarried, drawn to athletic young men, and thirty years old (the same age as Vaslav's favorite teacher Sergei Legat when he committed suicide). Lvov had seen Nijinsky dance, admired him from afar, and wanted to arrange a rendezvous. It was not unusual for rich balletomanes to seek lovers, both male and female, among the young artists at the Maryinsky Theater, who were underpaid and often lived a marginal existence. Mikhail Alexandrov, one of the dancers who accepted money for such services, introduced Nijinsky to Lvov. Here was an opportunity for him to enter the highest stratum of society and mingle with people totally different from his family. It was also the beginning of his involvement with the adult world of homosexuality, which in St. Petersburg was tolerated but not openly approved.

Nijinsky certainly was ready for a sexual relationship. He had been abstinent for several years, since giving up masturbation, and was yearning for affection. Thus, he responded favorably to Prince Lvov, accepted fashionable clothes and other gifts from him, enjoyed the lavish parties in his palatial mansion, and allowed himself to be put up in an elegantly furnished apartment. Whenever Nijinsky was not dancing, he would accompany Lvov to the theater or other social functions. It seems to have been a satisfying but rather one-sided relationship. "He loved me as a man does a boy," Nijinsky wrote about his benefactor. "I loved him because I knew that he wanted my good.... He wrote me love poetry. I did not answer him ... I never read it. I loved him because I felt that he loved me. I wanted to live with him always because I loved him."[46]

Lvov's generosity was a godsend for Nijinsky's mother. One of her greatest worries had been that Vaslav might turn into a womanizer like his father. She warned him repeatedly not to cohabit with "loose" women because of the danger of acquiring venereal disease. Worse yet was Eleonora's fear that her son might marry a young ballerina, Maria Gorshkova, whom he said he "loved." Knowing only too well the hazards of being married to a dancer, Eleonora quickly put a stop to her son's romance with Maria. And Prince Lvov was more than a strong ally: she saw in him the benevolent father her children had never had. According to Bronislava, Prince Lvov spoiled the whole family with "chocolates or marzipan petit fours, or sometimes a basket of fresh fruit. He often gave Mother gift boxes filled with all kinds of delicacies—caviar, salmon, pâté de foie gras, cheeses—and French white wine."[47]

Physical relations between Lvov and Nijinsky seem to have been less than satisfactory, however. In addition to his moral scruples about homosexuality and his anxieties about masturbation, Vaslav seems to have had fears about anal intercourse (his notebooks allude to this). As for the Prince, he may have found the dancer less appealing in bed than when he was on the stage. Many people have commented on Nijinsky's surprisingly disproportionate physique, his long neck and thin torso supported by a pair of enormously overdeveloped thighs and calves. (His tailor recorded Nijinsky's body measurements as follows: chest 52 cm, waist 50 cm, waist length 42 cm, elbow length 46 cm, pants [between the legs] 69 cm.) When he was wearing a costume or moving rapidly and gracefully while dancing, these less attractive features could be cleverly disguised. As for what male dancers hide and at the same time advertise with the help of a "strap" beneath their tights, Nijinsky's penis, at least in its nonerect state, was said, by his sister, to have been undersize (she may have been remembering him as a child). Richard Buckle wrote that Nijinsky "was small in a part where size is usually admired."[48] (I have searched all of Nijinsky's medical records for confirmation, since it is important to rule out a pituitary tumor, which can inhibit genital development. Few of the doctors who examined Nijinsky described his genitalia, but those who did reported them as "normal." A nude sketch of Nijinsky at age twenty-two or twenty-three, made by Aristide Maillol in Paris, also shows him quite amply endowed.[49])

The friendship with Prince Lvov lasted less than a year. It seemed to benefit Nijinsky in a number of ways. He became less shy and more confident in himself. The experience of mirroring his body in that of another man and identifying with him probably boosted his narcissism. People were astonished to observe changes in his demeanor. He became more aware of his appearance, more stylish, and somewhat dandified. He groomed his hair in new ways and struck poses. He climbed socially into a milieu of luxury and affluence (or, as some biographers would have it, of decadence and "corruption"[50]). Changes also became apparent in Nijinsky's approach to dancing. He no longer seemed content simply to interpret the roles assigned to him; he began to make alterations in his costumes and to vary his movements and gestures in original ways, thus transforming the stock figures into daringly new portrayals. For example, as the Blue Bird in Petipa's famous ballet *The Sleeping Beauty,* he removed the traditional full skirt and large wings worn by his predecessors (including his illustrious teachers Legat and Obukhov) and invented a way of vibrating his arms from the shoulders, which gave the impression of a fantastic animal soaring across the stage. Nijinsky succeeded in creating "a whole new theatrical image of the Blue Bird" without changing Petipa's choreography in any way.[51]

Lvov was actually more interested in athletics than the ballet. (According to what Diaghilev told Bronislava Nijinska, after the Revolution Lvov became the president of a "prominent sporting organization" in Scotland.[52]) This influence, too, may have rubbed off on Nijinsky. One of the choreographies he later produced for Diaghilev, the *ménage-à-trois* ballet *Jeux,* emphasizes sports and the sexual games people play. But the liaison with Lvov also had undesirable effects. As was mentioned earlier, the Prince apparently grew tired of Nijinsky as a sexual partner and passed him on to other lovers—Nijinsky mentions a "Polish Count [who] bought me a piano."[53] This made him feel rejected and again depressed. His friend and fellow-dancer Bourman thought it was time for Nijinsky to "become a man," and they experimented with the underworld of gambling and prostitution in St. Petersburg. (Bourman, probably exaggerating, describes "fantastic excursions" and the "most depraved women."[54]) Unfortunately, Nijinsky soon got into trouble, as his mother had predicted. "I did not know how to cheer myself up, and visited a tart together with my friend Anatole Bourman."

> I fucked her. She gave me V.D.... I wept. I suffered. I did not know what to do. I went to a doctor, but he did nothing for me. He ordered me to buy an injector and some medicine. He ordered me to inject this medicine into my member. I injected it. I drove the disease deeper in. I noticed that my balls started swelling.[55]

The venereal disease was gonorrhea, a very serious infection in those days before antibiotics. (There is no evidence from any medical or laboratory reports that Nijinsky ever had syphilis.) He recalled the lengthy treatment with disgust. It included the application of leeches. ("The leeches sucked my blood. I said nothing, but I was horrified. I was afraid. I suffered in my heart.... I was ill for over five months with that disease.") Nijinsky thought of killing himself at one point, the first sign of a suicidal tendency. "I was frightened and decided to end it at all cost."[56] Lvov supported him and his family through this long illness and paid all the medical bills. He was "wonderful," writes Bronislava. "He proved himself more than a friend. He behaved as a dear parent to us. He had immediately called a famous specialist, and noticing that Vaslav was embarrassed and reluctant to be cared for by his mother, Lvov had sent his valet to stay with Vaslav day and night throughout his illness."[57] It was the end, however, of any further intimacy between the Prince and his protégé.

Lvov can be viewed as a significant transitional figure in Nijinsky's life, the man who replaced his father during a crucial phase of maturation from adolescence into young adulthood, and also someone who for better or worse loosened the dancer's sexual inhibitions. Nijinsky's greatest strength was always his body and the prodigious kinesthetic intelligence he could use, publicly and privately, to get people excited, to "turn them on," to transmit his innate sensuality, to arouse violent emotions, both love and hate. Therein lay his charisma. In terms of his artistic development, the most important effect of Prince Lvov and the St. Petersburg aristocracy was that they led to his contact with that hugely resourceful individual Sergei Diaghilev, who knew instinctively how to transform a child prodigy into a man of genius.

NOTES

1. Vaslav Nijinsky, unpublished notebook on "Life," 24–25. (Hereafter, cited as Notebook on "Life.")
2. Bronislava Nijinska, *Early Memoirs*, 7–8. This book, hereafter cited as BNM, is the best source of information about Nijinsky's family and early development.
3. Ibid., 8.
4. Ibid., 12.
5. Notebook on "Life," 54.
6. Letter from Ian Ferguson to Mary Clarke, 21 February 1983. See also Ian Ferguson, "Nijinsky's Birthday?"
7. BNM, 12.
8. Eleonora Nijinska's attempt to produce a miscarriage was told to me by her granddaughter, Irina Nijinska.
9. See Daniel Stern, *The Interpersonal World of the Infant.*
10. Stanislav's tragic fall is described on page 18 of BNM, and his accident-proneness on page 33.
11. BNM, 19; David Henry Feldman, *Nature's Gambit*, 5; Prince Peter Lieven, *The Birth of Ballets-Russes*, 316.
12. BNM, 20.
13. Ibid., 51.
14. Maurice W. Laufer and Eric Denhoff, "Hyperkinetic Behavior Syndrome in Children." See also Paul Wender, *The Hyperactive Child, Adolescent and Adult.*
15. BNM, 45.
16. Notebook on "Life," 52. See also Romola Nijinsky (editor), *The Diary of Vaslav Nijinsky*, 43.
17. BNM, 57.
18. Vera Krasovskaya, *Nijinsky*, 1.
19. Unpublished notes by Romola Nijinsky, presumably written by her in Buenos Aires in 1913. Nijinsky Archives, Phoenix, Arizona.
20. BNM, 57.
21. Nicolas Legat, "Pages from the Memoirs of Nicolas Legat."
22. BNM, 81.
23. Anatole Bourman, in collaboration with D. Lyman, *The Tragedy of Nijinsky*, 4.
24. BNM, 85. According to Richard Buckle, *Nijinsky* (hereafter cited as RBN), 8, "Throughout his eight years at school [Nijinsky] never made a friend." Attributed to unpublished remarks made by Bronislava Nijinska, this statement is not entirely true. In addition to Bourman, who seems to have befriended Nijinsky, we read in the latter's autobiographical notes about a friend named Isayev, whom he met in church. Whether this boy was a student at the Imperial School is not known.
25. BNM, 87.
26. State Historical Archives of the USSR (hereafter cited as Archives USSR), Fond 498, Section 1, Unit 5052, p. 2. See also BNM, 100–103. Another description, perhaps somewhat exaggerated, as so much of this book tends to be, can be found in Bourman, 36–37.
27. Notebook on "Death," 25.
28. BNM, 102.
29. Archives USSR, Fond 498, Section 1, Unit 4903, pp. 2–3. Se also Notebook on "Life," 87.
30. Ibid., 89–90.
31. Bourman, 28.
32. Tamara Karsavina, *Theatre Street*, 189–190.
33. Bourman, 26.
34. Lenore C. Terr, "Terror Writing by the Formerly Terrified ..."
35. BNM, 142–143.
36. Karsavina, 177.
37. Anton Dolin, *Pas de Deux: The Art of Partnering.*
38. RBN, 42.
39. BNM, 190–191. For another, more fanciful, but probably less accurate description of the last meeting between Thomas and Vaslav Nijinsky, see Krasovskaya, 86.

40. Notebook on "Death," 37.
41. Notebook on "Life," 92–93.
42. Ibid., 90–91.
43. Interview with Romola Nijinsky, videotape of *Et liv*.
44. Notebook on "Death," 37. Information about the faux pas during *Swan Lake* comes from the Archives USSR, Fond 497, Section 3, Unit 223, p. 9.
45. Ibid., 37.
46. Ibid., 38–39.
47. BNM, 200.
48. RBN, 62. See also Richard Buckle, *In the Wake of Diaghilev*, 260.
49. Jean-Michel Nectoux, *L'Après-midi d'un Faune*, 28.
50. See, for example, Françoise Reiss, *Nijinsky: a Biography*, 53, and Arnold Haskell, *Diaghilev; His Artistic and Private Life*, 228.
51. BNM, 210.
52. Ibid., 262.
53. Notebook on "Life," 68.
54. Bourman, 135–141.
55. Notebook on "Death," 37–38.
56. Ibid.
57. BNM, 233.

*Never at any epoch in the whole
history of the art did one man, and
a non-dancer, so entirely dominate his
period, and the whole tragic story of
Nijinsky ...*

Arnold Haskell[1]

Chapter 2

Dancing for Diaghilev

Sergei Pavlovitch Diaghilev was born on 31 March 1872, in the province of Novgorod, south of St. Petersburg. He had two mothers. The one who gave birth to him died shortly thereafter as the result, he was told later, of injuries caused by his unusually large head. (To be so innocently mutilative may have been a burdensome fantasy for this sensitive, artistically inclined child, who as an adult would dedicate his life to the promotion of human enterprises and the support of other people.) His father, who came from a long line of civil servants, army officers, and "gentlemen" (as opposed to the larger population of Russian farmers, serfs, and untitled working people), married again when Sergei was two years old. Elena Panaev, "the best woman in the world" as she has been called,[2] came from a musical family. Her father had built a private opera house and her sister was a well-known soprano. Apparently, young Diaghilev was quite a handful, but his stepmother is said to have "found the way to tame his impulsive stormy nature, to discipline him, and to teach him to discipline himself."[3] He and his two younger half-brothers were exposed to music at an early age. Singers often performed in his house, sometimes entire operas, and Sergei came to know the works of Beethoven, of Schumann (who had actually been to Russia in 1844), of Tchaikovsky, a distant relative whom the boy remembered visiting in Klin, and of Mussorgsky, another composer he met as a child. He had relatively little contact with his father, a handsome, charming cavalry officer, who was often away from home on official duties. The family spent much time with relatives in St. Petersburg, then the vital and cosmopolitan capital of Russia.

Diaghilev's closest childhood friend was his cousin Dmitri ("Dima") Filosofov. They were the same age, and both were homosexual. As teenagers they traveled together, visited Europe, learned languages, went to concerts and museums, collected paintings and fine furniture, and established contact with other young people from well-to-do families. "This journey abroad marks the beginning of that deep friendship which united the two men for the next fifteen years," writes the Russian-born dancer Serge Lifar. "Both were tall, handsome, and well built, especially Dima, though there was something feminine in his looks ... people would often turn round to stare and gaze after them with open admiration."[4] Following their "Grand Tour," the cousins settled in St. Petersburg, where they lived in the comfortable home of Dima's mother. Sergei studied music at the conservatory, where the composer Rimsky-Korsakov was one of his teachers. He also took classes at the university and obtained a law degree. Dima, who was more interested in literature, poetry, and philosophy, had a close circle of friends in St. Petersburg, all previously schoolmates and several of them gay, who regularly met for the ostensible purpose of talking about art, the theater, and other local cultural activities, and to find ways of developing their talents and expressing their ideas. The leader of this group was Alexandre Benois, a young painter with close ties to France, who later became an important scene designer for the Ballets Russes. Others included the writer and amateur musician Walter Nouvel, the artist Konstantin Somov (who had been an earlier romantic interest of Filosofov's), the critic Valentin Serov, the painter Léon Rosenberg (who later changed his name to Bakst and, as a designer of costumes and scenery, also became one of the leading figures of the Ballets Russes), and Nicolas Roerich (an artist and archaeologist best known today for having painted backdrops for the Nijinsky-Stravinsky ballet *Le Sacre du Printemps*). These were liberal, progressive young men, rather opposed to the conformist czarist bureaucracy, who admired the writings and philosophy of Leo Tolstoy and were much taken with Richard Wagner's ideals of a *Gesamtkunstwerk*, a "total work of art" that sought to integrate music, painting, literature, architecture, and dancing. In 1890 Filosofov introduced his eighteen-year-old cousin and lover to this fraternity.

The dynamic, self-confident, and socially adroit Diaghilev had an immense talent in the field of administration and public relations. Hugely energetic and highly intuitive, he knew how to get the best out of people, and he soon became the leader of the group. They involved themselves in a variety of projects. Filosofov wrote and published literary criticism. Benois designed sets and costumes for a performance of Wagner's *Götterdämmerung*. Diaghilev, too, worked at the Maryinsky Theater for a while. He edited an exceptionally attractive and informative yearbook, and with Benois gave advice about the production of operas and ballets. But after an administrative crisis in 1900, Diaghilev was abruptly dismissed under conditions that proscribed his ever again being employed by the Imperial Theaters, a hurtful experience that left its mark on the young man. He began to organize art exhibits, traveling all over the country to collect old Russian paintings, ikons, and other valuable items. Diaghilev's most successful venture by far was the lavishly illustrated and beautifully printed journal *Mir Iskusstva* (The World of Art), published by him and his group for six years. In this journal Diaghilev explained and promoted his ideals, a "belief in the autonomy and subjectivity of art, his worship of beauty, and his . . . vision of art as an act of communication between the personality of the artist and that of the spectator."[5] *Mir Iskusstva* not only had a strongly positive influence on the younger generation of Russian artists and writers, but also alerted foreign readers to their work, especially in Paris, with its traditional ties to the culture of St. Petersburg and its large colony of Russian émigrés. In 1906, a year after the "Bloody Sunday" massacre, Diaghilev and his colleagues brought to Paris a collection of Russian paintings, ikons, and other art objects, which were exhibited in twelve halls of the Grand Palais, redecorated for this occasion by Léon Bakst. The exhibit was partly subsidized by funds from the czar. It marked the beginning of Diaghilev's so-called "artistic invasion" of Europe.

In 1907 he exported an entire festival of Russian music. (Diaghilev had by now abandoned the hope of becoming a professional musician himself.) It was a tremendously ambitious undertaking for so young and relatively inexperienced an impresario. Funds had to be raised abroad, since money from Russia was beginning to dwindle, and Diaghilev had good luck with an agent in France, Gabriel Astruc, who helped him to book the magnificent Paris opera house for this festival. Feodor Chaliapin, the greatest singing-actor of his day, performed arias from Mussorgsky's *Boris Godounov*. The brilliant virtuoso Sergei Rachmaninov played the piano. The celebrated Austro-Hungarian conductor Arthur Nikisch led the orchestra in music by Scriabin and Rimsky-Korsakov. Parisians, with their cultivated taste for what is traditional as well as avant-garde, were wildly enthusiastic, and Diaghilev quickly became their man. He seemed to know exactly how to show to the French the product of a country that stretched all the way from Europe to the Orient.

Diaghilev was a driven man, driven by an ambition to excel, to make himself and his ideals known to the world, to command others, and to be involved in enterprises that were ever novel, exciting, and popular. He was ruthless and perfectionistic in trying to achieve these goals, which required a coterie of loyal and devoted co-workers—imaginative and resourceful people he needed to supply him with new ideas and at the same time carry out his plans. Filosofov's circle of friends, which Diaghilev had come to dominate, served this purpose admirably. Diaghilev also had a strong appetite for physical gratification. He enjoyed good food, comfortable surroundings, fine clothes, and attractive men and women. He tried, with never-ending ingenuity, to maintain as luxurious a life-style as possible (sometimes, when he ran out of money, it was not possible). And always, even though he could be sexually promiscuous, he sought to ally himself with a steady lover, someone to share his vitality and reflect back his own radiance. These men had to be diamonds. In the course of his relatively short life—Diaghilev died at age fifty-seven—he attached himself to many glittering figures, beginning with his cousin Filosofov, and including over the years and for varying lengths of time the dancers Vaslav Nijinsky, Léonide Massine, Anton Dolin, and Serge Lifar, the writer Boris Kochno, and the musician Igor Markevitch. Diaghilev would be "enthralled" by gifted young men, writes one of them (Lifar), and "wish to bring that genius to life and reveal it to the world ... to love the possessor of that genius, tenderly, timorously, self-sacrificingly ... to be his, all his."[6]

Diaghilev's transition from Filosofov to Nijinsky is relevant here, not only because of the enormous impact it had on the latter's career and reputation as a dancer, but also because it coincided with the period when Diaghilev was moving his base of operations away from Russia and closer to the heart of Europe. Two important members of his group were pulling in different directions at this time. Alexandre Benois, its original leader, had long been encouraging them to take more interest in opera, ballet, and aspects of French culture, whereas Filosofov, Diaghilev's lover and the co-editor of *Mir Iskusstva,* was more inclined toward literary projects and the culture of St. Petersburg, in particular the circle of writers and philosophers congregating around Zinaida Gippius, a prolific memoirist who, like the nineteenth-century French novelist George Sand, wore men's clothes and adopted attitudes that were considered "unfeminine."

Gippius (also spelled Hippius) seems to have appealed to Filosofov in a special way. According to the Slavic literary scholar Simon Karlinsky, she considered herself to be androgynous, "a man intellectually and emotionally, but with a woman's body ... she could assume either a male or a female sexual role." Karlinsky conjectures that Gippius might actually have been "physically a hermaphrodite, with sexual characteristics of both sexes. Yet in outward appearance she was a very pretty and elegant young woman."[7] Gippius was married to Dmitry Merezhkovsky, author of a book about Tolstoy and Dostoyevsky, the trilogy *Christ and Antichrist,* including *Leonardo da Vinci.* He too was something of a mystic. It was well known that Merezhkovsky did not have sexual relations with his wife. Gippius evidently was attracted to the very good-looking, highly intelligent, and homosexual Filosofov, and succeeded in wooing him away from Diaghilev. Under her spell, Filosofov immersed himself in religion and philosophy, while Diaghilev (whom Gippius, in her letters, refers to as "the devil") shifted his interests increasingly toward opera and ballet. According to Professor Karlinsky, it was "in order to be away from St. Petersburg and to avoid seeing Gippius and Filosofov together" that Diaghilev put so much of his energy into organizing the Russian Seasons in Paris.[8] If that is true, it is a good example of how creative people can turn their personal loss into something of social value.

These years were critical for Diaghilev. In 1908 he brought a

magnificent production of the complete *Boris Godounov* to the Paris
Opéra and began planning other productions for the 1909 season,
including some ballets. To maintain the momentum of what some felt
was almost an "invasion" of Russians into the cultural life of France, he
had to woo singers, dancers, musicians, stage designers, and other
artists away from the Russian Imperial Theaters during their vacations
or other available times. This was not too difficult, since many
performers welcomed the opportunity to show their talents abroad as
well as the extra income that foreign tours could provide. Diaghilev
tackled the project with his customary zeal. He approached major
dancers such as Anna Pavlova, Tamara Karsavina, Adolph Bolm, and
Mikhail Mordkin, offering them attractively high salaries and an
opportunity for international fame. He engaged Michel Fokine as ballet
master and Sergei Grigoriev, a friend of Fokine's who had already
helped him to stage several innovative productions, as stage director.
Fokine was the most original and compelling choreographer in Russia,
an advocate of "realism" as opposed to the make-believe world customarily shown on the Maryinsky stage. (In his youth, Fokine had been
strongly impressed by the work of Konstantin Stanislavsky, a theater
director who advocated the expression of genuine feelings.) Fokine
urged his dancers to dramatize the roles he created for them, not just
use the stereotypic mimicry that had become a ballet tradition. He
wanted them to bring these characters to life, to portray flesh-and-
blood human beings rather than costumed dolls, and he had his eyes on
Vaslav Nijinsky, his former pupil and the most gifted dancer-actor at
the Maryinsky.

Obtaining the necessary funds was a tremendous challenge for
Diaghilev. Astruc, whose connections in Paris were impeccable, said he
would be willing to guarantee Fr. 100,000 for the 1909 season. To do so,
he had to seek support from Baron de Rothschild and other financiers.
A number of rich and influential women also became contributors to
Diaghilev's cause, including the Polish-born Madame Edwards (Misia
Sert), soon to be one of his most loyal friends, and the immensely
wealthy American-born Princesse de Polignac (daughter of Isaac
Singer, inventor of the sewing machine).

How did Nijinsky become part of Diaghilev's entourage? He had
undoubtedly seen Diaghilev at the Maryinsky Theater and heard about
his wish to form a traveling ballet company. The two may also have been
introduced to each other at the Cubat, St. Petersburg's most fashionable

nightclub, or during a party in Prince Lvov's mansion. According to the way Nijinsky recalled it some twenty years later, the arrangements for his first rendezvous with Diaghilev were made by Lvov: "He forced me to be unfaithful to him with Diaghilev because he thought Diaghilev would be useful to me. I was introduced to Diaghilev by telephone."[9] We do not have the other side of the story, but Nijinsky claims to have felt intimidated by the older man, and implies that Diaghilev proposi- tioned him. "I hated Diaghilev from the very first," Nijinsky writes, "because I knew Diaghilev's power ... he abused it. I was poor. I earned 65 rubles a month ... not enough to feed both my mother and myself." Diaghilev spoke about his sexual preference for "boys" and Nijinsky "pretended to agree with all his views. I realized I had to live and therefore it did not matter to me what sacrifice to offer."

> I hated him for his voice, which was too sure of itself, but I went in search of fortune. I found fortune there because I immediately loved him. I trembled like an aspen leaf.[10]

Bartering one's body for financial or social benefits was not unusual among young actors and actresses, ballet dancers, or singers, and I daresay it still happens today. A combination of poverty, insecurity, ambition, and desire to please makes performing artists especially vulnerable to sexual exploitation. But was Nijinsky homosexual? The question is often asked, especially because his wife regularly stated that he was not. However, as his own frank (and I believe honest) notebooks show, sexual intimacy with men was acceptable when a reward ("fortune") was offered. In other words, Nijinsky had sex with both men and women. He was bisexual. His wife's expurgated version of Nijinsky's notebooks has him saying about the first encounter with Diaghilev not "I immediately loved him," but "I allowed him to make love to me," making it sound as if Nijinsky was the more passive partner.[11] One would assume, however, that he had acquired enough experience with Prince Lvov, and perhaps with other men as well as from contacts with female prostitutes, also to take the active role in homosexual relations. How much he enjoyed it is another question. There is no evidence that Nijinsky deliberately sought men for sex or preferred them over women. Indeed, his masturbation fantasies suggest a heterosexual orientation as well as a narcissistic one. Nijinsky writes, "I was no more than 19 years of age when I started masturbating once every 10 days."

I liked lying in bed thinking about a woman, but I came afterwards and decided that I should make myself my own object of lust. I looked at my own erect penis and lusted.[12]

Excitement over his own erections, and exhibitionism, may have been important elements in Nijinsky's sexuality. But there were conflicts. He mentioned not only hostility but also anxiety (trembling "like an aspen leaf"), symptomatic perhaps of a fear of being rejected or of submitting physically. If anal intercourse was expected, it may have been difficult for Nijinsky to be receptive. He writes that his "back passage was not large" and that he "suffered from pain in [his] back passage." (These remarks, it must be noted, were made in connection with aspects of digestion, rather than sexuality.[13]) Was Nijinsky merely "pretending" to enjoy sex with men? Considering his great talent for acting, that possibility must be seriously considered. On the other hand, it seems likely that he enjoyed sharing the ecstasy of orgasm with others, men as well as women. In *L'Après-midi d'un Faune,* the first ballet Nijinsky choreographed for Diaghilev, he pretended to have (or perhaps did have) an orgasm on stage. (In his later years, when Nijinsky was a psychiatric invalid, he was occasionally observed to be masturbating openly, apparently with no inhibitions.) One can well imagine that this marvelously mobile dancer, so eager to "sacrifice" himself, was a satisfying lover when he was in good health. His wife certainly described him that way.

For Diaghilev, of course, it was a masterstroke to obtain the services of an attractive man not only as his lover, but also as a member of his ballet company. Nijinsky's short muscular physique, savage Tartar features, shyness, unsophisticated manners, and vague Polishness were probably tantalizingly different and perhaps made him even more desirable than the elegant, tall, and erudite Dima Filosofov. Recently, Diaghilev had been satisfying himself with a live-in "secretary," Alexis Mavrine. On 16 April 1908 Nijinsky asked for permission from the Imperial Theater to go abroad, presumably with Diaghilev, for two months. On 25 May 1908 his salary was increased to 75 rubles a month, probably as a way of trying to keep him in St. Petersburg. On 10 October 1908 he concluded a contract with Diaghilev. (Nijinsky signed it not once, but five times!) He was to be paid Fr. 2,500 for participating in Diaghilev's Paris enterprise and to receive a second-class railway ticket. Diaghilev agreed to take care of any additional expenses. It was customary for him to outfit his boyfriends in smartly tailored clothes, to have them stay in his hotel, and to allow them to join his inner circle to the extent that they were sufficiently cultivated to make a good impression on his patrons and advisers. Like the Greek mythological figure Pygmalion, who sought to transform the objects of his love, Diaghilev usually went to considerable trouble to educate his youthful companions, guide them in their reading, travel with them, take them to museums where he would point out his favorite paintings and sculptures, and try always to give them the benefits of his own rich cultural heritage.

With Nijinsky there was little time to lose. Rehearsals had to begin at once to prepare the Russian singers, dancers, musicians, and stage personnel for the tour. Fokine was commissioned to choreograph several new ballets especially for Paris, and the young composer Igor Stravinsky was recruited to help with orchestration for one of these ballets (*Les Sylphides*) and compose new music for another (*The Firebird.*) Diaghilev being persona non grata at the Imperial Theaters (and permission for him to use the Hermitage Theater having been withdrawn at the last minute), rehearsals had to be held in Catherine Hall on the Ekaterinsky Canal. Those were exciting weeks of preparation, with great enthusiasm and everyone pitching in to make suggestions, very different from the artists' customary work environment at the Maryinsky Theater. "From the ballet-master and *premiers danseurs* to the last dancer in the *corps de ballet*," writes Alexandre Benois, "everyone seemed to unfold and become utterly devoted to the art...we felt something was maturing that would amaze the world."[14] Nijinsky's sister had just graduated from the Imperial Ballet School. She, too, was engaged to join Diaghilev's company, and to chaperone her as well as keep an eye on Vaslav, their mother also decided to go to Paris. It was a welcome relief from their dreary and lonely life in relative poverty.

Bronislava Nijinska had some reservations about the influence of Diaghilev on her brother. Before meeting him, Nijinsky had been "carefree and more relaxed ... unconstrained, and particularly popular with young ladies."[15] Now he was "quite a different person," completely under Diaghilev's control, frequently absenting himself from the Maryinsky Theater so they could travel together, and of course not allowed to go out with girls. Nijinsky's mother, on the other hand, seems to have had no objections to this arrangement. If anything, she was happy to see him in such good company, staying at deluxe hotels, dining in the best restaurants, and wearing the finest clothes, all at Diaghilev's expense, while she and Bronia had to live much more modestly on the Left Bank and take their meals with the other dancers. One might say that in the long run Nijinsky was the ticket to a better life for the women in his life, first his mother and sister, later his wife.

The Russians took Paris by storm. Astruc had booked the Châtelet Theater for their highly publicized first season of operas and ballets. The orchestra pit had to be enlarged for the many musicians. The stage had to be renovated in order to accommodate the magnificent sets, replete with flowing fountains and other special effects imported from St. Petersburg. Tickets sold out quickly. A mixed audience of be-jewelled aristocrats, connoisseurs, artists, intellectuals, and nouveau-riche snobs sat and waited impatiently on opening night, 18 May 1909, a *répétition générale* (final dress rehearsal), as these gala events were called.[16] Nijinsky made his debut in the spectacular ballet *Le Pavillon d' Armide* (sets and costumes by Benois, music by Nicholas Tcherepnine). Wearing white tights, striped short pants that covered his ample thighs, a gorgeous silk-embroidered jacket, a feather turban, and a delicate jewel-encrusted choker around his slender long neck, Nijinsky per-formed the role of Armide's "slave." He danced superbly, with an air of detachment that made him look even more exotic. In the pas de trois (with Karsavina and his sister), he did something so sensational that the audience's attention was drawn completely to him: instead of just walking off the stage to await his solo as was customary, he took a flying leap into the wings. "He rose up," writes Karsavina, "described a parabola in the air, and disappeared from sight. No one of the audience could see him land; to all eyes he had floated up and vanished. A storm of applause broke; the orchestra had to stop." Nijinsky was an instant celebrity. During the intermission a horde of admirers swarmed onto the stage and invaded the stars' dressing rooms. It was known, of course, that Nijinsky was Diaghilev's lover, and many men as well as women wanted to get a closer look at him. Someone asked Nijinsky whether it was difficult to stay in the air after jumping. He seemed not to understand at first—he spoke little French—but then answered slyly, "No! No! not difficult. You have just to go up and then pause a little up there."[17]

His next appearance was in *Le Festin*, a kind of sampler consisting of selections from various classical ballets. One of them was the famous Blue Bird role from *The Sleeping Beauty*. The audience was electrified by Nijinsky's performance. Such dancing had not been seen since the days of Auguste Vestris, the great French virtuoso, who in the eighteenth century was called the "God of the Dance." Since then, male dancers had all but disappeared from the Paris stage, their roles usually taken by women dressed to look like men. It seemed miraculous to see someone like Nijinsky, a "second Vestris," and before long he too was called "God of the Dance," a "wonder of wonders, breaker of the record in *entrechats.*"[18]

Two other ballets featured Nijinsky that first season in Paris. In *Les Sylphides* (music by Chopin, sets and costumes by Benois), he was the only male dancer on stage, surrounded by ballerinas in flowing dresses. Wearing a black velvet jacket over white tights, a loose-fitting white blouse, and a wig with shoulder-length blond curls, he danced the role of a sensitive poet, absorbed in his own reveries, yet strongly supportive of the women. In many ways this was a new and somewhat ambiguous image for a male dancer, one that heightened the androgyny suggested by Nijinsky's physique. His very prominent thighs and legs, conspicuously masculine in tights, contrasted with the upper part of his body, which was more slender, curvaceous, and feminine-looking, with graceful lines in the arms and wrists. This combination of delicacy and power was irresistible. "With *Les Sylphides*," his sister writes, Nijinsky "became the idol of the public. As soon as he was seen onstage ... he caused a sensation. They went wild, screamed, cheered."[19]

In the ballet *Cléopâtre* (sets and costumes by Bakst, music by seven different Russian composers), Nijinsky played another "slave." His sister described him "crouching low as a black panther at the feet of his Cleopatra." (The role of the Egyptian queen was played by a rich amateur actress named Ida Rubinstein, who had been studying privately with Fokine.) Nijinsky's talent for mimicry made him stand out in this ballet. While defending his queen he would snarl and bare his teeth "like a dog."[20] It was one of those character roles that allowed him to act out his latent aggressiveness. His animal-like ferocity, the pent-up violence, and killing instincts alluded to by his gestures were elements that drove audiences to the point of hysteria. He also seemed very erotic. As Arlene Croce puts it, "Nijinsky made the relation between ... sexuality and the dancer's art absolute."[21] His leaping and soaring had phallic qualities. His dancing of certain roles was passionate, orgiastic. He emanated an enticing and at times shocking virility.

Although it was clear from the start that Nijinsky's participation was a major reason for the success of the "Imperial Ballet," as Diaghilev billed the company in Paris, his status remained ambiguous not only within the company, but also at the many social events he was expected to attend. As Diaghilev's protégé, he had privileges as well as obligations far greater than any of the other dancers. For example, he was invited to post-performance conferences with Bakst, Benois, Nouvel, and others from Diaghilev's inner circle. Current projects were critiqued, policy matters were discussed, and plans for the future were outlined at these meetings. Being younger and less well educated than the others, Nijinsky seemed and felt out of place. He had been performing and often was tired. He seemed listless and uncommunicative. Making frothy conversation and being deceptively polite did not enter his repertoire. Usually he had little to say and remained silent, or merely smiled. When Nijinsky did open his mouth, he seemed clumsy, struggling for words, almost disorganized at times, which was embarrassing for him as well as Diaghilev. There were times when he tried simply to parrot the older man. That only made matters worse. People thought Nijinsky did not have a mind of his own. One of the inner circle (Misia Sert, allegedly) called him "an idiot of genius."[22]

In addition to his regular appearances in the theater, Nijinsky, along with other solo dancers, was frequently obliged to perform at private receptions organized by Diaghilev's wealthy and influential friends. There seemed to be something "scandalous" about his charisma. As Richard Buckle points out, "It had been the woman, the Muse, the diva, the ballerina who had been worshipped; to admire a man for his grace and beauty was unheard of and in some circles unthinkable." Besides, Diaghilev (again to quote Buckle) "had become overnight a leading figure of the Paris homosexual set, and it rather went to his head."[23] The rough-mannered Nijinsky found it difficult to adjust to the polished and sometimes pretentious society through which Diaghilev moved so easily, but he kept trying. Where Diaghilev was smooth and diplomatic, Nijinsky tended to be blunt and caustic. (At a party in London he once told a dowager that she reminded him of a camel, or a "giraffe," depending on which version of the story one reads.[24]) He was thought to be rude, when in fact he was probably bored or disinterested. Yet wherever he went with Diaghilev, he was immediately surrounded by admirers who flattered him and wanted in turn to be admired, or at least acknowledged. An interesting example is reported by Bronislava Nijinska. In Paris she was puzzled to see a thin, fashionably dressed young man, wearing rouge and lipstick, "almost always" hanging around her brother. "This is Paris," Vaslav explained. "He advises me to do the same . . . to put some make-up on my cheeks and lips. . . . This is the poet Jean Cocteau."[25]

Indeed, the dapper and intrusive Cocteau soon became a leading member of Diaghilev's Paris circle. He twittered and criticized, often sarcastically, and drew many amusing caricatures, including one of the elephantine Diaghilev arm-in-arm with the diminutive Nijinsky. Cocteau also wrote the libretto for one of the ballets, *Le Dieu Bleu,* in which Nijinsky later starred. Other gifted and gay Parisians who frequented the ballet and became enthusiastic admirers were the novelist Marcel Proust and the composer Reynaldo Hahn (who composed the music for *Le Dieu Bleu*).

On the whole, the relationship between Nijinsky and Diaghilev was untroubled until the end of their first season in Paris. During the heyday, they visited art galleries, spent time in aristocratic homes, and basked in each other's success. Nijinsky's performances gave luster to Diaghilev's showmanship, while Diaghilev's ingenuity boosted Nijinsky's reputation as a "God." But just before he was to dance at a special gala in the Paris opera house, Nijinsky came down with an illness that was to have a marked effect on his relationship with Diaghilev. The first symptoms were weakness and a bad sore throat. He went ahead with the performance anyway, but Diaghilev excused him from dancing the next day at a private garden party. Soon, the illness was much worse, with vomiting, diarrhea, severe malaise, and terrible abdominal cramps.

Knowing how susceptible Nijinsky was to emotional stress, one might ask at this point, Was his illness physical or mental? In my opinion, a dichotomization of this sort can be unproductive when one tries to understand or help a patient. Body and mind exist in the same locus within the individual human being, and are inseparable. Bodily pathology, whether it is a fracture, a hemorrhage, a tumor, or an infection, affects the way we think, feel, and behave. Our mental processes, what we call fantasies, emotions, memories, desires, hopes, and regrets, influence the way we move the muscles, bones, and other organs of the body, including those within the chest and abdomen. Neural and chemical messages flow constantly, transmitting information through the entire "mind-body" system. Thoughts, feelings, and actions are interconnected. There is a tradition, of course, especially prevalent in Western medicine, for separating the mind from the body. It has philosophical and religious underpinnings. The official medical nomenclature classifies so-called "mental" diseases separately from "physical" ones. While there are practical as well as economic reasons for adhering to this dichotomy, psychosomatic medicine, and especially the discovery of an immune system that mediates between the way we feel and how our body responds, argues against it.[26]

Ever since March 1908, starting around the time of his first serious involvement with Diaghilev, Nijinsky had from time to time been reporting himself as being "sick" and unable to dance at the Maryinsky Theater. Entries pertaining to health problems can be seen in his St. Petersburg personnel file on 29 March 1908, 3 September 1909, and 18 August 1909, interspersed with repeated requests for "vacations." These were treated with increasing suspicion by the Imperial authorities as it became clear that the dancer, still on full salary, was using his absences primarily to fulfil engagements abroad with Diaghilev. But not until the end of that first spectacular season in Paris and the onset of the major illness about to be described were Nijinsky's so-called "delinquencies" punished by withholding his salary whenever he failed to appear for rehearsals or performances in St. Petersburg.[27] It was Diaghilev's physician friend, Dr. Sergei Botkin, who usually would examine Nijinsky to ascertain his fitness for performances. This time, in Paris in June 1909, Botkin made a diagnosis of typhoid fever. This is an infectious disease transmitted by contaminated food and water. It was serious and sometimes fatal in those days before effective antibiotics. (Nijinsky wrote later that he had been too "poor" to buy mineral water and had contracted typhoid by drinking out of a "jug."[28]) Quarantine and good nursing care were required for patients with the disease. Nijinsky had to be moved out of his hotel into a private apartment, where he was confined for a month and provided with a nurse, all at Diaghilev's expense, of course. Fortunately, it was a mild case of typhoid; by the time his sister was allowed to see him, Nijinsky "was cheerful and smiling and looked like a little boy; his head had been completely shaven and he had lost weight."

Vaslav seemed to be enjoying his convalescence and all the attention of everybody fussing over him all day long. Laughingly, he told me that throughout the length of his illness Sergei Pavlovitch [Diaghilev] had never once entered his room but had talked to him from outside, through the door, only slightly ajar. Even now that Vaslav was allowed visitors, Sergei Pavlovitch kept his distance.[29]

Diaghilev was deathly afraid of germs. He often held a handkerchief in front of his nose and mouth to avoid contamination, probably a factor in avoiding intimacy and a source of conflict when seeking sexual partners. There were other problems Diaghilev had to confront during Nijinsky's illness. His "secretary" Mavrine had eloped with one of the ballerinas. More serious was that Diaghilev's extravagant 1909 season of Russian operas and ballets had incurred an enormous deficit. It amounted to Fr. 68,000, over half the amount Astruc had lent him. Diaghilev needed to reorganize his life and his finances.* During Nijinsky's convalescence Diaghilev proposed that henceforth they should live together, an arrangement that he hoped would reduce expenses. Nijinsky no longer was to be under contract and receive an income. Instead, Diaghilev paid for his room and board, clothing, spending money, and a stipend for his mother. These conditions were kept secret from the other dancers. To agree to bind himself so closely to Diaghilev was a decision Nijinsky later recalled taking reluctantly.

> Diaghilev made me an offer in that house when I was lying in a fever. I agreed. Diaghilev realized my value and was therefore afraid that I might leave him, because I wanted to leave even then, when I was 20 years old. I became frightened of life.... I did not want to agree. Diaghilev sat on my bed and insisted. He inspired me with fear. I was frightened and agreed.[31]

Nijinsky's recollections of this turning point in his life were written down ten years later, when he was undergoing a kind of psychotherapy

---

*Lynn Garafola's book gives much information about the complicated situation. Astruc was bothered not only by Diaghilev's debt, but also because the Russian ballets and operas had been competing with his own enterprises in Paris, notably a season of performances by the Metropolitan Opera Company. To recover some of the money he had lent him, Astruc "at the bargain price of Frs. 20,000, [sold] Diaghilev's entire stock of matériel to ... the longtime director of the Monte Carlo Opéra [who] quickly brought to the stage his own version of *Ivan the Terrible* using the costumes and settings acquired from the Russian upstart." Following the 1909 season, Astruc actually attempted to wrest control of the touring company away from Diaghilev by negotiating directly with some of the performers in St. Petersburg and sending letters critical of Diaghilev to highly placed persons there. "In his eagerness to quash competition in the marketing of Russian ballet talent abroad, Astruc's ruthlessness knew no bounds."[30]

in Switzerland (see Chapter 8). He associated the memory of his typhoid infection in Paris with that of his earlier, post-traumatic hospitalization in St. Petersburg: "I sobbed and sobbed because I understood death.... I slept for a long time. I did not understand what was the matter with me. I lost consciousness. I was afraid of Diaghilev and not of death. I knew that I had typhoid fever because I had it in childhood...."[32] Nijinsky may in fact have had a delirium, not uncommon with typhoid fever, that can affect the brain. The role of Dr. Botkin in directly managing the dancer's health problems, and indirectly his relationship with Diaghilev, seems only too clear. Botkin wrote to St. Petersburg that Nijinsky was "not yet well" in July 1909 and needed "a very long rest, maybe for two months" in a warm climate. No until 26 September 1909 did Nijinsky return to work at the Maryinsky.[33] Later, Nijinsky wrote, "I did not know what the matter was with me. Serge Botkin looked at me and realized everything. I felt afraid. I noticed the doctor and Diaghilev exchanging glances. They understood without words."[34])

One can assume that Nijinsky's illness made Diaghilev not only more protective, but also more wary. There was an altruistic element in his offer to have the young dancer share his life as well as a self-seeking one. He loved Nijinsky and yearned to develop his full potentials as an artist. At the same time he depended on him as one of the primary attractions of the ballet company, and illness served the goal of detaching Nijinsky from the Imperial Theater.

Writing about it ten years later, Nijinsky emphasized the cumulative hatred and fear he had developed toward Diaghilev, and downplayed the helplessness and probable gratitude he felt when Diaghilev offered to take care of him. According to Bronislava Nijinska, their love-compact was sealed by a "massive new platinum ring with a sapphire from the jeweler Cartier," which Diaghilev placed on Vaslav's finger after removing "the gold ring with the diamond given him by Lvov." Nijinsky took Diaghilev's ring off "only just before going onstage for a performance."[35] They spent a two-week "honeymoon" (as Buckle calls it) at the health spa of Carlsbad, and then traveled to Venice, Diaghilev's favorite vacation place.[36] Léon Bakst, who had come along, made a painting of Nijinsky on the Lido beach, wearing scarlet bathing trunks. They went to museums, churches, and numerous parties. At one of these social events the unrestrained Isadora Duncan, who had visited Russia in 1904 and startled everyone with the freedom of her dancing, invited Nijinsky to make a baby with her. Nijinsky indicated (we do not know how tactfully) that he was not interested.

After returning to St. Petersburg in the fall of 1909, he resumed his place at the Maryinsky Theater, dancing in the traditional repertoire of ballets. But now there were new problems. On 1 November 1909, Nijinsky showed up so late for an orchestral rehearsal of the ballet *Amulet* that he was punished with a "fine." Two weeks later he was reprimanded for "taking pieces from two different costumes to make his own costume. This was prohibited, but he did it also at the second performance." In December there was another episode of "illness," and on 10 March 1910 Dr. Dvukratov (who identified himself as "personal physician to the Imperial family") rendered what was to be the dancer's first psychiatric diagnosis:

> Vaslav Nijinsky, age twenty [he had in fact just turned twenty-one], suffers from an acute form of cerebrospinal neurasthenia. This illness has been progressing very quickly. He has anemia. It is necessary for him to have rest and treatment by climate change and baths at the Riviera.[37]

The fact that Nijinsky himself submitted this document to the Imperial authorities, together with a request for "vacation abroad, with pay, from 14 April 1910 to 28 April 1910," makes one suspect that Diaghilev was behind it. (The diagnosis "neurasthenia," literally "nervous weakness," will be dicussed later, in the context of Nijinsky's first major breakdown, in London, at age twenty-five. See Chapter 5.)

Ever since the end of his first season of ballets in Paris, Diaghilev had been seeking new sponsors for the next season, to begin in April 1910. He was successful. A number of wealthy backers were willing to support him, including the very enthusiastic but somewhat irresponsible Baron Dmitri de Gunsbourg, who in exchange for being named "co-director" agreed to pay off Diaghilev's remaining debt to Astruc and buy back the scenery and costumes, which had been sold. A contract was signed, this time with the Paris Opéra. New productions were immediately planned, including two ballets, *Schéhérazade* and *Carnaval*, that featured Nijinsky in roles he was to make world famous and perform until the end of his career as a dancer.

Schéhérazade, an exotic-erotic ballet in the style of "The Arabian Nights," was set to music by Rimsky-Korsakov. It takes place in a harem. Nijinsky played the role of the Black Slave (later renamed the

Golden Slave), a sensuous and dangerous male concubine, who is briefly let out of his cell by an old eunuch (usually played by Enrico Cecchetti) and allowed to make passionate love to the queen of the sultan's harem (played in the early performances by Ida Rubinstein). It was both shocking and titillating to see the dancers openly caressing and petting on stage. The costumes heightened their sexual appeal. (Some of Bakst's drawings show exposed breasts.) Nijinsky wore baggy gold pants tight at the waist and ankles, a kerchief round his head, and a kind of brassiere suspended by thin straps from his naked shoulders. In the early productions his belly and arms were sheathed by brown tights; in later productions they were bare but painted a bluish color. Those who witnessed Nijinsky's impersonation often compared him to an animal—he seemed "half-cat, half-snake, fiendishly agile, feminine and yet wholly terrifying" (Benois), "undulating brilliantly like a reptile" (Vaudoyer), "a stallion, with distended nostrils" (Fokine), "I never saw anything so beautiful" (Proust).[37] At the end of *Schéhérazade,* after their orgy, the slaves who were cavorting with the harem girls are slaughtered. Nijinsky danced his dying paroxysm on his head and neck, with his legs thrust up in the air (an early example of break dancing?). It "invariably aroused a storm of applause," the London critic Cyril Beaumont wrote. "Apart from the rare skill obviously essential to its performance, it looked dangerous in the extreme." (After Nijinsky became a psychiatric invalid, Beaumont wondered "whether that tremendous strain on his spine could possibly have affected his brain."[38])

The other great Fokine ballet, *Carnaval,* was premiered on 20 May 1910 in Berlin. After 1911 Nijinsky starred in the role of the clown Harlequin, and it was in this role that Romola de Pulszky, the woman who pursued him for two years and then married him, first saw him dance in Budapest. The music was by Robert Schumann, written when the composer was in love with two girls and a boy at the same time. *Carnaval* seemed the perfect vehicle for Nijinsky's ambisexuality and also gave him a means to externalize his manic tendencies. Dressed in checkered tights, black cap, and a flowing blouse with cravat, he fluttered, bounced, darted back and forth, shredded bits of paper, balanced on one foot, and grinned fatuously behind his Harlequin mask. *Carnaval* consists of a string of brief dance episodes, set by Bakst in a Biedermeier salon and loosely choreographed to resemble scenes from *commedia dell'arte.* Each dancer was given the freedom to develop his or her role according to personal taste, which was a challenge. Bronislava Nijinska, coached by her brother, danced very successfully the flighty role of Papillon, and in demonstrating it to her his hands were said to move so fast they resembled the wings of a hummingbird.

While it can be said that Nijinsky "created" the roles that made him world famous, until he began doing his own choreographies this was more of a collective effort than an individual creative process. All of Diaghilev's ballets were the product of teamwork. Librettists, musicians, choreographers, scenery and costume designers, and solo dancers worked so closely together that it was often impossible to say who had provided the original impulse or idea for a new work. It also happened, with *Schéhérazade* for example, that when a ballet was especially successful one or another individual might try to claim the credit. Hurt feelings and jealousy were the inevitable result. By and large, however, Diaghilev's artists worked well as a group, inspired and goaded to strive for excellence by his imaginative leadership. Nijinsky received inspiration from many sources, but what he did with a role was always the result of his own originality.

Alexandre Benois has described how Nijinsky created a role by undergoing a kind of personal transformation. At first, during the early rehearsals, he seemed tentative, insecure, hesitant, and unsure of what he was doing. Advice and direction from others, particularly Fokine, who had been his teacher, were essential. But gradually Nijinsky's creative instinct took over. At the final rehearsals he "seemed to awaken from a sort of lethargy; he began to think and feel." An essential part of the transformation had to do with putting on his costume—a "metamorphosis" took place.

> At these moments the usually apathetic Vaslav became nervous and capricious ... he gradually began to change into another being, the one he saw in the mirror. He became reincarnated and actually *entered* into his new existence, as an exceptionally attractive and poetical personality.[39]

Other dancers have commented that getting into costume or putting on a wig allows them to "feel like someone else."[40] It was Benois's assumption that Nijinsky's metamorphosis was "predominantly subconscious ... the very proof of his genius." How truly unconscious it was we will never know. Nijinsky himself did not describe it. But in my opinion the transformation involved a considerable amount of conscious practice and preparation. We know that Nijinsky worked indefatigably on his roles for many months before presenting them to the public, and that he continued making unexpected changes or improvisations, which added to the excitement of his performance. One never knew exactly what would happen next. Probably his creation of a role involved both conscious planning of the effect he wished to produce and unconscious dissociation. There may have been times when he actually felt himself to be the person he was dramatizing. But these impersonations had to be brief, since in one evening he was often required to portray several different and contrastive characters. To "lose himself" in a role or "enter" it completely, as Benois suggests, would have been undesirable. In this early stage of his career, Nijinsky was able to emerge from his transformations without difficulty, as was readily apparent at the conclusion of a ballet, when he quickly reverted to his normally restrained, shy, and self-effacing behavior. It was impressive, for example, to see Nijinsky taking his bows. Unlike some of the other dancers who stayed in character while acknowledging the applause, he usually presented himself as a refined and modest person, smiling gently and deeply appreciative. There were no fancy flourishes or mannerisms.

In certain ballets the audience felt that Nijinsky may actually have been portraying himself. This was noticeable, for example, in the classical ballet *Giselle,* set to a story by Heinrich Heine about thwarted love and tragic madness, which Diaghilev revived for the 1910 Paris season. While dancing the role of Albrecht, a young man who loses his girl to suicide, the chameleonlike Nijinsky exuded such heartrending pathos that it was assumed he had torn away his mask and was expressing "his individuality to the full."[41] Indeed, it was during a performance of *Giselle* in St. Petersburg, on 5 February 1911, that Nijinsky revealed one aspect of himself, his submissiveness to Diaghilev, that was to cost him his tenured appointment at the Maryinsky Theater and his security of future employment in Russia. It came about in the following way.

As mentioned earlier, Nijinsky's frequent "illnesses," "vacations," and travels abroad caused concern among the directors of the Imperial Theater. At first they were lenient about it, but in August 1909 (after his bout of typhoid) they started to document his "delinquencies" more carefully and to withhold his salary whenever he was on "vacation."

Three months later, he received his first "fine" for missing a rehearsal, and the following year his name appeared on a printed list of artists whose salaries had to be restricted because of missed performances. Nijinsky failed to heed these warnings. On 15 September 1910, he sent a letter from the Grand Hotel in Venice stating that "the state of my health does not permit me to serve my duty at the theater. Three weeks ago, when the weather was very hot in Venice I had a sunstroke, and today the physician who treated me informed me that I am very weak, and he cannot allow me to go to Russia earlier than in two weeks." (It was clear that he wanted to stay longer with Diaghilev.) Nevertheless, his annual salary was raised that year to 960 rubles, probably because the Maryinsky was afraid to lose him. Nijinsky was one of the seven highest paid male dancers in St. Petersburg.[42] (Some of the ballerinas received more; for example, Vaganova, who unlike Nijinsky served also as a teacher, was paid 1,320 rubles beginning in 1909.)

After his highly publicized success abroad, audiences in Russia eagerly awaited Nijinsky's debut in the role of Albrecht in 1911. The *St. Petersburg Gazette* reported that what distinguished him from "common male dancers" was not only "the phenomenal lightness and rare gift of plastique" but his "more perfect understanding of the style of classical ballet."[43] The royal family was expected to come to this performance. A dispute arose, however, over Nijinsky's costume. Diaghilev, who was not on good terms with the managers of the Maryinsky Theater, wanted him to wear the attractive, Renaissance-style costume Benois had designed for the Paris production of *Giselle*. It was lighter and easier for Nijinsky to dance in, but also more revealing of his thighs and genitals than the dark tunic and heavy pants Albrecht was expected to wear in Russia. Word leaked out that Nijinsky would dance in his Paris costume, and he was warned not to do so. (Today, this seems like a tempest in a teapot, but under the czarist regime individual initiative was unwelcome, and frank display of the body, especially when there were rumors of homosexuality, was frowned upon.) "I wanted to create the most favorable conditions for my debut," Nijinsky naively told a reporter, "and for that reason requested permission ... to appear in the costumes in which I appeared five times, and not without success, on the stage of the first theater of the world—the Paris Grand Opera."[44]

There are different versions of what happened next. Igor Stravinsky said that "Nijinsky appeared at the Imperial Theater in the tightest tights anyone had ever seen (in fact, an athletic support padded with handkerchiefs), and little else."[45] One of the psychiatrists I interviewed in Leningrad, a leading authority in the field of adolescence, told me his mother had seen Nijinsky dance in this performance of *Giselle*, and she could remember him wearing "nothing more than a bandage" (i.e., his jockstrap). The costume can be seen in London's Theater Museum. No one today would judge it to be "indecent" as the St. Petersburg audience (and Stravinsky) evidently did in 1911. According to most reports, the Grand Duke Andrei, a cousin of the czar, went backstage to see Nijinsky, but the dancer denied him a closer look by covering himself grandly with a large cloak, thus further aggravating a delicate situation. The next day he was asked to apologize, and threatened with dismissal for his "improper" behavior. The director, Vladimir Telyakovsky, told reporters that "the self-willed appearance of Nijinsky in an unbecoming costume caused censure from the audience... what is suitable in Paris can turn out to be unacceptable here." There were other complaints as well. It was noted that Nijinsky had often excused himself from performing because of "prolonged illnesses." Telyakovsky spoke disparagingly about his "absenteeism as well as his whims."[46] In fact, Nijinsky still owed the Imperial Theaters four years of service for the education he had received there at government expense. But he knew that were he to leave the Maryinsky, Diaghilev would support him, indeed would offer him roles and opportunities undreamed of by Telyakovsky. Thus, despite the latter's last-minute efforts at diplomacy, and rumors that Nijinsky's salary might be raised even higher, he resigned. "My business is to dance and to dance well," he told reporters. On 24 January 1911 Nijinsky was officially dismissed from the Imperial Theater.

Bronislava Nijinska writes that their mother was "heartbroken" when she heard the news. "Every hope, every dream, every ambition she had had for her son was shattered."[47] Diaghilev, on the other hand, exploited Nijinsky's dismissal by sending telegrams to Paris, announcing that henceforth dancers would no longer be borrowed from the Imperial Theaters on a temporary basis. He was going to offer them full-time employment in an independent company of his own, called the Ballets Russes, with headquarters in Europe. Beginning in 1911, new productions were often rehearsed and sometimes premiered in the small, elegant Théâtre de Monte-Carlo, on the Riviera, then taken to various European capitals, and a few years later to the United States and South America. Diaghilev was always looking ahead. Long before the scandal over Nijinsky's costume he had started to work with Stravinsky, Benois, and Fokine on a most unusual ballet, to be called *Petrushka,* that he knew would appeal greatly to the Parisians. The music for this ballet, which is about a Russian street carnival, became one of Stravinsky's most popular works, often performed in orchestral concerts and by piano soloists. The choreography combined elements of the traditional storybook ballet, which usually had several scenes and included pantomimes, with the more modern trend toward naturalism, improvisation, and genuine display of feeling. There were to be milling crowds, street dancers, vendors, animals, and a magician's puppet show in which the doll-figures come to life. The sad-faced clown Petrushka, with wooden hands and feet moving in disjointed, mechanical gestures, came to be Nijinsky's favorite role. The way he held his body, swaying from side to side with feet turned inwards (and sometimes even on pointe), the harsh positions of his arms, his drastic pounding on walls and floor—all were a radical departure from the classical style of ballet and forerunners of choreographies Nijinsky himself would soon be inventing. Ironically, *Petrushka* also symbolized his enslavement to Diaghilev. In this ballet Nijinsky's very existence is controlled by a "magician," and his portrayal of Petrushka emphasized the puppet's suffering. Fearing the magician, he makes a gesture of being decapitated. Petrushka is in love with one of the other puppets, the Ballerina, but cannot possess her. She prefers the big, hypermasculine Blackamoor, who in a fit of jealous rage kills poor Petrushka on a crowded street in St. Petersburg. But the little fellow has the final word. Before the curtain falls, we see his ghostlike image teetering on the frame of the theater, high above the crowd. Petrushka has found freedom in death.

Another important ballet to be inaugurated that season was *Le Spectre de la Rose.* Set to music by Carl Maria von Weber and based on a poem of Théophile Gautier, the story* takes place in the boudoir of a girl in love. She inhales the perfume of a rose, falls into a trance, and experiences a fantastic dream: her lover flies in through an open

*It was written by Jean-Louis Vaudoyer, a Parisian journalist friend of Diaghilev. *Spectre* always reminds me of the nineteenth-century ballet *La Sylphide,* the antecedent of so many famous works, including *Giselle, Swan Lake,* and Fokine's *Les Sylphides,* all of them vehicles for Nijinsky's genius. In the much earlier *La Sylphide,* however, the roles are reversed. It is the man who snoozes and dreams, while the girl seductively whirls around him, only to disappear up the chimney, and not through a window as the Spectre of the Rose does.

window, whirls around her, then takes her in his arms. They dance together for a while, but her eyes remain demurely shut throughout this ecstatic union. It was a showcase ballet for Nijinsky and Karsavina, and became extremely popular. Nijinsky invariably completed it by ascending in one of his most spectacular leaps that took him out the window (a symbolic and probably unconscious reenactment of his brother's catastrophic fall). Exhausted by the time he was finished, Nijinsky had to land either on a mattress placed backstage or in the arms of a strong man, usually Vasili Zuikov, his valet and bodyguard. Diaghilev had assigned Zuikov, an unhappily married man about Diaghilev's age, to watch over Nijinsky, get him out of bed, shave and dress him, supervise his daily massage, and check any flirtations that might ensue while he was practicing with a ballerina.* Zuikov was the first of many men hired in the course of Nijinsky's life to take care of his daily needs, watch over him, and keep him out of trouble. After he became a psychiatric patient, these were "male nurses" and constant "attendants."

Although Nijinsky's impersonation of the Spèctre was a vehicle to great success, he generally felt some embarrassment in playing this role, especially when people came up to him afterwards and wanted to inspect his legs, hoping thus to find the secret to his extraordinary leap. His costume, with pink rose petals stuck onto his brief décolletage, was like a ballerina's, and some of his gestures—sensuously puckered lips and limp-wristed arms encircling his head—lent a feminine aura to this role as well. Cocteau marveled at the mystery of his disguise: "One would never have believed that this little monkey with sparse hair, wearing a skirted overcoat and a hat balanced on the top of his head, was the idol of the public."

> On the stage his overdeveloped muscles became slim. His figure lengthened (his heels never touching the ground), his hands became the fluttering leaves of his gestures, and as for his face, it was radiant. Such a metamorphosis is almost unimaginable for those who never witnessed it.[49]

The first time Diaghilev took his company to London was in the summer of 1911. The timing could not have been better, since it was the

---

*The Polish-born dancer Marie Rambert, who joined the Ballets Russes in 1913, after Nijinsky had become a choreographer, wrote that they "couldn't rehearse for twenty minutes" without being interrupted by Vasili.[48]

coronation of King George V. Performances of both operas and ballets were held at the Royal Opera House in Covent Garden and made a tremendous impression. Audiences, which included royalty, government officials, wealthy business people, writers, and artists (if they could afford the very high cost of tickets), were less demonstrative but equally enthusiastic as those in Paris, and very genuine in their appreciation of the company Diaghilev had assembled and the visual splendor of his productions. Many loyal and devoted friendships ensued. The Ballets Russes returned regularly each year until World War I broke out, appearing also at the British Opera House in Drury Lane. In addition, there were the usual performances at private parties, where the contrast between Nijinsky's charisma as a dancer and his generally reserved and inhibited offstage personality became especially noticeable. "He was very quiet and rather ugly," writes Lady Ottoline Morrell, a prominent figure in London society. "He always seemed lost in the world outside ... although his powers of observation were intensely rapid.... Many years later I found in Charlie Chaplin something of the same intense poignancy as there was in Nijinsky."[50] Nijinsky appealed strongly to the Bloomsbury circle. Lytton Strachey took a fancy to him, sent flowers, and bought a new, purple suit in anticipation of a possible romance, only to be disappointed by the man he later called "that cretinous lackey."[51] Duncan Grant made paintings of Nijinsky and John Maynard Keynes came to London to ogle his legs. Nijinsky, in turn, may have absorbed something of English country life and manners when he observed Grant and his friends playing tennis. He had not yet leaned to play tennis himself, but some of the movements probably entered into the choreography he made for a ballet called *Jeux*, in which he carried a tennis racket. In the United States, in 1916, Nijinsky began playing this game with a passion, and later, while hospitalized in Switzerland, he often amused himself by watching other patients play tennis.

Diaghilev had two other ballets designed for him. In *Narcisse* (1911), Nijinsky played the role of a gorgeous youth who becomes so enamored with his own reflection in a pool that he ignores his Echo, played by Karsavina, leans over too far, falls into the water, and drowns. It may have reevoked memories of his near drowning as a child in St. Petersburg when his father threw him into the Neva. (While dancing in South America during a tour in 1917, Nijinsky became so obsessed with the idea of actually falling through the stage and being killed at the end of *Narcisse* that he had trouble performing the ballet.) In *Le Dieu Bleu* (1912), the ballet based on a story Jean Cocteau had written (Reynaldo Hahn composed the music), Nijinsky was painted blue and dressed in a magnificent costume with a dazzling crown. He emerges from a lotus pond to confront a crowd of monsters. "His gestures are alternatively gentle and frantic," Cocteau writes. "He leaps from one to the other with supple and terrible bounds. He glides amid their groveling mass. Now he fascinates them with cabbalistic poses, now scares them with imperious threats. They try to drag him down, but he escapes them."[52]

These words also are prophetic of Nijinsky's madness. The groveling and "cabbalistic" threats were to be incorporated into terribly disturbed and frightening behavior he sometimes displayed in hospitals. Fokine later commented that a "lack of masculinity which was peculiar to this remarkable dancer" made Nijinsky "unfit for certain roles,"[53] but of course it was Fokine who choreographed the many Diaghilev ballets that capitalized not only on Nijinsky's androgyny, but also his capacity for violence.

It can be concluded that the years of dancing for Diaghilev brought great distinction to Nijinsky. His name became a household word among balletomanes in London, Paris, Budapest, Vienna, and other major European cities where the Ballets Russes performed. Fashions changed as a result of their influence. In Paris especially, clothes made of crimson and pink material could be seen. Bakst's original color schemes also led to an "oriental style" of furniture. Cartier began to handcraft green and blue jewelry. But along with the success came a shift in the leadership of Diaghilev's company. Alexandre Benois was beginning to feel more like an outsider, and sometimes was treated as such. Nijinsky, in addition to dancing, was being groomed to become Diaghilev's principal choreographer, much to the dismay of Michel Fokine, who had been his teacher in St. Petersburg and had crafted the ballets that made Nijinsky so popular. Diaghilev always demanded something new, exciting, and fascinating for the public. He, as well as Stravinsky, was growing tired of Fokine's style. They hoped Nijinsky could improve on it. These shifts of equilibrium affected not only Diaghilev's finely tuned organization, but also his relationship with the "God of the Dance," upon whom so much love and attention had already been lavished and for whose security, both artistically and financially, Diaghilev was wholly responsible.

NOTES

1. Arnold Haskell, in collaboration with Walter Nouvel, *Diaghilev: His Artistic and Private Life*, 240.
2. Richard Buckle, *Diaghilev*, 6.
3. Haskell, 11.
4. Serge Lifar, *Serge Diaghilev: His Life His Work His Legend*, 38.
5. Lynn Garafola, *Diaghilev's Ballets Russes*, 26.
6. Lifar, 33.
7. Simon Karlinsky, "Sergei Diaghilev; Public & Private."
8. Vladimir Zlobin, *A Difficult Soul: Zinaida Gippius*, 15.
9. Notebook on "Death," 39.
10. Notebook on "Life," 69.
11. *Diary*, 49. In unpublished notes titled "Vaslav remembers following incidents," Romola Nijinsky mentions "how he was asked by Prince L. to take part in his party and is disgusted [sic] of the perverted atmosphere ... how he is frightened when [Diaghilev] makes his advances." These notes, in English, are dated "1913, Buenos Ayres."
12. Notebook on "Death," p. 95.
13. Ibid., 75.
14. Alexandre Benois, *Reminiscences of the Russian Ballet*, cited in RBN, 81.
15. BNM, 306.
16. For the kinds of audiences that swarmed to Diaghilev's productions in Paris, see Garafola, 279–289.
17. Tamara Karsavina, *Theatre Street*, 235–236.
18. See RBN, 105.
19. BNM, 275.
20. BNM, 278; RBN, 117.
21. Arlene Croce, *Going to the Dance*, 277.
22. Prince Peter Lieven, *The Birth of Ballets-Russes*, 323.
23. RBN, 107–8.
24. Sandra Jobson Darroch, *Ottoline*, 126.
25. BNM, 266.
26. William A. Green et al., "Psychosocial Factors and Immunity."
27. Archives USSR, Fond 497, Section 3, Unit 2223, pp. 10–33.
28. Notebook on "Death," 85.
29. BNM, 277.
30. Garafola, 178–179.
31. Notebook on "Death," 85–86.
32. Ibid.
33. Archives USSR, Ibid., 29, 33.
34. Notebook on "Death," 86.
35. BNM, 278.
36. RBN, 122.
37. Archives USSR, ibid., 35–36.
38. Cyril W. Beaumont, *Memoirs 1891 to 1929*, 108. See also RBN, 160–61.
39. Benois, 289.
40. See Bruce Marks, interviewed in Barbara Newman, *Striking a Balance*, 210.
41. Vera Krasovskaya, *Nijinsky*, 150.
42. Archives USSR, ibid., 53–60.
43. Roland John Wiley, "About Nijinsky's Dismissal."
44. Ibid.
45. Igor Stravinsky and Robert Craft, *Memories and Commentaries*, 34.
46. Roland John Wiley, 243–244.
47. BNM, 320.
48. Marie Rambert, *Quicksilver*, 57.

49. Jean Cocteau, *The Difficulty of Being*, 44–46.
50. Lady Ottoline Morrell, cited by RBN, 306.
51. Michael Holroyd, *Lytton Strachey*, vol. 2, pp. 94–109.
52. RBN, 277.
53. Michel Fokine, *Memoirs of a Ballet Master*, 155–156.

Great as he was in the province of the performing dancer, Nijinsky was far greater as a practicing choreographer, in which function he either demonstrated or implied theories as profound as have ever been articulated about the classical theatrical dance.
                    Lincoln Kirstein[1]

Chapter 3

Nijinsky as Choreographer

Three events of the greatest importance for Nijinsky's developing sense of himself and his place in the world occurred in 1912, when he was twenty-three years old. They were closely related in time, and psychologically. First, on 29 May, he made his debut in the role of the Faun in a ballet he had personally choreographed. *L'Après-midi d'un Faune* (The Afternoon of a Faun) surprised everyone because of its unorthodox movements. It also evoked sharp criticism, something he had seldom experienced before. Second, on 15 July, his sister married one of the Ballets Russes dancers, Alexander Kotchetovsky. It was a formal, Russian Orthodox service. Nijinsky served as best man, and Diaghilev, standing in for their father, led Nijinska to the altar. Her marriage signaled the beginning of a separation between these two remarkable siblings, who since infancy had been closely intertwined in their thoughts, their feelings, their training, and their careers as dancers. The third critical event that year was the death of their father, Thomas Nijinksy, on 15 October. He had been touring the Ukraine with his dance company. His death, according to Bronislava Nijinska, was caused by the rupture of an abscess in his throat. He was fifty years old.[2]

Nijinsky's response to the death of his father will be discussed first because it led to one of the earliest judgments that there was something wrong or inappropriate about his emotional reactions. He had received word of Thomas Nijinsky's unexpected death by way of a telegram from his mother, handed to him just before a performance of *Schéhérazade* in Cologne, Germany. His first impulse was to protect his sister. According to her memoirs, he wanted to wait until the end of the performance before conveying the "tragic news," which he knew would be a shock to her. Nijinsky recognized that his sister felt a greater attachment to their father and loved him more deeply than he did. But when he came on the stage in his costume, he noticed that the dancer Adolph Bolm was talking to Bronislava about their father's death and trying to express condolence. Apparently the news had already reached other members of the company as well as the audience. Bronislava writes that a ballet critic from Odessa came backstage and spoke admiringly about their father, saying "he was a great *maître de ballet*" and pointing out that one of the ballets he had choreographed, *The Fountain of Bakhchisarai*, was "a forerunner of *Schéhérazade*, preceding it by many years."[3]

Coming at a time when Nijinsky was just starting to establish his own identity as a choreographer, and considering the ambivalence he felt toward the man who had been his father as well as his teacher and the betrayer of his family, Nijinsky's violent reaction is more understandable today than it was then. He exploded with rage, flew into a tantrum, turned angrily on Bolm, and called him an "idiot." But he just as quickly calmed down, and while leading his sister away from the other dancers said to her gently, "We must send Mama a telegram immediately and ask her to join us."[4] Later, he tried to apologize to Bolm for his outburst, but the older man thought it odd that Nijinsky smiled while apologizing. Sadness and a feeling of regret would have been more appropriate. We know that Nijinsky had very contradictory feelings toward his father, love and admiration on one hand, fear and hatred on the other. It may be that the hostile prong of his ambivalence was at this moment jabbed into Bolm.

Such displays of uncalled-for temper were not only upsetting to other members of the company, but also very difficult for them to understand. Was Nijinsky being deliberately provocative? Did he lack sensitivity for the feelings of others? Was his explosiveness a byproduct of the great talent he had for playing roles? In the theater, where time is compressed, the ability for shifting abruptly from one mood to another may be an asset, enabling quick changes to be made from a tragic character, say Petrushka, to a comic one, like Harlequin. In real life, however, one expects more sustained and predictable emotional responses. Here Nijinsky was at a disadvantage. It seemed to be difficult for him to modulate his feelings. They tended to dominate him. For long stretches of time he would be sullen or gloomy. Then there would be quick flashes of humor, excitement, or anger, followed again by a sort of apathy. Many people commented that he came truly alive only while dancing. The roles he played seemed to coagulate his emotions, and sometimes, especially after he began to create his own ballets, he seemed to have difficulty stepping out of them. After the curtain came down and long after the other dancers had gone to their dressing rooms and removed their makeup, Nijinsky might still be seen jumping, gesticulating, or practicing his pirouettes. Such behavior may have been needed by him to regain his stability after a performance. It also tended to confuse and alienate those who wanted to be close to him.

Nijinsky's interest in creating his own ballets probably grew out of a partial identification with his father, and certainly was stimulated when Diaghilev, a kind of father figure, invited him to choreograph *L'Après-midi d'un Faune*. Much has been written about the exciting fall of 1910, when Diaghilev and Nijinsky, then very much in love, spoke with Bakst about doing a ballet in the Greek style.[5] It would have to be a departure from Fokine's more conventional approach. Some of their colleagues, including Stravinsky, thought that Fokine, having to create so many ballets, was losing his originality. Why not let Nijinsky design a role and a ballet for himself? Diaghilev took him to the Louvre. They looked at Greek vases and Egyptian and Assyrian frescoes. They listened to music together, and read poetry. Nijinsky did not know enough French to understand Stéphane Mallarmé's poetic *L'Après-midi d'un Faune* (1865), which was popular in France at the time and had been a source of inspiration to Édouard Manet and other painters. So

Jean Cocteau explained the poem to Nijinsky and helped him to develop the scenario for a ballet. The music chosen was by Claude Debussy, who had composed a *Prélude à L'Après-midi d'un Faune,* and fully orchestrated it in 1895.

More than a year was needed for Nijinsky to work out the details of his ballet and perfect his role as the Faun. His sister describes him returning to St. Petersburg in 1910 looking rather glum, "more reserved, more pensive and aloof." There was "something different about him." (He had been diagnosed "neurasthenic" in March and had a "sunstroke" in August.) All he wanted to do was talk about Tolstoy, the great writer and philosopher who had just died. Tolstoy was a monumental figure, and his death in November 1910 was experienced as a personal loss by many Russians. After graduating from the Imperial Ballet School, both Nijinsky and his sister had received an eight-volume edition of Tolstoy's works as a present. It is not known how much Nijinsky read of Tolstoy, but there can be little doubt that he venerated the old man. Bronislava writes that in 1910 Vaslav "remained uncommunicative," except for talking about him. (A similar but more ominous preoccupation was to occur some six years later, when Nijinsky, while touring the United States, decided he must stop his career with the Ballets Russes and return to Russia, where he wanted to live like Tolstoy, celibate and vegetarian, on the land, like a peasant.) At the same time, there seemed to be "a new air of happiness" about Nijinsky, "a certain inner glow." It was related to the idea of choreographing *L'Après-midi d'un Faune.* He was inundated with ideas and fantasies. He could not communicate them verbally and asked his sister to help him express them through movements and gestures.[6]

She agreed. Between rehearsals at the Maryinsky, to which both of them still belonged before the scandal in 1911 involving Nijinsky's costume, they would go home to work on configurations for what was to become one of the most revolutionary ballets in dance history. They knew Debussy's *Prélude* "quite well," having heard it played for them by a pianist. To keep Vaslav's mind focused on the music, Bronislava would repeat several bars at a time while he "danced or demonstrated the movements." Then she repeated these movements, without the music, as best she could. The rehearsals were an ordeal for her, not only because of his inability to explain what he wanted, but also because he was so terribly demanding and perfectionistic, unable as she says "to take into account human limitations." Nijinsky used his sister literally the way a sculptor works with inanimate material. Sometimes they spent "all evening on the floor in front of the mirror trying out different poses." (Before the premiere of his ballet in 1912, he did the same sort of body molding and sculpting with the dancer Alexander Gavrilov. Similar behavior was to be noted by the doctors and nurses in the hospitals where Nijinsky was later confined.) Bronislava Nijinska wrote in her diary during the winter of 1910–1911:

> I am like a piece of clay that he is molding, shaping into each pose and change of movement . . . we are completely absorbed in our work . . . but sometimes emotions run high and we lose our tempers with each other. Vaslav . . . is unwilling to realize the tremendous distance separating his vision from the means that are at the disposal of the artist.[7]

Where did the "vision" for Nijinsky's unusual choreography come from? It is known that he had seen Isadora Duncan perform in 1909 and been astonished, as were all the Russian dancers, by her unorthodox way of expressing moods and interpreting music. The roles given to him by Fokine also allowed him to experiment with new poses and gestures. While visiting the Louvre with Bakst and Diaghilev, Nijinsky undoubtedly saw some of the friezelike positions, angular postures, and faces in profile that were incorporated into the choreography for *L'Après-midi d'un Faune*. This ballet is about a half-animal and half-human creature, the young Faun, who is aroused by seven nubile women, Nymphs, taking a bath. One of them shows an interest in him, and they dance together briefly. She drops her scarf and runs away. The Faun picks up the scarf, fondles it, takes it to his lair, and uses it as a fetish for autoerotic excitement. For Mallarmé, *L'Après-midi d'un Faune* was a fantasy; Nijinsky made it real. The Faun lies on top of the scarf and ejaculates. Could this have been Nijinsky's masturbation fantasy? It is hard to believe that his constant "molding and shaping" of his sister would not have led to a certain amount of sexual arousal that had to be inhibited, disguised, or expressed symbolically. Some of the Faun's aggressive approaches to the Nymphs were clearly based on Hellenic vase paintings Nijinsky had seen. As Jean-Michel Nectoux has convincingly demonstrated, a photograph of Nijinsky dancing the Faun, with head erect, arms extended, hands in profile, thumbs up, and fingers held together, resembles almost exactly the figure of a satyr on a 430 B.C. Greek vase in a collection from the Louvre.[8]

Another possible source of inspiration must be considered. Nijinsky and his sister occasionally visited the hospital where their brother Stanislav had to be confined. In 1911 he was transferred to the very large (960 beds) city asylum, Novoznamenskaya Dacha, near Ligovo. These visits were moving as well as troubling. Bronislava's memoirs describe how Vaslav would "turn pale" and sometimes be "reluctant" to see his brother, whose hospital room was "shared with several other adult patients."[9] It was customary in those days to house patients with neurological diseases together with psychiatric patients. Thus, more likely than not, the Nijinskys—mother, brother, and sister—would have seen cases of cerebral palsy, postencephalitic Parkinsonism, torsion spasm, dystonia, and other neurological deformities as well as epilepsy, mental retardation, catatonia, and dementia. Pathological movements associated with these conditions can be very striking, and Nijinsky, who felt considerable empathy with his brother and had a great interest in movement, probably remembered them well. "I like lunatics because I know how to talk to them" he wrote in a notebook shortly before he himself was hospitalized. "When my brother was in a lunatic asylum I loved him and he felt [i.e. understood] me. His friends liked me.... I understood the life of a lunatic. I know the psychology of a lunatic."[10]

One can also assume that certain ideas incorporated into Nijinsky's controversial ballets, for example the hyperextended wrists in *Jeux*, the turned-in feet in *Le Sacre du Printemps*, and the twisted neck in *Till Eulenspiegel* (not to mention some of his more extreme poses in *Schéhérazade, Petrushka, Les Orientales*, and other Fokine ballets), may have been derived, at least in part, from conscious or unconscious memories of pathological movements observed in his brother's hospital. While working on *L'Après-midi d'un Faune*, Nijinsky's wish to expand the repertoire of expressive gestures, and his fascination with contorted if not abnormal movements, were probably held in check by Diaghilev's demand for the more formal, stylized poses suggested by museum pieces. With growing independence, however, Nijinsky began using movements that often were awkward, grotesque, and difficult to carry out, at least by the classically trained dancers at that time. The similarity of these movements to expressions of disease seems inescapable, and spectators probably responded to that intuitively, often in a negative way.[11] (During the notorious premiere of *Le Sacre du Printemps* in Paris, some members of the audience shouted, "Call a doctor! call a dentist!")

Nijinsky's new position with the Ballets Russes as a choreographer and director of ballets (in addition to his usual work as a dancer) necessitated his being able to assume authority and give leadership to other members of the company. This proved to be difficult because of his youth, his inarticulateness, and his fluctuating moods. Rehearsals were agonizing. Of the seven Nymphs in *L'Après-midi d'un Faune,* only one, Bronislava Nijinska, knew exactly what was expected of her. Nijinsky would try to explain, but could not, so every movement, every pose, every gesture had to be demonstrated, over and over again, until the dancers got it right. He wanted "each position of the dance, each position of the body down to the gesture of each finger," to accord perfectly with his strict choreographic plan.[12] This meant that years of classical training had to be unlearned. In utter defiance of the rules of ballet, Nijinsky expected the dancers to hold their heads and feet sideways, in profile to the audience, while their bodies, with elbows held at an angle, had to face forward. There was to be no dancing on pointe, no facial mimicry of emotion, and no jumping, except for a single leap by the Faun. The task of learning to perform this ballet was aggravated by the languid and atmospheric quality of Debussy's *Prélude.* The music is a wash of sound, with no precise rhythm. Nijinsky liked its voluptuousness, but was frustrated by its blurriness. His dancers had to listen closely and count very carefully. *L'Après-midi d'un Faune* was a complete break with tradition, a much more radical approach than anything Fokine had ever done, and the true beginning of what is now called modern ballet.

Nijinsky worked incessantly to prepare himself for the Faun, a role with which he identified completely—"the Faun is me," he wrote later.[13] Bakst designed the costume for him: large brown spots painted on skin-colored tights and on his bare arms. Makeup was used to accentuate the heaviness of Nijinsky's mouth and obliqueness of his eyes. He wore a golden wig with two horns, and his ears were elongated with wax. Around his neck was a braided necklace, and a short tail jutted from his back. He carried a flute and fondled a cluster of grapes. His feet were in sandals (the Nymphs danced barefoot). Even when he was not rehearsing, Nijinsky sometimes behaved like a skittish beast. One evening at a dinner party, for example, Cocteau noticed that he was holding his head lowered all the time, and very slowly moving it back and forth. What was the matter, wondered Cocteau. Was Nijinsky sick? Was he in pain? There was nothing wrong with him, Nijinsky told

Cocteau. He was only "getting into the habit of behaving like a faun with its horns."[14] (Here is another example of the way certain of Nijinsky's dance movements were intuitively perceived as pathological. A not uncommon neuromotor disease called spastic torticollis consists of involuntary twisting of the neck.)

Rehearsals for *L'Après-midi d'un Faune* were inordinately time-consuming, and Diaghilev tried at first to keep this a secret from Fokine. The older and more experienced choreographer was preparing his own new ballet, *Daphnis and Chloë*, with Nijinsky dancing the male lead. When Fokine discovered that his star pupil was being groomed as a choreographer, he reacted with undisguised jealousy, which raised tensions within the company even higher. Fokine wanted *Daphnis and Chloë*, a ballet in two acts and also on a Greek theme, to have first place in the 1912 season. But a great deal of rehearsal time—some say more than one hundred hours—had to be allotted to Nijinsky's twelve-minute *L'Après-midi d'un Faune*, and still the ballet was not ready. Stories began to circulate that Fokine was going to take over the rehearsals, and Diaghilev, with one eye always on the public, suggested some last-minute changes in Nijinsky's ballet. This precipitated a crisis. "I will leave everything and quit the Ballets Russes," Nijinsky told his sister. She tried to get him to control himself: "Vatsa, no one can force you to change your *Faune,* so why are you in such a rage? Don't lose your temper."[15] Nijinsky got his way. His ballet was produced exactly the way he wanted it, and earlier than Fokine's. And instead of Nijinsky quitting, Fokine resigned instead, after the premiere of *Daphnis and Chloë*.

L'Après-midi d'un Faune was performed publicly for the first time on 29 May 1912, at the Théâtre du Châtelet in Paris. It produced only feeble applause and some aggressive booing, which in Diaghilev's experience was unheard of. He became visibly upset, but with his magisterial approach and quick instinct for publicity, Diaghilev ignored the catcalls and simply ordered the brief ballet to be shown again right away, as an "encore." He also made arrangements for a statement to be published by the famous sculptor Auguste Rodin: "Nijinsky has never been so remarkable.... Form and meaning are indissolubly wedded in his body, which is totally expressive of the mind within ... he is the ideal model, whom one longs to draw and sculpt."[16] Other remarks in the newspaper were less complimentary: "We have had a faun, incontinent, with vile movements of erotic bestiality and gestures of heavy shamelessness," the powerful critic Gaston Calmette wrote, "an ill-made beast, hideous from the front, and even more hideous in profile."[17] Calmette was referring mainly to the ending, when Nijinsky, while lying on top of the Nymph's scarf, put his hands under his pelvis and jerked his body in a way that suggested he was having an orgasm. Such behavior in public was considered scandalous in 1912, even in Paris. Nijinsky had told no one about it in advance; it is possible that he himself had not planned the climax to be so explicit. Cocteau used the term "panic episode" in reference to Nijinsky's ballet, an apt appraisal.[18] Fear can and does lead to sexual arousal. Even ejaculation has been known to occur when a performer gets unduly excited on stage, but usually the audience is unaware of it. In Paris, the police threatened to stop further showings of Nijinsky's ballet unless he toned down the ending. He complied, but not before the French Foreign Office got into an argument with the Russian Embassy over this issue. National honor seemed to be at stake in the mini-scandal. The rest of the season was sold out.

The publicity for Nijinsky's ballet far exceeded anything Diaghilev had planned, and the dancer as Faun was again the talk of Paris. He was allowed to pose in the nude for the artist Aristide Maillol, whose sketch shows distinctly the disproportion between Nijinsky's upper and lower body (as well as a perfectly normal set of genitalia). He was also invited to Rodin's studio, with less satisfactory results. Diaghilev suspected Rodin of being sexually attracted to the dancer, and after finding the two asleep on a sofa refused to let Nijinsky go back to his studio.[19] Nijinsky was to write later that Rodin did not care for his body: "He looked at my naked body and found it was wrongly proportioned and therefore crossed out his sketches. I realised that he did not like me and left...."[20]

Two other works were being planned for him to choreograph at that time. One was the lighthearted *Jeux,* a ballet on the contemporary theme of a tennis game, with dancers appearing for the first time in modern dress, again a departure from ballet tradition. The symmetry of the tennis court and the contrast between players on the ground and balls in the air seemed an appropriate challenge for Nijinsky's inventiveness. The other work, *Le Sacre du Printemps* (The Rite of Spring), was a brainchild of Stravinsky and the archeologist-painter Nicolas Roerich. This ballet was to plumb the depth of the Russian soul by reaching back to an archetypal, pre-Christian paganism. Diaghilev had commissioned *Sacre* in 1911. He gave Stravinsky permission to use as large an orchestra as he might need, sent Roerich to the Slavic hinterlands in search of

authentic fabrics, colors, and costumes, and instructed Fokine to work
on the choreography. But Stravinsky regarded Fokine as "an exhausted
artist, one who traveled his road quickly, and who writes himself out
with each new work."[21] Thus, after Fokine's departure in 1912,
Nijinsky was asked to take over this ambitious project.

Lincoln Kirstein, with his profound understanding of the history and
practice of ballet, describes Nijinsky as "an artist and a naive philosopher with ultimate aspirations toward sainthood." Kirstein finds that
the three ballets Nijinsky choreographed for Diaghilev parallel the
sequence of psychosexual maturation proposed by Sigmund Freud: "in
Faune, adolescent self-discovery and gratification; in Jeux, homosexual
discovery of another self or selves; in Le Sacre du Printemps, fertility and
renewal of the race."[22] This is a valuable insight. It was in the course of
working on these three ballets that Nijinsky actually tried to move away
from his narcissistic position toward a more heterosexual orientation.
We have already heard about the Faun's autoeroticism. Jeux was to be
about three people flirting, making contact, separating from each other,
and playing the "game" of sex.

Three-way sexuality may be an archetypal symbol for the basic
triangularity in evolving human relationships (father/mother/child). It
also seems to have been a personal predilection of Diaghilev's. Nijinsky
wrote that Jeux was meant to show "the lusting of three young men. . . .
Jeux is the kind of life of which Diaghilev dreamt. Diaghilev wanted to
have two boys. He told me many a time of this aim of his, but I showed
him I was angry. Diaghilev wanted to love two boys at the same time and
wanted these boys to love him."[23]

Today it is possible to produce a ballet that is so frankly homoerotic—
Judith Lynne Hanna's splendid book Dance, Sex and Gender describes a
number of contemporary ballets that show physical affection between
men as well as ballets with a lesbian content[24]—but in 1913, the year
Jeux received its premiere, audiences were not ready for a candid look at
erotic behavior. Thus, for better or worse, it was decided to "camou-
flage" the homosexual meaning of Jeux by having two women dance two
of the male roles, while the third "boy," actually a portrait of Diaghilev
himself, would be danced by Nijinsky.[25] A ballet of such subtlety would
require collaborators of the greatest tact and skill; but both Debussy,
whom Diaghilev had commissioned to write the music, and Bakst, who
designed the sets and costumes, turned out to be less than ideal for this
project.

Debussy was fundamentally unsympathetic to Nijinsky's ideas. In the first place, he had thoroughly disliked Nijinsky's choreography for *L'Après-midi d'un Faune*, and when Diaghilev commissioned him to compose *Jeux*, he was already moving away from orchestral writing and concentrating on smaller forms, piano pieces and chamber music. Debussy's score for *Jeux* is filled with clichés taken from his earlier works, plus attempts to sound like Stravinsky. He rewrote the ending of *Jeux* several times in an effort to please Diaghilev, but the music does not fit well the idea of a "tennis game." Even when played as a concert piece, *Jeux* has had little success.[26] Moreover, Debussy was opposed to Nijinsky's recent interest in eurhythmics, an experimental method for coordinating the pulse of a musical composition with movements of the body. Eurhythmics was invented by the Swiss composer Émile Jaques-Dalcroze, who had been running a school for dancers near Dresden, Germany. He favored a kind of automatic obedience to the time constraints of music. The rhythm of a piece was supposed to be indicated by arm gestures, while movements of the legs were to show the note values. Eurhythmics enjoyed considerable vogue in music education for a while, and Diaghilev thought it might help Nijinsky to solve some of the rhythmic problems of Stravinsky's extremely complex score for *Sacre*. Diaghilev actually took Nijinsky to Dresden to meet Dalcroze, and he hired one of Dalcroze's students, Miriam Ramberg (she later changed her name to Marie Rambert), to work with Nijinsky. But Debussy objected strenuously. After seeing rehearsals of *Jeux* for the first time, he wrote that "Nijinsky has given an odd mathematical twist to his perverse genius. . . . I hold Monsieur Dalcroze to be one of the worst enemies of music!" Debussy also seems to have recognized some similarities between Nijinsky's choreography and the pathological movements of neurological disease. He wrote that the dancer moved "as if suddenly *struck by paralysis on one side.*"[27]

The two ballerinas assigned to dance with Nijinsky in *Jeux*, Tamara Karsavina and Ludmilla Schollar, had the greatest difficulty learning their parts. Karsavina, surely one of the most intelligent and capable of Diaghilev's dancers, recalls that at rehearsals Nijinsky "was at a loss to explain what he wanted of me. And it was far from easy to learn the part by a mechanical process of imitating the postures as demonstrated by him." Again one senses the pathological origin of certain gestures the dancers were asked to reproduce. "I had to keep my head *screwed on one side,* both hands curled in *as one maimed from birth,*" Karsavina writes.

"In ignorance of my purpose I occasionally lapsed into my *normal shape,* and Nijinsky began to nourish a suspicion of my unwillingness to obey him."[28] She does not mention, and may not have been aware of, his sexual interest in her. "I know that Karsavina is an honest woman," wrote Nijinsky later in reminiscing about this dancer. "I lusted after her a little because she has beautiful forms.... I courted her in Paris.... I used to quarrel with Karsavina."[29] From her side, their impasse was described as follows: "Best of friends on and off the stage, we often fought during the preparation of our parts. On this occasion our collisions were worse and more ludicrous than ever."[30]

Jeux (premiere in Paris on 15 May 1913) was not considered a successful ballet. Bakst's scenic design for a garden looked gloomy and seemed too spacious for only three dancers supposed to be in close proximity or pairing off. Nijinsky's costume displeased Diaghilev, who at the last moment demanded that his short pants, heavy knee-length stockings, red suspenders, and red wig be discarded in favor of a simple white outfit, with a red tie. The tennis symbolism was confusing. Although Nijinsky carried a tennis racket, his movements did not resemble this game, and the ball—"a great white india-rubber thing, bouncing heavily over the hedge there"—resembled a volleyball more than a tennis ball.[31] Nijinsky's choreography received mixed reviews. Some people liked its sculptural effects, the "stylized gestures" and interlocked bodies.[32] Others thought it was contrived and too mechanical. In London, the critic Geoffrey Whitworth treated *Jeux* as a spoof—"the moon's so wonderfully bright tonight, and it makes one feel so queer, not like a real person at all, more like a nymph, or a fairy"— while Cyril Beaumont criticized it: "Nijinsky had clearly studied the Dalcroze method, but had interpreted it in the letter rather than the spirit, the movements being so meticulously phrased with the beats in the music that the dancers were reduced to the level of automata."[33] The ballet was dropped from the repertoire after only a few performances and has never been revived, which is a pity.* The historical importance

---

*A revival of *Jeux* would have posed problems, to be sure. Nijinsky did not write down the choreography. But drawings and photographs are available, and surely the ballerinas who performed it would have remembered certain details. Karsavina, as already mentioned, wrote about *Jeux* in her autobiography. Bronislava Nijinska, who had originally been groomed to dance the other "girl," had an excellent memory for her brother's work. Ludmilla Schollar, who replaced Nijinska after the latter became pregnant, became a ballet teacher in San Francisco and could have been consulted by Nijinska, then living in Los Angeles.

of this ballet lies not only in Nijinsky's experimental use of Dalcroze's ideas, which he did in *Sacre* as well, but also in his attempt to rebel against Diaghilev. Nijinsky later wrote that he had sought to impersonate the homosexual impresario in *Jeux:*

> the two boys are two young girls and *Diaghilev is the young man.* I camouflaged these personalities on purpose because I wanted people to feel disgust. I felt disgust and therefore could not finish that ballet. Debussy did not like Diaghilev's aim either, but he was given ten thousand francs for that ballet and therefore he had to finish it.[34]

It seems that around this time Nijinsky was starting to play some sexual games of his own. He no longer wanted to be intimate with Diaghilev. "I used to lock my door," he later wrote, "because our rooms were next to each other. I did not allow anyone in. I was afraid of [Diaghilev] because I knew that all practical life was in his hands."

> Diaghilev noticed that I was a boring man [i.e. not interested in him sexually] and therefore left me alone. As I was alone, I masturbated and chased tarts. I like tarts. Diaghilev thought that I was bored, but I was not bored. I was busy with dancing and composed ballets by myself.[35]

Nijinsky's *Diary*, published in 1936, omits most of what he had written about prostitutes. His original notebooks disclose that he was "chasing" them in Paris, but not without the fear of being discovered or that he might contract a venereal disease (he had already had gonorrhea). "Diaghilev thought I went out for walks, but I was chasing tarts," he wrote.

> "I used to rush around Paris looking for cheap tarts because I was afraid my actions might be found out. I knew that the tarts had no diseases because the police had them under observation. I knew that what I was doing was horrible. I want to describe my escapade with tarts. I was very young and so did silly things. All young men do silly things. I lost my balance and went about the streets of Paris looking for tarts. I looked for a long time because I wanted the girl to be healthy and beautiful. Sometimes I would look for one all day long and not find one because I had no experience in looking for tarts. I made love to several tarts a day. I know these were terrible things to do. I did not like what I was doing, but my habits became more complex and I took to looking for them every day.[36]

Nijinsky's need for intimacy with a woman probably was accentuated by his sister's recent marriage, which deprived him of the only satisfying female relationship he had ever had. To avoid discovery of his visits to "terrible place[s] where there were tarts," Nijinsky "resorted to all kinds of ruses." Rumor has it that Diaghilev's valet, Vasili Zuikov, knew what was happening but did not interfere.[37] Perhaps he felt that Nijinsky needed these occasional flings with women. (Zuikov had been married.) "I did not want to be dressed richly because I was afraid people would notice me," Nijinsky wrote later.

Once I was pursuing a tart who turned in the direction of LaFayette [shop]. I suddenly noticed someone looking at me very intently—a young man who was sitting in a cab with his wife and two children, if I am not mistaken. He had recognized me. I received a mortal blow for I turned and blushed deeply. But I continued to hunt for tarts.... I found rooms in a small Paris hotel. Paris is full of such small hotels. People living in such small hotels are simple. I know many such small hotels which exist by letting rooms for a short time for free love."[38]

It seems that Nijinsky also pursued these practices in London, or tried to, with somewhat unexpected results. According to Nesta Macdonald, who has collected information about the Ballets Russes in England, one of Nijinsky's nocturnal adventures led to his being taken "unconscious—not really ill but somehow the worse for wear" to a shelter for vagrants, now a hospital, in Chelsea. The ward attendants, not realizing who their "inmate" was, were astonished when "a figure suddenly leapt right over one bed, occupant and all—did the splits in the space, then leapt the next bed, and so on right up the twenty beds on one side and up the twenty beds on the other." He spoke no English, but communicated in pantomime and wrote something down on paper, probably the name of his hotel. "A little while later several well-dressed gentlemen arrived in cabs, one of whom said his name was Diaghilev. He extracted golden sovereigns from a sovereign purse, tipped lavishly, and distributed largess, and collected V. Nijinsky, thanking everyone for the care that had been taken of him."[39]

The greatest challenge, by far, to Nijinsky's ingenuity and creativity was his work on Le Sacre du Printemps, the fabulous score Igor Stravinsky had composed for a ballet that would require nearly forty minutes of dancing (compared to twelve minutes for Faune and eighteen for *Jeux*). *Sacre* shows spring returning after a glacial prehistorical winter in Russia. The earth is budding with fertility, squirming with new life. There are processions and dances of people awakened. Youths and elders convene. A young virgin is chosen for the ritual sacrifice, and she dances herself to death. With Fokine's departure from the Ballets Russes the responsibility for preparing *Sacre* had fallen on the relatively inexperienced Nijinsky. In spite of all of his other commitments, which included dancing in a new production of *Swan Lake* in London (with Kchessinska as the Swan Queen and Mischa Elman playing the violin solos), Nijinsky rose brilliantly to this challenge. Stravinsky said that his choreography for *Sacre* was "incomparable."[40] Many have considered it to have been his masterpiece, the work that ultimately established Nijinsky as one of the most important choreographers in the history of ballet.

In keeping with the idea of an integral connection between the human body and Mother Earth, he forced the dancers to the ground, feet turned in with knees unbent, hands, elbows, and faces pointing down. Stravinsky's hammerlike rhythm and shrieking orchestra provided the impulse, Roerich's bulky costumes the weight. As if to stress the aboriginal quality of these primitive rites, Nijinsky thrust the dancers into circles, single, double, triple, and interlocking loops of seething humanity. All the conventions of classical ballet, symmetrical arrangements and pleasing repetitions, were eliminated. There was something ruthlessly primitive, "almost bestial," about his choreography. His sister wondered if Nijinsky had been thinking of the "trained animals, or horses and elephants in the circus, or of the maneuvers of the army regiments" they had seen when they were children in Russia.[41]

Diaghilev's engagement of Dalcroze's student Marie Rambert to assist Nijinsky in training the dancers was a wise decision. Rambert could speak Polish as well as Russian and possessed the patience and verbal skills Nijinsky lacked. Each day after a general rehearsal of the company, Rambert would "stay for an hour or two and listen with Nijinsky to the score of *Sacre*." He then demonstrated to her what he wanted the dancers to learn during their next rehearsal. "The rhythms were very difficult, and I had to study the rhythm with each artist individually," wrote Rambert.

They soon nicknamed me "Rythmichka." There was no melody to hold on to—so the only way to learn it was to count the bars all the time. The movements in themselves were simple, and so was the floor pattern. But the basic position was difficult to sustain in movement, and the mastering of that rhythm almost impossible.[42]

In spite of Rambert's assistance, Nijinsky found it extremely frustrating to train the dancers. He now had the entire company of dancers to contend with, not just a handful of women as in the two Debussy ballets, and his rapport with them was minimal. As Bronislava Nijinska explained:

> Over the years, being always in the company of Diaghilev, Vaslav had kept to himself and rarely seen his colleagues outside the theater, and now that he was working with them as choreographer he was not able to establish a contact with them, to create a favorable atmosphere among the *corps de ballet,* loyal for the most part to Fokine. He was unable to reach them personally and obtain their cooperation, so they might believe in him and be supportive of his work and ideas, so essential during the process of creation ....[43]

Some of the dancers complained of headaches and other symptoms caused by the physical demands Nijinsky was making. And when Stravinsky arrived to watch the rehearsals, he "flew into a rage," started to bang his fists on the piano, and "yelled," trying to correct the tempo, which Nijinsky had slowed down so as to make it easier for the dancers. Nijinsky became "very nervous."[44] He himself was not planning to dance in *Sacre,* but it was necessary for him to demonstrate over and over again the steps he wanted. Under these stressful conditions he flared up repeatedly with anger and even accused his colleagues of wanting to "sabotage" him. Diaghilev often had to intercede. Nijinsky did not seem to understand that the unconventional movements and fantastic leaps he was creating went far beyond what ballet dancers in those days were trained to do. It was one of the drawbacks of his genius. His vision of *Sacre* was several generations ahead of its time.

Bronislava Nijinska's marriage destabilized the situation even further. Nijinsky wanted his sister to play the role of the Sacrificial Virgin, the innocent girl chosen by the primitive horde to dance herself to death in the second act. It is a moot point whether either of them appreciated the parallel between the Virgin's self-sacrifice and their own personal drama. As fate would have it, Bronislava became pregnant while rehearsals were in progress, in the fall of 1912. On hearing the news,

Vaslav erupted in an unbelievably frenzied rage. "There is no one to replace you," he screamed. "You are the only one who can perform this dance, only you, Bronia, and no one else." She tried to explain to him that being pregnant would make it impossible for her to do justice to his choreography, which required the Virgin "to dance with complete abandon" and throw herself violently to the ground. Bronislava wanted to reason with him, but "Vaslav did not seem to hear a word I was saying." He fumed and raged: "You are deliberately trying to destroy my work, just like all the others."[45] Here, temperament seemed to verge on paranoia.

Whether Nijinsky had overstepped the limits of behavior permissible for a performing artist and behaved irrationally at this point is debatable. (Later, as we shall see, his extremely disturbing temper tantrums, coupled with suspiciousness and inaccessibility, were indeed called "paranoid," "maniacal," and "catatonic.") Apparently it was impossible to calm him down for some time after the crisis precipitated by his sister's pregnancy. His mother, who after the death of his father had come to join them, "tried in vain" to do so. When Bronislava's husband, Alexander Kotchetovsky, came into the room and attempted to restore order, Nijinsky "turned on him and looked ready to strike him."[46] Marie Rambert writes that when she saw Nijinsky after this crisis he looked "pale as a ghost."

> "What on earth is the matter?" I asked.
> "I very nearly killed a man."
> "How can you say such a thing? Anyhow, who was it?"
> "A blackguard, a brigand, who has prevented Bronia from dancing *Jeux* and *Sacre.*"[47]

As far as we know, this was the first time that Nijinsky, then twenty-three years old, manifested any homicidal tendencies. The violence of his temper—and the real danger that he might kill someone or himself—was one of the chief reasons for his later confinement to psychiatric hospitals. In 1912–1913 it was most likely assumed that his murderous rage was an expression of his frustration while working on *Sacre*, an overinvolvement perhaps with the brutal content of this ballet. With so much at stake, Diaghilev did his best to protect Nijinsky. He would step into the melee, forcefully tell him to stop his raving, and make him apologize to the dancers, including on one occasion Tamara Karsavina, whom Nijinsky had managed to insult deeply. Replacements were quickly found for his pregnant sister. Ludmilla Schollar, as already mentioned, was given her role in *Jeux;* Marie Piltz, a ballerina from St. Petersburg who had recently been assigned solo roles with the Ballets Russes, was trained to take Nijinska's part in *Sacre.* Would Nijinsky himself have wanted to dance the Sacrificial Virgin? This question crossed Marie Rambert's mind while she was watching him rehearse with Piltz and, considering Nijinsky's close identification with his sister, it makes sense. While discussing this with Richard Buckle, Rambert said it looked as if a male sacrifice at the end of *Sacre* "might have been Nijinsky's most wonderful creation." One can well imagine that dancing himself to death at the end of *Sacre* might have been a remarkable sublimation of Nijinsky's terrible distress.

> With clenched hands across his face, he threw himself into the air in paroxysms of fear and grief. His movements were stylized and controlled, yet he gave out a tremendous power of tragedy.[48]

Diaghilev was understandably apprehensive about the premiere of *Le Sacre du Printemps.* He scheduled it for 29 May 1913, the anniversary of Nijinsky's debut in *Faune* a year earlier. Diaghilev was superstitious about such things. Anticipating a recurrence of audience disapproval, he instructed the conductor Pierre Monteux to make certain the orchestra would continue to play no matter what happened, and he told the dancers that under no circumstances were they to stop what they had to do on stage. In spite of these warnings, the ferocity evoked by *Sacre* came as a shock to everyone. Stravinsky's music began with a mournful bassoon solo in high register. Murmurs of dissent were soon heard, then a quick crescendo of intrusive whistling, raucous catcalls, and shouted insults. Suddenly the theater "seemed to be shaken by an earthquake."[49] The audience split into two antagonistic factions, one in favor, the other opposed to the new ballet. The way spectators were seated in the recently built Théâtre des Champs-Elysées seemed to favor such a polarization. The "old guard" of wealthy patrons, critics, and overdressed snobs sitting in one section felt violated by the extreme modernity of *Sacre* and took sides against the younger, poorer, and more radical "advance guard" of artists, musicians, and writers in another section. Fistfights broke out. Dowagers were mauled. Gentlemen stood on their chairs screaming and pummeling their neighbors. The savagery of the dancers on stage was nothing compared to the rioting of the public evoked by Stravinsky's score and Nijinsky's choreography.

To prevent a disaster, Diaghilev ordered the houselights to be turned on, which reduced the commotion somewhat. During the pause after the first act, policemen entered the theater to eject the most serious troublemakers. Nevertheless, people continued to behave deplorably for most of the second act. When a group of women dancers came on stage with their feet turned in, their heads twisted sideways, and their hands supporting their cheeks, someone in the audience screamed, "Call a doctor." Someone else yelled, "Call a dentist—call two dentists." Soon there was a chorus of derision. Women traded insults, and men challenged each other to duels. "You dirty Jew," someone shouted at the composer Maurice Ravel. Pierre Monteux (who *was* Jewish) continued steadfastly to conduct, but the audience drowned out the orchestra. "Please, let them finish the performance," Diaghilev pleaded from the wings. Nijinsky was "in a state of extreme anxiety" as his sister tells us. He nearly rushed out on the stage to direct the dancers. In order to keep them from losing the rhythm, he had to shout instructions and beat time. "The noise and tumult continued," writes Bronislava Nijinska, "and it was not until near the end of the ballet, when Maria Piltz began to dance her solo, that the public quieted down."[50] During the intermission afterward, Nijinsky had to don his rose-petaled costume and get ready to dance *Le Spectre de la Rose*. By then order had been restored.

Reports differ as to Diaghilev's reaction to the unruly reception of *Sacre*. Cocteau claimed he was in tears. Stravinsky asserted he was content to have a scandal; it was exactly what Diaghilev wanted because of the publicity. The second performance, six days later, went more smoothly, with "unexpected tranquility of the audience which had come because of real interest and to try to penetrate the music of Stravinsky and the choreography of Nijinsky."[51] There continued to be protests, however. After the fourth and last Paris performance, Diaghilev proposed that an abridged version of the ballet be prepared for London, but Monteux threatened to quit if there was any tampering with the score (Stravinsky was sick in bed with the flu). The Londoners turned out to be more polite than the Parisians, but equally dissatisfied with *Sacre*. "Those members of the audience who had gone to the theater expecting to be charmed with light and graceful movements . . .

bitterly resented Nijinsky's new production," wrote Cyril Beaumont.[52] After three performances in London, Diaghilev took *Sacre* out of the repertoire. "All the friends of the Ballets Russes," he told Bronislava Nijinska, "agree that *Sacre* is not a ballet and it would be a mistake to follow this path of Nijinsky's. They say I am destroying my ballet company!"[53]

Seven years later Diaghilev revived *Sacre*, without Nijinsky's original choreography. The new version was by Léonide Massine, whose choreography Stravinsky said was preferable to Nijinsky's. (In 1913 Stravinsky had called Nijinsky "an admirable artist ... capable of revolutionizing the art of ballet. He is not only a marvelous dancer, but he is able to create something new. His contribution to *Le Sacre du Printemps* was very important."[54]) There have been other interpretations of this ballet, including an animated film version in Walt Disney's *Fantasia*. But it was not until 1987—thanks to the persistent championing of Nijinsky by Lincoln Kirstein and Richard Buckle—that anything like the first *Sacre* was again shown in public. This was a remarkable piece of detective work. To reconstruct the choreography, Millicent Hodson meticulously pieced together everything she could find from photographs and drawings. She consulted with Marie Rambert and anyone who could remember something of the original *Sacre*. Miraculously, Rambert's score with notes from rehearsals with Nijinsky and Stravinsky showed up in London. Kenneth Archer, who later married Hodson, made an invaluable contribution by redesigning the costumes and sets for the ballet, based on Roerich's paintings (in the Roerich Museum in New York) and other sources of visual information. *Sacre* was rehearsed and performed to immense acclaim by the Joffrey Ballet, and has remained in the repertoire of that admirable company. It may not be exactly the way Nijinsky would have wanted it—he was an impossibly difficult man to please—but his position as perhaps the most innovative choreographer of our time has surely been vindicated.[55]

Nijinsky's association with Diaghilev was clearly coming to an end in 1913, months before the dancer's fateful voyage to South America. The intimacy of their relationship had already been undermined by Nijinsky's "disgust" with homosexuality. Now, with the failure of *Jeux* and *Sacre,* their ability to collaborate effectively was imperiled by Nijinsky's struggle for independence and his impetuous behavior, which collided with Diaghilev's need to control him and keep the company going. As we read in Nijinsky's notebooks:

Diaghilev liked showing that Nijinsky was his pupil in everything. I did not want to show that I agreed with him in everything and therefore often quarreled with him in everybody's presence.... I began to hate him quite openly and once pushed him on a street in Paris. I pushed him because I wanted to show him that I was not afraid of him. Diaghilev hit me with a stick because I wanted to leave him. He felt that I wanted to go away and therefore ran after me.[56]

Such fighting in public was not only distasteful but sometimes dangerous. (This pattern was to recur during Nijinsky's quarrels later with his wife.) "I can no longer endure Nijinsky's unpredictable behavior and his violent outbursts," Diaghilev told Bronislava Nijinska in 1913. "With each passing day it becomes more and more difficult to reason or deal with him. This is the end. I must part with Nijinsky! .... Me, Diaghilev, to be insulted by this young man. He is no longer a boy...."[57]

Yet something held them together. Part of it was neurotic: Diaghilev's masochistic devotion to young men; Nijinsky's adolescentlike need for parental figures he could both abuse and depend on. But another part of it had to do with their mutual striving for artistic excellence. Another ambitious ballet had already been planned for more than a year, a biblical extravaganza to be called *La Légende de Joseph*. The impetus for this work came from the Austrian playwright Hugo von Hofmannsthal, who considered Nijinsky to be "the greatest miming genius on the modern stage (next to Duse, and as a mimer above Duse)."[58] Hofmannsthal wrote librettos for the German composer Richard Strauss, and in 1912, even before Nijinsky's *succès de scandale* in Paris with *Faune*, he recommended to Strauss that they should work together on a ballet. Hofmannsthal first wanted it to be based on the Greek tragedy about Orestes and the Furies, the *Eumenides*, but Strauss had already written his opera *Elektra* and did not want to pursue this theme once more. After preliminary discussions, it was decided that a more appropriate story for the ballet would be *"Joseph in Egypt*, the episode with Potiphar's wife; the boyish part of Joseph of course for Nijinsky, the most extraordinary personality on the stage today."[59] Diaghilev commissioned Strauss to write the music, instructed Bakst to design the costumes, and spoke with the Spanish painter José-María Sert, the lover and future husband of Misia Edwards, about preparing the scenery. During the excitement of getting ready for *Sacre*, Diaghilev also told Nijinsky to think about creating choreography for *Joseph*. It promised to be a magnificent opportunity to develop yet another "slave" role for himself, that of young Joseph who is sold into slavery by his brothers, purchased by the Egyptian Potiphar, and seduced by Potiphar's wife. (The shy Joseph escapes her embraces by leaving his robe in her hands, a curious reversal of what happens in *Faune* when the Nymph drops her scarf for Nijinsky.)

A lot of money was at stake in *La Légende de Joseph*. The years 1912 and 1913 were precarious for Diaghilev's company, and short-term bank loans had been required to pay for his new productions of operas and ballets.[60] With the failure of Nijinsky's *Jeux* and *Sacre*, Diaghilev was having second thoughts about his desirability as a choreographer. It had become clear to everyone that while Nijinsky could come up with extraordinary ideas for innovative dance movements, he was not able to produce ballets as quickly as Diaghilev desired, and lacked the qualities of a teacher and ballet master. Nijinsky was needed, of course, as the company's most outstanding male soloist. In order to provide a sufficiently varied program for the 1913 season, Diaghilev had already invited another choreographer, Boris Romanov, to work on the ballet called *La Tragédie de Salomé*, set to music by the French composer Florent Schmitt. Diaghilev had also been consulting about future projects with the veteran Moscow choreographer Alexander Gorsky. Such collaborations, unless undertaken with the greatest of tact, could easily stir up professional jealousies, Fokine's angry departure after Nijinsky's elevation to choreographer being an example. Now it was Nijinsky's turn to chafe under Diaghilev's sometimes less than openhanded negotiations with other artists. "I realized that Diaghilev was deceiving me," he wrote later. "I trusted him in nothing...."[61]

In July 1913 Diaghilev called Bronislava Nijinska to his hotel and asked her to listen to some unpleasant news, which he wanted her to relay to her brother. He was too fearful of Nijinsky's irascibility to speak to him directly. Diaghilev felt under great obligation not only to the entire ballet company but to his host theaters in Paris, London, and Monte Carlo. They no longer could afford to be "sponsors for Nijinsky's researches," he told his sister. According to the terms of a new contract, Diaghilev would have to produce two new ballets for the next season in London, and Fokine was to choreograph both of them. One of these ballets was going to be *La Légende de Joseph*. "My heart fell," writes Nijinska. "I knew this ballet had been promised to Nijinsky and that he had already begun working on it. And now Diaghilev had been forced to entrust its realization to Fokine." The moment he heard about this, Nijinsky went into an "angry tirade." Nijinska describes how he "thrust his hands into his pockets and flung his shoulders back aggressively. He went pale and threw his head back; he stood tense, facing me as if he were confronted by Diaghilev rather than his sister. . . . He drew his hands out of his pockets and, clenching his fists, paced back and forth across the room, his voice from time to time rising to a shout."

> Why is Diaghilev deceiving me all the time, making up all sorts of nonsense about my ballets? Why doesn't Diaghilev speak with me himself about all this? Why does he transmit it through you? He is a coward. He is not sincere with me. He is dishonest and is afraid to tell me of his intentions.[62]

What these eyewitness reports suggest is that Nijinsky could not understand the complexity of Diaghilev's task in running the Ballets Russes. Ballets, like operas, are collective enterprises, dependent on the combined efforts of numerous people working together in a spirit of cooperation. Diaghilev was exceptionally gifted in running so diverse an organization, and the reason he succeeded is that the welfare of his entire company was always put ahead of the interests of any individual member, including his own. Understandably, this led to terrible conflicts at times. But having been so intimately involved with Diaghilev, Nijinsky in 1913 no longer seemed able to perceive his own position in the company from the proper perspective. To continue to mature as an artist, he would have to adapt to the realities of making a living in the theater. There was no company comparable to the Ballets Russes at that time, and Diaghilev was his only source of support, paying for all of Nijinsky's living expenses, his travel, clothing, costumes, and dancing shoes (a new pair for each performance), plus an allotment of Fr. 500 each month for his mother in St. Petersburg.

The lack of success of his last two ballets had been a severe blow to Nijinsky's self-esteem, and there now loomed another threat, that Fokine, his rival and a discarded father figure, would be rehired. Small wonder that Nijinsky felt "deceived" and could no longer contain himself. His sister, with greater psychological maturity, observed that Nijinsky was responding to the instability of his situation with excessive anxiety. "I realized that Diaghilev's personal friendship with Nijinsky was over," she writes. "I had become increasingly aware of Vaslav's heightened state of nervousness these past few months, as if he felt that a net was being woven around him and was about to envelop him." (A "net" symbolizes both safety and confinement.) Bronislava talked to him about his forthcoming voyage to South America. The entire company would be sailing in August, but unfortunately she was not going to be able to come along. Her baby was due in October. "Don't worry too much about the future," she advised her brother. "Don't concern yourself too much with work on the new ballets, enjoy the ocean, become closer acquainted with the artists, make friends, don't be alone so much." Finally, she warned him not to get into any more "spats" with Diaghilev. Perhaps the tide would change, and Nijinsky might still be asked to choreograph some new ballets.[63]

NOTES

1. Lincoln Kirstein, *Dance*, 283.
2. BNM, 448.
3. Ibid., 447.
4. Ibid.
5. Jean-Michel Nectoux, *L'Après-midi d'un Faune*.
6. BNM, 314.
7. Ibid., 316.
8. Nectoux, 18.
9. BNM, 110, 214, 215.
10. Vaslav Nijinsky's unpublished notebook on "Feeling," 15. (Hereafter, cited as Notebook on "Feeling.")
11. See, for example, S. A. Kinnier Wilson, *Neurology*.
12. BNM, 427.
13. Notebook on "Death," 97.
14. Susan Lee Hargrave, "The Choreographic Innovations of Vaslav Nijinsky," 36.
15. BNM, 429.
16. RBN, 286.
17. See Jennifer Dunning, "Essay on 'L'Après-midi d'un Faune,'" 27.
18. Nectoux, 17.
19. Ibid., 28.
20. Notebook on "Death," 93.
21. For Stravinsky's letter to his mother, 17 March 1912, see Vera Stravinsky and Robert Craft, *Stravinsky in Pictures and Documents*, 30.
22. Lincoln Kirstein, *Four Centuries of Ballet*, 199.
23. Notebook on "Death," 96–97.
24. Judith Lynne Hanna, *Dance, Sex and Gender*.
25. Notebook on "Death," 97.
26. Oscar Thompson, *Debussy*, 217.
27. Letter from Claude Debussy to Robert Godet, cited in BNM, 469. Emphasis added.
28. Tamara Karsavina, *Theatre Street*, 285. Emphasis added.
29. Notebook on "Death," 88–89.
30. Karsavina, 285–286.

31. Geoffrey Whitworth, *The Art of Nijinsky*, 70.
32. RBN, 339–340.
33. Cyril W. Beaumont, *Bookseller at the Ballet: Memoirs, 1891–1929*, 132.
34. Notebook on "Death," 97. Emphasis added.
35. Notebook on "Life," 67.
36. Notebook on "Feeling," 29–31.
37. Personal communication from Kyra and Tamara Nijinsky.
38. Notebook on "Feeling," 31–33.
39. Nesta Macdonald, *Diaghilev Observed*, 84.
40. Vera Stravinsky and Robert Craft, 102.
41. BNM, 459.
42. Marie Rambert, *Quicksilver*, 56–57.
43. BNM, 460–461.
44. Vera Stravinsky and Robert Craft, 513.
45. BNM, 462.
46. Ibid.
47. Rambert, 58.
48. RBN, 335.
49. From a broadcast by Valentine Gross, cited in RBN, 357.
50. Quotations from BNM, 470, and Françoise Reiss, *Nijinsky*, 121–123. There have been many descriptions of the extraordinary rioting caused by *Sacre*, which has become almost symbolic of the world conflagration ushered in with the beginning of World War I a year later. See Modris Eksteins, *Rites of Spring*.
51. Vera Stravinsky and Robert Craft, 101.
52. Beaumont, 137–138.
53. BNM, 472.
54. Vera Stravinsky and Robert Craft, 511.
55. See Arlene Croce, "Footnotes in the Sands of Time."
56. Notebook on "Life," 67, 80.
57. BNM, 472.
58. *The Correspondence Between Richard Strauss and Hugo von Hofmannsthal*, 121.
59. Ibid., 134.
60. See Lynn Garafola, *Diaghilev's Ballets Russes*, 187.
61. Notebook on "Life," 79.
62. BNM, 473–474.
63. Ibid., 475.

Marry in haste, repent at leisure.
                    English Proverb

Chapter 4

Marriage

On a Saturday, 16 August 1913, Nijinsky boarded the steamship *Avon* for South America. It was the Ballets Russes's first overseas tour, an ambitious undertaking that had been planned for more than a year and would require their absence from Europe for over two months. Some important personnel changes had been made, including the engagement of several new dancers and a substitute conductor, Rhené-Baton, to replace Pierre Monteux. Nijinsky felt rested and relaxed. Evidently he had heeded his sister's advice and behaved decently toward Diaghilev during a week's vacation spent in southern Germany, where Benois and Nouvel joined them. Plans for a new ballet were discussed. It was to be danced to music by Johann Sebastian Bach and performed in a setting that Benois hoped would suggest "all the elaborate splendour of Court Festivals of the Rococo period." The question arose, Who would be the choreographer? Benois doubted that Nijinsky "possessed the necessary knowledge" of the style. Nevertheless, he was allowed to participate in selecting the appropriate pieces, all keyboard works transcribed for piano, and instructed to begin working on some of the dances as soon as possible. Diaghilev, as was his custom, took Nijinsky to museums and palaces where appropriate paintings, costumes, and architecture of the period could be seen. All four of them assumed, of course, that he would be dancing in the Bach-Benois ballet. Thus, Nijinsky's artistic future with the Ballets Russes seemed assured for the moment.[1]

But Diaghilev was not planning to sail with the company to South America. The reason usually given for his absence on this fateful trip is that he was "mortally afraid of sea travel (a gypsy had prophesied that he would die on the water)."[2] Even crossing the English Channel had usually been an ordeal for him. But a more compelling reason has been suggested: Diaghilev's ambivalence toward Nijinsky, with whom there had been much arguing lately, and little if any physical affection. Richard Buckle surmises that Diaghilev "was doubtless drawn to spend the rest of August and September in Venice, where perhaps adventures with pretty dark-eyed boys awaited him."[3] (A few years later, traveling with a new friend, Diaghilev was able to cross the Atlantic without too much trouble.) In Nijinsky's first letter home, he told his mother that Diaghilev had not even come to the boat to say goodbye, which led his sister to worry that the hoped-for reconciliation between him and Nijinsky had failed, and that their "long friendship was indeed ended forever."[4] Bronislava did not yet know about a new and very different kind of friendship involving her brother, one that was to alter her own relation to him and drastically upset his entire career.

From the beginning of the voyage, Nijinsky had sensed the presence of someone who was ready, if not determined, to fill the vacuum left by Diaghilev. She was a beautiful young woman named Romola Pulszky, who had been following him constantly for the past eighteen months, hoping that he might reciprocate the adoration and desire she felt for him. Nijinsky mentions her for the first time in a letter to his sister from Madeira, the island off Portugal where the *Avon* made its last stop before sailing to South America. The woman was "also alone" (in fact, she was traveling with a female companion) "and we are often together."[5]

Almost everything that we know about Romola Pulszky's amorous pursuit of Vaslav Nijinsky, their shipboard romance, and their precipitous marriage less than a month after leaving Europe comes from the popular book written by her twenty years later (it was published in 1934). By then, their marriage had failed, he had gone mad and was no longer dancing in public, and she was trying to support herself and earn money for his psychiatric care. Separated from him, Romola had gotten involved in a complicated lesbian relationship, and her lover, Frederica Dezentje, encouraged her to write the book with the hope of having it made into a movie. It was dedicated to Frederica, but largely ghostwritten by Lincoln Kirstein, and one must be cautious in interpreting the content. In spite of its many inaccuracies, Romola Nijinsky's book gives a fairly convincing picture of what it must have been like for this idolizing and persistent woman as she pursued her elusive and distracted future husband. Missing, however, is an explanation of her own personality and its development. Romola never asks what it was in her background that motivated her to choose Nijinsky. What did she think (or did she think about it at all) that a partnership with him would lead to? Why was she so persistent in forcing herself on this particular man?

Romola Ludovika Polyxena Flavia Pulszky was a year younger than Nijinsky, almost exactly the age of his sister. She, like Bronislava, had been born in 1891, but that is where the similarity ends. Romola's mother was Emilia Márkus, Hungary's most famous actress of the time, a glamorous star of the Budapest theater, who later also made films. Her father was the eminent Charles Pulszky, member of parliament and director of the Hungarian National Gallery of Art. Both were devoutly Catholic. Count Pulszky (he rarely used the title) stemmed from a distinguished Polish family of French Huguenot origin ("de la Poule") that had acquired considerable wealth by developing mines in what is now Czechoslovakia. The Pulszkys moved in very sophisticated social circles, and Charles's marriage to Emilia had been a high-society event. "Everybody who was anybody would pay court to them," says their granddaughter Tamara Nijinsky, who grew up in the palatial residence that Emilia built after her husband's death. It was like a museum, filled with art objects he had acquired through his international contacts. Emilia Márkus received guests in a Renaissance costume, like an actress on stage. But behind the scenes was personal friction and unhappiness. According to what Tamara learned from her grandmother, she did not genuinely love her husband; indeed, he sometimes seemed repulsive. "I hated it," Emilia would say, "when Charles was drunk and wanted to make love." Her life was in the theater, where she had many adventures and "little affairs on the side." He was unpredictable and unstable.[6]

Charles and Emilia had two children, both girls. The first, named Tereza ("Tessa"), was blond, vivacious, fun-loving, and "almost a carbon copy of her mother." But Emilia seems to have had relatively little interest in her. Romola was born eight years later. There had been a miscarriage in the interval, and it is possible that the couple had expected or wanted a son. (It is also possible that Emilia, who was then at the peak of her acting career, did not want to have another child.) Romola was born at seven months. She was a pale and sickly child who grew up to resemble her father more than her mother in looks and temperament. He pampered and spoiled her; she adored and idolized him. Emilia, too, tended to favor Romola over her older sister, which Tessa deeply resented. (In later years, when Romola turned against her mother, this situation was reversed and Tessa became Emilia's favorite.)

Long before starting school, Romola had already acquired something of Charles Pulszky's independent spirit, idealism, and reverence for the arts. "She was brought up to be a Renaissance princess and became an avant-garde feminist," says Tamara. She also tended to identify with his aloofness. But her attachment to him was tragically broken by age five, when Charles went abroad to buy paintings for the National Gallery, and upon his return to Budapest was arrested for allegedly having embezzled government funds. (According to the information available, he made some very good deals for the museum, but kept no records, and was pushed by his brother and sister into purchasing several pieces that ended up in private collections. Whether public funds were in fact used for this purpose is not clear.) Hoping to avoid further scandal, Pulszky moved to London, where he had been born and educated, leaving behind his properties and accumulated wealth. His wife refused to join him, we do not know why. Was it because of her status as Hungary's leading actress—Emilia Márkus was multilingual; why could she not have made a name for herself abroad?—or for more personal reasons related to their marriage? In any event, after the crisis in 1896 Charles Pulszky seems simply to have "disappeared." There was no word from him for three years. Where he was and what happened to him were total mysteries.

For Romola this was a highly traumatic separation from the father she loved. Undoubtedly there were fantasies and gossip about the missing parent. The girl became disconsolate and restless, had difficulty adjusting in school, and tried to offset the pain of her loss by turning for affection to her aunt Polyxena Pulszky, an intelligent, forceful, but rather homely spinster (she later did marry and have children), who from the beginning had disapproved of Charles's marriage to the actress Emilia Márkus. In his absence, Polyxena became a controlling influence on Romola's life, guiding her education and gradually turning her against her mother. Then, suddenly, when Romola was eight years old, her father surfaced. He wrote a letter from Australia, where he had been living and trying to start an insurance business. Apparently the business had failed; Pulszky's letter indicated that he was bankrupt, destitute, and deeply depressed. A second letter was a suicide note. He wanted to apologize for his failures, say farewell to his family, and die. Pulszky killed himself with a revolver allegedly given to him by "friends" in Budapest, who at the time of the museum scandal suggested he ought to end his life "honorably." It was a shattering experience for Romola. Her capacity for trust and human attachment seems to have been permanently damaged by this event. When her mother remarried a few years later, Romola developed an intense hatred for her stepfather, Oscar Párdány. He was a civil servant, eleven years younger than Emilia, and a Jewish convert to Catholicism. "Nobody can ever replace my beloved father," Romola would say. (Her marked antipathy to her stepfather as well as to her mother, both of whom would make repeated efforts to help Romola and her husband, was to create innumerable problems during both world wars, when the Nijinsky couple took refuge in the Pulszky residence in Budapest.)

Romola grew into a lanky, flaxen-haired, blue-eyed adolescent. She learned to disguise her hostility behind a façade of cold beauty. She became unapproachable, "frigid, like a Greek statue," says her daughter Tamara. At age sixteen, while in Paris to learn French, Romola took to worshiping Napoleon. She bought a costume for herself to look like the emperor, which she wore around the Pulszky mansion like her mother, who also wore costumes. Boys did not seem to interest her at all. In this respect Romola was very different from her sister, who is described as warm, outgoing, and rather flirtatious. (Later, Nijinsky often expressed a preference for the vivacious Tessa over the more somber Romola.) Tessa had great talent for music and was an excellent pianist. (She later married, and divorced, the Danish singer Erik Schmedes, a leading Wagnerian tenor at the Vienna Opera.) Romola, by contrast, seemed to lack any particular talent, had little sense of direction, and remained so isolated that Aunt Polyxena finally implored her to hire a chaperone and get away from home so she could further her education abroad.

Romola went to England, where she learned to speak the language fluently. Then she moved to Paris and took drama lessons with the famous actress Réjane but made no progress toward a career in the theater. She also studied in Germany, where in Bayreuth she met Cosima Wagner, whose imperious manner and devotion to her dead husband made a lasting impression. But something always drew Romola back to Budapest, and at age twenty-one, hoping to stabilize her existence there, she became engaged. Her fiancé was a baron—the title had been purchased by his family. It would probably have been a loveless marriage. She mainly wanted wealth and the prestige of marrying into the nobility. He was deceitful—it later turned out that he was a homosexual who sought mainly to climb socially by marrying into the Pulszky family.

In March 1912, the year of Romola's engagement, the Ballets Russes came to Budapest for the first time. Her aunt Polyxena had seen them in Vienna and urged her to attend these spectacular performances. Romola went on opening night, as a guest of her fiancé's mother. It was an overwhelming experience for her, the revelation of a new art form that seemed to blend many of the aesthetic values in drama and painting with which she had grown up. Particularly impressive, as Romola recalls, was that "an equal number of male dancers shared with the women important and dominating parts,"[7] an observation consistent not only with the sexual equality favored by her mother, but also with the democratic spirit championed by her late father when he was active in Hungarian politics. On a less conscious level perhaps, Romola may also have been responding to her own bisexuality. Nijinsky was rumored to be the most fascinating member of the company, but he was not dancing on opening night because of an illness that had detained him in Vienna. So Romola, went expectantly again the next day. Her first sight of him was unforgettable.

> Suddenly a slim, lithe, cat-like Harlequin took the stage. Although his face was hidden by a painted mask, the expression and beauty of his body made us all realize that we were in the presence of genius. An electric shock passed through the entire audience. Intoxicated, entranced, gasping for breath, we followed this superhuman being ... the power, the featherweight lightness, the steel-like strength, the suppleness of his movements ....[8]

As she contemplated the welter of emotions stimulated by this fascinating man, Romola noted an "uncanny feeling of apprehension."

He symbolized everything that the Ballets Russes had achieved, and compared to his, her own life seemed meaningless and empty. But by looking at Nijinsky and relishing the beauty of his movements, she was able to keep unpleasant thoughts and feelings at a distance. The experience transformed her in some magical way. It was almost like a religious conversion. She felt an irresistible calling, a purpose to her existence that was new to her—*this magnificent vision was Nijinsky.*"[9] Turning to her woman companion, Romola said, prophetically, "That man will be my husband."[10]

After discussing her infatuation with Aunt Polyxena, Romola decided to break her engagement to the "Baron." Soon she was a camp follower of the Ballets Russes, attending every performance and trying to get into rehearsals with the hope of catching a glimpse of her idol. Her goal was to get as close as possible to Nijinsky and to share the aura of his magnificence. In that respect she resembled a modern "groupie." Romola followed the Ballets Russes everywhere—to London, to Paris, to Monte Carlo, to Berlin, to Vienna, and back to Budapest. She quickly discovered that Diaghilev kept what she calls "an impenetrable Chinese wall around Nijinsky" to deter anyone who might get too close to him. This puzzled but did not discourage her. If anything, Nijinsky's inaccessibility seems to have made him even more alluring, and the chase more exciting, than if he had been an easy prey. "I could not understand this strange air of isolation around Nijinsky," Romola writes, "but I realized one thing very clearly: that I would have to proceed with the utmost caution. Nobody noticed my adoration for Nijinsky."[11]

Trying to insinuate herself between Nijinsky and Diaghilev (she did not yet know they were lovers), Romola developed a strategy that became increasingly brazen. First, she befriended Adolph Bolm, who had accepted an invitation to the Pulszky mansion while the company was in Budapest. Bolm was very "moved" by Emilia Márkus's hospitality, liked the actress, and sent her flowers.[12] He considered himself obligated to reciprocate and agreed to take Romola backstage. There she worked to create the illusion that it was Bolm and not Nijinsky she was very much interested in. In due time, both Nijinsky's mother and his sister noticed her intrusiveness—Romola was constantly trying to make conversation, sitting backstage on top of the costume-filled clothes hampers, smoking and laughing loudly, and generally making a nuisance of herself[13]—but neither of them realized what she was up to.

Nijinsky himself seems to have been unaware of what was happening. When Romola finally managed to get someone to introduce her to him, Nijinsky thought she was the prima ballerina of the Hungarian Opera and greeted her cordially. After this mistake was explained to him, he reverted to his usual way of avoiding contact with strangers, barely acknowledged her presence at rehearsals, and ignored the fact that they had ever met.

Frustrated by his lack of response, Romola finally decided to pose as a student of ballet. She began taking lessons, and because she had money and contacts she was able to persuade Enrico Cecchetti, the venerable old maestro who daily coached Diaghilev's dancers, to let her attend his classes as an observer. Cecchetti evidently recognized Romola's true purpose fairly quickly and warned her not to get too close to Nijinsky, who was "like a sun that pours forth light but never warmth."[14] So she finally approached Diaghilev himself and, while flattering him with praise, boldly announced her intention to become a dancer. Diaghilev had his suspicions. The first thing he told her was to take private lessons with Fokine in St. Petersburg, which would have kept her as far away from the Ballets Russes as possible. Romola pretended to agree. "I misled him deliberately," she writes. She told him that it had always been her "dream" to go to Russia, and anyway it was Adolph Bolm and not Nijinsky who appealed to her "as a man." Diaghilev had a soft spot for attractive women, and he always needed the support of wealthy balletomanes. Thrown off by her deception, he said something that Romola later characterized as "the fatal words."

> I will speak to Maestro Cecchetti. He has taught all our greatest artists. I am sure he will take you as a special, private pupil. This way you will have not only a marvelous teacher, but also the possibility of travelling with us and closely studying our work.[15]

Romola relates that Nijinsky actually objected to her entering Cecchetti's classes and traveling with the company. She was only a dilettante, he told Diaghilev (who would have known that himself), but Diaghilev presumably told him about her prominent family and that she was a daughter of the famous Emilia Márkus.[16] Thus, Nijinsky came to regard Romola with a certain amount of respect, if not awe, and probably found her attention flattering. It also was clear that Romola had singled him out. She sought every opportunity to make contact with him and always instructed her maid-companion Anna to find out in which train compartment he was traveling so theirs could be booked as close to his as possible. She would then loiter in the corridor, nonchalantly smoking a cigarette and smiling to attract his attention. They seldom spoke, not only because of Nijinsky's general disinclination to communicate verbally, but because of the language barrier. Romola spoke French but no Russian or Polish, while Nijinsky was dysfluent in French and knew no Hungarian. Mostly they communicated with pantomime or body language. They looked and gestured at each other. One time, when she indicated that her leg was sore after a lesson, he took hold of the foot and fondled her ankle. After a while, he took it for granted that she, like a typical groupie, was "here, there, and everywhere where he appeared in public."[17]

Romola also befriended some of the other dancers, but mostly in order to learn as much as she could about Nijinsky's tastes and habits. Marie Rambert, who was then working closely with him on *Sacre,* had more access to him than any of the others. (She herself was secretly in love with Nijinsky.) Romola pumped her for information and thus probably discovered what was generally believed among the dancers, that he was a homosexual who "had no interest in us women." Far from discouraging Romola, this information only made him seem more alluring. "Where others failed, why shouldn't I succeed?" she writes, her earlier feelings of apprehension by now replaced by a sense of mission, an "invincible desire to awaken Nijinsky's interest."[18] Her ambition and perseverance were remarkable. It reminds one of another go-getter at that time, Alma Schindler, the daughter of a Viennese painter, who acquired a string of famous men, including Gustav Mahler, Walter Gropius, Oskar Kokoschka, and Franz Werfel, as lovers or husbands.[19] Romola Pulszky's desire to have the "God of the Dance" for herself was like religious zeal. She writes that she would kneel before her little picture of Jesus at night and pray: "Make Nijinsky happy some way, somehow; to save him from the way of life he was leading with Diaghilev." She was fully determined to convert him to heterosexuality and possess him.

> Unacknowledged even to myself, I wanted to reform him for myself, but cunningly I thought I might deceive God with my unselfish prayer, taking it for granted that the Almighty Himself had an orthodox attitude towards sexual relationship, and would condemn a form of it which He himself created.[20]

These apparently were her conscious motives, or at least what she wanted her readers to believe. Unexpressed (and perhaps unconscious) was Romola's desire for someone who could love her in a special way, someone as glamorous as her mother and hopefully more reliable than her father, someone whose greatness could vicariously make her feel more important and valuable. Romola evidently believed that she had found such qualities in the glittering Nijinsky, and his alluring androgyny probably reinforced her narcissism. By coupling herself to a man whose dance movements ranged from the most assertively masculine to the most demurely feminine, and who dressed in costumes that suggested both maleness and femaleness, she could bring herself closer to attitudes that at this point were still repugnant and immoral to her. (Only many years later, after Nijinsky had become an invalid and was no longer available as a sexual partner, did Romola allow herself to enter lesbian relationships, and as far as is known she remained exclusively homosexual after that.) In her quest for him, she may also have been motivated by a maternal instinct. She often referred to Nijinsky as "le Petit," the little one. His diminutive stature and probably his emotional immaturity appealed to her. She yearned in some magical way to have a baby by him: "If ever his genius should be perpetuated, I wanted to be the medium of this transmission."[21] Finally, it must be said that Romola was interested in luxury and money. Extravagance had been part of her heritage, but great wealth had been denied her by Charles Pulszky's catastrophe (he left her only a small inheritance). Diaghilev seemed to attract the rich and the famous. The Ballets Russes was the most prestigious theatrical enterprise in Europe, and Nijinsky its most glamorous, adorable star. Romola was convinced he would bring her luck.

Aboard the steamship *Avon*, their cabins were in proximity. "Fate was kind," Romola writes. "I could quite well supervise his door.... The day Nijinsky came on board I said to Anna [her maid and traveling companion] 'Now here is my chance. Twenty-one days of ocean and sky—no Diaghilev. He can't escape. By the time we arrive I will have a flirtation with "le Petit." *Ce que femme veut Dieu le veut.*'"[22] With obsessive interest she watched him like a hawk. In the mornings Nijinsky exercised on the open deck; afternoons he worked in a lounge, with Rhené-Baton at the piano, on dances for the Bach-Benois ballet. Romola was always there. When she saw him lying on a deck chair, she would stroll by, talk or laugh loudly, and wave to him. "I was determined not to give him any peace until he noticed me." She even took pains to befriend his masseur, Mr. Williams.

> I had suddenly developed an interest in athletics. For hours I listened about the boxers and their matches ... the difference between the Swedish school and the medical massage ... in return for my enthusiastic listening, I learned about the whole musculature of Nijinsky, which Mr. Williams knew and loved, each muscle separately.[23]

Gradually Nijinsky began to reciprocate, shyly at first, reticent and inhibited with a girl of her upper-class background, but flattered by the idea that she was interested in him. Romola spoke fluent French, which he could not. She seemed at ease and readily conversed with Baron de Gunsbourg, Rhené-Baton, and the other important passengers on the boat. Romola was much like Diaghilev in her snobbishness. Nijinsky may have noted the resemblance, but she was obviously more like the girls he had recently been "chasing" in Paris, and that attracted him. He acknowledged her, promenaded with her on deck, lit her cigarette, and tried speaking to her. The fact that Romola traveled first-class, unlike the women dancers who were in the tourist section, gave her more exposure. One evening she showed him a ring on her finger, removed it, gave it to him, and explained that it was a good luck charm her father had found in Egypt. "It will bring you happiness, surely," Nijinsky said to her in Polish while slipping the ring back on her finger. Then they stood silently watching the phosphorescent sea. Another time, with one of the dancers serving as translator, they chatted about a little pillow that Romola had lifted from his hotel room in Monte Carlo. It was a gift from his mother; Nijinsky was used to sleeping on it, and "cherished" the pillow.* Romola offered to return it, but Nijinsky told her that she could keep it.[25]

---

*Sentimental items such as dolls, pillows, security blankets, or special toys, which pass between people and serve as symbolic reminders of a past or present attachment, have been called "transitional" or "linking" objects."[24] They are helpful in establishing a sense of security and may be important for the experience of creative playfulness. One also observes that the fans or "groupies" who pursue famous people often take things that have been in contact with their idols, to be used as linking objects. For example, Franz Liszt's female admirers stole the covers off chairs he sat on, and framed them. They also gathered his discarded cigar butts to stuff in their bosoms. More recently, bedsheets used by the Beatles were cut into small squares and sold to their admirers. Similarly, Liberace's sought-after personal belongings generated a small fortune at auction.

Friends and passengers on the boat were astonished to see the usually taciturn and asocial Nijinsky so often "in animated conversation with Mademoiselle Pulszky."[26] Especially intrigued by this unexpected turn of events was Baron de Gunsbourg, who may have had reasons of his own for encouraging the liaison. Gunsbourg had invested a small fortune in Diaghilev's Ballets Russes, but was not always happy with the way the company was managed. It was rumored that he may have been thinking of taking over, perhaps even forming a ballet company of his own, with Nijinsky as his leading dancer. What better way to accomplish this than to get the young man married and thus sever his dependence on Diaghilev once and for all.[27] Whether Nijinsky knew about these intrigues is difficult to say. He seems to have trusted Gunsbourg. Before the *Avon* reached South America, Nijinsky asked him to talk to Romola and propose that they get married. It was obviously a rash and hasty decision, but Gunsbourg, whose job it was to inform Diaghilev of everything concerning the dancers, agreed *without* notifying him. What motivated Nijinsky to do this? He never explained it in his notebooks, so we can only speculate: her sex appeal; his loneliness; the fact that she had come along on the trip as one of the "dancers"; his need for intimacy with someone like his sister; an illusion (shared by others on board the *Avon*) that Romola was a very rich girl; his opportunism, similar to the impulsiveness that had led to sexual relations with Diaghilev five years earlier? Romola first thought that Nijinsky's proposal was a joke; she describes it this way.

> We were sitting together in the bar, before lunch ... Gunsbourg came up. "Romola, please come. I have to talk to you." I became quite upset. My God, what had I done?... I followed Gunsbourg silently on deck. There he stopped, and with a terribly formal face he said, "Romola Carlovna, as Nijinsky cannot speak to you himself, he has requested me to ask you in marriage." We looked at each other, and then I burst out: "No, really, Dmitri Nikolaivitch, it's awful. How can you?"; and blushing, half crying, I ran as fast as I could down to my cabin, where I locked myself up for the rest of the day.[28]

This habit of locking herself into her room when under stress was to have fateful consequences. (A similar incident later led to Nijinsky's first psychiatric hospitalization.) Romola assumed that Gunsbourg was teasing her, but she wanted to respond positively, and did so that evening when Nijinsky himself approached her "unexpectedly" on the promenade deck, pantomiming the gesture of a ring being placed on a finger of his left hand and saying, "Mademoiselle, voulez-vous, vous et moi?" ("Miss, would you, you and me?") She nodded and waved both of her hands. "Oui, oui, oui." He took her hand, and they sat in silence on two deck chairs. It seemed unbelievable—"was this all only a dream, or was it really true?" When the boat docked in Rio de Janeiro, they were driven to a jeweler's shop to look at wedding rings. Nijinsky picked out "two rather flat, dull gold bands" and had them engraved with the date, "1/9 [i.e., 1 September] 1913."[29]

Speed was of the essence. Some of the dancers thought that what Nijinsky was doing was crazy, and that he should be stopped before it was too late. An inexperienced woman like Romola Pulszky, a socialite and an outsider to the ballet world, was not the right match for him. Surely it would end in disaster. Marie Rambert did not believe him when he told her about being in love with this girl, but after the terrible shock of learning about their impending marriage, she cried "hot tears" and thought about drowning herself in the ocean. "We all knew he was Diaghilev's lover.... I suddenly realized that I was hopelessly in love with him, and had been for a long time."[30] Adolph Bolm took it upon himself, as a friend of Romola and her family, to issue warnings about Nijinsky's special connection to Diaghilev. It was more than a mere friendship, he told Romola, and she had better be careful. Nijinsky was known for being cruel and "utterly heartless" in human relationships: "It will ruin your life."[31] Gunsbourg worked fast to complete the formalities, which meant getting Emilia Márkus's permission (by telegram) and hurriedly organizing a civil ceremony in Buenos Aires, their next stop, to be followed by a church wedding. The company disembarked on 6 September. Rehearsals were to begin only two days later, and a dress rehearsal for the opening performance had been scheduled for the tenth. That was the day of the wedding. (It had originally been announced for 19 September, but was pushed forward to preclude any interference from abroad.) A reporter from the *Gazeta de Buenos Aires* commented on the unnatural haste: "The couple and their party ran as fast as they could into the church," and after the ceremony "the mad dash began as before. Nobody knew the customary manner of leaving the church. The bride was giggling at her mistake; the bridegroom followed timidly, letting himself be dragged headlong."[32]

Romola later explained to her sister-in-law, Bronislava, that it would have been stupid to give "advance notice of our wedding plans to

Diaghilev or to Vaslav's family and risk you stopping us...."[33] Her
apprehensions were well founded. With more time there would
undoubtedly have been stronger protests and the marriage delayed or
prevented altogether. Now, the deed was done. Newspapers were
announcing it all over the world. Nijinsky's mother "burst into tears"
when she read the news. She thought it was a publicity stunt. What
was a "lonely socialite" doing on board the boat with the dancers? How
could a "well-brought-up girl ... force a wedding in South America,
somewhere on the other side of the world, and not wait for their return
to Europe among family and friends?" How could she get married
"without parental blessing"? Her son must be "surrounded by enemies,"
and she predicted great unhappiness for the newlyweds. "It was
impossible to console her," Bronislava writes, who, having recently
gotten married herself, was more tolerant of Nijinsky's most recent
escapade. She felt great joy upon learning that she had a new sister-in-
law and "deeply wanted to share this happiness with Vaslav." It was
characteristic of Bronislava to want to align her feelings with her
brother's. She hoped that his bitterness toward her for having gotten
pregnant and forsaking him during the work on *Sacre* would now
disappear. She probably was also pleased to know about her brother's
turn toward heterosexuality. Bronislava knew about Nijinsky's instability in love relationships. He had a way of becoming "infatuated
with someone on first acquaintance." He projected all kinds of fantasies
and endowed his love objects with "a wealth of imagined qualities, and
then just as quickly became disenchanted."[34]

News of Nijinsky's marriage struck like a thunderbolt, Alexandre
Benois wrote in a letter to Stravinsky. There had been "no hint about
the coming event" when he, Diaghilev, and Nijinsky were talking about
the Bach ballet just before the South America trip. Benois worried
about its impact on Diaghilev. "How deep was the shock? Obviously
their affair was coming to an end, and I doubt that he was really
heartbroken... as head of the company, he must be completely
bewildered. The whole story is so fantastic that I sometimes think I
have read it in a dream and am insane to believe it."[35] Stravinsky,
correctly assuming that Diaghilev would now dismiss Nijinsky, wrote
Benois with obvious disappointment that "for me, the hope of seeing
something valuable in choreography has been removed for a long time to
come."[36] Diaghilev felt tricked, rejected, and humiliated by his ex-
lover's impulsive decision to marry Romola Pulszky, which probably

opened up old scars remaining from the time of Diaghilev's earlier abandonment by Dmitri Filosofov. He tried to stop the marriage by sending frantic telegrams to Argentina, but it was too late. According to witnesses, the forty-one-year-old impresario "gave himself to a wild orgy of dissipation" and swore to take revenge on the miscreant in some way. "Sobbing shamelessly in Russian despair, he bellowed accusations and recriminations; he cursed Nijinsky's ingratitude, Romola's treachery, and his own stupidity for allowing Nijinsky to travel without him."[37]

Nijinsky himself seems to have been disturbed by the sudden turn of events in his life. There had been no honeymoon. Because rehearsals had already started, he was obliged to go into harness immediately and perform for the public. Romola too, having come to South America ostensibly to dance with the Ballets Russes, was obligated to make appearances. She acted more than danced in the larger productions like *Swan Lake* and *Schéhérazade,* which required supernumeraries among the corps de ballet. All too soon Nijinsky discovered that the woman he had married "quite by chance [and] without thinking" was incapable of truly sharing the major interest that made his life meaningful. She could not really dance! Unlike his sister, with whom he had cavorted since childhood and created novel ballets, Romola did not have the instinct for making beautifully coordinated body movements. Her deficiency was remembered as a cruel disappointment: "The first time I felt grief was three or four days after our marriage. I asked her to learn dancing because for me dancing was the highest thing in the world." He recalls wanting to teach Romola "good dancing, but she became frightened and no longer trusted me. I cried and cried bitterly." In looking back on his marriage, Nijinsky wrote that he had "the intimation of death. I realized that I had made a mistake, but the mistake was irreparable. I had put myself in the hands of someone who did not love me. I realized my mistake."[38]

In terms of sexual intimacy, problems came to the surface very quickly. Romola seems to have been relatively inexperienced. Most likely she was still a virgin. She wondered whether to feel "flattered or offended" by her husband's avoidance of intercourse. "Perhaps, after all, Bolm was right." On their wedding night he politely kissed her hand and then left the room without making love. She felt relieved and "almost cried from thankfulness." Equally confusing was his behavior toward her in public. At rehearsals he treated her with respect but aloofness. When they met, it was as though "a strange person stood before me. There was no recognition in his face; the impersonal look of a master towards his pupil." During performances he lost his personality and entered completely into the roles he was playing, Harlequin in *Carnaval*, the Golden Slave in *Schéhérazade*, the Prince in *Swan Lake*, and the others. "He was no longer my husband," Romola writes; "he lived his part, and everything else for him ceased to exist." She was not even permitted to enter his dressing room. Only some time later, after Nijinsky had proved his greatness to the Argentinian audiences, was she invited into his private five-room hotel suite.

> The center of the apartment was a large drawing-room, where we used to take our meals. On both sides the adjoining chambers were turned into living-rooms, and each of us had a bedroom at the opposite end of the apartment... the evening he chose to remain I felt I was making an offering on the altar of happiness.[39]

Romola reports that her "fear of Nijinsky began to vanish," as he became more relaxed in her presence. But his difficulties in verbal discourse, plus the language barrier, continued to be an impediment. Gunsbourg often had to be asked to explain and translate certain things for them. That apparently was how Romola gained information about Nijinsky's past relationship with Diaghilev. She also discovered that his brother Stanislav was "insane."[40] In the book she later wrote, Romola praises Nijinsky's honesty for confiding painful secrets. There was one thing, however, that he apparently had to withhold from her and could disclose only in his notebooks—his sexual promiscuity: "If my wife reads all this she will go mad. I lied to her when I said she is the first woman I had loved. I knew many others before my wife. They were simple and beautiful [prostitutes]."[41]

Romola belonged to a different category of women. Distant, sphinx-like, yet constantly adoring, she seemed more mysterious than anyone he had ever known. She was neither a dancer like his mother and sister or the other ballet girls with whom one was expected to be chaste, nor was she a whore with whom one could be frankly erotic. ("Once I fucked a woman who had her periods. She showed me everything. ...")[42] Romola was a refined, upper-class, and well-educated woman, and she was domineering, again similar to Diaghilev. One had to obey someone like that. But she lacked Diaghilev's managerial genius and his artistic temperament. Although Romola sensed from the beginning that her relationship with Nijinsky was a sacred trust that required her undivided attention, she used him more as an ornament, a way to enhance her own self-esteem. "I began to rave about all the Callot dresses, Reboux hats and Cartier jewels," she writes, "and all the *mondain* life I was going to lead in the future. I was brought up to believe that this is what marriage meant." Motherhood no longer had much appeal to her. "I became so enraptured in him that I did not wish to have a child."[43]

Knowing next to nothing about birth control, Romola asked the older women on the ship for advice, but they seemed to be of no help whatever. Either they feigned ignorance and laughed at her, or they sermonized about "how marvelous it must be to become a mother." Finally, she had to approach Baron de Gunsbourg with her questions. The older man talked with Nijinsky about the problem, and instructed him what to tell Romola (at least that is how she remembered his little speech).

> For five years we shall live for art and our love, but the supreme happiness and the fulfillment of life and marriage is to have a child, and, after that time, when we will be in our permanent home, we shall have one.[44]

It was too late. Romola had gotten pregnant right away. In Montevideo, where Nijinsky was scheduled to give two performances in October, she already experienced symptoms of faintness, pallor, distaste for certain foods, and hypersensitivity to odors, especially coffee. By the time they reached Rio de Janeiro, by boat, she felt truly ill. Nijinsky responded with symptoms of his own, as many husbands do when their wives are pregnant. Some gain weight, vomit in the morning, and even protrude their abdomen like a pregnant woman. Nijinsky complained mostly of fatigue and headaches. "I have been ill for two months," he was to write to Stravinsky in December.[45] During a train trip that month, he had a migraine attack and fainted because of "the smell of cigarettes."[46]

In some cultures, in which this condition (called "couvade") is openly acknowledged, men expecting a baby are given special privileges such as rest and time off from work. The Ballets Russes did not share so humane a tradition. The attitude in general toward signs of psychophysiological distress among artists was not very enlightened. Management as well as the dancers themselves often pretended that disabilities did not exist. One went on stage regardless of one's aches and pains. There was no such thing as a tour physician or nurse. Dancers had to concoct their own remedies. Ballerinas could be seen with little pots of claylike adhesive that they heated and applied to their injured, sprained, or even fractured ankles. Men were expected to be even more stoical. A dancer's salary was much too small to allow consultation with a physician, and touring in South America was especially arduous because of the unaccustomed climate, the long distances, and the language problems. One never knew where to turn when symptoms arose, except to Baron de Gunsbourg or the stage manager, Serge Grigoriev, who were supposed to handle everything and cable Diaghilev for further advice if necessary, which could take days.

It was of course well known that Diaghilev "objected to his artists being married."[47] Affairs were tolerated, up to a point. When it became apparent that a dancer had gotten seriously involved with someone inside or outside the company, that usually was the end of his or her tenure with the company. Diaghilev himself had lovers, but they were considered his private domain. Exceptions were also allowed if a match resulted in social and financial benefits.* In Nijinsky's case, it was rumored that he had married a very wealthy girl. ("Why can't Nijinsky be both a ballet master and a Hungarian millionaire?" Benois asked Stravinsky.[48]) Pregnancies among the dancers had to be denied as long as possible, lest they lose their jobs. Nearly every book about the history of Russian ballet tells of Matilda Kchessinska's miraculous performance in *Les Élèves de Monsieur Dupré* before the Imperial family, in 1902. She was wearing a tutu, and she was pregnant. "I had carefully to calculate each of my attitudes so as not to let them see the change in my silhouette."[49]

Romola's pregnancy and Nijinsky's empathic response to it—learned perhaps at a very early age, when his mother was pregnant with Bronislava—were among the factors leading up to his tragic dismissal from the Ballets Russes. The problems began in Rio de Janeiro, shortly before they were to sail back to Europe. Boat trips were particularly ghastly for the expectant Romola, and Nijinsky asked whether he could

---

*For example, ballerina Lydia Lopokova, who married the influential British economist John Maynard Keynes, was allowed to remain with the company.

be excused from a performance one evening and stay with her in the hotel. What explanation he gave for wanting to take the night off is not known, but according to Grigoriev, who had to be consulted immediately, the request greatly agitated Baron de Gunsbourg. Why Gunsbourg got so upset is not clear, but in her memoirs, Bronislava Nijinska suggests that one reason was that her brother had coupled his request with a demand for wages: "The time had come for Vaslav, now that he was married, to think of his new responsibilities and expect to be paid his regular salary—as did Karsavina, Bolm, and all the other artists, and the administrative staff." Nijinsky was not under contract like all the others. It was Bronislava's belief that, before her brother left for South America, "Diaghilev had advised him to be firm in demanding that Baron de Gunsbourg pay him the money due for the several years he had worked in the Ballets Russes."[50] But did Gunsbourg have the money? Bronislava's opinion seems consistent with the idea that there was disharmony between Gunsbourg and Diaghilev and that Gunsbourg, behind Diaghilev's back, may have been trying to detach Nijinsky from the company, in which case he should have been paid on the spot. (Romola was always very insistent that Nijinsky be paid properly for his work.)

The ballet *Carnaval* was scheduled for the night he wanted to be excused. Since no understudy had been prepared to substitute for Nijinsky in the role of Harlequin, Grigoriev asked the dancer Alexander Gavrilov to begin rehearsing the part while Grigoriev went to Nijinsky's hotel to "try to persuade him to perform after all." Nijinsky refused adamantly; it was an obstinate, headstrong, and risky thing to do, a power struggle with the stage manager. "Despite all my entreaties," Grigoriev writes, "to which I added warnings that Diaghilev never forgave his dancers who missed performances without good reason, Nijinsky and his wife both insisted that he would not on any account come to the theater that night. Gavrilov accordingly appeared in his place."[51]

Grigoriev was a hard-boiled administrator, extremely loyal to Diaghilev (for whom he worked until Diaghilev's death in 1929, when the company was dissolved). "According to the rules of the company and the items of our contracts," Grigoriev wrote in his memoirs, "the non-appearance of any dancer at a performance, unless he could produce a doctor's certificate of illness, was the gravest offense he could commit and one that led to dismissal."[52] There was of course no medical certificate to produce; the illness, officially, was Romola's. Nor was there any contract to break; Nijinsky was dancing solely at the discretion of Diaghilev. On arriving back in Europe, he blithely assumed that everything would be as before, that his having gotten married would make no difference to Diaghilev. Nijinsky's reception should have been a warning. Diaghilev was not in Paris to greet him, as had been expected. Nor did Diaghilev answer his letters, asking when rehearsals were to begin for the Bach-Benois ballet he had been working on during the South America trip. Nijinsky also wanted to know about the Strauss-Benois ballet *La Légende de Joseph*, which he assumed he would be asked to choreograph.[53]

Without instructions, Nijinsky was helpless, and his wife took over. She suggested they go to Vienna to meet her sister Tessa, and then on to Budapest to see her mother and stepfather. "A crowd of reporters, camera-men, and photographers awaited us." To Romola's great relief, her mother quickly made arrangements for a doctor to terminate her pregnancy. "I had made up my mind not to have a child." But then Romola changed her mind. "I became suddenly terrified," she writes. Probably Nijinsky, with his more orthodox Catholic faith, had objected to the abortion. "An immense relief and pleasure was expressed in his face," Romola writes. "He kissed me gently, and whispered: 'Thank God. What He has given, nobody has the right to destroy.'"[54]

Nijinsky was eager to see Diaghilev and get back to work. He sent a telegram to St. Petersburg asking when rehearsals were to begin for the two new ballets, and also demanding, rather imperiously, that the company "should not be employed on anything else."[55] Receipt of this telegram provoked harmful wrath. Diaghilev was in the midst of contract negotiations for the upcoming 1914–1915 seasons. The London and Paris theaters "were demanding four new ballets in the repertoire and that at least two of them should be choreographed by Fokine."[56] It was a bitter pill for Diaghilev to swallow. He knew that Fokine was past his prime and that his recent departure from the Ballets Russes on account of Nijinsky's controversial ballets had produced a schism within the company. Some of the dancers were continuing to support Nijinsky, while others preferred the older man's more traditional choreography and wanted him back as their ballet master. An additional complication was Baron de Gunsbourg; he too was pressing for Fokine's return to the Ballets Russes. A decision had to be made. Money and the future of the company were at stake. In haste, and still smarting from what he felt as Nijinsky's betrayal, Diaghilev made a tragic mistake. He decided to dismiss Nijinsky, the company's stellar male dancer, and he did it in an unbelievably cruel way. Diaghilev dictated a telegram, and asked Grigoriev to sign it: "Monsieur Diaghilev considers that by missing a performance at Rio and refusing to dance in the ballet *Carnaval* you broke your contract. He will not therefore require your further services."[57]

Grigoriev had observed the presence of a new boyfriend, "an Italian valet looking after him," when he entered Diaghilev's apartment. After signing the fateful telegram he noticed that Vasili Zuikov, who had once been so protective of Nijinsky, was smirking. "Your telegram won't improve Madame Nijinsky's sleep," said Zuikov.[58] Not only did Romola lose sleep, she was petrified to realize that her husband was now "an outcast" from Diaghilev's company. It was an unmitigated disaster, which demolished her hopes for a brilliant social career and led to innumerable problems for her husband, including his first nervous breakdown, for which she felt partly responsible. "Now, for the first time, it dawned on me that perhaps I had made a mistake; I had destroyed, where I had wanted to be helpful," wrote Romola when she looked back on it years later.[59]

NOTES

1. Alexandre Benois, *Reminiscences of the Russian Ballet*, 351.
2. Ibid.
3. RBN, 372.
4. BNM, 477.
5. Ibid., 478.
6. Tamara Nijinsky, personal communication.
7. Romola Nijinsky, *Nijinsky*, 4. (Hereafter, cited as RNN.)
8. RNN, 5.
9. Ibid., 5, 6.
10. Michael Cenner, personal communication.
11. Ibid., 13.
12. See letter from Adolph Bolm to Emilia Márkus, 27 December 1912. Nijinsky Archives.
13. BNM, 479–480.
14. RNN, 13.
15. Ibid., 16.
16. Ibid., 196–197.
17. Ibid., 212.
18. Ibid., 218.
19. Alma Mahler Werfel, *And the Bridge Is Love.*
20. RNN, 233.
21. Ibid., 218.
22. Ibid., 220.
23. Ibid., 226–227.

24. Donald Winnicott, *Playing and Reality.*
25. Ibid., 232–234.
26. Serge L. Grigoriev, *The Diaghilev Ballet 1909–1929,* 86–87. I have changed the spelling of Romola's name, which Grigoriev gives as "de Pulska."
27. Ibid., 87.
28. RNN, 235.
29. Ibid., 236–239.
30. Marie Rambert, *Quicksilver,* 74.
31. RNN, 240.
32. *La Gazeta de Buenos Aires,* cited in Cyril Beaumont, "The Wedding of Nijinsky."
33. BNM, 480.
34. Ibid., 478–479.
35. Letter from Alexandre Benois to Igor Stravinsky, 11 October 1913, in Vera Stravinsky and Robert Craft, *Stravinsky in Pictures and Documents,* 115.
36. Letter from Igor Stravinsky to Alexandre Benois, 3 October 1913, in Vera Stravinsky and Robert Craft, 512..
37. Arthur Gold and Robert Fitzdale, *Misia,* 160.
38. Notebook on "Life," 121.
39. RNN, 248–251.
40. Ibid., 255–256.
41. Notebook on "Feeling," 32.
42. Ibid.
43. RNN, 257–259.
44. Ibid., 257.
45. Igor Stravinsky and Robert Craft, *Memoirs and Commentaries,* 38.
46. RNN, 258–260.
47. BNM, 480.
48. Vera Stravinsky and Robert Craft, 115.
49. H.S.H. The Princess Romanovsky-Krassinsky, *Dancing in Petersburg,* 87.
50. BNM, 486.
51. Grigoriev, 89.
52. Ibid.
53. Igor Stravinsky and Robert Craft, 38.
54. RNN, 260–261.
55. Grigoriev, 90.
56. BNM, 483.
57. Grigoriev, 91.
58. Ibid., 90–91.
59. RNN, 261.

Chapter 5

Career Problems and the First Breakdown

It is difficult to imagine, three quarters of a century later, how limited the opportunities were for a solo dancer like Nijinsky to continue his career without the active support of an impresario-manager like Diaghilev. Independent ballet companies such as one finds today in many cities throughout the world did not yet exist. Classical dancing could be seen only in major opera houses, but rarely for more than one or two numbers, usually interspersed among the more important songs and choruses. Mass entertainment, the movies, and television programs, which nowadays will occasionally include a ballet, were unheard of. Troupes of trained dancers did occasionally find employment in a circus or vaudeville show, but only for brief appearances. Full-scale productions such as those sponsored by the Imperial Theaters of Russia were very unique events, virtually unknown to the rest of the world except for Diaghilev's recent exports. And the newer, more "modern" trends in ballet, those with which Nijinsky felt most closely identified, were an exclusive Ballets Russes specialty. Thus, to be expelled from this company produced a major crisis in his career. Coupled as it was to the termination of his relationship with Diaghilev, Nijinsky experienced his expulsion as a huge personal loss, one that probably opened scars left from his earlier traumatic abandonment at the hands of his father. Loss of the opportunity to dance and to continue developing himself as a choreographer also contributed to Nijinsky's massive insecurity, leading to a nervous breakdown in March 1914. On 9 December 1913, three months before the symptoms became disabling, he wrote anxiously to Igor Stravinsky:

> I do not believe that Serge can act that meanly toward me. Serge owes me a lot of money. I have received nothing for two years, neither for my dancing nor for my staging *Faune, Jeux,* and *Le Sacre du Printemps.* I worked for the Ballet without a contract. If it is true that Serge does not want to work with me—then I have lost everything.[2]

One alternative, now that Diaghilev was no longer protecting him, supporting and guiding his artistic development, was for Nijinsky to return to Russia and try to pick up where he had left off before joining forces with Diaghilev. That would have required a clarification of his military status as well as his position with the Imperial Theaters. War clouds were beginning to gather over Europe at this time. The tension between East and West had been building up for several years. During a visit to Vienna in October 1913, Germany's reckless Kaiser Wilhelm boasted to his Austrian allies that war was "inevitable" and the czar would be unprepared to defend his country.[3] Indeed, under the weak and inept leadership of Czar Nicholas II, Russia was exceedingly vulnerable and badly needed manpower for its army. As was the custom, artists of the Imperial Theaters were deferred from military service so that they could continue to perform their official duties as singers, dancers, and musicians. A request for Nijinsky's deferral had apparently been submitted, for his sister writes that during his trip to South America in 1913 she was told that his petition "was turned down." An

official from the War Ministry in St. Petersburg explained that since
Nijinsky was now "very wealthy" and no longer the sole supporter of his
mother, there was no justification for deferring him. "All Nijinsky can
do now is to return from abroad and serve his term in the military
service." Bronislava attributed this piece of official cruelty to "the long
antagonism between Diaghilev and the Directorate of the Imperial
Theaters," and related it to the effect of her brother's dismissal from the
Maryinsky in 1911 (Diaghilev had warned him at the time about the risk
of losing his military deferment). Thus, returning to Russia would have
exposed Nijinsky to the prospect of three years' service in the infantry
as a common foot soldier, clearly an undesirable course for a ballet
dancer.

His other alternative was to seek engagements in Europe or South
America, where he was by now well known. From Budapest, in
December 1913, Nijinsky sent telegrams to Paris, saying he was no
longer working for Diaghilev and would be available to take on other
responsibilities. As a result, a number of inquiries were received.
Romola, recalling those distressing months when she was just beginning to realize what their marriage had led to, wrote that many offers
were "showered" upon Nijinsky, from "impresarios, theaters, with
incredibly high salaries."[5] In fact, there were no definite offers, only
two tentative proposals, and neither of them seemed very appealing to
him. The first came from Alfred Butt, the owner of a vaudeville theater
in London, who invited Nijinsky to perform there for eight weeks
beginning in March 1914. The second was from Jacques Rouché, the
newly appointed director of the National Academy of Music and Dance
in Paris, asking whether he might consider taking a position at the
Paris Opéra, but not before 1915. The frantic letter Nijinsky wrote to
Stravinsky on 9 December 1913 shows his shocked disbelief over the
consequences of Diaghilev's rejection, and his wish that Stravinsky
might intercede in some way to get him back into the Ballets Russes.

> You understand the situation I am in. I cannot imagine what has
> happened, what is the reason for [Diaghilev's] behavior. Please ask Serge
> what is the matter, and write to me about it.... I am receiving
> propositions from every side.... But I won't give them a definite answer
> before I have news from you.[6]

By the time Stravinsky received this request, he was no longer in
Russia and was having his own problems with Diaghilev. There was

Thomas Nijinsky (1862-1912), the father of Vaslav Nijinsky. (Nijinsky Archives)

Eleonora Bereda (1856-1932), mother of Vaslav Nijinsky.

The three Nijinsky children Stanislav (left), Bronislava, and Vaslav (right). (Nijinsky Archives)

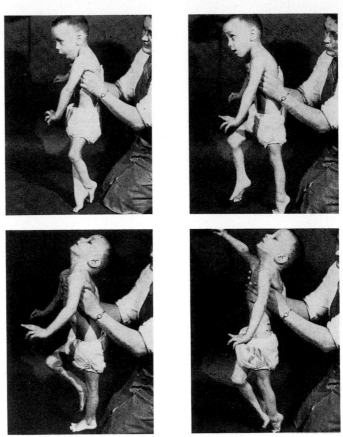

A child with cerebral palsy. Nijinsky probably saw such neurological diseases while visiting his disabled brother Stanislav in the hospital, and he may have incorporated some of the movements into his later ballets. (From Handbook of Clinical Neurology [Vinken and Bruyn, Eds. 1968])

Nijinsky when he was a student at the Imperial Ballet School in St. Petersburg, shortly before he had a near fatal accident at age 12.

(Nijinsky Archives)

Nijinsky, age 17, dancing the Blackamoor in *Le Roi Candaule* at the Maryinski Theatre in St. Petersburg. (Note the similarity in smile and facial expression in the later photograph of Nijinsky at age 49.) (Nijinsky Archives)

Nijinsky, age 18, dancing with Anna Pavlova in *Le Pavillon d'Armide* (first version). (Nijinsky Archives)

Nijinsky in *Le Roi Candaule*, c. 1908–1909. (Courtesy the Theatre Museum, Leningrad)

Nijinsky as the Golden Slave in *Scheherazade* around 1910.

Nijinsky at age 18, when he met Sergei Diaghilev. (Nijinsky Archives)

Sergei Diaghilev. (The Bettman Archive)

A break during ballet rehearsals at the "German Club" in St. Petersburg, when Diaghilev was forming his company in 1910. Nijinsky is to the left of the samovar and Stravinsky is standing to the right. (Courtesy the Theatre Museum, Leningrad)

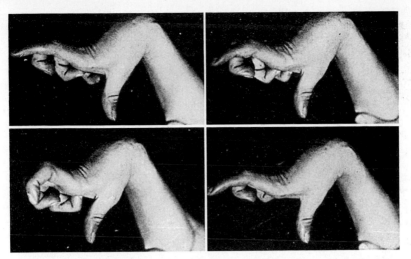

Hand positions of a patient with choreo-athetosis, another neurological condition that may have given Nijinsky ideas for future ballet movements. (From S.A. Kinnier Wilson, *Neurology*)

Nijinsky at a garden party, in costume for *Les Orientales*, 1910. (Fotoarchiv Rigal, Paris)

Romola Pulszky, Nijinsky's future wife, age 16, dressed in one of her "Napoleon" costumes. (Nijinsky Archives)

Nijinsky in his costume for Petrushka, with Igor Stravinsky (1911). (Nijinsky Archives)

Nijinsky in *Le Spectre de la Rose*, 1911.

Nijinsky with his sister Bronislava Nijinska, in the *Afternoon of a Faun*, Paris, 1912. (Nijinsky Archives)

Nijinsky as Harlequin in the ballet *Carnaval*, with Lydia Lopokhova. It was in this role that Romola Pulszky first saw him dance in Budapest in 1912.

Nijinsky, age 24, in *Jeux* his second ballet produced by Diaghilev, in Paris, in 1913. The women are Tamara Karsavina (left) and Ludmilla Schollar (right).

Nijinsky's notes for the Bach ballet he worked on while crossing the Atlantic to South America, where he married Romola Pulszky in 1913. (Nijinsky Archives)

Romola, Kyra, and Vaslav Nijinsky in 1916, on their arrival in the United States. (Nijinsky Archives)

Nijinsky, age 27, in the Hollywood studio of Charlie Chaplin.

little he could do to help. Whether Stravinsky felt motivated to do so is another question. In discussing this matter later with Robert Craft, Stravinsky said he could not remember what he had answered Nijinsky, and described the dancer's letter as "a document of such astounding innocence—if Nijinsky hadn't written it, I think only a character in Dostoievsky might have. It seems incredible to me even now that he was so unaware of the politics and sexual jealousies and motives within the Ballet."[7] Part of the politics of course involved the question of how to get Michel Fokine back as choreographer and ballet master for the company. This required many hours of tactful negotiating, some of it by telephone. Fokine was still smarting from his earlier displacement by Nijinsky. Now the shoe was on the other foot. He not only demanded that Diaghilev pay him a very high salary, but set conditions that were ruinous for Nijinsky. Diaghilev had to agree no longer to perform Nijinsky's three ballets, *Faune, Jeux,* and *Sacre.* From now on Fokine would be interpreting the solo roles in *Schéhérazade, Carnaval,* and other ballets that Nijinsky had made famous. But what about Joseph, Nijinsky's intended role in the lavish production of *La Légende de Joseph,* the Strauss-Benois ballet for which Fokine was now hired to provide the choreography? This role called for a lithe, sensual, and much younger man than Fokine. Diaghilev assigned it to the handsome seventeen-year-old Leonid Miassin (later Frenchified to Léonide Massine), a gifted actor he had recently discovered in Moscow and was now grooming to take Nijinsky's place as his disciple and lover.

Romola describes her husband's paralyzing indecision, his "pitying" looks, and reluctance to "do anything inartistic" at the end of 1913 while they were still in Budapest with her mother and stepfather. "I must first have the right ballets, artists to appear with me," she reports him saying. "I must think, create, and under no circumstances will I appear in a vaudeville house." Whether Nijinsky was already beginning to experience the fatigue, depression, chest pain, and other symptoms that were to plague him so much later on is unclear. His wife, pregnant at the time and unable to evaluate the early signs of his illness, says that he was "so harassed by everybody that we left for Vienna. But we did not find peace there either." Some of the harassment evidently came from Oscar Párdány, Romola's stepfather, whom she describes as having "an excellent business head." Párdány was saying that Nijinsky ought to start earning some money to support his wife and future child. Romola thought that was "very tactless of him, as Vaslav married me without a dowry."[8]

Finally, Nijinsky did sign a contract with the London theater magnate Alfred Butt, which obligated him to assemble his own ballet company and dance for two months at the Palace Theater, beginning 2 March 1914, for a salary of £1,000 per week. Considering that Nijinsky had no experience whatsoever in putting together a ballet company, it was a rash and unwise decision, but he was hoping to undo the damage resulting from his recent split with Diaghilev, and Butt's offer seems to have inflated Nijinsky's ego. He wrote to Stravinsky about "a very rich businessman, who offers one million francs to organize a new Diaghilev Russian Ballet. They wish me to have sole artistic direction and large sums of money to commission décors, music, etc."[9] Nijinsky knew that some of the Russian dancers, including Pavlova, Karsavina, and Lopokova, had appeared in vaudeville shows, but no male dancer of his quality had ever done so before, and he was fundamentally opposed to vaudeville. At the height of his success in 1911, a newspaper interview reports Nijinsky saying: "One thing I am determined not to do, and that is to go on the music-hall stage. I have had several tempting offers; but after all, what is money? I think more of my art than I do of money, and I refuse to be sandwiched between performing dogs and acrobats."[10]

Had his sister not agreed to help him, Nijinsky probably would not have been able to proceed in this direction. Her position with the Ballets Russes had also been jeopardized by Fokine's reappointment. Part of the deal was that Vera Fokina, Fokine's attractive but somewhat stoutish wife, would be assuming the solo roles Bronislava Nijinska usually danced. Nijinska had just had her baby and wanted to get on with her career. She missed her brother, resented Diaghilev's dismissal of him, and writes that she was "oppressed with doubts and worry about Vaslav, wondering how he would be able to live independently." Since childhood, when Bronislava used to help him with his schoolwork, she had regularly come to Nijinsky's rescue. "Up till now he had always been protected from everyday worries," she writes.

> I was somewhat reassured by the fact that Vaslav was not alone; he had a wife at his side, though we knew so little about her. In my letters to Vaslav I repeated to him my promise given in London that I would always be with him, and that if he needed me in his work, or for moral support, or even just to ask my advice, then I would leave everything and come to join him.[11]

In January 1914 Nijinsky sent a series of telegrams to St. Petersburg asking his sister to leave Diaghilev's company and work for him instead.

He proposed paying her eighty-thousand francs a year, plus forty thousand francs for her husband. Where that money was to come from was never clarified. Nijinsky's contract with Alfred Butt called for only nine weeks of dancing at the Palace Theater. Nevertheless, Bronislava accepted her brother's offer, and their "joyous" reunion took place in Paris. "I was immensely happy to see him again," she writes; "he assured me that from now on we would always be together." Thus, brother and sister, so alike in physical appearance, well matched in kinesthetic talent, and devoted to the creation of original ballets, teamed up once more. Their shared childhood fantasy of happily dancing together may have been reinforced by a mutual determination to get even with and possibly outdo Diaghilev, who like their father had betrayed them both.[12]

Their happiness did not last long, however. Bronislava had difficulty getting along with Romola, who except for being pregnant had changed little since the days when she used to make a nuisance of herself backstage at the ballet. Unlike Bronislava, Romola could not communicate with Nijinsky on artistic matters and seemed ineffectual in giving him practical advice. Soon there was a power struggle between the two women. Bronislava objected to the changes in her brother's life-style. "Vaslav and Romola were staying in the Hotel Scribe," she writes, "not nearly as luxurious as the hotels where he had stayed with Diaghilev."[13] Romola was put off by Bronislava's bossiness and "untiring" energy: "She spoke only Russian and Polish, but I soon noticed that she did not like me; she seemed to resent everything that happened and blame it on me. I was the intruder in the Russian Ballet, in the family." While Vaslav and Bronislava were working together, Romola felt like an outsider. "I used to await them for lunch sometimes until four or five o'clock in the afternoon."[14] Worst of all, in his sister's eyes Nijinsky could do no wrong, and she began to point her finger at Romola for letting him get involved in a full-scale theatrical enterprise without first planning any specific programs or hiring any additional dancers. "The performances were to begin on March 2," Bronislava writes. "There were only four and a half weeks to opening night, and Vaslav had not even started the work. To sign a contract with such a short time for preparation seemed to me to be pure folly, but it was too late to talk about it, least of all with Vaslav."[15]

That Nijinsky could have gotten his vaudeville act together without his sister seems unlikely. She took charge immediately, helped him organize a program, and went with him to engage the necessary musicians and designers. They visited the composer Maurice Ravel, who agreed to do a new orchestration of Chopin's music for *Les Sylphides*. (Photographs taken in Ravel's apartment show him playing the piano, four-hand, with Nijinsky.) Nijinsky also wanted to restage his *Faune*. To find dancers for the corps de ballet, Bronislava sped back to Russia without her brother; it was nearly impossible to locate competent personnel at such short notice, and she was able to convince only one fully trained ballerina, a woman named Bonni, to come along, plus five young women who had had no stage experience whatsoever. Returning to London, Bronislava found four men, "Kojuhoff, Abramovitch, Mozoroff, and Kaweki," who could serve as character dancers, and four women who had some training in classical ballet. Three of the women were English and had to be given Russian names: "Johnson became Ivanova; Jacobson, Yakovleva; and Doris became Darinska." Nijinsky arranged for each of the dancers to receive a contract for eight weeks, with the option that the contract could be extended for a whole year. "The four men and the three soloists, Bonni, Ivanova, and Darinska, were to receive seven pounds ten shillings," writes Bronislava, "and the other seven girls five pounds per week for the performances, and all were also to be paid for the rehearsal weeks at a reduced rate."[16]

Thus, a ballet company of fourteen untried dancers plus three soloists—Nijinsky, Nijinska, and Nijinska's husband Alexander Kotchetovsky—was hurriedly assembled. Flyers were posted in London announcing a "Saison Nijinsky" to begin at the Palace Theater in March, preceding the June visit of Diaghilev's Ballets Russes to the Drury Lane Theater. Nijinsky was hoping to put on a new show every two weeks, which meant that four different programs would have to be produced altogether. Each would last forty-five minutes. The first program was to consist of *Les Sylphides*, *Danse Orientale* performed by Kotchetovsky so that Nijinsky could change his costume, and *Le Spectre de la Rose*, with Nijinsky and his sister dancing the loving couple. (*Les Sylphides* had to be shortened, so that the three ballets could be squeezed into Nijinsky's allotted act, scheduled to run from 10:05 to 10:50 p.m.) To get all of this organized in time was a nightmare. Kotchetovsky at least spoke enough English to give proper directions to the costume designers, stagehands, and other theater personnel. But there were many unexpected complications. Freshly designed sets had to be fireproofed, which caused some of the paint to run and discolor.

There was a delay in the sale of tickets. Diaghilev made waves over Bronislava's abrupt departure from the Ballets Russes. Fokine threatened to sue Nijinsky for unauthorized use of his choreographies. Anna Pavlova sent a telegram, taunting Nijinsky with her best wishes to the "music hall artist." (This was Pavlova's revenge for Nijinsky's open disapproval of her earlier appearances at the Palace Theater.) Under the constant pressure of daily rehearsals from morning to midnight, without adequate rest and time for meals, he became "more and more nervous [and] distraught." As Bronislava observed, "It was frightening to see him trembling and the perspiration pouring off him."[17]

On Monday night, 2 March 1914, the curtain rose. Nijinsky and his sister were poised serenely amidst a group of sylphides, his hand on her waist and her head near his shoulder. Suddenly, they noticed a familiar face. It was Diaghilev, "nonchalantly sprawled in his seat." He had come to the theater to watch them. Bronislava reports that she felt Vaslav's fingers tighten nervously around her waist: "His shoulder jerked, touching my head, as his body straightened up. He took a deep breath and entered into his dance, the first *pas* of *Les Sylphides*."

> I watched Vaslav and listened to the "Nocturne" in Ravel's new orchestration, so perfectly in harmony with Nijinsky's new rhythms. From time to time I would tear my eyes from Vaslav and glance at Diaghilev, who was intently following Vaslav in his dance, his eyes never leaving him.[18]

What Diaghilev thought of that opening performance is not known, but Romola remembered being "blinded with tears to see Vaslav dance, in his exquisite program, after a clown's number, and before a popular cabaret singer's act."[19] As for the audience, there were two kinds of reaction that night. The first came from fans of Nijinsky who had seen him dance before as a member of the Ballets Russes. Their disappointment stemmed not only from the smaller and less glamorous production he and his sister had staged, but also from a subtle change in Nijinsky's performance. "He still danced with that rare *élévation* and feeling for line and style to which I have already paid tribute," observed the critic Cyril Beaumont, "but he no longer danced like a god. Something of that mystic fragrance which previously had surrounded his dancing in *Les Sylphides* had vanished... the old magic had departed."[20] The other half of the audience comprised people who had never seen Nijinsky before, music-hall habitués, who were more accustomed to the simple fare and snappy tempo of vaudeville. They objected to the long delays necessitated by scenery and costumes having to be changed between ballets. During such pauses it was customary to hear the orchestra play a medley of popular tunes, while the houselights were turned up so one could read the program, order refreshments, or go to the toilet. "Angry murmurs and expressions of disapproval broke the silence," Beaumont writes. "The audience ... became exceedingly restive at being kept waiting in a silent and darkened theater."[21]

The following night they were treated to quite a different experience. Nijinsky and the other dancers finished their first number, *Les Sylphides*. He then went backstage to get into his costume for the grand finale, *Le Spectre de la Rose*. His costume was covered with flower petals and had to fit tightly. To adjust it properly always took some time. The audience grew impatient, so the leader of the orchestra thought it might be better to fill the interval with music. Against Nijinsky's orders he began conducting a Tchaikovsky waltz, one that Anna Pavlova had always liked to hear during her entr'actes. Suddenly the audience heard a terrible noise coming from backstage. Nijinsky was enraged over the music. He had torn off his costume and was screaming so loudly that it "could be heard through the corridors and backstage." Bronislava rushed into his dressing room: "I found his Rose costume on the floor," she writes. "I pleaded with him to dance and finish the performance."[22] The stage manager, Maurice Volny, also came into the room to see what was happening. He found "Nijinsky's dresser and some of the company crying and wringing their hands, while the dancer himself, his costume dragged off, was rolling on the ground in a mad hysterical outburst of rage."[23]

In the past, Nijinsky's "hysterical" outbursts had usually been managed fairly expeditiously by Diaghilev's valet Zuikov, or if necessary by Diaghilev himself. A powerful man was needed to get the temperamental dancer to calm down and control himself. This time there was no one present who could do so. Kotchetovsky had gone on stage, Bronislava lacked the necessary strength, and the dresser and little group of novice dancers evidently were too upset to do anything to curb Nijinsky's excitement. It was up to the stage manager to take action, and he did: "Volny, fearing that Nijinsky was about to have a fit, snatched up a jug of water he saw on the table and, hurling the contents at the dancer, shouted, 'Lève-toi!' This stern treatment had its effect, for the dancer got up. Then, Volny barked a curt 'Habille-toi!' and left Nijinsky to dress."[24] Although he was able to finish his performance, there were additional disturbances as the week progressed, and his behavior became increasingly erratic. While rehearsing one day, Nijinsky suddenly attacked one of the stagehands. Romola says that it was because the man had tried to flirt with her. (He "patted my cheeks with an impertinent suggestion.") This might account for Nijinsky's rage, but would not excuse the violence of his reaction. According to Romola, he "jumped" on the stagehand, "knocked him down ... and a fight began." She describes herself as "dumbfounded. I had never seen Vaslav like that."[25]

Another temper tantrum was observed during a business conference in Alfred Butt's office. Romola, who stayed at the hotel, noted that Nijinsky always felt very uncomfortable at such meetings because he "could not make out what [was] wanted of him." He was unable to converse in English and may have felt that Butt was being critical of his performance. Kotchetovsky had to serve as translator. Butt apparently was asking why no Russian ethnic dances had been planned for any of the vaudeville shows. It was what the public expected. Nijinsky took this as an insult. Butt's request for a less refined way of dancing may have reminded Nijinsky of his childhood, when his father would ask him to perform peasant dances at country fairs or circuses. He became belligerent, "slapped away Butt's hand," and then "squatted down and performed two or three *pas* from the *prissyatka* [a folk dance], screaming angrily, 'Is this what you want to see from Nijinsky?'" He became so disorderly that Kotchetovsky had to restrain him by holding both of his arms. It was feared that Nijinsky was going to attack Butt physically.[26] After this incident, Nijinsky refused to have any further meetings with the owner of the vaudeville theater. He did, however, agree to make a program change consistent with Butt's wishes for something "more Russian." *Danse Polovtsienne*, a robust Slavic number with makeshift costumes, was substituted during the second week for Kotchetovsky's demure "oriental" dance. As Cyril Beaumont reports, Nijinsky's mood, judgment, and behavior continued to decline.

> His nerves were frayed by the innumerable cares of management and he detested the responsibility and the necessity for constant supervision of details that went with it. He became subject to moods of intense irritability and depression, and he flew into a rage over the most trivial

incident. It was said that in one such fit of temper he had smashed a table.[27]

Toward the end of the second week of the "Saison Nijinsky," an entirely new program was announced. It was to include excerpts from *Carnaval,* a *Danse Grecque* for six of the women (while the Nijinskys, brother and sister, changed their costumes), *L'Après-midi d'un Faune,* and the Blue Bird pas de deux. Preparing this ambitious and attractive program required an enormous amount of rehearsal time, as none of the women except Bronislava knew the difficult choreography for *Faune.* Nijinsky was very demanding as usual. His sister describes him looking so exhausted and being so "impatient" with her that she wondered how the new program could ever be gotten ready in time for its opening on 16 March. One day he suddenly flared up during a rehearsal and criticized her so unmercifully that she broke into tears and had to leave the stage. In an ensuing argument, Nijinsky and Kotchetovsky nearly came to blows. By now, even Bronislava, who up to now had been defending her brother, could no longer overlook the deterioration in his behavior. There was a noticeable change in his dancing: "The usual spark, the enthusiasm that filled his being, the elation felt in each dancing movement, was no longer there." His eating habits changed: where Nijinsky had previously been restrained and fastidious at meals, using alcohol sparingly or not at all, he now showed a ravenous appetite. Bronislava reports that he "would eat a whole young chicken by himself and order a half bottle of red wine. I had never before seen Vaslav drink wine with his meals. Usually he had mineral water, or sometimes at home, if he had a glass of red wine, it would be largely diluted with water."[28]

Over the weekend just before the new program was to be performed, Nijinsky's masseur noticed that he seemed feverish, and on Sunday, 15 March, Romola notified Bronislava that Vaslav's temperature "now was over 100 [degrees Fahrenheit]."[29] She gave him aspirin, which seemed to produce no relief. If anything he was getting worse. "By now Vaslav was unable to stand on his feet," writes Romola. She became very frightened and telephoned Lady Ripon, a personal friend who belonged to that segment of London high society that had expressed delight over Nijinsky's recent marriage.* Lady Ripon suggested that he be seen by a

---

*Misia Sert wrote, "In London, where people still remembered the shock of the Oscar Wilde trial and subsequent similar scandals, the matrimonial plunge of Nijinsky, who remained the darling of Society, produced a wave of fine Puritan approval."[30]

doctor, and recommended two of London's most eminent specialists, Sir Alfred Downing Fripp and Sir Harry Edwin Bruce-Porter. Dr. Fripp was a surgeon. He came from an artistic family, had been an outstanding athlete in college, and after graduating from medical school had treated a member of the royal family for an ankle dislocation, which led to his being appointed surgeon-in-ordinary to the Prince of Wales (King Edward VII). Bruce-Porter also was a surgeon, with a special interest in athletics and the problems of athletes. How much time these doctors actually spent with Nijinsky, and how they treated him is not known, but according to Romola, Fripp said she had "almost killed" Nijinsky by giving him too much aspirin. "He had an athlete's heart and was in an extremely dangerous condition. He was very, very sick. He tried to go and dance, but could not."[31]

Participating in the Monday morning dress rehearsal for his new program clearly was out of the question for Nijinsky. He rested in bed, leaving Bronislava to hurriedly reorganize the ballets for that evening's performance and to go on stage without him. Alfred Butt announced the disappointing news to a full house: "I heard by telephone eight minutes ago from Sir Alfred Fripp that Mr. Nijinsky is in bed with a temperature of 103 degrees. . . . Of course, anyone who wishes may have his money back. The rest of the dancers will perform their part of the program. I am sorry, but I knew nothing until eight minutes ago."[32] The next day Nijinsky again absented himself from the theater, and it was arranged to replace his act with a new show that featured two comedians, a pianist, and an actor who did "imitations of well-known artists."[33] On Wednesday, Nijinsky was feeling much better, but no one told this to the theater management, and the substitute vaudevillians again went on stage in place of the ballet.

The following morning, 19 March, Bronislava and her husband went to the Palace Theater to see Volny and tell him that Nijinsky was prepared to dance that evening. Volny's answer was that "the Saison Nijinsky had been cancelled" and that other acts would be replacing the ballet programs.[34] According to the conditions Nijinsky had signed with Alfred Butt, an absence of three consecutive days meant a breach of contract, and this gave the Palace Theater the right to release him and the other dancers. It is debatable whether Nijinsky understood what the consequences of his not performing for three days in a row might be. ("I know this boy all too well," Stravinsky wrote about him in 1916, "and he never remembers what he says or what he has done."[35]) A more charitable interpretation, by dance historian Nancy Van Norman Baer, is that "Nijinsky understood that he could miss three performing days because of illness. He did not realize, however, that these could not be consecutive days. This misunderstanding reflected Nijinsky's lack of experience with contracts."[36] Bronislava Nijinska always held it against Romola that the "Saison Nijinsky" had to close prematurely.

I have never been able to understand how his wife, Romola, who from the beginning of their marriage had shown herself to be so clever in business and financial dealings, and who also spoke English fluently, was able to allow Vaslav to sign such a difficult contract with a music hall theater.[37]

Cancellation of the contract produced economic hardship for the dancers. Out of the two thousand pounds Butt was obliged to pay for two weeks of ballet, Nijinsky had to cover the cost of new costumes, scenery, and the music he had commissioned as well as the salary of his dancers. He gave Bronislava and her husband one month's equivalent of the salary they would ordinarily have received from Diaghilev. The fourteen remaining dancers were paid a full month's salary, plus half-pay for their rehearsal time.* The company disbanded and Bronislava returned to Russia, never again to collaborate or dance with her famous brother. The timing of this calamity could not have been worse, since it coincided with the announcements of Diaghilev's very promising upcoming summer season in London, backed financially by the wealthy Beecham family (the conductor Sir Thomas Beecham was active in Diaghilev's opera and ballet productions). Invidious comparisons were made. "I am afraid that M. Nijinsky will regret that he is no longer in this social success," wrote one critic. "I hope none will be so vain as to ... think that they can be a music-hall Atlas and carry an artistic audience on their own shoulders. There are really very few Pavlovas, and as a male dancer has not got quite the same personality and charm, the chance of a success out of the general environment is very small." Speculation was rife as to why Nijinsky had stopped dancing. "Certainly it was widely considered that it was *not* influenza," says Nesta

---

*These figures come from Bronislava Nijinska's *Memoirs*. Romola Nijinsky wrote that Nijinsky paid "all the thirty two [sic] artists in full" for an entire year. Thus, she not only exaggerated his generosity, but also made it necessary to speculate where all the money came from. Richard Buckle asked Mme Nijinsky about this. "The answer is that for dancing at private parties such as the Aga Khan's [Nijinsky] had been paid enormous sums. As Diaghilev had always settled his hotel bills, fed and clothed him, and taken care of his mother's expenses, these were almost untouched."[38]

Macdonald, a dance scholar who mentions a newspaper report from America dated 4 April 1914, reporting Nijinsky's illness to be "much more serious than is generally realized.... He is said to be suffering from a nervous breakdown, induced by overwork in the planning and rehearsing of new dances."[39]

What kind of nervous breakdown was it? Most people think that Nijinsky was schizophrenic, but there is no evidence of this condition during this phase of illness, when he was twenty-five years old. According to a medical certificate signed on 3 October 1914, he was suffering from "neurasthenia with depressive states, insomnia and a nervous heart condition as well as chest-pain."[40] This diagnosis (similar to the one in Russia four years earlier) was made by Paul Ranschburg, M.D., a neurologist who examined Nijinsky after he and his wife returned to Hungary just before World War I.* Nijinsky's condition was also evaluated a number of times by Artur Isay, M.D., a professor at the medical school in Budapest, who wrote on 4 August 1914:

> I examined Mr. Vaslav Nijinsky and *as I have ascertained months ago,* his heart and nervous system presented a picture to me of a diseased (abnormal) change, which makes all kinds of vigorous physical activity unsuitable and forces him to spend the greater part of the day in bed.[41]

To understand these medical opinions we must make a brief excursion into the history of psychiatry. For centuries it has been known that patients may complain of fatigue, weakness, shortness of breath, and pain in the chest, abdomen, or other parts of the body without manifesting any physical changes that can explain these symptoms. When doctors relied only on methods like inspection, palpation, probing the body, or surgery, they were repeatedly baffled by such complaints. Those physicians who took the time to become personally acquainted with their patients, spoke with their relatives or friends, and looked more comprehensively at their lives often discovered that there were psychological, social, and emotional problems associated

---

*Romola herself had been seen by Dr. Ranschburg as a child, when she developed nightmares and other problems after her father committed suicide. He was the founder of a "psychophysical" laboratory in Budapest, where he worked extensively with children and became a Professor of Psychiatry. Dr. Ranschburg's major publication, in 1905, was on "Symptoms and Treatment of the Functions of the Mind." In 1928 he established the Hungarian Psychiatric Society, and remained its president for many years.

with their malaise. Labels like "hypochondriasis" and "hysteria" came to be attached to conditions in which patients complained a great deal but doctors could find no physical cause.

During the seventeenth century, a brilliant medical scholar in England named Thomas Sydenham reasoned that such diseases as well as a condition called "melancholia" (we now use the term "depression") were the result of disturbances and inconsistencies of the mind as well as the body. Efforts were made to remedy these illnesses through education, retraining, hypnosis, and other psychological methods. Two hundred years later, when the science of neurology assumed a more prominent position in clinical medicine, the American physician George Beard introduced the term "neurasthenia." It meant, literally, a state of nervous exhaustion. The diagnosis of neurasthenia became quite fashionable for a while. Different causal explanations were proposed, including heredity, intoxication, overexertion, and sexual conflict. Many people called neurasthenia "the American disease."[42] A Philadelphia neurologist, Silas Weir Mitchell, specialized in treating these patients with strict bed rest, social isolation, massage, and a diet of fermented camel's milk. Around the turn of the century, Sigmund Freud in Vienna established psychoanalysis as a way of treating many of the so-called "functional" disorders. At that time they were explained mostly in terms of sexual and aggressive impulses that were being blocked, unconsciously, by moral inhibitions. Freud had been trained as a neurologist. He believed that diseases of the mind would ultimately have to be understood as disturbances in brain chemistry.

Nowadays, the illness called neurasthenia no longer exists. Its place has been taken by new disease concepts, including "somatization disorder," which refers primarily to unfounded physical symptoms; "panic disorder," which focuses on crippling fears; and "affective disorder," which emphasizes disturbances in mood. All three diagnoses are pertinent to Nijinsky's in 1914. Especially prominent, as Dr. Ranschburg pointed out, was the commotion Nijinsky felt in his chest. It seemed to suggest that there was something wrong with his heart, an idea that Sir Alfred Fripp may inadvertently have reinforced by telling Romola that her husband had an "athlete's heart." Anyone who depends primarily on the integrity of his body in work and self-expression is likely to be terrified by the notion that there is something wrong with his heart and blood circulation. The recommendation that Nijinsky should take it easy and rest probably encouraged his latent passivity and dependency. Social withdrawal, escaping from responsibility, and staying in bed had been his way of coping with stress since he was a little boy. As an expert in the field of psychosomatic medicine recently pointed out, "A child who learns that being ill or complaining of physical symptoms is likely to be rewarded by increased attention or by avoidance of conflict or of some obligation may be predisposed to develop somatization as a coping strategy in later life."[43]

The physicians who examined and treated Nijinsky in 1914 clearly recognized that he was disturbed in both mind and body. Their reports call attention to his invalidism, his depressiveness, his sleeplessness, and his overconcern with discomfort in his chest. But they did not describe the causes. Most likely the unhappy circumstances of Nijinsky's life, including his recent separation from Diaghilev and the misadventure with his sister at the Palace Theater, had produced a devastating sense of failure. He felt dejected and pessimistic. He may have had disturbing ideas about bodily decay and death, similar to those he had experienced during the earlier depressive episode, following his graduation from ballet school in St. Petersburg. Unfortunately, there was little that could be done to treat him in 1914. Specific pharmaceutical agents for combating the psychophysiological effects of depression and anxiety had not yet been discovered. Some doctors prescribed sedatives, usually bromides or occasionally opiates for the relief of emotional distress, but these were relatively ineffective and produced undesirable side effects. Dynamic psychotherapy as we know it today was in its infancy. The few psychoanalysts then available tended to encourage free association and dream interpretation, rather than active coping strategies.

Were a patient like Nijinsky in therapy today, one would try to remedy his unfamiliarity with practical matters, encourage more effective communication in speech and writing, attempt to modify his chronic dependency and extreme perfectionism, help him to control his social irritability, and promote personal as well as artistic goals through improved interpersonal relationships.[44] Such a program of rehabilitation obviously takes time. Nijinsky moved so frequently from one place to another that it was next to impossible to develop even the basic relationship with a physician that is necessary for effective treatment. It devolved on his wife to provide whatever support, attention, and guidance he would need, something for which she was at first unprepared but soon came to accept as part of their marriage. "I now

insisted that Vaslav should rest, and live only to restore his health,"
Romola writes. "I could induce him to do this as I was approaching the
time of the birth of my baby, and Vaslav was willing to stay with me
constantly. We took long walks in Richmond Park, and used to picnic in
the beautiful Surrey country-side."[45]

During the hectic period before his breakdown, with the frenetic
stress of organizing and rehearsing a ballet company, Nijinsky's awareness of his impending fatherhood seems to have been pushed out of
consciousness. In April 1914, this was no longer possible. Romola was
now seven months pregnant. He expressed a need for greater privacy.
He wanted to be sure that "no stranger should witness this transformation [in his wife.]"[46] (Unconscious memories of his pregnant mother and
of the loss of his favored position as the youngest child in the family may
have activated some of these concerns.) He became increasingly
irritable and restless. He went with Romola to Semmering, a health
resort in the mountains near Vienna, where both of them benefited
somewhat from the secluded and tranquil environment. Before long,
however, an invitation arrived from the American Embassy in Madrid,
asking Nijinsky to come to Spain. He was wanted at a wedding
reception for Kermit Roosevelt, to dance for the guests, with the
Spanish King and Queen in attendance. It was an opportunity he could
not refuse. Romola writes that "the salary offered was three-thousand
dollars for one dance. We needed the money now that the savings were
gone." Because of Nijinsky's illness and the fact that he was unused to
traveling alone, Romola's stepfather, Oscar Párdány, offered to go with
him on the long trip of 1,600 miles by train.

What Nijinsky danced in Madrid, and how well, is not known.
Romola says that she received "a short note, written in Russian" every
day from him, which made her feel "proud, as I knew Vaslav never
wrote to anybody." From these letters, and from what she heard
afterward, she concluded that his brief appearance had been successful. "King Alfonso as well as the Queen led the others to make him feel
at home. I heard from witnesses that the dance on the stage, which was
placed in the beautiful gardens, was unforgettable."[47]

The knowledge that he could dance again and gain admiration seems
to have raised Nijinsky's spirits sufficiently to embolden him to remain
briefly in Paris before returning to Vienna. He wanted to attend the
opening performance on 14 May 1914 of the Ballets Russes. Most likely
he also wanted to see Diaghilev and other old friends. (Romola writes
that "Vaslav wanted to show the world that he was not afraid of

Diaghilev."[48]) It must have taken considerable courage for him to sit in the audience of the Paris Opéra, surrounded by people who could only stare at him with a mixture of curiosity and awe and no longer see him dance. On the program was *Schéhérazade*, with Fokine in Nijinsky's role of the favorite slave, a new ballet by Fokine, *Les Papillons*, set to the music of Robert Schumann, and the long-awaited premiere of *La Légende de Joseph*, the ballet Nijinsky was supposed to have starred in. (Before the dancer's dismissal as Diaghilev's choreographer, the librettist Hofmannsthal had urged Strauss "on behalf of ... the perturbed Nijinsky" to compose music "beyond all bounds of convention.... I must make myself the spokesman for Nijinsky who implores you to write the most unrestrained, the least dance-like music in the world."[49]) As it turned out, *Légende* disappointed almost everyone. The ballet was overly long (it takes more than an hour to play Strauss's score), and Fokine's choreography was generally considered "uninspired." One reviewer, however, praised Fokine for his "good taste" in bringing back to the Diaghilev's company "all the graceful attitudes and harmonious gestures which M. Nijinsky, with his grotesque ideas, sought to abolish."[50] Probably the best thing about the ballet was José-María Sert's opulent but old-fashioned decor.

As for Léonide Massine's performance in the title role, it could not have made Nijinsky feel very comfortable. Everyone knew that Massine was Diaghilev's new protégé and Nijinsky's successor. They expected miracles. Massine, however, had been trained more as an actor. He lacked experience as a ballet dancer and could not hold a candle to Nijinsky. Fokine simplified the choreography to make up for this. "Massine was overcome with nerves, but struggled through the performance," writes Richard Buckle. "What he lacked in dancing technique he made up in stage presence and beauty."[51] As a result of Massine's concupiscent posturing and brief costume, *Légende de Joseph* was quickly dubbed "Les Jambes de Joseph" by the Parisians. In London, where the ballet was conducted by Richard Strauss himself, it enjoyed more acclaim, partly because of the great enthusiasm for the composer, who was participating in a festival of his own. *Légende* was briefly revived in Berlin and Vienna in 1921, but had little success and was soon dropped from the Ballets Russes repertoire.*

During the intermission, Nijinsky, expecting that he would be

---

*In 1947, two years before his death, Strauss prepared a "Symphonic Fragment" of the music for concert performances, but it is almost never played.

welcomed with open arms by his old friends, went to the box where Diaghilev customarily held court. According to Romola's reminiscences, a "frozen silence" greeted the anxious dancer. Misia Sert apparently tried to engage Nijinsky in conversation. Then, Cocteau and "some other young men" began to laugh and taunt Nijinsky by saying, "This year, your creation is a child. The *Spectre de la Rose* chooses the part of a father. How utterly disgusting is birth." Nijinsky was understandably hurt and offended. He "stood up and answered, 'The *Spectre de la Rose's* child will be quite as beautiful as his own entrance, which you always admired.' He bowed and left them."[53]* As far as we know, Nijinsky never did get a chance to see Diaghilev during his brief stay in Paris. He did, however, take a lesson with Enrico Cecchetti, his old ballet coach. Diaghilev knew about this, of course, and sent Massine, who had never seen Nijinsky in action before, to observe what went on. Massine was deeply impressed by his extraordinary technique, and astonished by his courteous respect for Cecchetti, who had to point out some deficiencies in the way Nijinsky was positioning his arms. "Massine noticed that Vaslav accepted these corrections without ever answering back."[55]

While in Paris, Nijinsky also embarked on what turned out to be a long and difficult negotiation with Jacques Rouché, director of the Opéra, who had offered him a position earlier that year, before his debacle in London. (As we have already heard, anything having to do with administrative matters was an ordeal for Nijinsky, and his doctors had advised against it.) The theatrical agency H.B. Marinelli assisted in formulating a contract with fourteen clauses, and the business-minded Oscar Párdány did most of the bargaining. After Nijinsky rejoined Romola in Vienna, and his father-in-law returned to Budapest, the latter continued to handle all correspondence related to the dancer's future engagements in Paris and other cities.

According to his contract with Rouché, Nijinsky was to be employed four months a year, February through May, beginning in 1915. This meant that he would have ample time to rest, travel, and work on new choreography. His position was to be "prémier danseur (Étoile)," with

---

*This story must be taken cautiously, since it was written long after Romola heaped all kinds of blame on Diaghilev. Whether she heard it from her husband or her stepfather is not known. Romola Nijinsky was not alone in this attitude, however. Stravinsky, for example, told Robert Craft that "it is almost impossible to describe the perversity of Diaghilev's entourage—a kind of homosexual Swiss Guard—and the incidents and stories concerning it."[54]

an obligation to perform no more than thirty times during each four-month period. The contract specified that he was to "appear in the leading roles (acting, miming, and dancing)," of "new ballets ... not to exceed three altogether," and in any other "ballets, divertissements, lyrical works belonging to the repertory in which roles can be found for him." In addition Nijinsky was to serve as artistic adviser, with a "consultative voice" in selecting new ballets for the Opéra. He would be encouraged to produce his own ballets, but these could not be presented anywhere else in France or on any foreign stages until one month after they were first performed in Paris. The contract was to be binding for three years, 1915, 1916, and 1917, during which Nijinsky would not be permitted to dance "on any stage in Paris and France except that of the Théâtre National de l'Opéra."[56]

These conditions appear favorable, at least from our point of view, and stand in contrast to the marked uncertainty of Nijinsky's earlier employment with the Ballets Russes, where his talents were to some extent exploited and, as he characterized it later, he had "lived like a martyr" and "worked like an ox."[57] Why then did Nijinsky not sign the contract with Rouché and begin working in Paris in 1915? His wife claimed that it was for "artistic" reasons: "When Vaslav saw the material that the Opéra offered, he was obliged to refuse."[58] No doubt Nijinsky had misgivings about chaining himself to an organization having to cater to public taste and present numerous standard works, operas and ballets, each season. It would hardly have been as exciting and artistically stimulating an assignment as working for Diaghilev. (The dancer Serge Lifar, another Diaghilev protégé, did later accept a position at the Paris Opéra analogous to that offered to Nijinsky.)

A deeper reason for his reluctance, however, was his illness, which Dr. Ranschburg wrote had "recently become worse" and Dr. Isay said "was forcing him to spend the greater part of his day in bed (and) may require some treatment in a sanatorium."[59] In 1914 Nijinsky was far too troubled with fear, depression, and physical malaise to commit himself to a contract that would have been binding for the next three years. Two clauses in the Opéra contract look as if they would have been especially threatening to a dancer afflicted with "neurasthenia." One of them gave Rouché the right to cancel Nijinsky's engagement "without any restitution of damages" in case "the artist postponed or withdrew" from one of the performances. The other imposed a penalty of Fr. 100,000 "on either party" in the event that all obligations were not fulfilled "for the total duration" of the contract. These clauses most likely were meant to protect the Paris Opéra against the sort of emergency with which Grigoriev had to deal in South America, when Nijinsky suddenly refused to appear in *Carnaval*, or Alfred Butt faced when the dancer became disabled in London.

After returning to Austria, Nijinsky instructed Oscar Párdány to write to the Marinelli agency, requesting changes in the contract and asking if any other engagements were available on terms that were more desirable than those Rouché had offered. Marinelli's reply on 19 June 1914 shows the weaknesses in Nijinsky's bargaining position. He alluded to the difficulty in finding clauses "that would exclude unanticipated events from the contract." He mentioned that Rouché had every intention of remaining as director of the Paris Opéra for the next seven years, and that the only thing Rouché was willing to concede was that Nijinsky would have the same rights as he himself "to get out of the contract for any valid reason." But such a clause, in Marinelli's opinion, was "inappropriate." Nijinsky had asked for more freedom in attending or not attending rehearsals. Rouché was very firm on this point. Marinelli wrote Párdány that "you yourself must admit it is not very artistic when someone wants to withdraw from rehearsals."

> Surely Mr. Nijinsky must have sufficient sense of honor, and it must be so much in his interest to achieve great success, that he would in no way want to withdraw, but rather to step in as early as possible to participate in rehearsals, precisely because this concerns an artistic matter, and not an ordinary business. Or has Mr. Nijinsky changed his mind?[60]

Regarding other possible engagements, Marinelli mentioned that there might be opportunities for Nijinsky to dance "in America." He also asked Párdány to find out if Nijinsky "might eventually be willing to accept an engagement at the Wintergarten in Berlin." No definite commitments of any kind were made. Párdány had in the meantime contacted another theatrical agent, in London, who wrote back excitedly on 17 June 1914 to say that there were notices about the dancer in the London newspapers. It was rumored "that Mr. Nijinsky will be appearing here in the Drury Lane Theater. Is that true?"[61] What had happened is that Lady Ripon was putting pressure on Diaghilev to reengage Nijinsky. His dismissal was of great concern to her. Reports from Paris had suggested that the glamour of the Ballets Russes was diminished by Nijinsky's absence. ("He alone gave life to the whole company," one critic had written.[62]) Lady Ripon thought that by making peace between Nijinsky and Diaghilev she could remedy a situation that was having an adverse effect on the younger man's health and the older man's reputation. Her strategy was to appeal directly to Diaghilev's devoted friend and financial backer Misia Sert. She wrote to Misia in Paris, "You will understand that Nijinsky's marriage has predisposed everyone here in his favor."

> I am very much upset, for in spite of the failure of poor Nijinsky's ballets, the feeling against Diaghilev in London is acute because Nijinsky hasn't been re-engaged.... I had hoped that this whole business would pass unnoticed in London. But though Nijinsky has the good sense not to mention his quarrel with Diaghilev, everybody talks about it, and I am afraid it might do the ballet a great deal of harm.[63]

According to Romola, both Lady Ripon and Baron de Gunsbourg "were awaiting" the dancer in London. It was Romola's understanding that he would be asked "to dance *Faune* and *Spectre,* and some other parts."[64] There is no confirmation of this, and I suspect it was her fantasy. However, the ailing Nijinsky did make a trip to London, accompanied I assume by his father-in-law, only to be rebuffed once more during a rehearsal. "The company completely ignored Nijinsky," says Romola. "They did not speak to him; they did not even bow. Of course this was all done under the instructions of Sergei Pavlovitch. He was forced to call and tolerate Nijinsky, but he wished to show that he had not forgiven." Her bitterness is understandable. Grigoriev's description of the whole sad episode confirms the embarrassing position Nijinsky had gotten himself into.

> It is quite natural that the Marchioness of Ripon, a great admirer of Nijinsky's, should have done everything within her power so that he should dance some performances with us. Either she wished to rehabilitate him after his London failure, or she simply hoped that a reconciliation would take place. However, such a return was not possible at the time, not merely because Sergei [Diaghilev] did not wish it, but also because Fokine, who had come back to us as choreographer and dancer, was to replace Nijinsky, according to contract, in all the latter's roles.[65]

So far it had been a terrible year for the great dancer. Newly married, expecting a child, and pushed aside by his former lover Diaghilev, Nijinsky had fallen sick. He was fearful, depressed, and sleepless. He was worried about the discomfort in his chest, and probably afraid of dying. Much of the time he was resting in bed. In spite of his sister's heroic efforts, he had failed miserably to organize an independent ballet company. A contract to dance at the Paris Opéra and work there as ballet master and choreographer for three years seemed unacceptable. No alternatives were in sight. These cumulative stresses were eroding Nijinsky's self-confidence and ability to plan for the future. Only one thing seemed certain—he would soon be a father.

NOTES

1. Quotation from Mark D. Sullivan, "Organic or Functional? . . ."
2. Igor Stravinsky and Robert Craft, *Memoirs and Commentaries*, 38.
3. H.A.L., Fisher, *A History of Europe*, 1140.
4. BNM, 481–483; see also 382.
5. RNN, 262.
6. Igor Stravinsky and Robert Craft, 38.
7. Ibid., 37.
8. RNN, 262–263.
9. Igor Stravinsky and Robert Craft, 38.
10. Nesta Macdonald, *Diaghilev Observed by Critics in England and the United States*, 108.
11. BNM, 491.
12. Ibid., 492–494.
13. Ibid., 494.
14. RNN, 265.
15. BNM, 495.
16. Ibid., 496–497.
17. Ibid., 499.
18. Ibid., 501.
19. RNN, 267.
20. Cyril Beaumont, *Bookseller at the Ballet, Memoirs 1891–1929*, 149.
21. Beaumont, 150.
22. BNM, 506.
23. Beaumont, 150–151, describes this incident as occurring the second night of Nijinsky's appearances at the Palace, while BNM, 505, says it took place during a matinee on 14 March, when "for the first time during the Saison Nijinsky all the seats were sold out."
24. Beaumont, 150–151.
25. RNN, 266.
26. BNM, 504.
27. Beaumont, 151.
28. BNM, 502–503, 505.
29. Ibid., 506.
30. Misia Sert, *Misia and the Muses*, 122.
31. RNN, 267.
32. Macdonald, 110–111.
33. Ibid.
34. BNM, 507.
35. Vera Stravinsky and Robert Craft, *Stravinsky in Pictures and Documents*, 606.
36. Nancy Van Norman Baer, *Bronislava Nijinska*, 17n.

37. BNM, 507.
38. BNM, 508; RNN, 268; RBN, 407.
39. Macdonald, 111.
40. Dr. Paul Ranschburg, medical report (in German), 3 October 1914. Property of David Leonard, London.
41. Dr. Artur Isay, medical report (in Hungarian, translation by Kinga Gasper), 4 August 1914. Property of David Leonard, London. Emphasis added.
42. F. G. Gosling, *Before Freud*. For an excellent discussion of the evolution of concepts about diseases like hysteria and neurasthenia, see Henri F. Ellenberger, *The Discovery of the Unconscious*.
43. Z. J. Lipowski, "Somatization: The Concept and Its Clinical Application."
44. Peter Ostwald, "Psychotherapeutic Approaches in the Treatment of Performing Artists."
45. RNN, 268–269.
46. Ibid., 269.
47. Ibid.
48. Ibid.
49. *The Correspondence Between Richard Strauss and Hugo von Hofmannsthal*, 150.
50. Alfred Bruncan, cited in RBN, 411.
51. RBN, 411.
52. Bernard Taper, *Balanchine*, 61.
53. RNN, 272.
54. Igor Stravinsky and Robert Craft, 40n.
55. RBN, 410.
56. Contract proposal from Jacques Rouché to Nijinsky, 30 May 1914. Nijinsky Archives.
57. Notebook on "Death," 40.
58. RNN, 262.
59. Dr. Ranschburg; Dr. Isay, undated appendage to his report of 4 August 1914. Property of David Leonard, London.
60. Letter from H. B. Marinelli, Ltd., to Oscar Párdány, 19 June 1914. Nijinsky Archives.
61. Letter from P. Wollheim to O. Párdány, 17 June 1914. Nijinsky Archives.
62. Jacques Riviere, newspaper article quoted in RBN, 411.
63. Sert, 122–123.
64. RNN, 275.
65. Letter from Serge Grigoriev to Walter Nouvel, 5 April 1934, quoted in Arnold Haskell, *Diaghileff*, 237.

It was a nervous affliction that so
tormented him, one of those medically
indeterminate ailments that mock the
sufferer over the years and threaten to
make life unbearable, while never
actually putting life at risk.
                    Thomas Mann[1]

Chapter 6

Partial Recovery and Return to Dancing

Depression is a biological phenomenon, characterized by feelings of sluggishness, turndown in mood, and slowing of physical and mental activity. According to present-day scientific knowledge, the condition is caused by changes in the transmission of chemical signals across gaps, or "synapses," between cells in the brain and spinal cord. Many factors are involved, including the type of nerve cell, its age and function, the chemistry of neurotransmission, the integrity of the nervous system, and general health factors such as nutrition, presence of other diseases, stress, and immune responses. Small wonder then that more than one form of depression can occur at the same time, and that an individual may suffer from different forms of depression during a lifetime. These illnesses are called "affective disorders." One can think of them along a spectrum, with "normalcy" at one end and "madness" at the other.[2]

Nijinsky's symptoms at age twenty-five consisted of severe nervousness, moodiness, fatigue, irritability, fear, inability to sleep, and worries about his physical health. This illness was precipitated by a series of stressful life events: rejection by Diaghilev, ouster from the Ballets Russes, and failure of the "Saison Nijinsky." The term *reactive* depression seems applicable as a diagnosis, and since there had been similar depressive episodes during his childhood and adolescence, one wonders whether he might have been manifesting a *recurrent* form of affective disorder, the sort of disease that tends to run in cycles. The course his illness took in 1914 seems to have been influenced by several factors, including his age, certain limitations in his personality, the problems inherent in his marriage, and the deleterious effects of World War I.

On Thursday, 18 June 1914, the ailing dancer was still in Vienna, negotiating with Rouché in Paris and preparing to go to London for what turned out to be another exasperating contact with Diaghilev. Romola took Nijinsky to the opera that night. On the program was *Elektra,* the violent drama of a woman mourning her father's death and plotting revenge, by murder, against her mother. Richard Strauss's shimmering, seductive music impressed Nijinsky deeply; he was to devote his next choreographic effort to a Strauss ballet. Romola too was moved by the Greek tragedy. After returning from the opera she went into labor. Plans had already been made for her to spend several weeks in Dr. Loew's clinic, a private sanatorium. Two special nurses were engaged, one to look after the mother, the other a wet nurse for the baby. (It was decided in advance not to try breast-feeding.) Such arrangements were not unusual for a woman of her social class. Less attention was given to expectant fathers in those days, but Nijinsky of course had his own doctors. Both he and Romola thought their baby would be a boy. She wanted to call him Boris, while Nijinsky preferred the name Vladislav, a smaller version of himself.[3]

A baby girl arrived the next day: what a disappointment! Romola remembered being "very unhappy about it." When the nurse told Nijinsky that it was "only a girl, but a nice one," he had a little temper tantrum. Romola says "he lost his self-control, and threw his gloves on the floor." She also describes a very disagreeable incident precipitated when Emilia Márkus arrived, unexpectedly, at the hospital. Romola had told her mother to stay away. Why? I gather that the famous actress was then struggling to maintain a youthful image in the eyes of her adoring public. She probably had mixed feelings about becoming a grandmother (this was her first grandchild). But more important was Romola's smoldering resentment toward Emilia, which was to sour their relationship over the years and had a very bad effect on Vaslav, who liked and felt understood by his mother-in-law. When Emilia tried to pick up the newborn baby and hold her, Romola became "extremely upset." She says she jumped out of her bed, which "brought on serious complications." Evidently Nijinsky was so disturbed by all of this that he again flared up, and nearly got into a fist fight with Oscar Párdány. Unusual behavior, to say the least, on an obstetrics ward.[4]

The baby was given a Greek name, Kyra, as well as a Slavic middle name, Vaslavovna, in honor of her father, as is customary for Russians. Kyra turned out to be an unusually attractive child, with curly black hair and "beautiful green eyes, as strangely fascinating, as oblique as Vaslav's very own." She also was "extremely muscular," Romola says, and seemed to mirror her father's beauty: "The more she grew the more she resembled Vaslav."* Before long they were so closely attached to each other that the child seemed almost like an extension of the father, and the father seemed to lose himself in the child. "The world ceased to exist for him," writes Romola. They had moved back to Budapest, where "from morning till late evening he accompanied the baby everywhere, and watched over her sleep." He carved and painted small wooden toys for her, and played with her constantly. Romola says that Nijinsky was so "enchanted" with his daughter that he even participated in feeding her, unusual for a European man in those days.[6]

Both of the Nijinsky daughters remember Romola as a cold, remote, and indifferent mother, who left it to others to care for them. "She was terribly insecure," says Tamara, the second child.

---

*Even today Kyra has many qualities of Nijinsky. She is very energetic, powerful, and artistic. For many years she worked as a dancer, and her autobiographical film, *She Dances Alone*, gives evidence of a creative as well as headstrong personality.[5] Unlike Nijinsky, whose speech was often noticeably inhibited, Kyra (until she had a stroke at age seventy-five) was highly verbal and spoke many foreign languages fluently. In this regard, and in her ability to control and manipulate other people, Kyra more closely resembles her mother.

In my opinion, she was jealous of her own mother, not only because of Emilia's great talent—I think that was the lesser problem—but because she envied her mother's warm and charming nature, which made her attractive and loved by everyone she came in contact with. Romola also envied the fact that other members of her family had accomplished something, her father in art, her uncle in politics, her aunt and sister in music, while she had not distinguished herself in any way. It was only after she fell under the spell of Nijinsky that her life became meaningful. And while she became very fond of this exceptional, gentle human being, guilt and anger must have entered Romola's soul for maybe ruining his life.[7]

Romola did, of course, distinguish herself, with Lincoln Kirstein's help, as the chronicler of her husband's career. She reports a touching scene in which Nijinsky took the initiative in providing milk for Kyra. This happened after the wet nurse left. (They were all living in the Pulszky mansion in Budapest.) Nijinsky went to a pediatrician's office "and returned carrying under his arm a book about the upbringing and care of babies and a sterilizing apparatus. With infinite care he sterilized and prepared the bottles, and from that noon on he fed Kyra himself."[8] (Whether Nijinsky read the book about baby care is questionable, since he understood neither Hungarian nor German.)

Concurrent with Romola's failure to assume a maternal role was her continual feuding with her own mother. This came to a head after the outbreak of hostilities in August 1914. As a Russian citizen, Nijinsky was now a virtual prisoner of war. Unable to travel outside Hungary, and still too sick to work, he became totally dependent on Romola, who in turn depended on Emilia Márkus and Oscar Párdány for shelter and food. Instead of expressing gratitude, Romola (in her book) berated her mother for making life miserable for Vaslav and herself, for telling the servants not to feed them properly, for interfering with Kyra's upbringing, for spying on Vaslav, for reporting his activities to the police, for "screaming" at him "You hateful man, you damned Russian.... I wish you were out of my house forever, you silly acrobat, you circus dancer," and other terrible accusations.[9] How much of this was true is difficult to say. When, in 1916, Romola spoke to reporters in New York about the problems she allegedly had had in Budapest, they dismissed her complaints as "wild and arrant nonsense."[10] Tamara Nijinsky (who was born in 1920, grew up in Emilia Márkus's home, and later was adopted by her) also refutes Romola's stories: "My grandmother actually liked Vaslav very much and always had great respect for him as a fellow performing artist. They were kindred spirits, and maybe that's what bothered Romola so much. She never could share Vaslav with anyone."

No doubt it was stressful for Nijinsky to be confined to the Pulszky residence under wartime conditions and to have to report to the authorities each week. But the experience seems to have brought out a certain worldly wisdom, a sense of resignation. "I am destitute," he later wrote in a notebook about what he had felt in Budapest in 1914:

> I have no shelter or food, for I have nothing. My wife's mother has a three-floor house with marble pillars. She likes that house because it is expensive. I do not like that house because it is stupidly built. I know that many people will say that I do not understand the beauty of that house, for it contains many lovely old pictures and Gobelins. I shall say that I do not like anything old because old things smell of death. I know that many people will say that I am a man without a soul because I do not like old people.[11]

Nijinsky was not alone in describing the Pulszky mansion as an uncomfortable place to live; his son-in-law, Igor Markevitch, thought it resembled a museum; his daughter Tamara says it was "ugly." One way out of his discomfort was for Nijinsky to withdraw from the adults in the house and attach himself ever more closely to his child, with whom he could identify and whom he came to love in a very special way. Romola says that he "worshipped" Kyra, who "reciprocated" this devotion and showed no interest in anyone except her father. They played together "for hours. He threw her in the air, to Kyra's delight, rolled with her in the grass, and they pulled the carved colored duck together. She used to jump in her bed, arching her body." He wanted her to be a dancer and said: "You see, she will be a dancer; she is dancing already."[12] It was like a repetition of his own childhood.

During the winter of 1914, Nijinsky also spent a considerable amount of time with his wife, and they probably became really well acquainted for the first time since their marriage the year before, going for long walks and developing an interest in literature and philosophy. She started to learn Russian, which helped the process of communication, since he spoke no Hungarian and never mastered French, German, or English, the other languages Romola knew. She says that they "read together the works of Tolstoy, Chekhov, and Pushkin, and the marvellous treasures of the Russian literature unfolded before me." In spite of the improvement in their relationship, she continued to feel uncomfortable about having taken Nijinsky away from his Russian friends and family: "These were Vaslav's people, who felt and thought and loved unselfishly like he did. I understood him. But I could not help feeling, as we read Dostoevsky's *La Maison des Morts,* that I had brought a similar fate on Nijinsky." He was still depressed, and ruminated a great deal about death. Romola says that he passed his days "in complete isolation from the world and of [sic] all artistic manifestation. When I spoke about it, he bravely replied, 'Others are dying, suffering far more. I have my art in my soul; nothing and nobody can take it away. Happiness is in us; we take it with us wherever we go.'"[13]

Romola exaggerates the completeness of Nijinsky's "isolation." In fact, Diaghilev had been trying to contact him since October 1914. Wartime conditions were making it difficult for the Ballets Russes to remain intact, much less to obtain engagements in Europe, and Diaghilev had signed a contract with the directors of the Metropolitan Opera for appearances in New York, beginning in 1916. A great deal of money was at stake as well as the company's reputation. Diaghilev was thinking of producing a new ballet with music by Stravinsky, about a wedding ceremony in rural Russia, to be called *Les Noces,** but Fokine had decided to remain in St. Petersburg for the duration of the war and was not available to work on the choreography. Thus, Diaghilev wondered whether Nijinsky might again be useful to him as a choreographer. "The invention of movement in *Noces* is definitely for Nijinsky," he wrote Stravinsky, "but I will not discuss the thing with him for several months yet." Communication was a problem. Nijinsky would not answer Diaghilev's letters, and when Diaghilev sent a telegram he curtly answered, "Cannot come." Diaghilev jokingly wrote Stravinsky, "I am sure that his wife is busy making [Nijinsky] into the first ballet master of the Budapest Opera."[14] Only gradually did it dawn on him that special arrangements and much high-level diplomacy would be needed to get the dancer out of Hungary.

In 1915 Nijinsky's spirits began to lift. During the spring he was

---

Les Noces was not produced until 1923, by which time Nijinsky was too sick to collaborate. His sister did the choreography, in a format that Diaghilev was then bringing to perfection: a wedding cantata in peasant costume with some of the musicians on stage along with the dancers. This and *Les Biches* turned out to be Nijinska's most inspired creations.

moving again, dancing more, and regaining his interest in creative pursuits. Romola noticed that there were times when he seemed like "a changed person." He would adopt a "mischievous" expression and throw himself around wildly, with maniacal abandon. Sometimes he seemed compelled to dance like a woman. "He would suddenly be transformed into a wild, fierce, savage girl, trembling all over from the tips of his fingers to his toes, shaking his shoulders as if they were independent of the rest of his body." Romola liked these displays of femininity, a manifestation probably of Nijinsky's androgyny. She seemed to tolerate his contrasexual behavior as long as it did not include any intimacy with men. It was enjoyable, for instance, to see him imitate different ballerinas he had danced with at the Maryinsky.

> We often begged him to show us how Kchessinskaya danced. But we loved it most when he showed us how the peasant women flirt whilst dancing. He had an inimitable way of throwing inviting glances, and undulating in such a lascivious manner as to stir up the senses of the spectator almost to frenzy. [15]*

Another activity that occupied Nijinsky during his year of "isolation" was the design of a system of dance notation, a formidable intellectual exercise. He sought to make records of the ballets he had already produced, and intended to write down his ideas for future works. He may also have wanted to create his own language of the dance. This proved to be a daunting task. As can be seen from the scores Nijinsky composed (for example, see photo), he was handicapped by insufficient understanding of the principles of musical notation. Choreographic notation systems he was more familiar with, having become acquainted with a method of notation by Vladimir Stepanov used in St. Petersburg since 1893. This system did not suffice, however, for denoting the more recent innovations by Fokine, or Nijinsky's own unusual steps and unorthodox gestures. He worked assiduously at trying to perfect a system of notation in which every movement could be permanently recorded. He wanted to denote even the physical characteristics of the dancers, their placement on stage, and costumes as well

*It should be noted that these words were written after Romola Nijinsky had begun to acknowledge her own homosexuality by entering into lesbian relationships. Nijinsky's imitation of women dancers in 1915 may have stimulated her sexually, similar to the way some wives of transvestite men become excited when they see their husbands putting on brassieres and pantyhose or wearing nightgowns. [16]

as scenery. Nijinsky's first experiments with choreographic notation made use of musical symbols, which he put on lines similar to an orchestral score. For transcribing *L'Après-midi d'un Faune* this worked reasonably well, and he was able to complete the notation in 1915. For his other ballets, however, he never got past the preliminary sketches. Ann Hutchinson Guest, a notation expert, has made a thorough study of Nijinsky's choreographic writings. They show a very limited understanding of human anatomy and physiology. For example, in his notations of pliés, grand battements, and jetés one finds "a rather crude analysis of movement; the familiar steps are not analyzed correctly. The most noticeable evidence of carelessness is in connection with weight-bearing and free-leg movements.... One has the impression that because supporting on the half toe or on pointe gave a feeling of lightness, the feet did not seem to be supports at all."[17]

Many of Nijinsky's ideas about choreographic notation are set down in his notebook titled "Notation of All the Movements of the Human Body." Here he made another fundamental error by assuming that "the basis for all the movements of the human body and other bodies is a circle and square marked out in segments."[18] This led to a static configuration. Circles and squares cannot adequately denote the flow of events over time; they have no beginning and no end.* To approximate the linear patterns needed for denoting actions, Nijinsky had to superimpose a complicated system of grids and to add musical notes, numbers, and words. No one has been able to decipher fully this idiosyncratic system, and he himself had great difficulty using it. Romola thought his drawings looked "like geometry, like mathematics." She observed him "designing and counting, drawing with infinite care; sometimes very late at night." It disturbed her sleep and led to complaints that Vaslav was using up "too much electricity." Nijinsky's labors on choreographic notation even came to the attention of the Budapest police, who wondered if he might be working on a secret code for military espionage! "A real war-psychosis was raging," writes Romola. "Experts of music and mathematics were called in, and Vaslav explained to them his system. It took several days of investigation, and then those men congratulated him on his epoch-making creation."[19]

As Nijinsky's health improved in 1915, he began to think of producing

*The Hungarian dancer Rudolf von Laban worked on the problem of dance notation for many years. His book *Schrifttanz,* published in 1928, introduced a choreographic notation system that has gained general acceptance and is widely used today.

another full-length ballet. Romola's cousin Lilly Márkus, a concert pianist who had studied with Emil von Sauer (a former pupil of Liszt) in Vienna, played the piano for Nijinsky, and that is how he became acquainted with Richard Strauss's *Till Eulenspiegel*. Strauss had written this tone poem in 1894/5. The music is witty and highly dramatic. Originally intended to be a one-act opera, *Till Eulenspiegel* is about a mischief-maker—half-clown, half-hero—who drives the people of his village to distraction by playing various tricks on them. They finally decide to get rid of him. There is an execution by hanging, but Till's soul, symbolized by a characteristic staccato melody, survives. Both the music and the story appealed greatly to Nijinsky. According to Romola he was "enthusiastic" and able to visualize the entire ballet, which suggests a return of creative vigor. "Again he wished to use masses, not altogether as in *Sacre*, but in groups and by making twenty people do the same movements as if they were one." This is reminiscent of marching soldiers; possibly Nijinsky's creativity was being affected by the war. "He suffered intensely," writes Romola, "through the knowledge that thousands of people were daily killing each other, and he could not help, he could not prevent it." Nijinsky's choreographic vision of *Till Eulenspiegel* may have helped him to hold in check the rage and horror stimulated by fantasies of carnage on European battlefields. He demonstrated *Till*'s movements for Romola, and she remembered their "angularity" and "mediaeval" character. The postures he dramatized were stiff and corpselike, resembling "the attitude of statues on the purest Gothic cathedral."[20]

Diaghilev's efforts to have Nijinsky released from captivity were beginning to produce results by the end of 1915. Thanks to intercession by the American Embassy as well as people in very high places, including Emperor Franz-Joseph, the King of Spain, and even the pope, Nijinsky was allowed to leave Budapest in January 1916. He and Romola moved to Vienna, where they enjoyed greater freedom and certain luxuries such as permission to live rent-free at the Hotel Bristol. The dancer's fame was publicly acknowledged, and he was allowed to practice on the stage of a major theater. Romola says that he even had access to the Imperial Opera, where he coached her brother-in-law, the tenor Erik Schmedes, in dramatic interpretations of Lohengrin, Tristan, and other Wagnerian roles. Perhaps it was Romola's feeling of closeness to Cosima Wagner that led her to emphasize (or exaggerate?) Nijinsky's interest in working as a choreographer at Bayreuth after the war. He hoped to produce "dances for *Parsifal, Tannhäuser,* and *Die Meistersinger,"* she says.

While in Vienna, Nijinsky posed for the painter Oskar Kokoschka, who drew a serious-looking portrait of him. He also spent an agreeable afternoon with composer Arnold Schönberg, listening to twelve-tone music and looking at the "curious and mystic pictures" Schönberg was then painting. According to Romola, "a very heated discussion" broke out between the musician and the dancer on the subject of how much training is needed to compose and to play the piano, with Schönberg allegedly taking the position that any person with talent can succeed in music "without certain study." Nijinsky was a bit of a poseur when it came to the piano; he liked to have pictures taken of himself at the keyboard, and there is a famous one of him sitting next to a grand piano, pretending to read the score of *Till Eulenspiegel.*

Nijinsky also had the opportunity to confer with Richard Strauss, who was in Vienna in January. They spoke about a ballet based on *Till Eulenspiegel.* Strauss seems to have reacted favorably to Nijinsky's plans, and according to Romola even offered "to make changes, if necessary, in the musical score."[21] (A letter from Strauss's son Franz confirms the composer's high regard for Nijinsky, which went back to the time that Diaghilev and Nijinsky had visited Strauss in order to discuss *La Légende de Joseph.* Strauss is reported to have told the German minister von Bethmann-Hollweg that "among dancers, Nijinsky is what Frederick the Great was among kings."[22]

The month in Vienna was filled with activity. Nijinsky was generally in high spirits, bubbling over with creative energy and feeling optimistic about the future. He talked about producing numerous ballets, not only *Till Eulenspiegel,* but also a Japanese ballet in the style of Hokusai paintings. In addition he wanted to choreograph a medieval ballet based on the story of the Faust legend and set to Franz Liszt's *Mephisto Waltz.* Romola was greatly relieved to see her husband no longer so depressed and complaining so much of physical symptoms. To her delight, he demonstrated the various dances he had in mind: "a slight inclination of the head, a lowering of the eyelids, an unbelievable turn of the wrist, the fluttering fingers" for his Japanese ballet; "a living Dürer—full of fire, brilliant, flaming.... jumps, all toe dancing" for *Mephisto Waltz.* He impersonated all the different roles, "forty-five dancers" altogether, and he danced both the male and the female parts with enormous "strength, virility, exuberance."[23] It has to be emphasized that these spectacular dances that Nijinsky enacted for his wife were demonstrations of his fertile imagination, more like improvisations, and by no means finished works of choreography. When Romola tells us that *Mephisto Waltz* was "ready" to be produced in 1916, she is mistaking fantasy for reality. Nijinsky says nothing about this ballet in his notebooks, which comment on everything else he actually produced. He also does not mention a Japanese ballet, except for one passing reference to pornography: "I do not like a wife and a husband who do depraved things while they look at depraved Japanese and other books and then go through all the motions of bodily love."[24] (Nijinsky's sister did later design a ballet with Japanese costumes and dancing; it is possible that they discussed this at some time.)

The question arises whether, in the course of recovering from his depression, Nijinsky might have experienced a manic episode, the sort of frenetic excitement, overactivity, and flights of fancy observed in people with cyclic mood disorders called bipolar or manic-depressive disease. This diagnosis cannot be made on the basis of evidence available in 1916. We have only Romola's description of Nijinsky's behavior, and she does not characterize it as psychopathological. To my knowledge, no diagnoses other than "neurasthenia with depressive states" and "dancer's heart" were made at this period in his life. However, in view of Nijinsky's past history of depressive episodes, his recent nervous breakdown, the disturbances in his mood about to be described, and the full-blown psychosis he developed later, it can be postulated that he may have been cycling in and out of depression for some time before going mad. The question can also be raised whether the hypomanic states I suspect Nijinsky was experiencing just before leaving Europe in 1916 were conducive to his subsequent artistic performance and creativity in the United States. "Hypomania" refers to a state of elation that resembles pathological mania, but does not disrupt the personality as severely as a true manic psychosis. Among writers, painters, composers, and certain scientists, it has been observed that a depression followed by excitement (a sort of "creative mania") may be associated with exceptional productivity.[25] As long as an exalted state of mind provides fulfillment and leads to successful achievement, it seems unwarranted to call it an illness. But when a manic or depressive episode results in maladaptive behavior and leads to breakdown, it must be clinically evaluated and treated.

The circumstances of Nijinsky's departure for the United States were so complicated that an objective appraisal of his state of mind at that time becomes especially difficult. In order to have the Ballets Russes travel to New York and then go on a transcontinental tour, Diaghilev had received an advance payment of $30,000 from the Metropolitan Opera Company, to be augmented by additional payments of $45,000, spread out over three months in 1915.[26] Great pressure was put on him to reengage Nijinsky, who was the best-known male dancer and a much desired participant for the company's tour. However, to include Nijinsky required an exchange for another "prisoner of war," a delicate barter that had to be negotiated between the U.S. State Department and the Austrian government. At one point he was offered his freedom only on condition that Romola and Kyra stay in Europe, which Nijinsky refused. There was the additional stress of having to cross the frontier on a shabby train full of soldiers, and the fear of being arrested at the French frontier. "Traveling was always hard for him," Romola writes. "He could not stand being locked up in such a small place for many hours, and the motion of the train seemed to affect him, also he suffered from violent pains in his head."[27] After reaching neutral territory, they had to decide what to do about Kyra, not yet two years old. Nijinsky felt she ought to stay in Switzerland, so she could be spared the discomfort of touring with a ballet company. From his own childhood he knew only too well the discomforts of incessant travel and repeated environmental changes. He hoped that Igor Stravinsky, then living with his wife and four children in a village near Lausanne, might agree to keep Kyra for the duration, but Stravinsky turned him down.

> I told him that I would pay all Kyra's expenses [writes Nijinsky]. He did not want to agree. When I was alone with him, he advised me to give my Kyra to one of the governesses who would be living in the hotel. I told him I could not leave my child in a stranger's hands because I did not know whether that woman loved Kyra. I do not like people who leave their children in strangers' hands.... Stravinsky is a dry stick. I am a man with a soul.[28]

When they reached Paris, Romola went on a buying spree. She writes that "we were able to make a tour of the leading dressmakers and millinery establishments." Boarding the train, they were "elegantly dressed, and followed by sixteen trunks, loaded with flowers, and accompanied by our maid and nurse and escort, Mr. [Henry] Russell."[29] Nijinsky disliked such displays of wealth, and Romola's extravagance soon became a source of friction between them. She loved wearing expensive jewelry, and whenever there was a belt, purse, or pair of shoes that she liked, her habit was to buy one in every color, to match her various dresses. Nijinsky preferred to see his wife attired simply and modestly, in black or subdued colors like his mother and sister wore, according to the Russian style. Where did the money for Romola's prodigality come from? Some of it, from her family, she presumably took out of Hungary, but that could hardly have been enough. With the promise of Nijinsky's America tour, Romola was counting on a new era of economic affluence. She and her stepfather had urged Nijinsky to initiate a lawsuit, in London in 1914, against Diaghilev for "unpaid salary." A settlement agreement had just been reached. Romola hoped they would receive Fr. 500,000, which was the equivalent of nearly $90,000 in those days. (Diaghilev was not a legal resident of any country; there was to be difficulty collecting the money.)

The many troubles Diaghilev had been having since coming to the United States were as yet unknown to the Nijinskys when they crossed the Atlantic in March 1916. His autocratic style did not suit the administrators of the Metropolitan Opera, whose director, Giulio Gatti-Casazza, had been opposed to a visit by the Ballets Russes in the first place. (Gatti-Casazza's mistress and later wife, Rosina Galli, was the leading ballerina of the Metropolitan, and he was said to be "notoriously jealous" on her behalf.) The Russian ballet season had gotten off to a slow start in January, and the company's tour of sixteen cities from Boston to Kansas City was no huge success. Diaghilev's programs seemed poorly organized, and some of his best ballets were thought to be offensive. *Schéhérazade,* for example, with its sexual orgy between blacks and whites, had to be "tailored" before it could be shown in the southern states, and *L'Après-midi d'un Faune* (danced by Massine) had to be emasculated even more than in Paris to suit American tastes. In Chicago the Ballets Russes danced to nearly empty houses. Audiences regularly complained that the famous soloists they had been promised were not on stage. Thus, Nijinsky was most eagerly awaited when he arrived in New York on 4 April 1916. Before he had even gotten off the boat, reporters rushed to interview him. Romola did most of the talking, as Nijinsky spoke no English.

Diaghilev met him at the dock. They had not spoken to one another for nearly three years, and so much had happened to both men—Diaghilev now living with Massine, Nijinsky married and a father—

that the initial encounter was awkward. Diaghilev kissed his old lover warmly on both cheeks, in the Russian manner. Nijinsky reciprocated by proudly placing his daughter into Diaghilev's outstretched arms. (This gesture so embarrassed Diaghilev that he quickly passed the baby on to the nearest bystander.) It sounds incredible, but Romola was so preoccupied with the "beautiful bouquet of American Beauties" Diaghilev had given her that she was unable to hold the frightened child. (This was "typical of Romola," says her daughter Tamara.) The meeting soon became "cold and formal," Nijinsky merely asking about the dates and the ballets he was to dance, and Diaghilev giving noncommittal answers.[30] They all went to their respective hotels, and the next day Otto Kahn, president of the Metropolitan Opera Board, welcomed Nijinsky to his office to talk about his future participation with the Ballets Russes. The dancer had little to say, as usual. He seemed inarticulate and subdued, and may have been somewhat depressed. Romola spoke for him: "Vaslav would readily dance at the Opera, but not with Diaghilev, as long as he did not pay the amount he owed Vaslav for his past salary," in other words, the huge court settlement decided in London.[31] This produced consternation and placed the Metropolitan Opera in the embarrassing position of having to mediate between Diaghilev and his former lover. "NIJINSKY AT ODDS WITH BALLET RUSSE" headlined the *New York Times*. "He will not twinkle a toe at the Metropolitan until his price has been met and he has been accorded the respect he demands from his associates in the ballet."[32] Romola hired an attorney, while the company continued to perform without Nijinsky. Many of the dancers grumbled. They felt Nijinsky was being selfish, ungrateful to Diaghilev for getting him out of wartorn Europe, and just plain mercenary. It took a week before Nijinsky indicated that he would be ready to perform. Diaghilev agreed to pay him $13,000 owing on the lawsuit in London, plus $1,000 for each of his eleven performances scheduled for New York,[33] a staggering fee in those days.

Nijinsky's long-awaited American debut was on a Wednesday matinee, 12 April 1916, and he danced again that evening. The applause was ardent and prolonged. Newspapers were enthusiastic: "NIJINSKY CHARMS IN FIRST DANCES. Shows Prowess Probably Never Equalled in Ballet Here. 'Le Spectre' Seems Totally Different." But there also were complaints, especially from those who perceived (or imagined) Nijinsky's dancing to be unmanly. One disgruntled critic wrote that "a super-refinement of gesture and posture amounted to effeminacy. The costume of the dancer, fashioned about the shoulders exactly like a woman's décolleté, with shoulder-and-arm straps, even helped to emphasize this, as did certain technical details of the dancing, such as dancing on the toes, which is not ordinarily indulged in by male dancers." Another critic carped that "except for his legs, which are as palpably muscular as those of an athlete, Nijinsky's appearance, bearing and manner disturb by a most unprepossessing effeminacy," which shows how difficult it was for some people to accept grace and beauty in a male dancer in 1916.[34] Nijinsky's sensitive portrayal of the beautiful youth in *Narcisse* was "greeted by giggles." Even his virile eroticism in *Schéhérazade* evoked censure:

> The part of the negro who makes love to the princess is a repulsive one, but he tones down some of its unpleasantness. The impulse to jump on the stage and thrash him must be suppressed.[35]

One can imagine the effect of such criticism on the vulnerable Nijinsky, who had only recently recovered from a major depression. "He had grown heavier and looked very sad," wrote the English dancer Hilda Munnings (Lydia Sokolova) in her autobiography. "We felt sorry for him . . . . He never spoke a word to anyone and picked his fingers more than ever."[36] Photographs show that Nijinsky had indeed put on some weight since his recent breakdown. And of course he had not danced in public for two years. He had been working on his own to perfect certain movement patterns that were different from his customary roles, more angular, less elegant, and in opposition to classical ballet tradition. Thus, it is not surprising that Nijinsky felt nervous about having to resume his former position as Diaghilev's star, this time without the fringe benefits of special attention and favors. Nijinsky had come to New York expecting to see his own ballets, *Till Eulenspiegel* and *Mephisto Waltz*, produced. Diaghilev would hear nothing of it. Even the revival of *L'Après-midi d'un Faune* led to arguments. Massine had been dancing Nijinsky's role in his absence, and some changes had been made in the ballet which Nijinsky found objectionable. Additional rehearsal time would have been needed to restore the work properly, and this Diaghilev, already feeling exploited, was unwilling to grant. As a result, Nijinsky simply refused to dance in the one and only ballet of his that Diaghilev had retained in the repertoire, and he insisted that all further- performances of *Faune* be canceled in New York. Night after night, he simply repeated the familiar roles he had helped to popularize all over Europe and in South America, thereby quickly regaining his fabulous technique and awesome charisma. "There is something of transmutation in his performances," commented writer Carl Van Vechten.

> He becomes an alembic, transforming movement into a finely wrought and beautiful work of art. The dancing of Nijinsky is first an imaginative triumph. . . . He can look tall or short, magnificent or ugly, fascinating or repulsive. Like all great interpretative artists, he remolds himself for his public appearances. It is under the electric light in front of the painted canvas that he becomes a personality, and that personality is governed only by the scenario of the ballet he is representing.[37]

Having regained superstardom, Nijinsky was now much in demand socially. Mrs. Vanderbilt invited him to dance for a benefit in her New York mansion, where Romola showed off her Parisian gown, "a *chef d'oeuvre* by Callot Soeurs," while Vaslav lost his underwear to lady souvenir hunters. He met other celebrities, including tenor Enrico Caruso, violinist Fritz Kreisler, and theater director David Belasco. At a luncheon party, Isadora Duncan complimented Nijinsky on his tolerance for "us women," to which he reportedly replied, "I love everybody, as Christ did."[38] (Such statements, a blend of mysticism, grandiosity, and Russian craziness, were to characterize Nijinsky's talk for some years, both before and after the leap into madness in his thirties.) He thoroughly enjoyed the hubbub of New York's theater district, and happily promenaded up and down Broadway, gazing at the flashing lights and fast traffic. The cinema especially interested him, and he loved the films of Charlie Chaplin. Nijinsky was one of the first to recognize the value of motion pictures as a way to record dancers' work. Toward this end he urged Diaghilev to preserve on film all of the great ballets they had produced together, but Diaghilev evidently was slow to recognize the merits of cinematography. His preference was for seeing live dances in color, three-dimensionally, and not as black-and-white images projected on a flat screen. There are no films available of the great early Ballets Russes ballets, a tremendous loss to teachers and historians of this art. As for Nijinsky's dancing, only one short film was ever made, apparently while he and Diaghilev were visiting Dalcroze in Germany in 1912. It was recently televised in the Soviet Union.[39]

At the conclusion of the Ballets Russes's 1916 spring season in the United States, Diaghilev expressed a desire to have the company return later that year for a second tour. It would be much safer and more profitable than performing in Europe, where the war was still raging. Otto Kahn of the Metropolitan Opera Board said he would be willing to underwrite such a tour, from coast to coast, for six months beginning at the end of October. But Kahn insisted that Nijinsky had to be included. His name and fame were essential for the tour to be a financial success. A managerial crisis resulted from this demand. On one side was Nijinsky, firmly backed by his wife, who let it be known that were he to join the tour, he would want to have "complete control of the company" in order to produce new ballets and properly restore the earlier ones, all in accordance with his own exacting standards and innovative ideas. On the other side of the conflict was Serge Grigoriev, still stage director of the company, who felt that Nijinsky's temperament was incompatible with effective leadership on a transcontinental tour. (Grigoriev, we will remember, had already clashed with Nijinsky during the company's South America tour in 1913.) Diaghilev, who also did not trust Nijinsky and wanted to support Grigoriev, was caught in the middle. For the sake of the company, he could not afford to turn down Kahn's offer. Thus, a compromise solution had to be found. Since Diaghilev did not much care for being in the United States anyway, he offered to "retire" to Europe for the duration of the tour, taking along Massine and a few other dancers to prepare a repertoire of new ballets for the company's 1917 season.* Otto Kahn and the Metropolitan Opera Board were made responsible for organizing the tour and managing all performances by the Ballets Russes in the United States. If they wanted, they could appoint Nijinsky as "head of the company."[42]

The prospect of taking Diaghilev's place as head of the Ballets Russes, at a salary of $60,000, stimulated a great surge of enthusiasm in Nijinsky. He purchased a Peerless automobile and, without proper instruction in driving or servicing such a car, took it to New England. "I was aghast," writes Romola, "because while he could drive straight

---

*One also senses a more personal motive behind Diaghilev's willingness to return to Europe with Massine. His jealous possessiveness toward the young dancer had become quite apparent in New York, where a woman (teasingly nicknamed "Hotpants") seemed to be flirting with Massine and creating dissension.[40] Having recently lost Nijinsky to a conniving admirer, Diaghilev was understandably apprehensive about leaving Massine unattended. History repeated itself, however, in 1921, when Massine married the pretty dancer Vera Savina and was forced, like Nijinsky, to leave the Ballets Russes.[41]

ahead quite well, he would back the car round with a fearful swing...in a few small towns Vaslav drove on the wrong side, and was shouted at by the passers-by. He almost ran into a tramcar, but at the last moment pirouetted aside. I was so angry that I sat silent, but Kyra, alone in the back seat with all her dolls, was enjoying herself immensely." Whenever there was engine trouble, "Vaslav in an important and knowing manner opened the bonnet and disappeared from view. Then he lay under the car and made some mysterious repairs ... he was better able to take the car to pieces than to put it together again."[43]

Nijinsky seems also to have behaved in an excitable manner around the swimming pool, where crowds gathered to watch his leaping and dancing in the water. Perhaps to compensate for his childhood fear of drowning, he would suddenly dive and swim under water in such a way that people thought "he would never come up again." Another diversion was tennis. Nijinsky "was a constant winner, jumping high so quickly, with such a sense of speed and distance, that he was able to hit each ball, and make its return impossible." While vacationing in Bar Harbor, Maine, he and Romola had what she calls their "first and last domestic fight." (It was by no means the last.) She attributes this to her sudden, unannounced departure from the house. "I took a car and went some sixty miles away, only returning at dawn.... Vaslav was angry and scolded me, but I threw some pillows at him and we both laughed and made up." This is the first hint of marital problems, but we do not know what actually happened. Romola says that she left her husband and child because she felt "scared" when a dentist wanted to give her "an injection," not a very convincing explanation.[44]

The most formidable challenge to Nijinsky's capabilities that summer was the planning of *Till Eulenspiegel*. It would be necessary to produce this new ballet without any assistance from the two people who in the past had always helped him, Bronislava Nijinska and Diaghilev. Hoping to enlist a suitable designer, possibly Benois or Soudeikine, Nijinsky sent telegrams to Europe, but no one could or wanted to cross the Atlantic to work with him. An American artist would be needed to make the costumes and scenery. Fortunately, Nijinsky was introduced to Robert Edmond Jones, a young designer then living in Greenwich Village. Jones not only liked him personally, but considered Nijinsky to be "a genius." Their first meeting, when the dancer was twenty-seven years old, is revealing:

I see, first, an extremely pretty young woman, fashionably dressed in black, and, following her, a small, somewhat stocky young man walking with delicate birdlike steps—precise, anxious, excessively intelligent. He seems tired, bored, excited, all at once. I observe that he has a disturbing habit of picking at the flesh on the sides of his thumbs until they bleed. Through all my memories of this great artist runs the recurring image of those raw red thumbs. He broods and dreams, goes far away into reverie, returns again. At intervals his face lights up with a brief, dazzling smile. His manner is simple, ingratiating, so direct as to be almost humble.[45]

Jones was impressed with Nijinsky's "incredible" perfectionism, "the extraordinary nervous energy of the man—an almost frightening awareness, a curious mingling of eagerness and apprehension," and his terrible temper tantrums. "The maestro is waiting for me in a flame of rage. Torrents of Russian imprecations pour from his lips.... He lashes out at me with an insensate blind hate. It is a nightmare set in a blast furnace."[46] These were the same personal characteristics that made it difficult for Nijinsky to function as director of the Ballets Russes when Kahn appointed him to that position in 1916. After the company reassembled in New York in mid-September, many of the dancers were put off by his aloof manner, remoteness, self-absorption, and unpredictability in organizing or even attending rehearsals, and his unwillingness to listen to their complaints.[47]

Opening night was scheduled for 9 October, which gave them only three weeks to prepare their first program. Even though Nijinsky had not yet completed the choreography for *Till Eulenspiegel*, he wanted to include this ballet. Everything had to be demonstrated, as usual, by miming and gesturing. It was impossible for Nijinsky to explain his ideas. The dancers tried their best to cooperate, but his communication handicap proved so frustrating that they went on strike for two days. Further difficulty arose when conductor Pierre Monteux announced that he was unwilling to lead the orchestra for *Till Eulenspiegel*. Another conductor had to be found. The reason usually given for Monteux's refusal to conduct the music for Nijinsky's new ballet is that it was by Richard Strauss, a German composer, and since Germany was then at war with France, it would have been an act of disloyalty for a Frenchman to lead it. But I know from personal contact with Monteux that he greatly admired Strauss's music, and that even during World War II, and despite the Nazi holocaust, which killed many members of Monteux's family, he often conducted *Till Eulenspiegel* and other works by German composers. The real reason Monteux would not conduct the music for Nijinsky's ballet, asserts dancer Lydia Sokolova, was that he was "fed to the teeth with Nijinsky's bungling over Till ... and wanted to dissociate himself from the fiasco."[48]

Opening night had to be postponed for a week, at great expense and embarrassment to the Metropolitan Opera. Why? Nijinsky, tired and overwrought, had slipped during a rehearsal and twisted his ankle, one of those accidents a dancer dreads most. He briefly lost consciousness, and, according to Robert Edmond Jones, had to be "carried moaning and cursing to his suite at the Biltmore hotel."[49] It was thought that Nijinsky's foot was broken, but X-rays revealed no fractured bones. The injury was a ligamentous sprain, very painful and disabling. Surgery was not required, but for it to heal properly, Nijinsky was told to stay off his foot and rest in bed. "I worked like an ox," he wrote later. "I never let up. I slept little.... The ox was driven too hard for he twisted his ankle.... I rested and rested."[50] Nijinsky again became very nervous and depressed, and had serious trouble sleeping. It was "extremely difficult" to manage him in their hotel, writes Romola. The doctor "insisted on having day and night nurses ... but Vaslav would not tolerate anybody near him except me and his *masseur*."[51]

Two dancers, Dmitri Kostrovsky and Nicolas Zverev, both Russians, were also permitted to visit Nijinsky during his convalescence. Romola describes them as belonging to those members of the company who looked up to him as a vastly superior colleague, a man of great vision, "a saint." Kostrovsky often stayed in Nijinsky's bedroom for hours. He tried to comfort the ailing dancer by talking about their homeland, about religion, and about Tolstoy, whom so many Russians loved. This was the beginning of an important new friendship. Romola says that "Kostrovsky took to Vaslav from the first moment, and showed an adoration which was not only for his art but for his nature. He followed Vaslav everywhere like a dog, eagerly looking for a smile."[52] She resented their obvious attraction because it drew Nijinsky away from her and brought him closer to a circle of men she distrusted.

Nijinsky was not well enough to appear for the postponed opening on 16 October, nor could he perform for the entire first week, much to the disappointment of the New York public. Adolph Bolm substituted for Nijinsky's roles, and the world premiere of *Till Eulenspiegel* was postponed yet again for a week. There had been much advance publicity. The Metropolitan management expressed deep concern. On

Monday morning, 23 October, the sick Nijinsky limped to the opera house for a dress rehearsal of *Till Eulenspiegel*. Everything went well until his "terrified" colleagues realized that he had not yet worked out the details for the final scene. It seemed that he had run out of ideas. Romola rushed Nijinsky back to their hotel and put him to bed, while Otto Kahn and the management of the Metropolitan tore out their hair. The house had been sold out, and another postponement was simply out of the question. So the dancers were asked to get the ballet ready on their own. According to Lydia Sokolova, who danced one of the leading roles, they did this by "filling the gaps" and "piecing together" what had been rehearsed earlier. Nijinsky was told not to worry. He would not have to dance in any other ballet that night. Everything would be all right "so long as he knew what he was going to do himself in the second act [i.e., *Till Eulenspiegel*]. Perhaps that was the only time in ballet history when the dancers more or less improvised nearly half a ballet on its opening night."[53] It was a credit to the Ballets Russes that they succeeded.

The new ballet lasted eighteen minutes. Jones's crenellated gothic scenery looked stunning. The stage was crowded with villagers costumed in yards of billowing material and gigantic hats, all in vivid colors, primarily greens and blues. Nijinsky, wearing tights, a loose cravat around his neck, and a dark, unruly wig, darted about mischievously, upsetting the townspeople, creating confusion and havoc. His dancing was improvisatory, totally unorthodox, and very exciting. Here is Jones's description:

> I hear a crash of applause, fierce and frightening. The little figure in green begins its leapings and laughings. There is the scene of wild love-making, the confutation of the scholars, the strange solo dance, swift as the flash of a rapier, the hanging of the corpse on the gibbet—and last of all, the apparition of the ghost shooting upward through a foam of tiny lanterns, like a moth veering above a sea of fireflies.[54]

Nijinsky reappeared in different costumes, a monk's habit, a merchant's rich cloak, a professor's garb with a long, flat hat tied under his chin. People in the audience did not realize that what they were seeing was a ballet in the making. They applauded enthusiastically, and the dancers took fifteen curtain calls. Nijinsky had triumphed once more, thanks to his audacity, the disciplined teamwork of his company, and the generosity of the audience. "The American public loved me because it had confidence in me," he wrote later, without any illusions about his shortcomings.

> It saw that my foot hurt. I danced badly, but the public enjoyed it. *Till* was a success, but it was produced too soon. It was taken out of the oven too soon and therefore was raw. The American public liked my raw ballet because it tasted well. I had cooked it very well.[55]

The following week *Till Eulenspiegel* was presented again, along with other ballets in which Nijinsky performed, including *Petrushka*, but not *Spectre*—his ankle had not yet healed sufficiently. For the first time, American audiences were able to see him dance *Faune*, and they liked his impersonation better than Massine's, which had been censored. Nijinsky's performance, reports the *New York World*, was "refined, artistic, and masterful."[56] *Till Eulenspiegel* received two additional performances in New York and was repeated twenty times when the Ballets Russes toured the country later that year, but it was never produced outside the United States. (Jerome Robbins danced in another version, called *Tyl Ulenspiegel*, choreographed by George Balanchine, and Millicent Hodson tells me that a reconstruction of Nijinsky's *Till Eulenspiegel* is currently being planned.)

At the end of October 1916, the company started its long-awaited transcontinental tour, which was to take them to fifty-two American and Canadian cities in four months. It was an enormously complex operation, involving the transportation of over one hundred musicians and dancers, a stage crew of twenty-one, and a nine-person executive staff. They traveled in two separate trains—six coaches and two Pullmans for the passengers and seven baggage cars for the costumes, props, instruments, and scenery.[57] Stops in the bigger cities, such as Boston, Chicago, and Cincinnati, were long enough to find a hotel room and do some sightseeing. But in smaller places like Hartford, Des Moines, or Tacoma, where they usually stayed only one or two days, the musicians, dancers, and stage crew simply rushed from the train to the theater and back, feeling like a flying circus, disoriented and exhausted.

As the distance from New York increased, so did the disorganization of the company. Press notices were usually sent in advance, along with programs that showed which ballets were to be performed and who would be dancing. But Nijinsky often made last-minute changes, to show ballets that had not been announced or cancel some that had. Improvisation was the rule. The "director" had a way of unpredictably reassigning certain roles, and even exchanging his own parts (for example, playing the chief eunuch in *Schéhérazade*), so that in the course of time many of the lesser dancers had to appear as soloists. His "democratic" approach to casting rattled those who were unprepared or felt uncomfortable about taking on new roles at short notice. It also baffled the audience. Unaccustomed to ballet in the first place, many spectators did not know what they were seeing or who was dancing. There were many complaints about interminable delays before the curtain went up, and about unduly long intervals between ballets.

Unfamiliarity with the American language and culture led to amusing incidents. One time, an administrator of the company, Randolfo Barocchi, fell asleep in a barbershop. On awakening, he discovered that his long, flowing beard had been shaved off, and he became inconsolable. In Salt Lake City, Nijinsky shocked Romola by telling her that polygamy is "quite a sensible institution, and most suitable for artists" because it allows a wife to devote more of her time to her children and household duties! She in turn surprised him, in New Orleans, by asking to go to a bordello. Nijinsky thought that his wife would feel "disgusted" at the sight of prostitutes. "But how would you know?" she asked him naively. "You have never been in a brothel yourself."[58]

The Metropolitan Opera lost a quarter of a million dollars on this tour. "Much of the responsibility," writes Lynn Garafola, "lay with the Metropolitan's management: the higher ticket schedule it had insisted on, incompetent advance men who alienated local newspaper editors, and a failure generally to assess what the market would bear in Wichita and Tacoma. But part of the blame rested with Nijinsky...."[59] Artistically, however, the tour was a great triumph. It brought ballet to audiences who were totally unfamiliar with the art form. People throughout the United States were privileged to hear great music and see beautiful dancing for the first time. And Nijinsky received much praise. In Washington, D.C., President and Mrs. Woodrow Wilson congratulated him personally. In Philadelphia, a reporter wrote that "the star reveals a mimetic power which is remarkable and emphasizes the truth of the assertion that 'speech was given to man to conceal his thoughts.'"⁶⁰ An eyewitness, then seventeen years old, recalls that "Nijinsky floated effortlessly to the top of the stage, where he lingered as if held up by imaginary ropes." (I asked my informant from Philadelphia to compare Nijinsky's performance to others she has seen. "Today we don't think twice about a man jumping and dancing like that," said Mrs. Rick Sievert. "At that time it was something we had never seen before. And I have seen all the great men dancers since— Massine, Youskevitch, Eglevsky, Franklin, Nureyev, Baryshnikov, you name them. But no one ever equaled Nijinsky in the fluidity of his movements, his incredible leaps, the way he remained suspended in the air. It gave you the feeling that strings were pulling him to the top of the stage and holding him there."⁶¹)

Nijinsky also had to dance to half-empty houses. Hoping to stimulate attendance, the Metropolitan management sent special bulletins from New York: "FAMOUS DANCERS SEE THEIR FIRST FOOTBALL GAME," headlined the *Ballet Russe Courier;* "NIJINSKY THINKS GENIUS NO BARRIER TO WAR SERVICE." (He had been called briefly to Washington, D.C., to clarify his status in regard to the Russian army.)⁶² Just after Christmas 1916, the company reached California, midpoint of their tour. In Los Angeles, the Russians were astonished to see sunshine and flowers during the winter. Famous movie stars came to the ballet. Charles Chaplin took an immediate liking to Nijinsky, and described him as "a serious man, beautiful-looking, with high cheek-bones and sad eyes, who gave the impression of a monk dressed in civilian clothes."

> He was hypnotic, god-like, his somberness suggesting moods of other worlds. Every movement was poetry; every leap a flight into strange fancy.... No one has ever equalled Nijinsky in *L'Après-midi d'un Faune.* The mystic world he created, the tragic unseen lurking in the shadows of pastoral loveliness as he moved through its mystery, a god of passionate sadness. All this he conveyed in a few simple gestures, without apparent effort.⁶³

Chaplin's autobiography comments on Nijinsky's "hollow voice" and "gauche" way of speaking. He looked and sounded depressed. While visiting Chaplin's Hollywood studio, Nijinsky became "sadder and sadder," Chaplin noted. He feared that the dancer's "doleful presence would ruin my attempts to be funny." Therefore Chaplin told his cameraman not to put any film in the camera while shooting the scene. In Southern California, Nijinsky, like other wealthy European visitors, was offered real estate, oil wells, and orange groves. Romola told him not to buy any; too bad, for had she encouraged him to invest the money he was then earning, their later financial difficulties might well have been attenuated.

On New Year's Eve the company went north to San Francisco and stayed there for two weeks, performing also in Oakland, where Isadora Duncan had grown up. Many artists have been attracted to the Bay Area, with its steep hills, glorious views, and happy blend of American and foreign culture. (Pierre Monteux later came back to become conductor of the San Francisco Symphony; Romola returned after her husband's death; and their daughter Kyra, now seventy-six, still lives there.) Nijinsky was "much entertained by society," writes his wife. He seems to have experienced an agreeable upswing in mood while in San Francisco, becoming rambunctious again, and going flying for the first time in an airplane that "looked more like an abandoned sewing-machine." Up in the air he had "one of the most glorious, exhilarating feelings one could imagine." Romola says that she felt "really angry with him this time" and berated Nijinsky for taking such a "great risk" with his life by flying.[64]

Her concerns had been building up gradually. For much of the tour Nijinsky had been moody—"silent, meditative," and "gloomy." There were days when he did not want to have anything to do with her at all. He seemed to prefer the company of the two Russians who had comforted him when he was sick in New York. Kostrovsky and Zverev were now constantly visiting his train compartment, "sometimes the whole night through." What exactly took place when the three dancers were together we do not know, but that there was some homosexual activity is not unlikely. (Michael Cenner, who knew Romola and her family very well and also met Nijinsky during World War II, is convinced of it—"he had extensive sexual experience with men before his marriage, and surely afterwards as well, as many dancers do."[65] Romola says that Nijinsky reacted "like a sensitive plant" to these men, and that he was "folding himself up." They spoke Russian all the time, delving into a "very abstract philosophy ... repeating Tolstoy and the teachings of Christ."[66] She had difficulty following their conversation. In a notebook Nijinsky wrote two years later, he reports that "I would be sleeping and [Kostrovsky] would be writing and in this way I could do something else as well." Nijinsky goes on to say, "I am what Christ felt. I am Buddha. I am a Buddhist and every kind of God."[67] Clearly, there was an aura of religious mysticism to these nocturnal sessions from which Romola was excluded. She reports that Kostrovsky and Zverev ceaselessly talked to Nijinsky about highly personal matters until he "hardly slept or ate" and seemed totally "exhausted.... They were like leeches; it was impossible to get rid of them."[68]

Tolstoy's teachings, which combined the tenets of Protestant puritanism and oriental resignation, appealed very strongly at that time to people who favored nonviolence, and a return to nature, for example the Indian leader Mohandas Gandhi.[69] That such ideas would interest Nijinsky, who was in conflict about sex, love, obedience, and rebellion, and tended to see himself as a godlike figure, is therefore not surprising. What gave Romola the greatest concern was that her husband was discussing with his friends the possibility of going back to Russia and living there in a kind of commune. The three men seemed to be talking about abandoning their wives and their careers as professional dancers. They were dreaming of a simple life, working among the peasants, preaching the gospel, and, like Tolstoy, eating only vegetables and abstaining from sexual intercourse. Already during the tour Nijinsky had stopped eating meat, and he was probably no longer sleeping with his wife. He had begun to wear peasant-style clothes, shirts with round collars and no ties, consistent with his ascetic philosophy. Romola felt determined to put a stop to this.

> I spoke to Vaslav very frankly, and told him that with all my love and admiration for him I could not agree to his new idea that he should give up dancing and become a peasant farmer or live the life of a *moujik* in Russia. I could understand that he was exhausted by the caravan life which the Russian Ballet had led since his separation from the Maryinsky... but I could not believe that he wanted to throw away what he loved most—dancing.[70]

Her argument was ineffectual and when they reached Chicago, Romola decided to leave Nijinsky. "If he had really decided to live the life of Tolstoy I would return alone to Europe," she recalls telling him. "He could keep Kyra if he wanted, as I could never adjust myself to that life." She packed her bags, went to New York, and consulted an attorney, who (so she says) told Romola she was doing the right thing to "frighten" Vaslav by abandoning him.[71] The Ballets Russes continued on through the Midwest, south to Tennessee, then back east, where their last performance with Nijinsky as director took place in Albany, New York, at the end of February. "By then, the company was split into factions," writes Sokolova. "Nothing was danced properly anymore, and the takings were getting less and less."[72] It was now clear to everyone, Otto Kahn, the Metropolitan Board, and of course Diaghilev, that Nijinsky was not a capable administrator.

Nevertheless, Diaghilev wanted him to remain with the company. Nijinsky had proven himself to be as magnificent a dancer as ever, and a creative force to be reckoned with. Diaghilev intended to have him dance later that year in Spain and then go on yet another tour, to South America. This news had been cabled to Nijinsky in Cleveland, and he immediately called Romola for advice. She apparently was quite excited by it and told him "not to promise anything" without first consulting her attorney. When the couple was reunited in New York, Romola was pleased to see her husband wearing normal clothes again, "his silk shirts [and] rings." He was eating meat, no longer talked about Tolstoy all the time, and presumably seemed interested in having sexual intercourse again. His intention, Romola says, was "to settle down and do some creative work." She hoped that he had mended his ways and was no longer "under Kostrovsky's influence." But Nijinsky still seemed to be depressed, "rather lost," like an abandoned child, and so helpless that Romola promised him "until the war is over, I will stay with you whatever happens."[73]

NOTES

1. Thomas Mann, *Pro and Contra Wagner*, 114.
2. The literature on affective disorders is vast. In terms of contemporary understanding of these diseases, the reader may wish to consult the following books: John Rush and Kenneth Z. Altshuler (editors), *Depression: Basic Mechanisms, Diagnosis, and Treatment*; Anastasios Georgotas and Robert Cancro (editors), *Depression and Mania*; Frederic Flach (editor), *Affective Disorders*.
3. RNN, 273.
4. Ibid., 273–274.
5. Kyra Nijinsky, *She Dances Alone*.
6. RNN, 281–282.
7. Tamara Nijinsky, personal communication.
8. RNN, 286–287.
9. Ibid., 289.
10. *New York Times*, 6 April 1916.
11. Notebook on "Death," 104.
12. RNN, 292.

13. Ibid., 286.
14. Letter from Diaghilev to Stravinsky, 25 November 1914, in Igor Stravinsky and Robert Craft, *Memoirs and Commentaries*, 48–49.
15. RNN, 288.
16. For a sensitive discussion of androgyny in history and everyday life, see Carolyn G. Heilbrun, *Toward a Recognition of Androgyny.*
17. Ann Hutchinson Guest, "Nijinsky's Dance Notation," 127.
18. Vaslav Nijinsky, unpublished notebook on "Notation," 94.
19. RNN, 288, 297.
20. Ibid., 284, 287.
21. Ibid., 304–307.
22. Letter from Dr. Franz Strauss to Romola Nijinsky, 25 November 1962. Nijinsky Archives.
23. RNN, 302, 303, 306.
24. Notebook on "Feeling," 71.
25. An excellent discussion of this phenomenon may be found in Sir George Pickering, *Creative Malady.* See also Leon Edel, "The Madness of Art."
26. Lynn Garafola, *Diaghilev's Ballets Russes,* 202.
27. RNN, 310.
28. Notebook on "Life," 46–47.
29. RNN, 319.
30. Ibid., 323. See also Serge Grigoriev, *The Diaghilev Ballet, 1909–1929,* 110.
31. RNN, 324.
32. Nesta Macdonald, *Diaghilev Observed,* 168.
33. Garafola, 203.
34. Macdonald, 172–174.
35. Unidentified newspaper review, quoted in RBN, 434.
36. Lydia Sokolova, *Dancing for Diaghilev,* 77.
37. Carl Van Vechten, "The Russian Ballet and Nijinsky," 7–9.
38. RNN, 330, 333.
39. Georgii Vlasenko, personal communication. The movie, according to filmmaker Vlasenko, shows Nijinsky dancing the Faun.
40. Grigoriev, 111.
41. Sokolova, 75.
42. Richard Buckle, *Diaghilev,* 371.
43. RNN, 334–335.
44. Ibid., 335–337.
45. Robert Edmond Jones, "Nijinsky and Til Eulenspiegel," 46.
46. Ibid., 56.
47. Sokolova, 88.
48. Ibid., 89–90.
49. Jones, 56.
50. Notebook on "Death," 31.
51. RNN, 341–342.
52. Ibid., 340.
53. Sokolova, 90–91.
54. Jones, 60.
55. Notebook on "Death," 32.
56. Macdonald, 197.
57. Ibid., 202.
58. RNN, 351–352, 357. Romola's remark about the brothels has been paraphrased. Her exact words are, "I told him he could not know, as he never had been in any." I gather this was written before she discovered from Nijinsky's notebook that he had had earlier contact with prostitutes in Russia and France.
59. Garafola, 206–207.
60. Macdonald, 201.
61. Personal communication from Mrs. Rick Sievert.

62. Macdonald, 203, 204.
63. Charlie Chaplin, *My Autobiography*, 192–193.
64. RNN, 361.
65. Michael Cenner, personal communication.
66. RNN, 359.
67. Notebook on "Feeling," 53.
68. RNN, 360, 363.
69. James H. Billington, *The Icon and the Axe*, 445.
70. RNN, 360, 363.
71. Ibid., 364.
72. Sokolova, 93.
73. RNN, 365.

Great gifts are the fairest, and often
the most dangerous fruits on the tree
of humanity. They hang on the
weakest branches, which easily break.
                              Carl Gustav Jung[1]

Chapter 7

Warnings

On leaving New York for Spain in March 1917, Romola was crying "hysterically" while Vaslav tried "to hide his tears." They had made friends in the United States. The transcontinental tour, with Nijinsky nominally in charge of the Ballets Russes, had given them considerable prestige and success throughout the country, which was beginning to feel almost like "a second home." Now they would have to cross the Atlantic, infested by German U-boats, and work again for Diaghilev, whom Romola disliked. Nijinsky had agreed to begin dancing in Madrid in June, then go to other Spanish cities and finally on another lengthy tour of South America. Neither he nor Romola felt much enthusiasm. During the two-week voyage, in cold and stormy weather, on a rickety boat overrun with "well-nourished rats," Romola was frightened and uncomfortable, while Vaslav "stoically accepted the situation" and kept an eye on the not yet three-year-old Kyra.[2]

This atmosphere of unrelieved gloom changed almost as soon as they arrived in Madrid, where a wealthy couple, the Duke and Duchess of Durcal, cordially welcomed Nijinsky and his wife. They were relatives of the King of Spain. The duchess had seen Nijinsky dance during his earlier visit to Madrid, in 1914. She expected to see much more of him now that he was planning to be in Spain for a longer time. The duchess was infatuated with Nijinsky. She planned to travel with him and take him sightseeing. She also made it clear that she was interested in him physically. That seemed to bother Romola much less than the attention her husband had been receiving from male admirers in the United States, especially the two Russian dancers Kostrovsky and Zverev, with whom there was talk of a communal life, without women, in Russia. With the aid of an admiring female, thought Romola, Nijinsky's erotic interests could be reactivated. Furthermore, a liaison with the Duchess of Durcal might lead to important social connections, which Romola always valued. It was to take a while, however, before Nijinsky and the duchess became intimate.

The first two months in Spain were very pleasant. Diaghilev had taken the Ballets Russes to Italy and France, leaving Nijinsky and his wife free to take a vacation. They visited cathedrals and museums, attended the theater, and caught up on their reading. (Romola mentions books by Oscar Wilde, Selma Lagerlöf, and Rabindranath Tagore, which Nijinsky would not have been able to read, so one must assume that she read them to him.) Nijinsky danced and practiced by himself every morning on the stage of Madrid's Royal Theater. He worked not only on his usual routines, but also sought to master the "austere movements" of gypsy dancers he had been observing since coming to Spain. Always affected by new and unusual movements, he wanted to imitate the flamenco postures and gestures, which he had never seen before, and incorporate them into his dance repertoire. In Madrid he also met the Polish pianist Arthur Rubinstein, and they became friends. Rubinstein was in Spain at that time to give concerts. Like Nijinsky, he was a refugee, forced by the war to limit his concertizing. One day they went together to see the exciting jai alai games played by Basque athletes. Rubinstein never forgot Nijinsky's reaction.

> The violent leaping and running of the players excited him so much that once he actually fell off his chair. "They are the most perfect dancers," he screamed. "I would like to jump down there and dance with them right away."[3]

At quieter moments, Nijinsky contemplated the future. He spoke with his wife about his preference for a simple, peaceful life, away from the hustle and bustle of the theater, and hopefully in Russia. In spite of the absence of news from his mother or sister since the beginning of the war, he did not seem to worry about the unsettled situation there. Romola writes that Nijinsky wanted to retire from the stage after a few more years, and then devote himself exclusively to teaching and creative work. It was his dream to design a special theater made entirely of wood, "in the Russian style," and painted in gaudy colors. He talked about wanting to organize a "yearly festival where some of the performances would be entirely free." He hoped to finance these projects from accumulated savings, derived from the money he had received for dancing with the Ballets Russes in the United States.

Romola worried about Nijinsky's dependence on Diaghilev. He had never been a hard bargainer, and even now his approach to money seemed unrealistic. There had been no serious discussion about a salary for touring in Spain and South America. No contracts had been signed. The only thing Nijinsky really wanted was to dance and to design new ballets. His personal needs were very modest, and he thoroughly disliked Romola's incessant desire for luxury. "I give you furs, jewelry, and anything you wish," he told her, "but can't you see how silly it is to attach importance to them?" (She had been complaining about the damage to her elegant wardrobe after an invasion of mice!) Nijinsky was a conservationist at heart. He objected to the cruelty of hunters, who had to slaughter animals so that wealthy people could wear fur coats. He worried about the dangers to pearl divers and to miners, who sought jewelry and precious stones only "for the adornment of women." What he told Romola in Spain made her realize that "Tolstoy was still preying on his mind." She had no intention whatsoever to live like a peasant in Russia.[4]

When Diaghilev arrived at the Ritz Hotel in Madrid, there in the lobby he "embraced Vaslav passionately" and treated him like an old friend, as if "no misunderstanding had ever occurred." This immediately made Romola suspicious. The two men spoke in Russian about the future of the Ballets Russes, about Diaghilev's difficulties in keeping the company together under wartime conditions, and about Nijinsky's hoped-for participation in the forthcoming tour. "Have you composed anything new?" Diaghilev asked him. "I want you to do so." Romola began to wonder if this amiability was merely a façade to hide Diaghilev's cunning. Was he planning to exploit Nijinsky for his purposes, by promising the impossible? Everyone knew that Massine was now Diaghilev's friend and his principal choreographer. Original ballets by this splendid dancer were already in the repertoire. Massine's zany *Parade*—based on a story of Jean Cocteau, with music by Erik Satie and a cubist decor by Pablo Picasso—had just been premiered in Paris. This proved that Diaghilev meant to be progressive and experimental as usual, even if it meant having to lose money. Would he really endorse Nijinsky's choreographic experiments once more, especially after all the problems with *Till Eulenspiegel?* What Diaghilev obviously needed was a surefire star like Nijinsky, someone to dazzle the public with the standard and more popular ballets, and to help defray expenses while the company was on tour. According to Romola, Diaghilev assured Nijinsky that he could dance to his heart's content in Spain and South America. He would no longer have to worry about any planning or administrative responsibilities, as in the United States. Grigoriev was in Spain to see to that. "Vaslav was so happy," writes Romola, "that he would have done anything to please Diaghilev." As for discussions about a contract, these were simply "brushed aside."[5]

Spain was a neutral country during World War I, and a haven for people from all over Europe who had been displaced or, as Arthur Rubinstein puts it, were "waging their own little war in Madrid." Rubinstein talks of the "spying, intrigues, false alarms, and slanders" that were their "secret weapons."[6] It was in this heady environment that the battle for control over Nijinsky's future now began to take shape. Diaghilev, who had championed the dancer when he was younger and sexually available, now needed Nijinsky mostly for his on-stage charisma. Romola, who had seduced him when he was more glamorous and virile, needed him now as a breadwinner, spouse, and symbol of success. Between these powerful figures, Nijinsky, with his dependent personality, desire to please, and difficulties in dealing with practical reality, was in danger of suffocating. Romola kept pushing Diaghilev for a written contract—"did they expect him to dance for nothing as in the past?" She feared that without such an agreement, Nijinsky might "isolate himself from the rest of the world and live only with Diaghilev and the Russian Ballet."[7] Diaghilev would not budge. Always gracious, courteous, and looking after the interests of his entire company rather than any single individual, he regarded Nijinsky's wife as an outsider and something of a meddler. Would the catastrophe of Nijinsky's madness have been averted if these two highly intelligent people had put their heads together and worked out an amicable agreement for him to continue functioning in the way he knew best, as a dancer and occasional choreographer? The question remains rhetorical.

In Spain it seemed that Nijinsky was able to relieve his inner tension by acting out his aggressive, erotic, and submissive impulses on stage. Off stage, he maintained an outward appearance of poise and amiability. Massine describes his "calm assurance and complete understanding." Following a performance of Massine's ballet *The Good-Humored Ladies* in Madrid, Nijinsky came to his dressing room, embraced him, and asked if in the future he might be allowed to dance the role of Battista, a comic character in this delightful ballet. "I felt very honored," writes Massine.

> In return I told him how much I admired his dancing and particularly his ballet, *L'Après-midi d'un Faune*. After this exchange of compliments we had a long talk and I found him a most delightful and sympathetic companion.[8]

In unfamiliar settings, however, Nijinsky seemed unapproachable and fearful. For example, when Arthur Rubinstein took him to a bullfight, Nijinsky suddenly stopped at the entrance gate. He turned "ashen pale," his eyes looked terribly distressed ("a sign of madness," writes Rubinstein), and he whispered: "Let's go back. I couldn't stand that."[9] Grigoriev, too, comments on Nijinsky's irritability and fearfulness in Spain, and the disturbing look in his eyes.[10] Two years later Nijinsky himself described these symptoms. He feared bodily injury. He was obsessed with all kinds of fantasies about the slaughter of animals. He thought he could "feel the tears" of calves and pigs being killed, and therefore did not like to eat meat. These fantasies may have been stimulated, in part, by Kostrovsky's recent lectures on vegetarianism, as well as guilty memories of perverse sexual practices (as a child, Nijinsky, like many youngsters growing up on farms or in the circus, had masturbated with animals.) Nijinsky identified with the suffering of overburdened beasts and often referred to himself as an "ox," "dog," or "horse." When he worked very hard and had to dance in spite of his fatigue, he felt "like a horse which is forced with a whip to drag a heavy load." The violence of the Spanish bullfights obviously repelled him. Unlike Diaghilev and Massine, who thought of bullfighting as a "magnificent art," Nijinsky had little tolerance for the bloody sport. It

stirred his own aggression—"I am bullish," he said—and made him fear
losing control.

> Spaniards love a bull's blood and therefore like murders. Spaniards are
> terrible people because they carry out the murder of bulls. The church,
> with the Pope at its head, cannot stop taurocide.... I know many
> toreadors whose stomach has been ripped open by a bull. I said that I did
> not like the slaughter of bulls, they did not understand me then.[11]

As the battle shaped up between Romola and Diaghilev over the
matter of a contract, Nijinsky's anxiety increased. She was complaining
that Kostrovsky and Zverev had again "installed themselves" in his
apartment and were advising him on highly personal matters, including
sex and religion. "Every second sentence was a quotation from Tolstoy,
and Vaslav listened attentively." She thought they were in cahoots
against her, trying to take possession of Nijinsky, so that Diaghilev
could "own him both as an artist and as a man," and thus destroy their
marriage. "It was all a carefully laid plot to estrange Vaslav from me and
restore him to Sergei Pavlovitch's clutches." (In a television interview
many years after Nijinsky's death, Romola complained about "three
great world conspiracies—the Vatican, the freemasons, and the homosexuals.") Her jealous if not paranoid fear that Diaghilev might win the
tug-of-war over Nijinsky apparently motivated her to declare "open
war" on the Russians. Romola pressured the dancer to make a choice
between her love and the "diabolical influence" of these men. When
Nijinsky refused to take sides, and instead pleaded with his wife not to
withhold "hospitality" from his friends, she gave him an ultimatum: "If
within half an hour these people are still here I will leave you." And
leave him she did—"I went out into the night," she says. Where Romola
disappeared to is not known, but this separation seems to have been
briefer than the one in Chicago earlier that year, and it had a different
outcome. Romola says Nijinsky found her in the Prado Museum the
next day, and "begged" her to return. After that she engineered his
extramarital affair with the Duchess of Durcal.[12]

How a romp in bed with another man's wife was supposed to improve
Nijinsky's marriage is a bit of a mystery. Romola tells us that he had
been reluctant to have sexual intercourse unless it was for the purpose
of procreation—"either an ascetic life or a child every year was the right
way"—for which she blamed Kostrovsky. The setting for the affair with

the duchess sounds very romantic and a bit Wagnerian. Romola writes that after leaving Madrid the company motored up to the monastery of Montserrat, Parsifal's holy mountain. Women were not permitted there, so Nijinsky went there "alone" with his Russian friends. Evenings were spent with the Duchess of Durcal, who "was by this time desperately in love, and wanted to become Vaslav's mistress." Romola denies any feelings of jealousy. Perhaps it was her need for a female ally in the fight against Diaghilev (and her own latent lesbianism) that allowed her to "encourage" the duchess's "advances."

> I almost threw them together, because, unconsciously, I felt that two loving women could achieve more than one in holding back an idealist from falling into the abyss of utter day-dreaming to which these fanatics were dragging him.[13]

According to Romola, the Duchess of Durcal, a beautiful redhead, was happy and honored to have Nijinsky as a lover. But she seems to have made no lasting impression on the dancer, if one is to judge by his notebooks, written two years later, which contain lengthy descriptions of his intimacies with animals, childhood friends, Prince Lvov, Diaghilev, Romola, and even the Paris prostitutes, but barely mention the duchess. (What he wrote was not flattering: married couples "make mistakes" and do "depraved things."[14]) Wealthy admirers had used Nijinsky for their own enjoyment when he was a young man; to repeat this pattern now that he was married seemed distasteful. After his night of love with the duchess, Nijinsky appeared "mournful." Romola writes that "this escapade had quite a different effect on him than I had expected." He apologized to her: "I am sorry for what I did. It was unfair to her as I am not in love, and the added experience, that perhaps you wanted me to have is unworthy of us."[15]

The Duchess of Durcal accompanied Nijinsky and his wife to Barcelona, where six performances had been scheduled, which sold out in advance because of the dancer's great reputation. "His name was even better known here than in Madrid." notes Grigoriev.[16] Romola reasoned that Nijinsky's obvious popularity in Barcelona made it timely to press Diaghilev for an agreement about his salary for the South America tour that was to follow. A luncheon meeting was arranged to discuss the matter. All that we know about it comes from Romola. She says that Nijinsky was uncertain about whether he really wanted to go.

He did not like the prospect of being separated from Kyra again. What he really wanted was "a rest" (a rather incredible statement, considering that he had just had a two-month vacation). He objected that the South America tour was not going to be "a creative trip artistically." No new works, neither his own *Till Eulenspiegel* nor any of Massine's ballets, were scheduled to be performed overseas, only the old chestnuts. Diaghilev responded to these objections "with a freezing smile," and proceeded to lay down the law.

"But you have to go, you are under contract."
"Have to?" said Vaslav. "I have no contract."
"You cabled me from America agreeing in principle. That is a contract."
"But I also cabled that we would discuss the matter in Spain."
"That is beside the point. In this country, a cable is a binding contract... I will force you to go."[17]

Diaghilev could easily seem dictatorial or arbitrary with his dancers, and most of them took this in stride. But Nijinsky and his wife felt that it was beneath their dignity to be treated in such a way, especially after the laborious contract negotiations in New York, which had led to a very favorable salary arrangement. Would Diaghilev now revert to his old method, handing out unspecified amounts of money whenever it was convenient for him to do so? Nijinsky notified Diaghilev that "as no contract existed, he would take no further part in the Russian Ballet." The servants were told to pack their bags; Nijinsky wanted to leave immediately and return to Madrid. It was a precipitous and unwise decision, considering that the Barcelona public was waiting to see him dance that night. Diaghilev retaliated immediately by calling an attorney and notifying the governor of Barcelona. Before the Nijinskys could board the train, two policemen stopped them and threatened to throw him in jail. Romola says she saved the day by "dashing" to the telephone, calling Madrid, and begging the Duke of Durcal to intercede, which he gladly did. The police let Nijinsky go, and he returned to his hotel, protesting, "I can't dance now; I'm too upset." Nevertheless, under firm pressure from management, he did dance that night in a performance that was much delayed. (A telegram sent the next day to the Teatro Colón in Buenos Aires reads as follows: "Nijinsky has made enormous troubles. Police yesterday had to arrest him to prevent him from leaving so his arrival in Argentina improbable." Diaghilev went on to explain that he was prepared to make some monetary compromises and was planning to send Gavrilov and Idzikowsky, "the new stars who last year successfully replaced Nijinsky and Massine.")[18]

This needlessly brutal showdown in Barcelona was what finally severed the long, troubled, but undeniably productive relationship between Nijinsky and Diaghilev. Never again would the world's most famous male dancer be on "speaking terms" with the greatest impresario of his time.[19] Suspiciousness and hostility were to mark Nijinsky's overt attitude toward this man who had once loved him, while underneath lay a yearning for contact and support. Diaghilev coped with the loss of his star readily enough by finding other men to dance the leading roles, none Nijinsky's equal, however. For him the loss was more tragic. Nijinsky lacked the capacity for independent work and always needed someone like Diaghilev or Bronislava or Romola or later the doctors and nurses to help direct his energies.

After the crisis in Barcelona, Romola seems to have jumped in and tried to salvage what was left of his career. Their financial future depended on his continuing to perform. She succeeded in getting Diaghilev to agree to the same fee arrangement for the South America tour that Nijinsky had had in the United States, only this time, to avoid "any lawsuits later on," she demanded that all payments had to be in cash, "in gold dollars, one hour before the curtain rose at every performance." The contract also specified that a penalty of $20,000 had to be paid if Diaghilev were to default on Nijinsky's salary, or if Nijinsky canceled a performance. "The contract was so cleverly drawn up," Romola writes, "that, while it fulfilled all his stipulations, there was no possibility of any trick being played on Vaslav."[20] Her perspicacity (and greed?) are apparent if one checks her correspondence with Bankers Trust Company in New York. It shows that "Mrs. Romola Nijinsky had on deposit with our institution on March 5, 1917, cash and securities aggregating approximately $40,000," a sizable fortune in those days, especially for the wife of a performing artist.[21] After signing his new contract, Nijinsky attended a gala reception, then returned to Madrid with Romola. Kyra was sent to a private nursery in Lausanne, Switzerland. Diaghilev took Massine and a small group of dancers to Italy, while on the fourth of July the rest of the company, Vaslav and Romola included, sailed for South America.

Nijinsky's last tour with the Ballets Russes resembled a play within a play. In front of an audience, with the footlights blazing, he continued to dance magnificently, with his usual vitality. "It is the possession of the body by the spirit, and the utilization of the animal by the soul," writes the French poet and diplomat Paul Claudel, who saw Nijinsky dance in Brazil.[22] (Claudel was a leading French cultural figure, expected by some to become the second Shakespeare. His sister, a sculptress who had been Rodin's mistress, tragically went mad, like Nijinsky, in mid-career.) Another eyewitness, André de Badet, who was then living in Montevideo with his mother, wrote that Nijinsky "possessed wings on his heels like Mercury, and defied the laws of gravity by not letting himself return to the floor after he had leapt to the sky in one of those prodigious arcs, which reached eight meters."[23]

Behind the scenes, however, the great dancer seemed "more than usually quiet and absent-minded, as if forever brooding: he never smiled and his eyes had a frightened look."[24] Along with this depressiveness came a tendency to be mistrustful. Enemies seemed to be lurking everywhere. When Nijinsky stepped on a rusty nail, he suspected it had been put there by one of Diaghilev's henchmen. When a heavy weight from an overhead pulley fell and nearly hit him, this, according to Romola who shared his suspicions, surely was no "accident." Such incidents allegedly were meant to keep him from dancing. It was all part of a plot to make Nijinsky pay the twenty-thousand-dollar penalty specified in his contract. "Some people may have wanted to assist the hand of fate." Detectives were hired to protect the dancer, but even this precaution did not make him feel safe. During a performance of *Petrushka,* for example, the puppet theater on top of which he was dancing started to shake, and he nearly fell off. It had not been fastened securely to the stage, another "attack," asserts Romola.[25]

The accuracy of Romola's memory for these "accidents" has been questioned. Some of them may have occurred earlier, when Nijinsky was dancing in the United States.[26] For example, an article in the *New York Times,* 26 April 1916, reports that he stepped on a nail, certainly not an unusual event in the theater and something that may have happened on several occasions. But Nijinsky's hypervigilance in regard to real or imagined danger makes good sense if we remember his childhood injury on a ballet floor. Nijinsky also knew about other accidents in the theater. For example, while rehearsing in Italy, a man had fallen through an open trapdoor and been killed. Romola, too, was plagued by terrible memories, probably related to the suicide of her father. Today, one would recognize intrusive fears and unbidden fantasies of this kind as the symptoms of a stress-response disorder, a condition that may benefit from psychiatric treatment.[27] Nijinsky and his wife had no access to professional help in 1917. They were traveling in a foreign country and were surrounded by people who had their own worries, not to mention the jealousies and rivalries so often found among performing artists. Furthermore, an atmosphere of "intrigue" during the South America tour only seemed to make matters worse. Romola writes of someone on the boat who spread rumors about "liaisons that Vaslav and I were supposed to have had with various people." One man "tried to make love" to her and then to have "an *affaire*" with Vaslav.[28] How much of this was fantasy and how much reality is impossible to say, but one has the impression that the Nijinsky couple was driven to behave irrationally at times. André de Badet reports that Vaslav "avoided the other artists [and] believed himself to be persecuted by certain of his comrades."[29]

That his fears and suspiciousness interfered with certain performances seems clear from eyewitness reports. For example, during one of the rehearsals for *Narcisse,* at the point where the dancer had to sink into the lake and be transformed into a flower, Nijinsky refused to let himself be lowered through the opening in the floor. Grigoriev reports that Nijinsky "would lie on the stage saying he was frightened in case I should give the wrong signal, so that he would fall through and be killed." Another time Nijinsky procrastinated endlessly before mounting the rock at the beginning of *L'Après-midi d'un Faune.* Finally, Grigoriev raised the curtain, even though the dancer was "pacing up and down" and obviously not ready to begin. He fled to the wings, in full view of the audience, whereupon the stage director barked at him to start dancing. "This time he obeyed; the ballet started; and he performed his part as usual. After this incident it was obvious that Nijinsky was seriously ill."[30]

Yet no treatment was provided. His illness notwithstanding, Nijinsky had to go on dancing. Every appearance meant more money. Romola writes, "I used to sit in Vaslav's dressing-room with a watch in my hand, waiting for Vaslav's salary."[31] In due time almost everyone in the company was alarmed by his disturbed behavior. The conductor Ernest Ansermet, for example, recalls how Nijinsky forced him to repeat the music for *Faune* "twenty-three times, because he could not make it clear to the artists what he wished them to do." Finally, Nijinsky became completely fed up with what he perceived to be the musicians' and dancers' inability to produce satisfactory results. To stop any further performances of *Faune,* he took his position on stage, but refused to move, a legitimate way, he claimed as the choreographer of the work, to cancel a ballet without having to pay the default penalty. Ansermet concluded that Nijinsky was suffering from "a latent conflict between his genius as a dancer—that grace which nature had bestowed on him— and his critical faculties."[32]

The South America tour ended on 26 September 1917, with Nijinsky performing in *Le Spectre de la Rose* and *Petrushka,* after which the Ballets Russes sailed back to Europe. It had already been announced that Nijinsky would be leaving the company, and newspapers reported that he was planning to take a short rest in Switzerland. There were rumors that he would organize his own company and in 1918 take them on a tour of the United States, Mexico, Peru, Chile, Argentina, and Brazil.[33] Badet invited him to remain in Montevideo for a while and suggested that he might establish his own school of dance in Uruguay. An evening of original ballets was announced, including "*Minstrels* by Debussy [and] a scene from *Pelleas and Melisande,*" but nothing came of it.[34] To live and work in South America would have required considerable diplomacy, since Nijinsky had no legal permission to stay there. Claudel wrote letters on his behalf, and Romola made arrangements for him to participate in a benefit recital for the International Red Cross, thinking that might help. Nijinsky's letters about the Red Cross benefit to André de Badet and others were written in nearly impeccable French, suggesting either that Romola dictated and corrected them for him or that he was far more fluent in this language than is generally believed. ("I did not learn French because I felt a repugnance for it," Nijinsky was to write shortly, in Russian, in one of his notebooks.)

Arthur Rubinstein—the pianist was also in South America at the time—had been asked to appear on the same program with Nijinsky. Rubinstein agreed, albeit somewhat reluctantly because of an overly busy concert schedule. "My dressing room was next door to Nijinsky's, and I heard him exercising with great jumps which made my room tremble." The recital opened with Rubinstein playing a Beethoven sonata and two shorter pieces, after which the dancer was supposed to make his entrance. He did not come on stage. Evidently he was feeling sick, "something on his foot," Rubinstein was told, "it is wet or sore or something . . . he is so nervous that I am afraid he might decide not to dance at all." At first Rubinstein thought that Nijinsky might have been stalling deliberately, so he could "have the last ovation of the concert like so many ambitious virtuosos." But when after much delay he finally made his entrance, Rubinstein was alarmed by his obvious depression. "He looked even sadder than when he danced the death of Petrushka." He was wearing a makeshift costume, with pink tights from *Spectre* and a black tunic and white blouse from *Sylphides*. "I must confess," writes Rubinstein, "that I burst into tears. The horrible mixture of a seemingly endless farce with one of the most heartbreaking tragedies was more than one could bear. We gave him an endless ovation."[35]

The return voyage to Europe in October 1917 allowed Nijinsky to relax and rest "practically the whole day" in a deck chair. He worked on his choreographic notations, which seemed to improve his mood. Crossing the Atlantic was always risky in wartime, and Romola was especially afraid of submarine attacks, but he remained relatively unperturbed. She also worried about the possible theft of her jewels, and complained about having to put up with armed searches and hostile passengers. Before landing, they heard news of the recent Soviet take-over in Russia, which upset her because Nijinsky seriously contemplated going back there after the war. "He had already designed our future home in Russia, with a special apartment for Kyra," writes Romola, who noted that when Nijinsky was reunited with his daughter in Lausanne, he became quite elated and seemed totally at ease with the child, hugging and dancing around the room with her. "Kyra screamed with joy. It was remarkable how the child changed the moment Vaslav entered the room. It seemed almost as though they had been one person split apart, and constantly wishing to be reunited." Romola had to admit a certain discomfort in her role as wife and mother, and a marked disinclination to adapt herself to the Russian ways of her husband. She describes her alienation from Vaslav, and Kyra as well: "Sometimes I almost felt as if I were intruding on them. They were both essentially and fundamentally Russian—something we Europeans can never, never penetrate. They so easily adapted themselves to different circumstances, to joy, to sorrow, to luxury, to hardship." How could Romola, a Hungarian citizen accustomed to luxury, and with a large amount of money in her New York bank account, ever follow him to revolution-torn Russia, where he "dreamed" of making his home?[36]

For the time being, with Europe still at war, there was no alternative except to remain in neutral Switzerland. But where? Romola did not want to stay in Lausanne or one of the bigger cities. She had fond memories of the Swiss Alps, where her parents had often taken her as a child. Especially appealing was the village of St. Moritz, a ski resort high in the Engadine and a gathering place for the rich and famous. She yearned to go there, but Nijinsky objected immediately. He "hated" mountains, he said. "They hide the view. I want to see far, far away. I do not want to be shut in." Yet he assented and agreed to leave Kyra again so that Romola could visit her favorite vacation resort. They arrived just in time to witness a rare Alpine earthquake. It shook the village so violently that the hotels had to be emptied, leaving the guests "sitting in the snow with chattering teeth, more from the fright than from the cold."[37]

The uncanny sense of disorientation produced when the ground trembles beneath one's feet has been described by many earthquake survivors, including Charles Darwin, who, like Nijinsky, was afflicted with a recurring disorder and needed to be hospitalized from time to time (although he never decompensated psychotically).[38] To the high-strung Nijinsky, so sensitive to anything that moved and shook, the earthquake in St. Moritz signified a cosmic force unleashed. He wrote about it in a typically Russian hyperbolic style and with a prophetic foresight that is remarkably like modern-day conservationism: "The earth is disintegrating because its fuel is ceasing to burn. Fuel will continue to give heat for a bit, but not very much, and therefore God wants love before the earth loses all heat." Nijinsky equated the absence of movement with cosmic death: "I know that if there are no earth-quakes, the earth will be extinguished, the whole life of man will be extinguished too, because man will not have a constant supply of food." And he felt that there was a connection between the life-giving energy of the universe and the heat of his own pulsating body: "I am alive as long as I have fire in my head. My pulse is an earthquake. I am an earthquake."[39] Nijinsky was to have many supernatural experiences of this sort over the next few years. They denote a cosmic consciousness that is familiar to mystics, to certain artists and philosophers, and to people who strive for realms beyond personal existence. William James called them "conversations with the unseen, voices and visions, re-sponses to prayer, changes of heart, deliverances from fear." They have also been used to diagnose certain forms of psychosis.[40]

Why Nijinsky chose to remain in the Swiss Alps, since he disliked the mountains, is not clear. Perhaps the remoteness of St. Moritz satisfied his need for solitude. The deep winter snow may have reminded him of Mother Russia. His dependence on Romola certainly had something to do with it. (She points out that he could not speak German, and was "completely lost when he had to attend to the necessities of everyday life. To book a room in a hotel and to buy a railway ticket were experiences unknown to him."[41]) Another reason probably was their hope that living in the Swiss Alps might remedy Nijinsky's nervous condition. His doctors in London and Budapest had recommended protection from undue stress. Other artists and writers, notably Thomas Mann, have benefited from staying in this environment. Within walking distance of St. Moritz Dorf (the village) is St. Moritz Spa (the health center) with its curative mineral springs, mudbaths, massage and physiotherapy facilities. During the years the Nijinskys lived there, the spa was open only in the summer, whereas today it caters to visitors year-round. Medical services are close by, in the luxury hotels of St. Moritz or in nearby private clinics.

On 11 December 1917, Nijinsky signed a one-year lease, renewable annually, for a spacious, three-story house, the splendidly furnished Villa Guardamunt, situated 200 meters uphill from the center of St. Moritz Dorf. It has breathtaking views of the surrounding glaciers and a lovely garden. The rent was Fr. 4,500 a year, payable in two installments, plus the cost of all utilities, telephone service, insurance, and taxes.[42] A studio, living area, and bedroom for Nijinsky's exclusive use occupied the entire upper floor, and there were several balconies where he could get sunshine and do his exercises for two hours every morning. Frau Nelly Tröger, now living in a retirement community in nearby Samedan, remembers seeing the famous dancer practicing in full view of his neighbors. Kyra, too, recalls how Nijinsky would demonstrate his prowess by leaping and showing her how to dance. Romola describes how Kyra "used to cheer and clap her hands, then often Vaslav, forgetting his iron discipline, caught her in his arms and waltzed round singing [in a mixture of French and Russian] '*Votre amabilité, maia Kotyik, maia Funtyiki.*'" Their first winter in St. Moritz was "a very happy one." Nijinsky's mood improved, and he became more sociable.

Vaslav was simply worshipped by the servants. If he met the cook on the way up to the Villa, he carried the parcels. If the coal was too heavy to put on the fire, he helped the maid, and he even flirted with the old laundress, bought her chianti, and chatted to her of her native Italy. He would play with all the children of the village.[43]

While he practiced dancing and worked on his choreographic sketches, Romola usually went sledding, skating, or skiing. "I had decided to take part in all the winter sports." Then they would meet for a drink at Hanselmann's, a popular cafe, and have their midday meal. Romola emphasizes her pleasure in socializing with the "many interesting Swiss and foreigners" living in St. Moritz, including "President Gartmann," her next-door neighbor, and Dr. Bernhard, a well-known surgeon.* Nijinsky seems to have preferred to be with less sophisticated people, the servants and the children of the neighborhood. Unlike Romola, he eschewed the winter sports, wisely, since skiing and skating pose some risks for a ballet dancer. Twice a week the entire family went for a sleigh ride to the nearby lakes and mountain passes, where they usually stopped for lunch "at some roadside inn."[45]

Over the Christmas holidays, Vaslav and Romola were joined by Tessa and Erik Schmedes, Romola's sister and brother-in-law. Tessa was fun-loving and flirtatious, as usual. (Nijinsky commented how she could "excite lust." He nicknamed her "Tiger-Cub," and wrote rather indelicately that she "loves a prick. She needs a prick.")[46] It was a festive atmosphere. Nijinsky seemed to be "quite rested and soothed by the light-hearted gaiety of his *entourage.*" Romola fails to mention, however, a fifth member of this presumably happy group, an attractive young physician, Dr. Albert Greiber (not his real name—for reasons of medical confidentiality I cannot disclose it), who was to play an important role in her life and have a significant impact on the course of Nijinsky's illness. He was the hotel physician in an elegant resort just up the road from the Villa Guardamunt. Dr. Greiber was well trained in internal medicine and, since coming to work in St. Moritz, had been specializing in the problems of athletes, what is now called "sports medicine." He is described as "a bohemian, musical and nature-loving man," handsome, ambitious, a few years older than Nijinsky, married, and with a daughter exactly Kyra's age. That Greiber would be fascinated by the medical problems of this "world-famous" dancer and

*Oscar Bernhard, M.D. (1861–1939), was one of several enterprising medical men who had moved to St. Moritz because of the tourist clientele there, and to promote a new treatment for tuberculosis called "Heliotherapy," which consisted of fresh air and sunshine.[44]

"leader of the Russian ballet," as he called Nijinsky, and "the woman who married him because of her strongly hysterical disposition" is not too surprising.[47] St. Moritz is a small town, and Nijinsky was one of its most prominent guests. It was also comforting for Romola to have a medically trained person close by, an intelligent and well-meaning individual interested in the arts, to whom she could turn for advice whenever Kyra had a "cold," or Vaslav manifested troublesome behavior.

After the winter season, when the tourists go home and the rains begin turning the snow into slush, St. Moritz can become a rather dreary place. The big hotels close and many of the shops and restaurants are also boarded up. This is not an especially hospitable location for year-round living. For Romola, used to socializing with artists and people of means, St. Moritz now seemed "remote and five centuries back." For Nijinsky's career, it turned out to be a dead end. Mrs. Madeleine Grant, Kyra's nanny, tells of their unhappy "isolation" in the spring of 1918. "No one ever came to the house, and we did not even have a newspaper ... you could seldom meet anyone.... It was evidently a sad life for the Nijinskys. Vaslav looked like a caged animal at times. When he did come out of his shell he used to speak about his brother and his mother."[48] He kept working, however, practicing, trying to perfect his choreographic system, making sketches in his upstairs study. "He was full of ideas for new ballets," Romola says.[49]

Only from her recollections and from his drawings and notations that she managed to save can one obtain information about Nijinsky's St. Moritz ballets. First, he "composed a delightful version of Debussy's *Chansons de Bilitis*," in which Romola apparently was supposed to play a leading role, that of the androgynous Bilitis. Debussy had set to music three sensuous, erotic love poems by Pierre Louÿs. Nijinsky wanted them to provide the background for two contrasting scenes on a Greek island: Bilitis with a male lover, and Bilitis with a female lover who "shares her sorrows and her pleasures." This ballet, approximately ten minutes in duration, was to "obey the same basic choreographic laws as the *Faune*." Nijinsky's next "choreographic poem" was to be frankly autobiographical. Romola does not say anything about the music. He wanted to dance the role of a painter "in the period of the High Renaissance." At the beginning he is "a youth seeking truth through life." He dances with "his master, one of the greatest artists of the period, a universal genius," clearly a reference to Diaghilev. Then the painter meets a woman, "his mate, who finally carries him off." Romola describes the enormous amount of energy Nijinsky expended in planning this ballet, and how much he identified with the central role of "the painter." "He designed the scenery and costumes for it himself, modern, and yet correct to the period." He not only danced the "painter," he became one.[50]

While designing his costumes and choreography, Nijinsky seemed to be in a state of creative elation, but the rest of the time he was in a sad mood, depressed by his enforced isolation and the unavailability of other artists with whom to try out his ideas. Creating new ballets takes more than inventiveness and enthusiasm. One needs colleagues to work with. "No matter how much mental preparation a choreographer makes," writes dance critic Arlene Croce, "the real work is done in the studio, where real bodies are in play. It is a slow and exacting process, infinitely boring to watch."[51] There was no one with whom to share this process—not even Romola, whose approach to dancing was more that of an amateur than a professional. She mentions another ballet—Nijinsky wanted to call it *Papillons de la Nuit* (Nocturnal Butterflies)—which was to show the entire range and variety of human sexual behavior in a house of prostitution.

> The chief character was to be the owner, once a beautiful *cocotte,* now aged and paralysed as a result of her debauchery; but, though her body was a wreck, her spirit was indomitable in the traffic of love. She deals with all the wares of love: selling girls to boys, youth to age, woman to woman, man to man.[52]

Romola wondered how he was going to "express" this difficult subject. Such a ballet would have been considered extremely daring at the time, and even today might evoke censorship. Nijinsky tried to explain it to her by dancing all the different roles, quite effectively it seems, for she says that he "succeeded in transmitting the whole scale of sex life." Not only that, but he even tried to compose the music for *Papillons de la Nuit.* Having no staff paper available, he used large sheets of foolscap and crayons to draw the lines, placing the musical notes on them like dancers on a tightrope, with little awareness, apparently, that this music is disconnected, full of awkward leaps and missing beats. (Nijinsky's melodies sound like twelve-tone compositions in the style of Schönberg, whose music he may have had in mind, but one finds no tonerows as used by Schönberg and his followers.) Nijinsky also made crayon drawings of costumes and scenery. In addition he did many self-portraits, and drew sketches of Kyra and other people, some in vivid pastels, others in charcoal or pencil. These are impressive works of art, with good control of form and color. His abstract drawings, made with intersecting lines and circles, are also quite original, very delicate, like a spider's web. Nijinsky's work resembles the "nonobjective" art that flourished in Russia, briefly, after the revolution. Art historian Alessandra Comini calls it "unofficial Russian art." These painters used "archetypal geometrics such as the circle, the cross, the spiral, the square [to represent] a natural progression between two resonant chords of the collective Russian soul: mysticism and mathematics."[53]

That Nijinsky was able, independently, to create these kinds of symbols demonstrates his deep identification with the culture of his homeland. The persistence of circular forms in his art may also be interpreted as an attempt to maintain balance and personal integration in the face of an overwhelming threat to his existence. Rings, spirals, and magic circles have frequently been used to symbolize man's search for purity, for unification, for the grace of God, and for sanity. "Circular mandala symbols," writes Carl Jung, "often appear at moments of mental disorientation, when they serve as a compensatory and organizing factor."[54] Nijinsky even wanted to design a circular stage, resembling a Greek theater: "I do not like a theater with a square stage," he writes. "I like a round theater. I will build a theater which will have a round shape, like an eye." He equated the circle with an all-seeing cyclopean eye, an extension of his own brain, the narcissistic center of his universe: "I am the brain in the brain. I like to look closely in the mirror and I see only one eye in my forehead. Often I make drawings of one eye."[55] For most of the summer he was able to maintain reasonable self-control and a fairly optimistic attitude. "I work, I compose new dances, and I am perfecting the system of dance-notation," he wrote to a friend in Paris. "I wish to work independently of other troupes of dancers, in which intrigue prevents the creation of real art. I am planning to dance alone with a small company and achieve some interesting results."[56] In a quite similar letter to André de Badet, on 28 April 1918, he mentioned the recent death of composer Claude Debussy—"poor Debussy is dead, what a loss for all of us." Later that year there was a darkening of Nijinsky's mood, and outbursts of bad temper, accompanied by frenzied overactivity. "He used to work until late at night, and came to sleep only at dawn," says Romola. "He seemed to make a drawing in three minutes with a lightning speed. His study and rooms were literally covered with designs." He incessantly drew circles. He was beginning to spiral into mania.[57]

What precipitated Nijinsky's first true manic episode? We already know about his inclination to affective disorder, his separation from the world of ballet, and his isolation in the Swiss Alps. But the straw that broke the camel's back seems to have been an assault, real or imagined, on Nijinsky's marriage in 1918. He suspected that Romola and Dr. Greiber were in love and might be having an affair. How much justification there was for these suspicions is hard to say. Others in St. Moritz shared them, including Dr. Greiber's wife, and rumors have persisted to this day that Romola and the doctor were involved in a "passionate romance."[58] Greiber was giving her medical advice, and probably had a hand in what she later described as a "minor operation," carried out in Bern. What kind of an operation this was remains a matter of conjecture, since the relevant hospital records no longer exist. Romola writes that she had a gynecological procedure because "I had been suffering slightly ever since Kyra's birth."[59] (For four years? Kyra was born in 1914!) A more likely explanation is that Romola probably had gotten pregnant in 1918, and went to Bern for an abortion. We know that Nijinsky wanted her to have another child, he hoped a son, to be named Borislav, and that she was strongly disinclined. We also know (from medical records in Budapest, dated 1941) that Romola "gave birth to two children" (Kyra and Tamara) and had "an abortion from her husband," presumably in 1918.[60] They had been quarreling furiously because of his insistence on "going somewhere in Russia to farm." In one of these arguments Romola went so far as to "hurl" her gold Brazilian wedding ring at Nijinsky, saying, "I have had enough; I can't become a peasant. I was not born one. Even if I love you I will divorce you and marry some manufacturer."[61] Whether she accepted Dr. Greiber as her lover remains a moot point.

After returning from the hospital, Romola felt "not yet quite strong" and apparently did not resume having marital relations. It was during this period of abstinence that Nijinsky began to behave in what she calls "the Russian patriarchal way."[62] He would argue vehemently with the servants, barge into the kitchen to inspect the pots and pans, and throw out any meat they contained. To eat meat was "a terrible thing" in Nijinsky's opinion, since he felt that meat stimulated sexual desire and made him want to masturbate. It was an old obsession: "My lust has disappeared since I ceased to eat meat," he writes.

Meat is a terrible thing. I know that children who eat meat practice masturbation. I know that girls and boys practice masturbation. I know that women and men together and separately practice masturbation. Masturbation develops idiocy. Men lose feeling and reason. I used to lose my reason when I practiced masturbation.[63]

He worried constantly about Kyra, watched her suspiciously, and punished her brutally if he saw her crossing her legs or moving in a suggestive manner. Any meat put on the child's plate he would throw on the floor or toss out the window. He terrorized Kyra's nanny, one day suddenly "leaping" at her and holding her by the throat. "I tore out of the room," writes Mrs. Grant. "I was terrified." She left the household shortly thereafter.[64]

This crescendo of disruptive behavior was interrupted by news from beleaguered Russia. Nijinsky's sister and her family as well as his mother, now sixty-two, had survived the revolution and were in good health. The war was over; armistice had been declared on 11 November. But Nijinsky's brother had died. (The cause has been debated. The huge city hospital, where he had been confined for years, burned to the ground in 1917, destroying all records and killing many of the patients, including, I was told in Leningrad, Stanislav Nijinsky. Richard Buckle disputes this—"he died in bed of a liver complaint [not in a fire].") Nijinsky accepted Stanislav's death stoically, much as he had his father's in 1912, by smiling and saying very little. As a child he had witnessed his brother's violent tantrums, twisted movements, and shrieking imbecility. Stanislav had always been the "lunatic" of the family; now he was gone. Romola recalls the "strange and deep quietness" with which Nijinsky attempted to control his feelings, probably a mixture of regret and relief. "Do not cry," he told her; "[my brother] was insane; it is better like this."[65] Concurrent with the news about his family, Nijinsky also heard for the first time about the horrors of World War I, the ghastly trenches, the killing and maiming of soldiers, the bloody battlefields. All this added to his alternating depression and excitement.

Creative people may be able to subdue their grief and deal productively with the anguish of personal bereavement by engaging in a symbolic activity of renewal. Johannes Brahms, for example, composed his stirring *Ein deutsches Requiem* in response to emergent German nationalism and to commemorate his mother's death. Käthe Kollwitz, while mourning for a beloved son, made poignant portraits of children. Nijinsky tried to express his despair in drawings and ballet designs. During the winter of 1918–1919 his art became darker, more abstract, filled with images of horror, evil eyes and gaping mouths, "like the blood spitting of some enraged and outraged demon."[66] He was planning another ballet—Romola called it a "dance for life against death"—in which he would assault the public for sending young men to their graves, a symbolic expression of his survivor guilt. He was trying to sort out ideas and feelings in accordance with the unconscious dynamics of mourning, whereby the mourner incorporates certain qualities of the deceased into his own psyche and assimilates them into his personality.[67] During this process, he began to think and behave more erratically and to transform himself gradually into a new character. It was to be a variation on themes Nijinsky had enacted so convincingly in the past: capriciousness, enslavement, violence, and suffering. He said he wanted to play the role of "a lunatic."[68]

While preparing for what was to be the most enduring role of his career, Nijinsky "threw all his reserve to the winds" and became savagely excited. Having no stage to dance on, he used the natural environment, the ski slopes and mountains of St. Moritz. Aided by his superb sense of balance and muscular coordination, he rushed down the steepest terrain at breakneck speed. With the enthusiasm of a fanatic, he entered the famous skeleton races of St. Moritz. (The "skeleton" is a short sled, without steering mechanism. It can be controlled only by shifting one's weight while shooting headfirst down steeply twisting ice tunnels, at a speed often exceeding sixty miles per hour. This is an exceedingly dangerous sport, and there have been numerous fatalities.[69]) Nijinsky had several near-fatal accidents; once he almost capsized a horse-driven sleigh by running it into oncoming traffic. He also became assaultive toward Romola, shoving her, striking her, and one time pushing her violently down the steps of the villa. Not knowing what was "the matter" with him, she became angry, and terribly afraid. "You are behaving like a *moujik*," she yelled at him; "you ought to be ashamed!" In his maniacal mood, Nijinsky went on shopping sprees, buying hundreds of postcards, lavish gifts, enormous amounts of art material, "cases of paints and pastels," reams of paper, more than he would ever be able to use. Driven by what he called "a mysterious force," he rushed out of the house to climb the trails behind Villa Guardamunt, and while perched on a cliff he entertained fantasies of leaping all the way down to the village. He roamed around the village, preached religion, wore Kyra's large crucifix over his jacket, and told people to go to church, all of which set Romola's teeth on edge because it embarrassed her in the eyes of their neighbors. She did not yet realize how sick he was. "What is this new nonsense?" she asked him scoldingly. "Vaslav, won't you stop imitating that old lunatic Tolstoy? You are making yourself into a laughingstock."[70]

Romola's admonitions had no effect whatsoever in reducing Nijinsky's furor. If anything, they inflamed him even more, just as his mother's punishment had done when as a child he romped crazily on rooftops and climbed into trees. Romola became frantic. She realized that she could no longer handle him alone. She asked Dr. Greiber to help her. He was no psychiatrist, but he had seen emotionally and mentally disturbed patients in medical school. In his opinion, Nijinsky was in "a state of acute exhaustion," which could be attributed to his "uninterrupted dancing (sixteen hours a day) for several months."[71] Perhaps what Greiber heard from Romola about the dancer's earlier "neurasthenia" led to this mistaken diagnosis. He decided to tranquilize Nijinsky by administering large oral doses of chloral hydrate, a sedative. This was a commonly prescribed medication at the time. Like most sedatives, it increases depression. (Chloral hydrate was also one of the more popular "knockout drops," given to unsuspecting persons in what used to be called a "Mickey Finn" cocktail.) Another way to keep Nijinsky under control was to assign a male nurse, a "solid, tall, good-natured German," whose job it was to supervise him day and night and keep the dancer in bed.[72]

He became "very suspicious." He felt that Romola and the doctor were doing something behind his back. He tried to keep his notebooks from being read by Greiber. He disobeyed the doctor's orders. But under the watchful eyes of the nurse, who he was told was a "masseur," Nijinsky gradually became more tractable. After ten days of enforced sedation, Romola was delighted to see him stretched out on a sofa, "nonchalantly" drinking tea, and "making fun" of the visitors who had come to see him. His behavior had changed dramatically. "It almost seemed that he was now acting the part of a *blasé mondaine* aristocrat," Romola recalls.

You see, I am an artist [Nijinsky told his guests]; I have no troupe now, so I miss the stage. I thought it would be an interesting experiment to see how well I could act, and for six weeks I played the part of a lunatic, and the whole village, my family, and even the physicians believed it. I have a male nurse to watch me, in the disguise of a *masseur*.[73]

In this black comedy mood, with Romola wondering if it had all been an "artistic experiment" to drive her "crazy," Nijinsky made plans to perform his latest ballet about lunacy and the war. Romola and Dr. Greiber helped him to find a suitable place, the ballroom of Suvretta House, an elegant hotel on the outskirts of St. Moritz Dorf. The date was set for Sunday afternoon, 19 January 1919.

NOTES

1. Quoted by David Blum in a "profile" on violoncellist Yo Yo Ma, 61.
2. RNN, 366–368.
3. Arthur Rubinstein, *My Many Years*, 11.
4. RNN, 369–370.
5. Ibid., 370–372.
6. Arthur Rubinstein, *My Young Years*, 467.
7. RNN, 374, 379.
8. Léonide Massine, *My Life in Ballet*, 113–114.
9. Rubinstein, *My Many Years*, 11–12.
10. Serge Grigoriev, *The Diaghilev Ballet, 1909–1929*, 126.
11. Notebook on "Feeling," 68.
12. RNN, 375–379. Television interview "Et liv," 1974, Norway.
13. Ibid., 375.
14. Notebook on "Feeling," 71.
15. RNN, 380.
16. Grigoriev, 123.
17. RNN, 380.
18. Ibid., 381. Telegram from Diaghilev to Daroso Mochi, Bibliothèque de l'Opéra, Paris, *Fonds Kochno*, 1.
19. Grigoriev, 124.
20. RNN, 382.
21. Notarized affidavit from Bankers Trust Company, New York, 6 December 1921. Nijinsky Archives.
22. Paul Claudel, describing Nijinsky dancing in Rio de Janeiro, in RNN, xv.
23. Letter from André de Badet, Nijinsky Archives.
24. Grigoriev, 126.
25. RNN, 392–395.
26. John Fraser, "The Diaghilev Ballet in South America."
27. Mardi J. Horowitz, *Stress Response Syndromes*.
28. RNN, 384, 391.
29. Letter from André de Badet to Romola Nijinsky, 16 June 1953. Nijinsky Archives.
30. Grigoriev, 128.
31. RNN, 389.
32. Arnold Haskell, *Diaghileff*, 247.
33. Fraser, 18.
34. Letter from André de Badet, see above.
35. Rubinstein, *My Many Years*, 12–16. Letters from Nijinsky to André de Badet and others, Bibliothèque de l'Opéra, Paris. Notebook on "Life," 86.

36. RNN, 397–400.
37. Ibid., 401.
38. Ralph Cope, *To Be an Invalid; The Illness of Charles Darwin.*
39. Notebook on "Life," 71–72.
40. William James, *Collected Essays and Reviews*, 428.
41. RNN, 397–400.
42. See lease agreement in the Nijinsky Archives. The house is still standing and may be visited with permission of the owners. It has been modernized and remodeled slightly since the Nijinskys lived there.
43. RNN, 402–403.
44. Paul Ehrler, *Heliotherapie.* See pages 15–26 for details about the life and work of Dr. Bernhard.
45. RNN, 403.
46. Notebook on "Feeling," 77–78.
47. Letter from Dr. "Greiber" to Eugen Bleuler, 2 March 1919.Zürich University Archives.
48. Letter from Marta Madeleine Grant to Igor Markevitch, September 1979. Nijinsky Archives.
49. RNN, 404.
50. Ibid., 404–405.
51. Arlene Croce, "The Tiresias Factor," 58.
52. RNN, 409.
53. Alessandra Comini, "Mother Russia at the Dawn of the Twentieth Century ..." Catalog.
54. Carl Gustav Jung, "Die Schizophrenie," 239.
55. Notebook on "Feeling," 81.
56. Letter to composer Reynaldo Hahn, in Paul Magriel (editor), *Nijinsky*, 76. Hahn does not say when in 1918 he received this letter from St. Moritz.
57. RNN, 413, 416. Letter to Badet, Bibliothèque de l' Opéra, Paris.
58. Personal communication from colleagues and relatives of Dr. "Greiber."
59. RNN, 406.
60. Records from Budapest-lipótmezö Hospital, 14 August 1941.
61. RNN, 420.
62. Ibid., 406.
63. Notebook on "Death," 106.
64. Grant, letter.
65. RNN, 408. Richard Buckle, *In the Wake of Diaghilev*, 250.
66. Marsden Hartley, "The Drawings of Nijinsky," 72.
67. Sigmund Freud, "Mourning and Melancholia."
68. RNN, 421.
69. Jeremy Bernstein, "The Sporting Scene: Raking."
70. RNN, 413–418. See also Notebook on "Life," 116–117.
71. Letter from Dr. "Greiber" to Eugen Bleuler, 2 March 1919." Zürich University Archives.
72. RNN, 420.
73. Ibid., 421.

People like eccentrics and they will
therefore leave me alone, saying that I
am a "mad clown."
                              Vaslav Nijinsky[1]

Chapter 8

Playing the Role of a Madman

With its central baroque façade, twin towers, and two great wings
set against a backdrop of pine trees on snow-covered fields, the Suvretta
House resembles a gigantic stage, and appropriately so, for close to two
hundred people had gathered there on Sunday, 19 January 1919, to
witness Nijinsky's first public performance since returning to Europe
in 1917. It was a motley crowd: some skiers and hotel guests; a few local
people who were curious about this famous dancer living in St. Moritz;
wealthy visitors from abroad, a few with titles that would become
worthless once the boundaries of Europe had been redefined; some
refugees from countries recently ruined by the war; and various and
assorted social climbers who mostly wanted to be seen in the best
circles. It was a perfect day, with crisp, cold weather and clear blue
skies. Now, with the sun receding and the mountains casting dark

shadows over the frozen lake, they wanted to go inside, to relax, gossip, have a drink, and be entertained. Chairs had been set up in one of the big salons, but no program was announced or printed for the performance scheduled to begin at 5 p.m.[2]

Nijinsky felt very "nervous" in anticipation of his recital, and was wondering who would be in the audience. Were they mostly "townsfolk"—in that case he would wear a simple "townsuit"—or was he expected to impress Romola's sister and her friends, who had recently arrived from Vienna? In that case he ought to be dressed "in expensive clothes so that everyone will think I am rich." His nervousness was affecting his digestion. "I do not want to dance on a full stomach . . . I shall dance when it all calms down and when everything drops out of my bowels." Before going to the hotel, he took a nap, then visited a dressmaker's shop to pick up some material for decorating the stage. He liked the dressmaker, a woman named Negri. In his excitement, he had asked her to bring "hundreds of yards of gorgeous colored silks, velvets, and lamés" to the house. Nijinsky felt sorry for Negri because she was "poor," had two children, and was married to a violinist who had to work nights at the Palace Hotel. Nijinsky had given Negri "a present" for her husband, "a pair of underpants and a sweater." He wanted to give her a present as well, "a warm jersey and a cap," and "something else for the children . . . I like giving to poor people whatever they are in need of."[3]

As Nijinsky approached the hotel, his nervousness became unbearable. He wondered if he would be able to control his trembling. Would the public "feel" what he intended to express, his anguish, his suffering, his guilt over the wartime death of young men? He told Romola that he wanted to demonstrate "the pangs of creation, the agony an artist has to go through when composing." She did not understand, but went with him to his dressing room. With a mournful expression he turned to her and said, cryptically, "Today is the day of my marriage to God." A friend of theirs from Vienna who played the piano had volunteered to provide the music for his dancing. "Please tell me," asked Romola, "what Bertha Asseo must play for you." This angered him. Without warning he became menacing and thundered at Romola, "Do not speak. *Silence!*" The tension became unbearable, so she left his dressing room and went into the salon to greet their guests. The pianist sat down and waited for instructions. The lights were dimmed. All conversation ceased.[4]

Suddenly the great dancer appeared, still very attractive with his muscular body, slender torso, beautifully sloping shoulders, long neck, oval face, and catlike eyes. He wore a pajamalike costume of white silk with a black border, no belt, and white sandals. With the taut grace of a tiger he walked over to the pianist and told her to play something by Chopin or Schumann. The music started. Nijinsky felt so tense he could barely move. People were staring at him. He picked up a chair, sat on it facing the audience, and stared back without moving a muscle. Everyone sat quietly, wondering what to make of this mute, immobile figure, with his penetrating eyes looking at them. The pianist played on. Time went by. Then, the music stopped and there was dead silence. It seemed endless. The music started again. But nothing else happened. Nijinsky just sat there. He seemed to be in a trance, and the people in the audience, too, were behaving as if under hypnosis.

Waiting and waiting, Romola became increasingly apprehensive, wondering whether he was in one of those "dark moods" she was so familiar with. How embarrassing to have this happen in public, and in front of their socially prominent friends. Was he again playing the "lunatic" to impress her and the rest of the audience with his unique talent for mimicry? Or was he conducting an experiment in modern ballet, consistent with other audacious choreography like *Sacre* or *Till Eulenspiegel* he had staged in the past? For a dancer to come on stage, sit down, not move, and simply stare at the audience was unheard of in 1919. Today, we would not be so shocked by it. In 1957 Paul Taylor made a big splash with *Events I,* a ballet in which he and his partner did almost nothing visible. "The stillnesses are important," writes Taylor, "as important as the negative space in paintings, the yin of the yang."

> With no dance steps for us to hide behind, even more than is usual the sequences are revealing us as people. Undisguised, our individual traits are laid bare, and our shapes, spacings, and timings are establishing definite emotional climates.... Posture has become gesture.[5]

Again Nijinsky was way ahead of his time. Finally, Romola could stand it no longer and went up to him to suggest that he perform something familiar, say a number from *Les Sylphides*. With that, the dancer exploded. "How dare you disturb me!" he snarled at her. "I am not a machine. I will dance when I feel like it." She became frightened and nearly burst into tears. Trying to control her agitation, she went outside to join her sister and some of the other guests who had left the ballroom in alarm, wondering what to make of Nijinsky's strange performance. Romola decided it would be best to stop him and go home, but before she could do so, the pianist began playing a familiar Chopin prelude. And now Nijinsky started to move in time to the music, matching each chord with a gesture. First he stretched his arms forward, hands raised vertically, palms outward as if to ward off danger. Then he spread his arms out sideways in a welcoming gesture. Next he brought them up high over his head, reaching upward as if praying. Finally he let them drop noisily, making it appear that the joints were broken.[6]

Nijinsky thought that he was doing a fine job transmitting his nervous excitement to the audience, communicating his sense of oneness with the universe. His body and soul seemed to be fused with God. ("I am God; I am Christ who fulfills God's commandments," he had written in a notebook.) He took pride in "playing nervously on purpose, because the public will understand me better if I am nervous." But it soon became apparent that many in the audience did *not* understand, and were annoyed with what he was doing. Some left the ballroom, and that made him feel even more nervous. The thought crossed his mind that they wanted to be "amused." So he launched into a "joyful, merry" dance. They seemed to like it; a few even started to laugh. That made Nijinsky happy. He too felt like "laughing."

Then his mood abruptly changed again. Suddenly he felt remorseful and very sad. His sense of contact with the audience receded, and that was very frightening because he yearned to "love" them and be loved in return. He came prepared, however. He picked up the rolls of cloth he had brought from the dressmaker's, unfurled the black and white velvet on the floor, and made an enormous cross spread over the entire stage. Standing stiffly at the head of the cross with his arms wide open, he looked like a crucified Jesus. Then, to everyone's surprise, he launched into a sermon. Speaking in a hollow voice and broken French, he told the audience about the horrible war just ended. Millions had died, mostly young men. "Now I will dance the war," he said, "the war which you did not prevent and are also responsible for." He began to move, faster and faster, and suddenly rose into the air. It was one of those spectacular leaps that he knew would "arouse" the audience. Romola wrote that his dancing was "as brilliant, as wonderful as ever, but it was different. Sometimes it vaguely reminded me of that scene in *Petrushka* when the puppet tries to escape his fate."

> He seemed to fill the room with horror-stricken suffering humanity. It was tragic; his gestures were monumental, and he entranced us so that we almost saw him floating over corpses. The public sat breathlessly horrified and so strangely fascinated.... Vaslav was like one of those overpowering creatures full of dominating strength, a tiger let out of the jungle who in any moment could destroy us.[7]

As his movements grew wilder, more violent, and less coherent, the audience became petrified. ("They think I want to kill them," Nijinsky wrote afterward.) There was not enough space for him to leap the way he intended, and at one point he stumbled, for which he blamed himself. ("I danced badly because I kept falling on the floor when I did not have to.") He was beginning to feel exhausted, like a "tired horse," but could not stop. "I wanted to dance more, but God said to me 'Enough.' I stopped. The public dispersed. The aristocrats and the rich public implored me to dance again. I said I was tired."[8]

During the reception afterward, Nijinsky continued to behave very strangely. When an "aristocratic" lady came up to him and asked to be introduced, he thought she wanted to flirt with him. ("She seems to like young men.") So he extended his hand ostentatiously and told her that she was moving in a very "exciting" way. This embarrassed her. Then, he showed her his foot, which was bleeding, and began preaching again. ("She does not like blood. I made her realize that blood is war and that I do not like war.") This put the woman off even more. Finally, he burst into a "tart's dance" and collapsed on the floor, which caused great bewilderment. ("She knew I was acting. The others thought I would lie down on the floor and make love.") Romola was terribly agitated by his behavior, and wanted to take him back to the villa. "I did not want to complicate the evening," noted Nijinsky, "and therefore got up whenever it was necessary." Before leaving the hotel, the Viennese woman who had played the piano for him turned to Romola and said, "It must be very, very difficult to be married to a genius like Nijinsky. I almost wish you could be free to marry one of our nice, charming, inoffensive compatriots."[9] Thoughts of remarriage were also in Nijinsky's mind, but they were more spiritual: "I felt God throughout the evening," he wrote. "He loved me. I loved him. We were married."[10]

The ensuing weeks brought increasing dissatisfaction. Nijinsky stopped sketching and removed all his drawings and paintings from the walls of his upstairs apartment. Instead of designing new ballets, he began to engage in a great deal of soul-searching and reflecting on the past. Every day he worked "feverishly" on his notebooks, sometimes all night as well. Romola was startled to observe his extreme self-absorption in literary work. Writing had always been difficult for Nijinsky; his vocabulary was limited and he often made mistakes in spelling and grammar. Now he seemed to be writing "with tremendous speed, and always in Russian." She tried to decipher the text—it seemed "almost illegible" to her—and she showed it to Dr. Greiber, who was equally puzzled. Romola noticed that "the two names Diaghilev and God" dominated Nijinsky's writing. This worried her deeply. "What was happening to Vaslav?"[11] The answer is that since his brother's death the dancer's transformation into a "lunatic" had been progressing. Nijinsky vividly described the process in his notebooks titled "Life," "Death," and "Feeling."

Before we examine these documents, let me say something about the so-called diary of Vaslav Nijinsky, which many people have come to regard as the definitive statement about his transformation into a madman. Widely read, translated, and reprinted, this diary has been compared to the work of William Blake, Walt Whitman, and Léon Bloy.[12] It is "impossible to overestimate the historical and human value of Nijinsky's Diary," wrote the Russian dancer Serge Lifar. Colin Wilson's *The Outsider,* a best-seller about existentialism, extensively quotes the diary to explain problems of alienation in modern society.[13] Psychoanalyst Karl Abenheimer plumbed the diary for Jungian insights into Nijinsky's mental state, and other scholarly works, as well as films and ballets, have been based on it.[14] But *The Diary of Vaslav Nijinsky* actually contains only a limited selection from the dancer's three notebooks, plus six letters he wrote in St. Moritz. With the help of Jennifer Mattingly, Romola rearranged and censored this material, translated it, and published it in 1936. In a preface to the 1971 edition she expressed the hope that the diary might serve "as a textbook for students of psychiatry."[15] We now know that long before she edited the notebooks and removed passages felt to be incoherent or embarrassing, they had already been used for clinical purposes, by Dr. Greiber, who treated Nijinsky in St. Moritz, and by psychiatrists in Zürich, where he was briefly hospitalized. Generous selections from the notebooks were transcribed into Nijinsky's hospital records there. But in accordance with the rules of medical confidentiality, this material was never made public. Thus some parts of the diary very important for understanding Nijinsky's illness have remained completely unknown to biographers.

After Romola's death in 1978, Nijinsky's notebooks were completely translated for the first time by Kyril FitzLyon in London, who took pains to preserve their authentic organization and precise linguistic structure. Thus, it was discovered that Romola had "suppressed approximately one third of the original, excising long erotic passages, poems, including one on defecation, explicit sexual references and obsessive repetition, transposing or omitting whole pages or passages, often altering their sequence."[16] Nijinsky's original handwritten manuscript consists of 381 pages, forty-four in pencil, the rest in ink (except for thirty-one pages that are blank). By comparing it with the published *Diary*, one begins to appreciate the true purposes of the notebooks, and an important reason why Romola felt it necessary to censor them. Nijinsky wanted to keep an independent record not only of his mental disorder, but also of the triangle situation that had been developing between him, his wife, and his doctor. His opening sentence reads: "I can no longer trust my wife for I have felt that she wants to give these notes to Dr. Greiber for examination." He then described what he thought and felt about going "mad." Clearly, Nijinsky was trying to understand himself. The notebooks are his self-analysis, written in much the same way as would a person who is undergoing psychoanalysis, with all kinds of fantasies, memories, and free associations brought into the open.

One detects a running battle throughout the notebooks between Nijinsky and his doctor as well as with other men about whom he had strong feelings, Diaghilev quite understandably being one of the most important. Greiber was indeed trying to psychoanalyze Nijinsky. He had attended Professor Bleuler's lectures while a medical student in Zürich. He had heard about the use of free association, dream interpretation, and Rorschach (inkblot) projective testing used in this field. But Greiber was no expert in psychiatry; his specialty, as mentioned earlier, was sports medicine. Apparently he got caught up in a tremendously powerful transference, in which Nijinsky projected or acted out all kinds of unconscious fantasies and delusions. The countertransference was probably also highly charged, since Greiber apparently was in love with the patient's wife.

One of the first things he tried was to delve into Nijinsky's family background and explore his developmental history. "It is to be emphasized," Greiber wrote in a long medical report, "that [Nijinsky's] father betrayed his mother early on by taking a mistress, and after being very rough with his wife, he abandoned her in favor of his beloved. The mother seems to be psychologically intact [but] is said to have much influence over the patient. A brother died recently in an insane asylum...." Greiber also pumped Romola for information about what Nijinsky was like before their marriage.

> The patient's wife portrays him as always having been a strange, eccentric person. Nijinsky's valet, who knew him well, told her the same thing. Evidently his education in a Russian ballet-school was primitive, and his achievements in all subjects not connected with his dance development were mediocre.[17]

Greiber was impressed with the "sharp differences in education, intelligence, and culture" between Nijinsky and his wife. Romola, he wrote, "stems from a culturally high-standing Hungarian family and regards her husband as a type of Russian peasant; brutal, violent fits of temper." Greiber felt that because Romola "loved Nijinsky so much she accommodated herself for a long time to his incessant demands 'for her to be like him.' She allowed him to force his grotesque and abnormal theories on her. Yes, she even believed that *her* ways of thinking might be abnormal."[18]

Greiber made an effort to explore the couple's intimate relationships, and concluded that their "sexual life was normal." But he found that Romola was subject to "neurasthenic and hysterical tendencies." As for Nijinsky, "In his youth the patient showed a tendency to be moody.... Despite many opportunities throughout his career, he has always rejected women." This is an odd statement, considering that the doctor thought Vaslav and Romola were having a "normal" sex life. Perhaps he meant other women, but that was untrue, since Nijinsky liked prostitutes. The doctor mentioned nothing about the dancer's homosexuality. (Nijinsky was less squeamish in his self-analysis; he wrote very frankly about his relations with Diaghilev and other men.) Doctor Greiber did record a medical history of sorts, but missed the important facts about the dancer's early cerebral damage, gonorrhea, typhoid, and other major health problems:

> Somatically I find nothing of significance. Syphilis is denied. No drinking. Nicotine very rarely. Alcohol nearly abstinent. He does not hear voices. Sleeps generally well. Occasionally he eats enormous amounts, then again little ... he is ironic, mischievous, argumentative,

torments everyone with his remarks, suddenly pounds the table with his
fist ... stares at his wife, why? to impress her. In response to my
reproach that this makes his wife suffer, that he is torturing her and
bringing her close to distraction, he says that he intends nothing
harmful, he is no wild man, *she* is nervous. After one of his scenes he
locks himself into his study all night, and improvises on the piano.... He
claims that he does everything on purpose "in order to play the fool." His
wife says that he is a comedian from A to Z.[19]

About a week after the dance recital, Greiber started to psychoanalyze Nijinsky in earnest. Evidently he had heard about Carl Jung's
work with severely disturbed patients. It was believed in those days that
even psychotic patients could benefit from dream analysis and the
exploration of unconscious fantasy. The aim was to provide "insight."
(That insight does not necessarily provide relief, and may in fact be
harmful, was not yet well understood.) By the end of World War I,
Switzerland had become one of the few countries in the world where
psychoanalysis was an acceptable medical procedure, and could even be
practiced by psychologists and clergymen.[20]

Dr. Greiber tried to spend some time with the dancer nearly every
day. All this attention puzzled Nijinsky, and he resisted it. In his
notebook he wrote, "Dr. Greiber's questions were not rational. I
answered him quickly and logically. My wife answered him quickly and
illogically." He resented Greiber's attempt to examine his "brain," and
made an effort to examine the doctor's "mind" in turn. For a while
Nijinsky remained suspicious, said little, hid his notebooks, and
"pretended on purpose to be mad." The doctor tried different ways of
overcoming his resistance. He showed Nijinsky "obscene pictures," and
encouraged him to reveal his fantasies. (This may have been a way of
probing the dancer's sexuality.) Nijinsky wrote that his "heart would
break" when he looked at the "filth." The pictures reminded him of a
time in Vienna when he used pornography to overcome Romola's
"boredom." He had wanted her to "engage in debauch." (The notebook
does not explain what was meant by that, only that Greiber's "obscene
pictures" served to get Vaslav very excited, and that he remembered
having had to "force" Romola to become aroused.[21])

These and other sexual topics were recorded helter-skelter in
Nijinsky's notebooks. He describes his worship of the penis, and his
curiosity as well as dread regarding female sexual organs. He makes
many equations between the vagina, the mouth, and the rectum. There

are long discussions of homosexual "perversion," prostitution, bestiality (women copulating with monkeys; his own masturbation with dogs). Themes of incest abound; an erotic interest is expressed in Romola's sister, and in Kyra. (Almost all this material was deleted from the *Diary.*) Whether some of it came spontaneously, and how much was suggested by Greiber's clinical probing, is impossible to say. The doctor even tried to use word-association tests of the type invented by Carl Jung. These consist of strings of unrelated words, to which one must respond by saying or writing down the first word that comes to mind. There are two ways to respond. One is by way of semantic association. For instance, when hearing the word "tree," one might think of words like "elm, "wood," "green," or "climbing," all connected through meaning. The other way to respond is phonetically, according to the sound of the word, instead of its meaning. "Tree" can make one think of "free," "three," or "she." In ordinary conversation, one usually inhibits the phonetic associations in favor of the semantic ones. The opposite holds true for poetry, where equal or even higher values are placed on the way words sound.

As his notebooks show, Nijinsky was inclined to take Greiber's test words as stimuli for producing rhymes—"I wrote some poetry so that the doctor could observe the workings of my brain"—not surprising, considering first of all that Nijinsky was an artist, and second that the words were in a foreign language (probably French; possibly German). Greiber regarded Nijinsky's poetry (in Russian!) to be distinctly psychopathological, "various clang-associations . . . pages full of stereo-typed, monotonous, repetitive phrases,"[22] and Romola took pains to eliminate every bit of it from the *Diary.* Not that the world has thereby lost a great poet—Nijinsky was better at dancing than at writing—but the uncensored notebooks show more convincingly Nijinsky's struggle to express artistically his thoughts about love, religion, sex, and scatology. The first poem, four pages long, focuses on his adoration of Christ: "I am Christ's blood. . . . I love you, always. Rockabye, Rock-abye." (Because of copyright limitations I can quote only a few lines.) The second poem, three pages long, is about sleeping and "shitting." I have asked a Russian expert in linguistics, Professor Vyacheslav Ivanov from Moscow, to examine this work.

Nijinsky seems to be playing with words that have many possible associations. One observes numerous anagrams (ciphers). He uses spaces between words to indicate silence, which is a typical Russian cultural feature. For example, 'Gulia gulia gulia lia lia/Lia gu lia gu lia gu lia/.' These sounds refer to body movements; *gulia* alludes to 'walking'; *liagu* means 'I will lie down' (with possible erotic connotations). *Gu* also has a primitive association to baby-talk. *Ni gu gu* implies 'not a word, to be absolutely silent.' It seems that Nijinsky was struggling with the problem of whether to speak or express himself without words.[23]

Another Nijinsky poem is about "mother earth." In trying to make the rhymes, he often got stuck on certain words, or parts of words. (This is what Dr. Greiber called "stereotyped, monotonous, repetitive phrases.") For example, "I love everyone everyone everyone .... I want to tell all all.... You sleep sleep sleep sleep sleep sleep sleep." He seemed unable to stop a train of words, and behaved almost like a child just learning to speak, who feels compelled to "babble" new words over and over again. What caused this perseveration is hard to say. Part of it may have been due to Nijinsky's long-standing linguistic disability, probably a congenital dyslexia or some sort of stammering. Another factor may have been the chloral hydrate sedative Dr. Greiber was prescribing, for sedatives cause attention to wander. Finally, it must be pointed out that to practice certain moves and gestures over and over is adaptive, and consistent with a dancer's career.

Throughout his notebooks, Nijinsky emphasized that he was trying to communicate with an unseen audience. He sought to convey information about his life and his feelings to people who would never be able to see him dance. He seemed to be aware that a process had been set in motion that could go far beyond the immediate goal of his self-analysis. He wanted his discoveries to be published "soon" in a book that would bring "a lot of money" and make Romola "happy." He wanted "peace for everyone and the earth to be full of love." He realized that the sexually explicit content of the notebooks might make publication difficult, but might also bring him income (as the *Faune* had led to notoriety). "The Swiss will prohibit it."

Nijinsky was very sensitive to the calligraphy of his writing, the quality of the paper, and the feel of the pen or pencil as he moved it across the pages. He hoped that his manuscripts would be photographed rather than set in type, so that readers might appreciate not only what he had to say, but also the way he moved while expressing himself. Toward this goal, he even tried to design some special tools, to make his handwriting more legible. When he ran out of ink, he sought to invent "a perfect fountain pen" with a permanent supply of "thick ink." This was an imaginative forerunner of today's ballpoint pen. Without any formal knowledge of engineering, however, Nijinsky's sketches for a "new pen" look crude, like children's drawings, as do his designs for "a round pencil with ink," with which he hoped to replace the lead pencils that kept breaking as he labored over his notebooks day and night. Another facet of his inventiveness was to design a "bridge" that might connect Europe to America one day. He envisioned a heavy cable from which trains could be suspended. Nijinsky's interest clearly was in communication and contact, rather than withdrawal and isolation. (That is an important diagnostic point. There is nothing basically bizarre or "crazy" about Nijinsky's writing.) While the drawings he made for a transatlantic bridge look primitive, they do anticipate an age of undersea cabling and telecommunication, which other visionaries (Jules Verne even earlier than Nijinsky) were predicting.

Very prominent in his notebooks is a quest for identity—the search for answers to the question "Who am I?" Nijinsky characterized himself as a "simple" man, the helpless, victimized husband of a wife who cannot understand or "feel" as he does. He also saw himself as the maligned father of a child who will not obey him. His concerns about "feeling" seem typically Russian (one entire notebook is devoted to the subject). Do people understand him by what he "feels" or what he thinks? Feelings are tremendously important for Russians, perhaps more important than mind and intellect. In Russia, one criterion for believing someone to be "mad" is when that person stops feeling and thinks too much.[24] Nijinsky fretted over the question of whether he was an "artist" or a spiritual leader. He compared himself to Christ and Tolstoy. He felt he was a "God," who bears personal responsibility for peace and universal brotherhood. He yearned to involve himself in the armistice talks then going on in Europe. He wanted to advise the British Prime Minister David Lloyd George, and the French Premier Georges Clemenceau, and the Polish President-in-Exile Ignace Jan Paderewski. These were grandiose fantasies, inflated by Nijinsky's sense of self-importance. But they were also connected to his unresolved love-hate relationship with Diaghilev, which preoccupied him a great deal. Diaghilev was more crafty and had greater political skill than he did. Nijinsky thought that Lloyd George resembled Diaghilev; his "intentions are terrible." Clemenceau on the other hand "seeks the truth." Paderewski "is not a paederast" (an example of punning, or what Dr.

Greiber called "clang-associations"). Paramount in Nijinsky's estima-
tion was Woodrow Wilson, President of the United States, for whom he
had once danced and with whose pacifism he identified. "Wilson wants
to stop the war but men do not understand him."

Intermingled with these positive self-images are more negative ones.
Nijinsky viewed himself as a "clown," and a "lunatic." He recognized a
similarity between himself and his dead brother, whose "lunacy" he
could understand. (I have commented earlier on the impact of seeing
the psychotic Stanislav in the hospital, and the balletic use Nijinsky
may have made of his brother's pathological movements and postures.)
He feared that, like his brother, he might be crippled or bent out of
shape. Now that he was "playing" the role of a madman, Nijinsky
sensed that there were many things wrong with his body. His bowels did
not work properly. He was a "hunchback," a "monster," a "bandit." He
felt estranged from society. Logic no longer had any meaning. Everything revolved around pure emotion. "I kill my brain. I do not want
intellectualization." He experienced overwhelming fear and immense
sadness (some of this may have been medication-induced). There was a
profound "emptiness" in his soul.

Nijinsky's haunting memories of childhood, his family's poverty, his
archaic fear of "starvation" unless he provides for his mother, the
drowning episode with his father, and other key events of his developmental history were also mentioned in his notebooks and have been
described earlier. What use Greiber made of this information is difficult
to say. If Greiber gave advice, explanations, or interpretations, these
probably fell on deaf ears, for Nijinsky often commented that he was in
no mood for an "intellectual" approach and that "thinking" was not the
answer to his problems. (When the Jungian psychiatrist Karl
Abenheimer reviewed the Diary, he commented that Nijinsky seemed
"indefinite," showed "increased suggestibility," and had "histrionic"
tendencies. These would have made psychoanalysis very difficult.[25])
How the inexperienced Dr. Greiber handled the "God" Nijinsky's
inflamed pride and impotent rage is anybody's guess. Did he try to cut
him down to size by appealing to his sense of reality? Did he indulge his
grandiosity by flattering the dancer, thinking this would reassure him
and make him more tractable? Nijinsky wrote, "I think better than Dr.
Greiber," which may have been true, but could have been a source of
resistance to psychotherapy.

Additional resistance probably arose from the eroticized transference that developed in the course of Nijinsky's psychotherapy with Greiber. Not since Diaghilev had any man taken so much interest in him or encouraged him to use his imagination so freely. Thus, it is not surprising that both submissive and rivalrous attitudes were evoked toward the doctor, similar to what Nijinsky had experienced in earlier relationships with men. "I love Dr. Greiber," he writes. "He is a good doctor. He is beginning to feel me.... I love my wife and Dr. Greiber equally." Nijinsky yearned to be with him constantly. He felt he had to "obey his commands." He wandered around St. Moritz looking for him, and felt upset if he saw him talking to someone else. To "act nervous on purpose" was one way of attracting the doctor's attention. In a letter Nijinsky wrote at this time to "the Man" (obviously Diaghilev), he revealed mechanisms of approach-avoidance, simultaneous loving and hating, and playful ambivalence, which had probably characterized his earlier homosexual relationships.

> To the Man,
>   I cannot name you because I have no name for you. I am not writing you hastily. I don't want you to think that I am nervous, I am not.... I love you as one loves a human being, but I do not want to work with you.... I do not call you my friend, knowing that you are my bitter enemy, but even so I have no ill feelings toward you .... I am not writing in order to make you merry, I am willing to make you cry .... I know all your tricks. In the past when I was with you I often pretended to be nervous.... I am a tender being and want to write you a cradle song.... Sleep peacefully. Man to Man.[26]

After four weeks of treatment, Nijinsky seems to have been so thoroughly confused that he wondered if he might indeed be going "insane" (he used the Russian term for madness, literally "soul-sickness"). He felt that Greiber did not really "understand" him, and that Romola was no longer to be trusted either. "She thinks that Dr. Greiber is God. She trusts a stranger rather than myself. I do not like clever Romola.... She thinks that I am either mad or bad." In an oppressive mood of self-analytic melancholia (perhaps complicated by overmedication), Nijinsky wrote in his notebook called "Death":

> I want to weep but I cannot because my soul hurts so much that I fear for myself. I feel pain. I am sick in my soul but not in my brain. The doctor does not understand my sickness. I know what I need in order to be well.

My sickness is too great for me to be cured soon. I am not incurable. I am sick in my soul. I am poor. I am a beggar. I'm unhappy. I'm hideous. I know that everybody will suffer while reading these lines because they will feel me [i.e., feel what I feel]. I know well what I need. I am a strong and not a weak man. I am not sick in my body. I am sick in my soul. I suffer. I suffer. I know that Kostrovsky will feel what I feel and I also know that everyone will feel what I feel. I am a man and not a beast. I love everybody. I also have faults. I am a man and not God. I want to be God and therefore I work on myself. I want to dance. I want to draw. I want to play piano. I want to write verse. I want to compose ballets. I want to love everyone. This is the aim of my life. I know that socialists will understand me, but I am not a socialist. I am God. I have God's part. I love everybody. I don't want war. I don't want borders or separate states. I want Wilsonism, which will improve the whole earth. I am the earth. I have views everywhere. I live everywhere. I do not want to own property. I do not want to be rich. I want to love, to love. I am love and not bestiality. I am not a bloodthirsty animal. I am a man.[27]

Because it was obvious that Greiber's treatment had gotten nowhere, a more experienced physician would have to be consulted. Romola wanted Nijinsky to be seen by "somebody great like Lombroso, a genius who could understand and help him."[28] That was totally unrealistic because the Italian criminologist Cesare Lombroso had died in 1909. She then asked her mother and stepfather to come to Switzerland and advise her what to do. (Before going to St. Moritz, Oscar Párdány had to apply for funds from the Hungarian government. On 24 February 1919 he was granted a stipend of 10,000 Hungarian crowns.)[29] They arrived at the end of the month. At first Nijinsky refused to speak to his mother-in-law. He felt "angry" at Emilia Márkus and provocatively put food on her plate when they had meals together and then grabbed it away. (Nijinsky still was making a fuss over eating no meat.) He felt he had to match wits with a "very good actress.... She reminds me of Diaghilev.... I play-act because God wants me to, while my wife's mother play-acts for selfish reasons." After that he became childish and unpredictable, would talk to no one at dinner, glared at his wife, then suddenly smashed his fist on the table saying he had "to crack a nut."[30]

Very frightening was Nijinsky's threat to "shoot a bullet through my brain, if that is what God wants." He told Greiber that he could no longer "control his moods."[31] He thought (and may have talked) about Emilia Márkus being killed, fantasies that were stimulated, as we learn from his notebooks, by what he had learned from Romola about a jealous dresser at the theater in Budapest. This woman is said to have been "in love" with Emilia Márkus and threatened to kill her with a pistol. "The woman became angry and shot at the door." Nijinsky also mentioned that he could "understand" why Romola's father had "shot himself." Romola reacted with understandable terror when she read or heard about the homicide and suicide themes. Dr. Greiber shared her anxiety. On 2 March 1919 he sent a telegram to Zürich, followed by a letter, asking if Professor Eugen Bleuler, director of the Burghölzli University Psychiatric Hospital there, would agree to see Nijinsky in consultation.

Bleuler was one of Europe's foremost diagnosticians. He had recently coined the word "schizophrenia", literally "splitting of the mind," to describe a psychological process that he believed to be responsible for many mental diseases. "Schizophrenics," thought Bleuler, were people whose thoughts typically followed no logical sequence, veered off in unexpected directions, or got completely stuck. Such individuals tended to focus all their attention on themselves—he called this "autism"—and to have reduced or inappropriate emotional reactions as well as ambivalent social attitudes. Bleuler believed that many additional symptoms flowed from these "primary" psychopathological processes, including delusions, hallucinations, and disturbances of speech and behavior. He had presented his theory of schizophrenia in the form of a monograph, published in 1911, and included it in every edition of his widely read *Textbook of Psychiatry*.[32]

In his letter to Professor Bleuler, Greiber stressed that he did not know "whether one is justified to speak of schizophrenia" in Nijinsky's case. "The findings seem to me to justify the diagnosis of at least a psychosis with paranoid and catatonic content." Greiber made it clear that he wanted to have Bleuler take charge and get himself out of the difficult situation he had gotten into by trying to treat the patient in St. Moritz: "I ask you, honorable Professor, for your support [and] for your detailed suggestions in regard to therapy, which undoubtedly will be followed without reservation by the relatives."[33] Greiber wrote Bleuler that "the patient himself spontaneously expresses the wish for a psychiatric examination" and that Romola's parents intended "to stay in Zürich as long as necessary for making a diagnosis, and are completely at your disposal in respect to your orders."

The prospect of meeting Professor Bleuler seems to have animated Nijinsky. He wrote excitedly about wanting to "study in Zürich together with God." He planned to wear his "good suit," pretend to be a "rich foreigner," go to the Stock Exchange, and make lots of money. "My wife wants me to go to Zürich to see a specialist for nerves ... I promised her 100,000 francs if she is right about my nerves being in a bad way.... She wants to have a child, a little boy, a reincarnation of me, as she is afraid I will soon die. She thinks I am mad."[34] But a mix-up in the train schedule delayed their departure. The "silly" maid had forgotten to tell Romola's parents the correct time. This put Romola and Emilia in a "bad mood," and made Oscar "nervous." A quarrel ensued. Nijinsky told Romola that if she continued to be "afraid of him" he would willingly stay in a "lunatic asylum." Let them put him "in a prison" if necessary. What about Kyra? Romola told him to tell the child he would probably not be coming back to St. Moritz for a while.

> The maid came and stood near me, thinking that I was sick. I am not. I am healthy. I am afraid for myself because I know God's wish. God wants my wife to leave me. I do not want it, I love her and will pray that she may remain with me. They are telephoning about something. I believe they want to send me to prison. I am weeping, as I love life, but I am not afraid of prison. I will live there. I have explained everything to my wife about the revolver. She is no longer afraid, but she still has a nasty feeling....
> My little girl is singing: "Ah, ah, ah, ah!" I do not understand its meaning, but I feel what she wants to say. She wants to say that everything—Ah! Ah!—is not horror but joy.[35]

It takes four hours to get from St. Moritz to Zürich by train. Rooms had been booked at the fashionable Hotel Savoy Baur-en-Ville, not far from the railway station. Nijinsky with his wife and parents-in-law settled in on Tuesday 4 March. Two days later Romola took a cab to Burghölzli, a twenty-minute drive to the western outskirts of Zürich, for a conference with Professor Bleuler. "Vaslav did not want to accompany me. Bleuler was an old man [in fact only sixty-two] with an infinite understanding in his eyes. I spoke to him about Vaslav, myself, our marriage, and life for almost two hours."[36]

Eugen Bleuler was one of three German-speaking physicians whose ideas have left a deep imprint on the practice of psychiatry. The first was Emil Kraepelin (1856–1926), a descriptive psychopathologist and systematizer. His influential textbook—the first edition came out when Kraepelin was only twenty-seven years old!—put the many forms of mental disease described by his predecessors into neat categories based on causes, symptoms, course, and outcome of each condition. Psychiatry having come of age rather late in Germany, Kraepelin's great contribution was to bring logic into a somewhat disorganized field of medicine. One of his most brilliant ideas had been to separate "manic-depressive psychosis," a recurring and more benign form of madness beginning in adult life, from "precocious dementia," a more malignant disease of childhood and adolescence. The second great pioneer was the Viennese neurologist Sigmund Freud (1856–1939), who made his mark on psychiatry by establishing plausible connections between mental diseases and psychological conflicts. Freud emphasized the role of sexual frustration and inhibited aggression. Especially valuable was his invention of psychoanalysis, a verbal dialogue that aimed at reducing unconscious discord between biological drives ("id"), adaptational resources ("ego"), and moral-ethical demands ("super-ego"). Eugen Bleuler (1857–1939), a Swiss psychiatrist only a year younger than Freud and Kraepelin, attempted with his dynamic concept of "schizophrenia" to integrate the somewhat divergent approaches of these two men. Bleuler believed that the course of many illnesses previously thought to be incurable (for example, "dementia praecox") could be altered by psychotherapy and social rehabilitation. He wanted psychiatrists to use their personal influence to improve the lives of patients in all sorts of practical ways, by changing their family environment, finding work for them, having meals together, even picking out their clothes. Bleuler thought that it was far better to treat mentally ill people within the community, rather than in a hospital, where confinement tended to foster dependency and expose the patients to a regressive lifestyle. Other dangers to mental health, in Bleuler's opinion, were indolence, dishonesty, alcohol abuse, and what he called "autistic and undisciplined thinking," the tendency to stray away from logic and reality. [37]

While listening to what Romola had to say about Nijinsky, Bleuler noted some discrepancies. Dr. Greiber's letter said the dancer had attacked his mother-in-law. Romola told Bleuler this was a "misunderstanding." He asked her to describe Nijinsky's behavior at Villa Guardamunt, and noted that "she can no longer tolerate it."

> For example, he stares at his child, says bring me this or that, but does not say what, and when in despair she brings him something, he accuses her that it isn't the right thing, that she is supposed to guess his thoughts. [38]

Bleuler also expressed interest in Nijinsky's recent ballet recital. His conclusion was that "according to the unanimous report of the relatives, Nijinsky's expressions and also his performance had become obscene, he no longer danced, but produced peculiar mimicry, threw pieces of cloth around himself, tied a bow to his leg, and did similar things which were supposed to represent something, but nobody could understand the connections." The way Romola remembered this interview, Bleuler seemed concerned but not overly "worried" about Nijinsky. "The symptoms you describe in the case of an artist and a Russian do not in themselves prove any mental disturbances," she recalls him saying. She felt "relieved," and after returning to the hotel told Nijinsky how nice Bleuler was: "he thought I was healthy and that we could now have a son." Considering the magnitude of the dancer's suffering, her comments seem both naive and inconsiderate. Romola writes that "in a happy mood, we went out shopping, and I noticed that Vaslav stopped before the window of a great department store where babies' layettes were exposed; he smiled, and I knew he was thinking of the son he so ardently desired."[39]

The next day, 6 March, both of them went to Burghölzli. Here is Professor Bleuler's report:

I was consulted on Thursday. The man came up with a few difficulties, showed fear of being declared mentally ill and answered my questions for the most part with a flood of words behind which there wasn't much substance, or with evasions. He constantly had to ask me how I can recognize mentally ill people etc., explains that he acted like a mentally ill person in front of his wife in order to see how she reacts to that, and therefore sometimes just stared into a corner. He guarded himself against giving information about any delusions. Intelligence evidently very good in the past, now he is a confused schizophrenic with mild manic excitement.

The term "confused schizophrenic" must be put in a historical context. Bleuler did not say that Nijinsky was hearing voices, having persecutory delusions, talking about bizarre ideas, experiencing intrusive thoughts, or behaving incoherently—all signs of schizophrenia (unless some other condition like epilepsy, intoxication, mental deficiency, or organic brain disease can account for them). It was the "flood of words" containing little "substance," the evasiveness and guardedness, the querulous asking "how do you know when someone is mentally ill," and the inappropriate mood (plus of course what Romola and Dr. Greiber had told him about Nijinsky) that alerted Bleuler to the presence of a psychosis. That the dancer did not speak German and could not communicate very well in French made it extremely difficult to find out what was really on his mind, whether he was truly psychotic or simply pretending to be mad. Bleuler appreciated Nijinsky's "very good" intelligence, but thought he was "confused." He seemed to be in an elated mood, and smiling, which together with his pressured speech called for the diagnosis of a "mild manic excitement," leaving the door open to the possibility of manic-depressive psychosis rather than schizophrenia. (It is not an easy distinction, even today.[40])

Perhaps even more important than the ambiguity of Bleuler's diagnosis is the recommendation he made in regard to treatment. He did not believe that Nijinsky should be hospitalized. He felt that the dancer was confused, inappropriately excited, making his family miserable, and behaving "obscenely." To confine him with people who were even more disturbed might lead him to acquire other deplorable habits. Bleuler recognized Nijinsky to have powerful histrionic instincts, aggressive fits of temper, and great physical strength. Trying to control someone like that in a hospital would surely lead to trouble. The dancer lacked empathy for his wife and daughter, had abused them, and had been assaultive toward others as well. "Just let him go," Bleuler advised Romola. She should get a divorce. It would be far better for Nijinsky to be free of family obligations. The idea of having him father another child was totally unacceptable. (Bleuler was so worried about the inheritance of mental disease—there had been psychosis in his family— that he advised his own son not to marry until reaching the age when schizophrenia—or dementia praecox as it was also called—could be ruled out.) Bleuler emphasized to Romola that it would be far better to let the dancer go on with his career any way he wanted, as long as this did not endanger him or harm others.

She was horrified by the professor's recommendation. For seven years she had devoted herself to this capricious man, who first eluded her and then impulsively married her. Now he seemed deranged and was blaming *her* for being "nervous." It was "brutal," she writes, for Bleuler to advise her, after just a brief consultation, to let him go. "I did not listen; I had to get out of there quickly. I felt the place was going round with me faster and faster in a circle." Romola thought she heard Bleuler say: "Now my dear, be very brave. You have to take your child away; you have to get a divorce. Unfortunately I am helpless. Your husband is incurably insane."[41] This is an overstatement. "Incurable insanity" not only contradicts what Bleuler wrote in his clinical report, but also runs counter to his well-known therapeutic optimism. Bleuler was only too well aware that many prominent men and women continue to function admirably after a mental illness (composer Robert Schumann was one of the examples he gave in his famous monograph).

Bleuler explained to Romola how a marital separation could be achieved without further endangering Nijinsky's reputation. He knew of an excellent private sanatorium in Kreuzlingen, a village on the Lake of Constance near the Swiss-German border, where the dancer could live comfortably, be well taken care of, work on his choreography, and recover from his present state of psychosis. Such an arrangement would allow Romola to return to St. Moritz with her parents and take care of Kyra without having to be unduly worried about her husband. This sanatorium, called Kuranstalt Bellevue, had been founded in 1857 by the grandfather of its current director, Dr. Ludwig Binswanger, a psychoanalyst noted for his special interest in the lives of people with unusual creative ability. Binswanger was a close friend of Freud, whose own patients he occasionally took into the Kuranstalt. Surely this humane physician would find a way to rehabilitate Nijinsky and help Romola to cope with the stress of separation and divorce. But Romola indicated that this was unacceptable. "She did not want to take my advice," Bleuler wrote in his file on Nijinsky; "She feared that in his present confusion he will go to pieces, and then most surely would blame himself at performances."[42]

How would Nijinsky have fared had Bleuler's advice been accepted? One can only speculate. We know that he yearned to go back to Russia. In a letter written to his mother from St. Moritz (but never mailed) he expressed his wish to be reunited with her. His notebooks also comment on his sister and her family, who had "escaped from Moscow to get away from the Maximalists."[43] (They had moved to Kiev, where in February 1919 Bronislava Nijinska opened an École de Mouvement to teach her brother's ballet technique.) It seems reasonable to assume that they might have teamed up again. She, too, had had marital problems. (Bronislava was happier with her second husband, with whom she had a son.) Possibly Vaslav might also have remarried. But life in postrevolutionary Russia would have been unbearably grim for him. Those were the years of famine, fuel shortages, complete breakdown of the

Nijinsky, age 27, as *Till Eulenspiegel*, in the ballet he premiered in New York and took on tour throughout the United States, 1916–1917.

St. Moritz in 1917, when Nijinsky moved there. The Villa Guardamunt, where he, Romola, and Kyra were living, is the smaller of two houses uphill to the right of the thin church steeple, near the road ascending to the Chanterella Hotel, where Nijinsky often went walking. (Author's collection)

The Villa Guardamunt, St. Moritz, today. (Author's collection)

One of the many "circular" drawings made by Nijinsky in St. Moritz in 1918. (Nijinsky Archives)

Nijinsky's handwritten score for *Les Papillons de la Nuit*, one of several ballets he worked on in St. Moritz in 1918. (Nijinsky Archives)

Ludwig Binswanger, M.D., Director of the Bellevue Sanatorium in Kreuzlingen, Switzerland, who supervised Nijinsky's treatment and was his psychiatrist in 1919. (Binswanger Archives)

The Parkhaus where Nijinsky lived when in the Bellevue Sanatorium in Kreuzlingen. (Binswanger Archives)

Lounge of Villa Bellevue, Bellevue Sanatorium, where Nijinsky danced before invited guests and patients of Dr. Binswanger. (Binswanger Archives)

Drawing made by Nijinsky in 1919, after Romola signed him out of the Bellevue Sanatorium against medical advice (note the disorganization of form, compared to earlier drawing). (Nijinsky Archives)

Vaslav Nijinsky, age 34, with his daughter Tamara, age 2-1/2, taken in Paris in 1923. (Nijinsky Archives)

Vaslav Nijinsky, age 37, during a phase of catatonic depression in Paris while Romola was in the United States. (Nijinsky Archives)

Nijinsky, age 40, on the stage of the Paris Opera, with (left to right) Benois, Grigoriev, Karsavina and Diaghilev. (Nipnitski, Paris)

Manfred Sakel, M.D., the inventor of "insulin-shock," at the Bellevue Sanatorium where he treated Nijinski in 1938. (N.Y. Public Library, Lincoln Center)

Nijinsky, age 49, at the time of his first course of insulin-shock treatment with Dr. Sakel in Switzerland. (Nijinsky Archives)

Nijinsky, age 50, when Serge Lifar visited him at the
hospital in Münsingen.

Karl Kämpf, the male nurse to whom Nijinsky became attached while a patient at the
Münsingen hospital. (Nijinsky Archives)

Nijinsky, at age 51, with his wife, while living with Emilia Márkus (right) in Budapest, 1940. (Courtesy Dr. Michael Cenner)

The house in Budapest, owned by Nijinsky's mother-in-law Emilia Márkus, where he and Romola lived during the First and Second World Wars. (Nijinsky Archives)

Wreckage left by one of Nijinsky's temper outbursts at the Márkus house in Budapest in 1941. (Nijinsky Archives)

The last photograph of Nijinsky, in London with his wife shortly before his death at age 61 in 1950. (BBC)

railways, "drastic enforcement of absolute State monopoly," and whole-sale political terrorism. Many artists tried to escape (as Nijinsky's sister did in 1921), were imprisoned, or committed suicide.[44]

Another possibility would have been to take refuge in Paris, Vienna, London, New York, or one of the other world capitals where he had made a name for himself. But what sort of an adjustment would have been possible once Nijinsky reached the age where dancing in public was no longer feasible? (Ballet dancers, men especially, tend to retire early, often in their thirties or forties.) Given Nijinsky's personal handicaps, would be have been able to support himself as a teacher, a painter, or a writer? Only with the greatest difficulty, I suspect. We have already heard about his borderline social adjustment, wandering the streets of Paris, entering a London poorhouse, drifting around St. Moritz. Romola knew Nijinsky far better than Bleuler did, and she was probably right in wanting to protect him from what might have led to a vagabond existence. Another pessimistic prediction, considering his severe mood disorder and violent temper, is that he might have committed suicide. Romola writes that after seeing Bleuler, Vaslav said to her, "*Femmka*, you are bringing me my death warrant."[45]

On returning to the hotel, both of them apparently were in a very bad mood. Bleuler writes that Romola decided to sleep in "another room." During the night Nijinsky tried to "break into her room, but found it was locked." He then started to make "some noise," yelling, "I want to see my wife," which caused great consternation. Romola and her mother were terrified and tried "to flee from him." After that, Nijinsky locked himself up in *his* room, and refused to come out.

> He only allowed his breakfast to be brought in, but otherwise did not answer those who knocked. He had purchased a fairly big knife, and showed it to his relatives in a somewhat noticeable way, claiming that he was planning to use it for sharpening pencils. That was another reason to be afraid of him.[46]

For twenty-four hours he remained isolated, while Romola and her parents became increasingly "frantic." Who finally decided to intervene by calling the police is not clear. (Romola accused her mother of having done this behind her back.) After the ruckus of a forcible entry into Nijinsky's room, an associate of Bleuler, Dr. Emil Oberholzer, was called to examine the dancer. From Oberholzer we have an excellent description of his "somewhat manneristic and theatrical" behavior when trapped in an embarrassing situation. (Compare this to Romola's observation of Nijinsky putting on airs in St. Moritz, "acting the part of a *blasé mondaine* aristocrat.")

> In a grotesque way he enacts for us the unexpected surprise: "I am a man of the world and not accustomed to being treated this way." He makes use of a peculiarly scanning and saccadic speech-style, articulating slowly, with exaggerated clarity, and accenting the individual syllables and words with irregular and unfitting pauses, all in a pompously serious and lofty tone of voice, accompanied by stiff mimicry.[47]

After this initial show of haughtiness, however, Nijinsky seemed to relax and become more "trusting." Oberholzer told him that Romola had "taken to her bed due to a nervous crisis," and therefore he would have to "forgo speaking to her." This made Nijinsky very "sad," and he kept pleading with the doctor that he really "loves his wife very much" and did not mean to cause her "any harm." Oberholzer explained that on Bleuler's advice the couple should remain separated, and Nijinsky accepted this "without offering any resistance, or asking what we intend to do with him and where he will be taken.... He also calmly accepted my statement that he is nervously unwell, and should be brought to Burghölzli for medical treatment by Professor Bleuler, whom he consulted two days ago."[48]

Nijinsky arrived on the psychiatric ward at four that afternoon. The admitting doctor noted him to be "in high spirits, calm, very polite, without any extremes of behavior." The Burghölzli was a Cantonal Hospital where well-to-do private patients seldom stayed for any length of time. Bleuler came personally to "apologize" for the inconvenience of having no single rooms available. "You would have been better off to take my advice and go to a sanatorium." It was amazing to the staff "how little the patient seemed to be impressed with the reality of his confinement." He was friendly and cooperative: "One notices nothing whatsoever of any defiance. Nijinsky indicates that it doesn't matter to him where he stays, and that he likes it here." Later that day, when the ward physician made his evening rounds, the dancer's mood had shifted. Now he was angry, and expressed "indignation about the primitive accommodations." This attitude persisted until he was released, a day and a half later. [49]

During this period of forty-eight-hour observation, the psychiatrists examined Nijinsky's notebooks and the letters he had written in St. Moritz. (He had brought all this material along, hoping to get his "book" published in Zürich.) The medical chart contains an evaluation of his writings, which, along with a careful description of Nijinsky's behavior, led to the first definitive diagnosis of his mental disorder. The doctors were impressed with Nijinsky's marked handicap in verbal communication. "He speaks with peculiar difficulty and slowness in French, but even more laboriously in German."

> Even in [writing] the Russian language, which he has spoken since childhood and studied in school, he makes orthographic errors. French he writes only phonetically, without any knowledge of correct spelling or grammar. In a letter to a Polish singer [Jean de Reszke] he stresses that he is Polish, but has never learned the Polish language.... This letter abounds with mistakes, but shows that he can speak Polish.[50]

The psychiatrists commented on the "chains of association" in Nijinsky's notebooks, which seemed to them illogical: "He writes about himself: I am God, I am a peasant, a factory-worker, a servant, a gentleman, an aristocrat, a God, a Czar, an Emperor, Life and Eternity, I am Everything." They also noted the repetitions in Nijinsky's poetry, which they called "verbigeration," a term coined by the nineteenth-century German psychiatrist Karl Kahlbaum to depict the way psychotic patients repeatedly shouted certain words or phrases. (This was a sign of "catatonia," a mental disorder Kahlbaum first described in 1874.) It is true that Nijinsky repeated himself when writing poems—I have commented on this earlier—but that was never part of his behavior while speaking. The "flood of words" noted by Bleuler, and the "saccadic" (like stuttering) way of speaking described by Oberholzer are not "verbigeration." In any case, it is hazardous to make a psychiatric diagnosis on the basis of written documents. Letters and notebooks can help us to understand how people think, remember, and deal with problems; they have little diagnostic validity.[51]

There were other features of "catatonia" the Burghölzli psychiatrists thought they could detect in Nijinsky. One was the dancer's remarkable passivity. "He lay in bed the entire time he was with us, and refused to go to the ambulatory unit.... He kept emphasizing that although he is not mentally ill, we can do with him whatever we want." Nijinsky also seemed to be holding back his resentment toward Romola. "He had every reason," the doctors wrote, "to be angry at his wife, since she had no longer allowed him to visit her at night." And he was making gross errors in social judgment: "At St. Moritz he had studied how to present himself as a madman; he did this so convincingly that one actually took him to be one." Finally, Nijinsky's notebooks showed evidence of what the psychiatrists thought were "systematized delusions." He had written that his father-in-law "and other relatives own the records of a madhouse, therefore I am being put in an insane asylum." He seemed deluded about himself—"I am an animal, a wild beast, an idiot"—and there were guilty sexual preoccupations, the sign of a deep conflict. "When I was a child I showed a dog how to masturbate and masturbated myself at the same time.... My impresario [Diaghilev] taught me all sorts of perversions which I abhor."[52]

Considering all of these findings, and Nijinsky's lack of insight into his obviously disturbed condition, Bleuler felt it would be most unwise for him to return to the hotel in Zürich, where a repetition of the marital crisis that had brought him to the hospital seemed inevitable. Therefore, arrangements were made for him to go directly to Dr. Binswanger's sanatorium. Nijinsky boarded the train for Kreuzlingen on Monday, 10 March 1919. His discharge diagnosis was "catatonia." It was Dr. Greiber, not Romola, who accompanied him on the trip.

NOTES

1. Notebook on "Feeling," 15. See also *Diary*, 166.
2. Descriptions of the hotel and tourist resort are based on personal observations, photographs, and information available in archives of the Kurverein in St. Moritz.
3. Notebook on "Feeling," 4–6; RNN, 423.
4. RNN, 424; Notebook on "Feeling," 9.
5. Paul Taylor, *Private Domain*, 77–78.
6. RNN, 424. See also RBN, 493–495, and Françoise Reiss, *Nijinsky*, 178–181.
7. RNN, 425–426.
8. Notebook on "Feeling," 8.
9. RNN, 426.
10. Notebook on "Feeling," 8–9.
11. RNN, 426.
12. Reiss, 184–186.
13. Colin Wilson, *The Outsider*.
14. Karl M. Abenheimer, "The Diary of Vaslav Nijinsky."
15. *Diary*, xv.
16. Sotheby auction house, Catalogue, London, 24 July 1979.
17. Letter from Dr. "Greiber," to Eugen Bleuler, 2 March 1919. Zürich University Archives.
18. Ibid. Emphasis in the original.
19. Ibid.
20. Peter Loewenberg, "A Creative Epoch in Modern Science."

21. Notebooks.
22. "Greiber," letter to bleuler, 2 March 1919.
23. Vyacheslav Ivanov, Ph.D., head of the Department of Structural Typology of the Institutes of Slavonic and Balkan Studies, USSR Academy of Science, personal communication.
24. James H. Billington, *The Icon and the Axe.*
25. Abenheimer.
26. *Diary,* 70–72.
27. Translated from the original Russian by Professor Simon Karlinsky, Department of Slavic Languages, University of California, Berkeley. Nijinsky's recurring grammatical mistakes, such as "I *is* a man," have been corrected.
28. RNN, 426.
29. Párdány correspondence, Nijinsky Archives.
30. Letter to Bleuler. Zürich University Archives.
31. Medical records. Zürich University Archives.
32. Eugen Bleuler, "Dementia Praecox, oder die Gruppe der Schizophrenien."
33. "Greiber," letter to Bleuler, 2 March 1919.
34. *Diary,* 7, 6. I have restored the words "a little boy" from the unpublished notebooks.
35. Ibid., 183–184. "About the revolver," referring to Nijinsky's recent suicide threat, appears in the Notebooks. Romola deleted these and many other references to Nijinsky's potential and actual violence.
36. RNN, 427.
37. Eugen Bleuler, *Autistic Undisciplined Thinking in Medicine and How to Overcome It.*
38. Bleuler report. Zürich University Archives.
39. RNN, 427–428.
40. Allen R. Doran, Alan Breier, and Alec Roy, "Differential Diagnosis and Diagnostic Systems in Schizophrenia."
41. RNN, 429.
42. Bleuler report. Zürich University Archives.
43. *Diary,* 167.
44. D. S. Mirsky, *A History of Russian Literature,* 505.
45. RNN, 429.
46. Bleuler report. Zürich University Archives.
47. Dr. Emil Oberholzer, medical report, 8 March 1919. Zürich University Archives.
48. Ibid.
49. Nijinsky hospital record. Zürich University Archives.
50. Ibid. His letter is reproduced, minus the linguistic errors noted by the doctors, in *Diary,* 66–70.
51. Carol North and Remi Cadort, "Diagnostic Discrepancy in Personal Accounts of Patients with 'Schizophrenia.'"
52. Nijinsky hospital record. Zürich University Archives.

Madness is a question, not an answer. ... What distance separates man from God? What separates life from death? Madness from truth? And words from silence?

Chapter 9

Catatonia and the Bellevue Sanatorium

"Catatonia" has had a checkered career in psychiatry. The term was invented by Dr. Karl Kahlbaum (1828–1899), an astute psychiatrist who taught at the University of Königsberg and later worked in a private asylum in Görlitz, a small town on the present border between East Germany and Poland. In 1874 Kahlbaum published his famous book *Catatonia, or Tension-Insanity*, which describes twenty-six patients whose illnesses all seemed to follow a predictable course.[2] The first symptoms invariably were mood disturbances, usually a severe depression or sometimes a short spell of mania followed by depression. Then, these patients entered a peculiar state of muscular rigidity or immobility. They were very tense, would not talk (Kahlbaum called this "mutism"), and stood, lay, or sat in a fixed position as if they were completely paralyzed. Although they were alert and conscious, these patients seemed impervious to external stimuli. One could stick them with a needle and they did not budge. They seemed numb, frozen, as if dead. This was called a "catatonic stupor."

While methods of physical examination were relatively primitive in those days (no blood-pressure cuffs, X-ray machines, or electrocardiograms), Kahlbaum and his associates realized that something was the matter physiologically. These stuporous patients had a very slow pulse and breathed very slowly. Their skin often turned cold and blue. Fluid collected in their motionless legs. In their paralysis they stared ahead with a fixed expression, seldom blinking. Sometimes they would contort their face or squeeze the mouth and eyes tightly shut, a symptom called "grimacing," or even twitch and convulse like epileptics. If one attempted to feed these patients, to change their posture, or to move their limbs, they would resist fiercely ("negativism") or comply only very gradually ("waxy flexibility"), passively adopting whatever position one chose to put them into ("catalepsy"). A catatonic stupor might last for hours, days, or even weeks. Then, suddenly, for no obvious reason, these patients would explode into a violent outburst of raving madness. This was called a "catatonic excitement." They shouted obscenities, screamed incoherently, ran around in a wild frenzy, and tore their clothes off ("nudism"). If one succeeded in calming them down, these patients often began to behave like robots. They moved mechanically, imitated every gesture they saw ("echopraxia"), or followed the doctors around like mindless zombies ("mitgehen"). Sounding like a broken phonograph record, they repeated what one said to them ("echolalia"). Catatonia was considered a life-threatening disease. While in a stupor, patients could become dehydrated, lose weight, develop infections, have fevers, and die. An "attack" of catatonic excitement made them extremely dangerous. They smashed things, injured themselves, cut off parts of their bodies, ripped out their eyes or genitals, struck other people. Some of them were violently homicidal, or suicidal.

In searching for a cause, Kahlbaum adopted the medical model, which assumes that all diseases have physical causes. This model had paid off handsomely in the nineteenth century, when it was discovered that two of the most rampant and virulent diseases, tuberculosis and syphilis, could be explained as infectious processes. Bacteria entered the body; there was a period of latency, while they worked insidiously; then overt symptoms would appear—sores, coughing, bleeding, weight loss, paralysis, and death. Doctors worked busily to detect each phase of a disease as quickly as possible. They prescribed remedies for whatever symptoms were treatable, and comforted the patient and his family if the disease progressed. In France, psychiatrists had taken the lead in identifying the clinical course of syphilis, which in its final stages could produce "general paralysis," a particularly gruesome form of progressive madness. French psychiatrists had also pioneered in introducing concepts such as "circular insanity," which was a recurring form of madness, and "precocious dementia," which tragically affected young people. The causes of these conditions were not understood, but Kahlbaum felt that they, too, could be explained in terms of pathological processes within the brain. (It was already known that strokes, head injuries, and other brain diseases could lead to marked changes of personality and behavior.)[3]

Kahlbaum worked assiduously to pin down the many problems presented by the patients in his asylum. In doing so, he coined a number of new descriptive terms. One of these, "verbigeration," we have already seen applied, rather loosely, to Nijinsky's poetry. (As defined by Kahlbaum, verbigeration meant that a patient *"makes a speech* which is composed of often repeated, meaningless words and sentences."[4] As far as is known, Nijinsky never talked like that.) Other neologisms invented by Kahlbaum include dipsomania, cyclothymia, and catatonia. They are still part of our vocabulary. But today we think of these words only as descriptive terms. In the nineteenth century they were thought to represent actual diseases. In working out his theory of "catatonia," Dr. Kahlbaum observed that some of his patients recovered, left the hospital, and remained well for the rest of their lives, while others had to be readmitted from time to time with the same condition. They never recovered completely. Still others alternated between stupor and excitement all the time, without letup, making it necessary for them to stay in the hospital indefinitely. Over the years these chronic catatonics seemed to become more and more confused, until they ended up in a state of "dementia," which Kahlbaum thought was the final phase of catatonia. In that respect, this disease resembled syphilis, but the fact that males and females were equally susceptible suggested that catatonia was *not* a form of syphilis. (Syphilis was much more common among men than women in the nineteenth century.) Nor did catatonia seem age-related. Although there was "a preference for early middle age," young people as well as older people could develop this disease. Heredity did not seem to be an important factor, which made catatonia different from certain forms of imbecility. What then could be the cause? After carefully studying all of his patients, Kahlbaum concluded that a "very strong religious excitation might be included among the decisive factors." He had often observed a "preaching urge." Many catatonic patients seemed to come from religious families, and showed "a tendency to isolation and contemplation." Another "decisive" factor, thought Kahlbaum, was "sexual overstimulation." He noticed that catatonics liked to masturbate or to engage in lewd behavior, and that "their religious tendency is often connected with a sexual perversity."[5]

Kahlbaum's books were not widely read, and he had no university professorship from which to disseminate his ideas about catatonia. But Emil Kraepelin, the great classifier and system-builder in psychiatry, knew of Kahlbaum's work and incorporated some of it into his own nosology. Considerable progress had by then been made in physical diagnosis, so that some of the patients previously called "catatonic" were recognized to have tuberculosis, brain tumors, and other diseases. The rest, Kraepelin thought, were manifesting "only a special, quickly-passing form of dementia praecox," by which he meant that they were basically schizophrenic. Bleuler, who had invented the term "schizo-prenia," was not so sure about that. He thought that catatonia might be a form of manic-depressive psychosis or schizophrenia, depending on which symptoms came first. If the disease started with thought fragmentation and other basic signs of schizophrenia, one could call it "catatonic schizophrenia," but "as a rule, catatonic symptoms mix with the manic and the melancholic conditions," said Bleuler, "and one can speak of a manic or a melancholic catatonia."[6] In the United States, the eminent Swiss-born psychiatrist Adolf Meyer (1866–1950) questioned whether catatonia actually was a "specific illness"—"there always were some dissenting or warning voices pointing beyond this assumption." Meyer preferred to regard it as a failure in adjusting to "psychobiological problems," and wondered about hormonal factors. "The fact that sex tension, usually with efforts at suppression, is frequently found in the beginning especially of the catatonic crisis, might rouse suspicion of possible gonadal influences."[7]

Freud did not have much to say about catatonia, but other psycho-analysts who worked with these patients discovered developmental problems going back to childhood and inhibitions in emotional expression. "The mood is essentially that of self-depreciation, covering infantile egotism, sensitiveness, self-pitying, having hurt feelings, being sorry for themselves, moroseness, pouting, sulking, wishing to be sick, helpless, and loving to fantasize about dying."[8] These patients often seemed to depend on primitive defense mechanisms in trying to manage outbursts of rage. "The impulse is to move, to strike. The defense is its opposite—complete inaction."[9] Only a handful of gifted therapists, often women, were able to tolerate the overwhelming aggressivity and unbridled need for attention manifested by catatonic patients. Thus, large numbers of them began to accumulate in mental hospitals, and it was not until the discovery of insulin and electro-convulsive therapy (in the late 1930s) that they could be treated effectively.

During World War II, it was frequently observed that inmates of Nazi concentration camps who were starving, terminally ill, or in a mood of hopeless despair would begin to manifest behavior that resembled a catatonic stupor. They stopped talking, moved very slowly or not at all, stared into space, and had a fixed, zombielike posture. Since then, "catatonia" has also been described among patients who are suffering in an overwhelming way from cancer, AIDS, or other life-threatening diseases.[10] Today, most psychiatrists think of catatonia as a nonspecific disturbance in self-regulation of emotion and body movement brought on by a number of potentially devastating biological and psychosocial stressors.[11] "Catatonia" is no longer a useful diagnosis and, with the availability of much more specific and reliable treatments for the underlying diseases, is fast fading into history.

When Nijinsky arrived in Kreuzlingen, on Monday afternoon, 10 March 1919, for admission to the Bellevue Sanatorium, Dr. Greiber told the examining psychiatrist how difficult it had been to transport the dancer from Zürich, and that some of his behavior during the trip seemed "catatonic."

> He made himself quite conspicuous: first he didn't speak at all, but then he followed willingly. While getting out of the train in Romanshorn, he was completely "catatonic," held peculiar postures, made himself stiff, gave no answers, did not allow himself to be led, so I called for a car, because I couldn't very well bring the patient by train in this condition.[12]

It will be remembered that Greiber had already mentioned in his letter to Bleuler that he suspected "a psychosis with paranoid and catatonic content" while treating Nijinsky in St. Moritz. (Romola's assertion, in 1936, that Nijinsky had his "first catatonic attack" *after* being hospitalized by Bleuler is misleading.[13]) But the admitting psychiatrist at Bellevue, Dr. Kurt Binswanger (a cousin of the hospital director), evidently was not much impressed, and did not use the term "catatonic" in describing Nijinsky: "On arrival, the patient says almost nothing, greets me ceremoniously with a friendly smile, and later, when I can see him alone, speaks a little bit more. He does not consider himself to be 'crazy,' but thinks he is only somewhat nervous. He had not done anything wrong, one only misunderstands him." Binswanger did not think it necessary to watch Nijinsky "very closely." He recommended, however, that a male attendant should "sleep in the same room" with the dancer in the Parkhaus, a spacious building reserved for twenty-six men, where Nijinsky was to have his room. Such arrangements were customary when a new patient, who might be unpredictable and potentially violent, was admitted to the sanatorium for the first time. The responsibility for doing Nijinsky's initial medical and psychiatric work-up was assigned to Dr. H. Reese, a clinician "of the old school," as a colleague describes him, "stiff, somewhat inhibited and rigid in his attitudes, but very devoted and sympathetic to his patients."[14] Nijinsky offered no objections. He "slept well," reports Dr. Reese, and the next day was allowed to rest in bed. "He doesn't speak much, also doesn't eat especially much; mood fairly good during the medical visit. Otherwise he sleeps a lot."[15]

The Bellevue Sanatorium is situated on a wooded, gently sloping, thirty-acre estate overlooking Lake Constance. Founded in 1859 by Dr. Ludwig Binswanger, Sr., it consisted at the beginning of one magnificent villa, with elegant and well-furnished rooms for fifteen patients, a luxurious parlor, a billiard room, a superb dining pavilion, and beautiful lawns and gardens, all expertly organized along the lines of a well-run Swiss hotel. The purpose of this "asylum," as it was first called, was to provide "a place of shelter and protection for any individual who has been defeated in his fight against the forces of nature, the hatred of political persecution, or the paralyzing effects of illness, age, and misery of any kind." Bellevue was a family enterprise, where Dr. Binswanger and his wife, with the assistance of well-trained nurses and attendants, cared with "love, good-will, and sympathy" for their "so-called mentally-ill" guests.[16] Around the turn of the century, under the management of Ludwig's son, Dr. Robert Binswanger, the Bellevue Sanatorium grew into one of the world's most outstanding psychiatric hospitals, with seventeen buildings: homes for the patients, residences for the doctors and their families, a central kitchen and bakery, workshops, barns, machine shops, a hydrotherapy center, a gymnasium, laboratories, and maintenance facilities. Bellevue was a "therapeutic community" in the best sense of the word. Its population, ranging from forty to eighty patients, was quadrupled by the abundant treatment personnel, doctors, psychologists, nurses, teachers, coaches, and rehabilitation therapists, all of whom lived there, either on the grounds of the sanatorium or in the immediate vicinity. "Service to the sick" was their life's calling.

The guiding spirit of this model institution was to seek "utmost individualization" in the management of every patient, and to approach each new problem with "absolute clinical thoroughness." Psychotherapy, education, and reintegration of the "suffering individual" into his or her family and community were the goals of treatment. There were strict rules of conduct while one lived at Bellevue, and although medical care was always available, a policy of "no mechanical or chemical restraint" prevailed. Many patients stayed at Bellevue for years and received treatment indefinitely. For those who could not tolerate moving to a less sheltered social milieu, the Binswanger family was prepared to erect private villas, where patients were able to reside with their own families and servants, an arrangement that obviously catered to a very upper-class clientele.[17]

Dr. Ludwig Binswanger (1881–1966), the chief medical director while Nijinsky was a patient there, brought to Bellevue an unprecedented humanistic and philosophical attitude. Binswanger had been trained by Bleuler and Jung in Zürich, and later by his uncle, Otto Binswanger, a professor of psychiatry in Jena, Germany. In 1907, Ludwig Binswanger had traveled to Vienna with Jung for the purpose of meeting Freud, and that led to his passionate interest in psychoanalysis. He and Freud became lifelong friends. Some of Freud's more difficult patients were hospitalized at Bellevue, and he himself stayed there briefly in 1912 as a guest of Dr. Binswanger, who took Freud on "long walks along the Bay of Constance and an automobile ride along the lake, which particularly enchanted him."[18]

In spite of their mutual high regard, the two men differed sharply in several respects. Binswanger, coming from a medical family and thoroughly identified with clinical practice, found it difficult to show hostility toward patients, whereas Freud, a more detached and re-search-oriented scientist, admitted quite openly that he "could wring the necks of all of them."[19] The two men also disagreed about the connections between psychoanalysis and philosophy. Trained as a neurologist, Freud regularly cast his theories into a rational-scientific mold, while Binswanger, a philosopher at heart, always insisted that psychoanalysis is a hermeneutic enterprise, one of many ways to find meaning through the interpretation of symbols. Binswanger was strongly influenced by the phenomenologist Edmund Husserl and the existentialist, Martin Heidegger. In eleven books and more than one hundred articles, he created the foundation for what is called Daseins-analyse, the existential analysis of "being-in-the-world."[20]

> In this context we do not say that mental illnesses are diseases of the brain (which, of course, they remain from a medical-clinical viewpoint). But we say: in the mental diseases we face modifications of the fundamental or essential structure and of the structural links of being-in-the-world as transcendence. It is one task of psychiatry to investigate and establish these variations in a scientifically exact way.[21]

When Binswanger assumed the directorship of Bellevue Sanatorium in 1911, he was still under the sway of orthodox Freudian psychoanalysis and believed that "almost every patient must be analyzed." This he proceeded to do with the help of four associates (including his cousin Kurt), only to discover innumerable obstacles. There never seemed to be enough time. The analytic hours tended to conflict with the doctors' other duties, and they felt overburdened. Psychoanalysis requires imagination and flexibility. One of the doctors (H. Reese, Nijinsky's first psychiatrist at Bellevue) turned out to be too "old-fashioned" for this kind of work. There were also many patients who resisted the psychoanalytic approach, which calls for initiative, willingness to free-associate, and the capacity to observe oneself objectively, all qualities that may be impaired with serious illness. Misunderstandings as well as complicated transference and countertransference problems often arose between patients and their doctors. How to deal with these was not yet well understood. There were further difficulties for foreign patients, like Nijinsky, who were insufficiently fluent in German, French, or English to collaborate effectively with a treatment based essentially on verbal discourse. (Only during his third hospitalization was Nijinsky assigned to a Russian-speaking psychiatrist, and by that time his illness was already very advanced.)

Finally, there were difficulties related to Dr. Binswanger's authoritarian personality. According to colleagues who knew him well, he "talked a lot about good psychotherapy, but preferred to spend his time poring over case records, and writing books, rather than actually taking care of patients." He was considered more of a philosopher and methodologist than a psychologist. He also had a reputation for being "unbelievably strict, a real son-of-a-bitch." A somewhat feudal atmosphere reigned at the Bellevue Sanatorium. "The staff was paid little; your life was with the patients."[22]

Dr. Reese tried to obtain a psychiatric history shortly after Nijinsky's admission, but the patient did not tell him very much and it is possible that Dr. Greiber supplied the following facts: "His father is supposed to have been very brutal; his brother died in an insane-asylum, mentally-ill since childhood; his sister is an outstanding dancer; his 4-year-old daughter is very nervous." Nothing was recorded in Nijinsky's chart about his own childhood, his education, his career as a dancer, or his marriage. Perhaps it was assumed that this information would emerge in the course of subsequent psychotherapy. Documentation of the physical examination also seems very brief, when compared with the way psychiatric patients are examined today. Reese described Nijinsky's "small, graceful body-build, pale skin, very strong and well-developed muscles." The only abnormal findings recorded in the chart were an "irregular pulse," a "slight tremor of the tongue," and "very lively reflexes." No blood-pressure reading is shown, which is surprising in view of the observation of a pulse irregularity. Most likely, this finding, along with Nijinsky's tremor and brisk reflexes, was attributed to hyperarousal, or he may have had withdrawal symptoms after coming off the high doses of chloral hydrate prescribed by Dr. Greiber. A blood test for syphilis was negative. But there was a "trace" of albumin in Nijinsky's urine, which suggests mild kidney dysfunction.[23] Today these findings would be followed by chemical and metabolic tests as well as an electrocardiogram.

Within forty-eight hours after his admission, Nijinsky was noted to be "more talkative," and his mood seemed "changeable ... in conversation one cannot hold him to anything." Dr. Reese tried to get information about his family and came to the conclusion that "he has no real interest in them." The dancer did, however, write "a long letter to his wife (in French, orthography and style very awkward, like a small child), in which he repeats the same sentences over and over, and in which the paranoid view of his situation becomes more evident than in his conversation."[24]

Two days later, on 15 March 1919, Nijinsky was "getting out of bed more" and talking to Dr. Reese "about his wife, with natural affection. Otherwise childlike . . . doesn't need to be watched closely, but may not leave his room unaccompanied." He asked for permission, which was granted, to speak with Romola over the telephone, and Dr. Reese was "very astonished" to hear "the patient talking from the beginning in a tearful, plaintive voice, like a tiny, helpless child."

> First he says only "Romola, Romola." Then he wails. "I am sad, imprisoned." He pleads with his wife to come and get him immediately, which she then promises. (In reference to this phone-call, the wife actually wanted to have the patient picked up. She changed her mind only after she noticed that the patient may leave at anytime, and that things really are not going badly for him.)

The telephone conversation was "good for him," Reese noted the following day.

> He is very happy . . . in a bright mood, talkative, goes walking in the park a little. Talks to the attendants, and plays the piano. He makes many drawings, ornamental symbolism, which he himself obviously values quite highly. He is very proud to demonstrate these productions, and when one shows interest in them, his entire face radiates pleasure.

The following day was uneventful. On 18 March, however, while Nijinsky was walking in the village of Kreuzlingen with his attendant, he suddenly "leaped" into the air and rushed away, leaving the younger man breathlessly trying to catch up. He did this twice and the attendant became alarmed, saying he would have to tell Dr. Reese about it. Nijinsky tried to "swear him to silence," and told the attendant "the whole thing was a joke." Then he teasingly suggested, "it might do you some good to have to jump once in a while."

The medical staff found out about Nijinsky's prank soon enough, there being almost no way to keep anything secret at Bellevue. The doctors conferred every morning at 8:15 for about an hour before making their "rounds," which consisted of visiting all the patients and reviewing with the nurses and attendants how they were doing, their progress or regress, any problems that had come up during the night, and their plans for the day. Whatever time was left in the morning was taken up with individual treatment sessions, record-keeping, correspondence, and other administrative duties. The midday meal was a "big occasion" at Bellevue, insofar as all members of the staff had to attend and thus interact with their patients in a less clinical setting. The afternoon was again devoted to psychotherapy, group meetings, admission of new patients or discharge of old ones, and conferences with family members and referring physicians. The time to make "evening rounds" was left to the discretion of the individual doctor. Some chose to begin at four p.m. and continue until suppertime. Others, including Ludwig Binswanger, preferred to do it later.[25]

Dr. Reese did not think that Nijinsky's jumping and running was a "joke." He interpreted it as an "escape attempt," and warned the attendants that the dancer might become "violent." It had been noted that "before jumping Nijinsky always looked around attentively." Wouldn't any dancer, especially in an unfamiliar environment? But the rather unimaginative Reese concluded that Nijinsky had "persistent thoughts about running-away" and would therefore have to be watched very closely. More likely, Nijinsky was beginning to experience increased levels of anxiety and tension and needed a physical outlet. The hospital records show "strong excitement, fast respiration, fearfulness in the evening, temperature 37 degrees, fast and very irregular pulse (100 per minute), he complains about headache." It might have been more helpful if Dr. Reese had empathized with Nijinsky's obvious discomfort at being confined and commented on the problem of his marital separation and probable sexual frustration. At least, he might have acknowledged Nijinsky's special gift for leaping and his expressed desire to have the attendant join him in dancing.

There is nothing in Reese's notes to suggest that his discussions with or about the patient went in this direction. Instead, he described Nijinsky's vexing pattern of mood swings. One day the patient would "rest in bed" and complain about feeling "physically unwell." The next day he would be "very lively and cheerful, talking with other people, playing the piano a little. He even danced once." In these "high moods" he often showed what Reese called a "silly gaiety" (*läppische Heiterkeit*) before swinging back again into angry depression. "Suddenly he becomes negativistic, first won't go to his room for dinner, but then lets himself be talked out of it. Mildly stuporous, assumes crazy body postures, twists himself like a snake, says nothing. Laughs when one speaks with him, but almost never gives an answer." Reese wondered if Nijinsky might be "hallucinating," a relevant question when someone stops talking and acts "crazy." Nijinsky had not complained of any intrusive voices, noises, visions, or other hallucinatory phenomena. "At least he sometimes looks attentively in a certain direction," noted Reese, but that was not enough to confirm his suspicions. No further notes appear in the hospital chart during the last week of March, suggesting that Dr. Reese may have gone on vacation, been ill, or lost interest in the case. At the end of the month, Dr. Ludwig Binswanger personally assumed responsibility for Nijinsky's treatment.

It should be emphasized that by today's medical standards, a patient as disturbed as Nijinsky, with a history of manic attacks and showing marked mood swings, would most likely be taking psychoactive medication after three weeks of hospitalization, probably lithium salts to reduce his emotional ups and downs, an antidepressant, and an anxiolytic drug for the control of fearfulness. But we are talking about 1919, when specific symptomatic treatment was not yet available. Patients at the Bellevue Sanatorium were expected to benefit from the controlled social environment, various recreational and occupational activities, and psychotherapy. All were treated as "members of the family," with the hope that their illness would gradually remit. When Dr. Binswanger saw him for the first time, Nijinsky was in the billiard room of the main building, Haus Bellevue, where patients and staff mingled freely. At a nearby piano sat "Miss B." (one of the nurses), "playing music" for the dancer. Dr. Binswanger's handwriting is not easy to read—Freud called it "atrocious" and "schizophrenically rejecting"[26]—but one can be sure that his approach to psychotherapy differed markedly from Reese's. In the first place, Binswanger saw "nothing whatsoever pathological" about Nijinsky's behavior. He thought of him as a great artist, a man deserving of respect and needing to express himself through movement. Thus, without a moment's hesitation, he asked Nijinsky if he might be "interested in preparing a dance-recital." It was customary at Bellevue for talented patients as well as staff members or visitors to participate in concerts, plays, poetry readings, or other forms of entertainment. Nijinsky was more than eager to be invited. Binswanger writes:

> He is exaggeratedly amiable and very flattered when one mentions his fame. He would gladly dance for us. He very much misses having an audience. He was four years old when he began dancing, and at age nine was admitted to the Imperial Ballet School in St. Petersburg. The way he looks around is *not* paranoid or otherwise remarkable.[27]

Not since performing at the Suvretta House in January had Nijinsky had the opportunity to dance in public. Now, on 1 April 1919 (April Fool's Day!), he made his debut in Kreuzlingen, appearing in the central foyer of the sanatorium's main villa. Sofas, lounge chairs, and coffee tables were moved aside, the Persian carpets were rolled up, and "a large audience" of guests, patients, and personnel with their familes gathered to watch him. Again, as in St. Moritz, Nijinsky entered the room quietly and greeted the audience "in a friendly way." He then went to the piano and began playing, or rather "pounding on it," as Dr. Binswanger says. (Binswanger himself was a pianist, and, like Stravinsky, Ansermet, and others who have criticized Nijinsky's musical abilities, he did not think much of him as a keyboard artist.) We are not told how long the "pounding" went on, but another pianist (I assume it was Miss B., if not Binswanger himself) finally took over, playing "the E-minor Intermezzo by Brahms, and then some music by Reger" for Nijinsky to dance to. By this time he was performing what Binswanger called "a suicide-madness scene."

> He is in a state of clouded consciousness (*Dämmerzustand*) while dancing. To get into this takes him a long time, until he is "inspired." Afterwards he is very pale, done-in, kaput, and extremely excited. Then he can't sit still, devours one cigaret after another, and has a marked tremor in his crossed legs and hands.[28]

Binswanger's observations remind us of earlier descriptions of Nijinsky when, as a member of the Ballets Russes, he first seemed listless or distracted, then gradually became inspired, "entered" a role, and was "transformed" into another person, after which he would dance magnificently and sometimes violently for a while, before collapsing into a state of agitated depression. The physiological concomitants of such behavior are not yet well understood, but there have been many descriptions of so-called "peak performance" by Olympic champions, trapeze artists, concert pianists, and others who regularly drive themselves to the limit of endurance, including racehorses.* There is a surge of adrenalin and other neurohormones, which may cause waves of anticipatory "performance anxiety." Endogenous opiates (endorphins) are secreted that partially anesthetize the body. After the peak event comes a phase of physical depletion, felt as postperformance depression, and sometimes extreme irritability, due to postexertional hypoglycemia. Many performers crave company, while others need solitude when they are in this state. Horses must be properly "walked" after a race in order to maintain their health. The long-term effects, both physiological and psychological, of repeatedly going from anticipation through peak performance to tumult and exhaustion is an important subject for clinical research. An understanding of these dynamics may also be important for work and creativity in general.[31]

After Nijinsky's performance, Binswanger asked himself, "What is this patient trying to tell us?" His first thought was that the dancer was imitating someone who is insane, someone who indeed had been catatonic. "When Nijinsky enters a room," wrote Binswanger, "he goes to the open piano and bangs on it like a catatonic patient. At first, I was continually reminded of scenes from the closed wards, when old catatonics would fling themselves on the piano." It was a consummate piece of acting: "The impression he makes, and the complete art of his pantomime, is most thoroughly studied and 'truthful.'" When it was all over, Nijinsky stopped being "catatonic" and let himself be taken back to the Parkhaus by a nurse, where he spent "a normal night."[32]

Binswanger could not explain this behavior. He lacked precise information about Nijinsky's exposure to a mentally ill brother, his training in St. Petersburg (which included the "truthful" imitation of people in emotional distress), and his choreographic invention of unusual movements. However, Binswanger did intuitively appreciate the dancer's extraordinary talent for assimilating the expressions of disease. Apparently, Nijinsky's month of mingling with psychotic

---

*Psychiatrist Jurgen Ruesch first suggested this analogy between human and animal performance to me. Since then, I have come across a number of examples. Composer Gustav Mahler, while conducting, reminded people of an "animal ... stray and half wild."[29] Choreographer George Balanchine once told his biographer Bernard Taper, "You should think of your task as if you were writing the biography of a racehorse."[30] Nijinsky himself used the term "tired horse" after performing.

patients at Burghölzli and Bellevue obscured the boundary between art and madness. It now was possible for him to dance a "suicide-madness scene" with absolute conviction, and one could never be sure exactly which state he was in. After his dance recital, for example, he was "very pleasant all day." The next evening, however, Binswanger found him "in a psychogenically charming *stupor-condition.* . . . He sits in the billiard-room with his forehead leaning on the edge of the table, while Miss D. and Mr. W. are making music together. He won't let himself be shaken out of it and doesn't react to commands."[33]

Was the music putting Nijinsky into this "charming" mood or was he having a true catatonic stupor? One way to tell would be by stimulating him to move, since stuporous catatonics typically resist, or comply only very slowly and then stay rigidly in one position (catalepsy). Binswanger tried this experiment, and it showed that Nijinsky was not truly catatonic: "He allows himself to be placed in an upright sitting position without any negativism or catalepsy." Another sign of catatonia was when patients jerked spasmodically, as if they were having an epileptic seizure. Binswanger looked carefully for "convulsive movements (*Zuckungen*)," but found none. He did detect signs of intense emotional arousal, however: "marked sweating, and very prominent veins on his forehead." He also noticed "a soft but deep moaning," which suggested that Nijinsky was in pain, or trying to express sadness, or perhaps both. But as soon as the doctor left the room, it was noted that "the patient awoke from his stupor." Clearly, Nijinsky seemed to be motivated by an awareness of who was watching him. This, more than anything, convinced the staff that an element of deliberate playacting was involved: "When Miss B. asked him why he does such stupid things, Nijinsky raised his finger roguishly and made 'pst, pst' as if to tell her not to betray him."[34]

The next day he again seemed "somewhat downcast," and during Binswanger's evening visit communicated only with body language. He said nothing, but "fell into an abnormal condition, standing in the corner on one leg, with his right hand stretched out as if he were holding something in his fingers." One can be reminded here only of a dancer rehearsing a ballet. "What are you trying to tell me?" Binswanger asked. Nijinsky gave no answer. Binswanger pushed him to make him lose his balance, which evidently sufficed "to shake the patient out of this state." Nijinsky seemed startled at first, then began to talk (in French): "What do you want? I'm just being an artist." Thereafter, he "conversed normally." Binswanger asked if he could remember what he was feeling the day before, while in his "stupor" at the billiard table. "I had a stomach ache!" Nijinsky replied. "He does remember the dance recital," Binswanger noted, "but he is much more reserved, 'stranger' than before; distracted and apparently less attentive."[35]

The patient's remoteness puzzled the Bellevue staff. Did it indicate that he was losing contact with reality and withdrawing into schizophrenia or was he simply dramatizing his disinterest in the hospital or his rebelliousness, as if to say, "I don't care for this place; let me go home." It might be helpful, reasoned Binswanger, for his wife to visit him at this point. She had not yet been to Kreuzlingen, and by observing them together Binswanger could perhaps come closer to the psychodynamic meaning of Nijinsky's "strangeness." Already, while telling him about his wife's impending visit, Binswanger was able to observe something of interest. "The patient reacts with remarkably little affect and seems not to listen. The disclosure that his wife is coming invariably produces the same expressions of astonishment: 'So! Really? Oh!'"

Binswanger's plan was to have Vaslav and Romola spend the weekend together in Heiden, a pleasant mountain village only thirty kilometers southeast of Kreuzlingen. An attendant from Bellevue would be asked to go along, to observe the patient and to help his wife in case of any disturbing behavior. In explaining this to Nijinsky, Binswanger again noted his strange apathy, his lack of interest in leaving the hospital and spending time with his wife. "He likes to think about staying here, where there are many people." When Binswanger told him about the attendant, Nijinsky "indicated no resistance," and jokingly said that Bellevue is really such a fine place to stay that "he would advertise it whenever he goes." Throughout this conversation Nijinsky seemed to be somewhat out of it. "He continues to impress me," Binswanger noted, "as a patient who is in a state of mildly clouded consciousness, rather than epileptic. His catatonic postures do not impress me as truly catatonic. They are more psychogenic."

The term "psychogenic," which Binswanger used frequently, was employed in those days to connote behavior thought to be motivated by conscious or unconscious desires, as opposed to the symptoms resulting from "organic" changes in the brain. This distinction was of importance for therapeutic reasons. According to the older school (Kahlbaum, Kraepelin), catatonia was an organic brain disease similar to syphilis or epilepsy, while the newer approach (Bleuler, Jung, Freud) regarded it as a product of psychological conflicts. "Psychogenic" cases ought, on theoretical grounds, to respond to psychoanalysis, which was available at the Bellevue Sanatorium, whereas "truly organic" catatonias required custodial care and could be treated only symptomatically. It was after Nijinsky's weekend outing with Romola that Dr. Binswanger finally convinced himself that his illness was "truly psychogenic." There seemed to be many volitional, goal-directed elements, designed not only to impress, but also to manipulate the social environment.

Nijinsky's spouse had arrived at Bellevue on Thursday, 3 April. She struck the staff as gloomy, pessimistic, and not altogether trustworthy. After spending some time with Nijinsky she told Binswanger that she felt "very depressed." Especially disturbing to her were his "stupors." She "claimed never to have seen him this way before," true to the extent that, by virtue of his hospital experience, his mimicry had become more foreign to her, but untrue in the sense that she had observed similar eccentricities many times, and Binswanger knew it. (On his desk was a copy of Dr. Greiber's letter to Professor Bleuler, describing Nijinsky's many pathological behaviors in St. Moritz.) Furthermore, Romola seemed to display no faith in her husband's recovery: "I do not believe he will ever get well," she told Binswanger. Nevertheless, Binswanger felt it would be worth the risk to let Nijinsky leave the hospital for a weekend pass, so that he could spend some time with his wife, as long as the two were never alone together. Dr. Greiber telephoned to say that he and his wife were taking the train to Rorschach (within walking distance of Heiden), and would gladly meet the Nijinsky couple there. Binswanger warned Greiber about "the need for close supervision."

Even with these well-laid plans, Nijinsky kept balking. "He was extremely unwilling to leave here," reports Dr. Kurt Binswanger, the Bellevue psychiatrist responsible for admissions and discharges. "He made no secret of the fact that he has an aversion to going to Heiden. He even tried in all sorts of ways to get to the train too late." During the trip he behaved "in a most peculiar way, especially after Dr. Greiber joined them in Rorschach." Nijinsky "sat down ostentatiously opposite Mrs. Greiber, pointed his index finger at her, made clownish faces, grimaced menacingly, and chattered." Upon leaving the train station, he deliberately chose to walk in the muddy street, rather than on the sidewalk. When Greiber asked him to stop doing this he "began ostentatiously to march and beat time," which made Romola "extremely frightened." After arriving in Heiden, Romola "declared that she could not stand being alone with him for even an instant. It was now perfectly clear to her that taking him out of the hospital had been a mistake." She was angry at Dr. Binswanger for having recommended it. But by now no other arrangements could be made, so the two couples had dinner together and went to their rooms, where "the patient slept alone, next to Dr. Greiber," while the women stayed separate. At 11:30 p.m. Kurt Binswanger received a telephone call from Greiber saying that "the patient should be picked up again."

Early Saturday morning Kurt Binswanger got in his car for the half-hour drive along Lake Constance to Rorschach, and then up the hill to Heiden, where he was surprised to see "the whole company walking toward me, the patient cheerfully arm-in-arm with Mrs. Greiber." Apparently, they had spent a comfortable night at the hotel and were all feeling much better after a good breakfast.

> Dr. Greiber immediately explained to me [writes Kurt Binswanger] that he hardly thinks the patient can be returned today; today he seems so good that his wife no longer wants to be separated from him.... During our communal lunch the patient behaved very correctly, and played the amiable host.[36]

Binswanger had his suspicions that Nijinsky was again pretending or putting on an act, so after their meal he quizzed him thoroughly in private. What was he planning to do? Did he want to go back to the hospital? Absolutely not! "He explains that he wants to go back to St. Moritz," writes the psychiatrist. "He wants to be alone with his wife and have sun-treatments there. That is what he needs more than anything. He no longer wants to go back to Bellevue. Yesterday he did not want to leave at all because he was told that he has gotten much better. Now he doesn't see why our judgment has changed so suddenly." Evidently, Nijinsky had no insight into the effects of his unpredictable behavior on others. "If you don't agree to my returning to St. Moritz," he told Binswanger, "I could look for some other place in Switzerland." Throughout this entire discussion, Nijinsky "remained very friendly and correct," but whenever Dr. Greiber wanted to join in and advise him what to do, Nijinsky's attitude changed completely and he exploded with rage. (Apparently the dancer still suspected that Romola and Dr. Greiber were having an affair, and perhaps they were.) When Greiber tried "to tell him that the climate in St. Moritz would not be good for him, Nijinsky attacked him with hostility." Afterward, still in an angry mood, he disclosed to Binswanger his "hatred and enmity, i.e. his jealousy toward this man.

Above all, he did not want his wife to stay together with Dr. Greiber. (While saying this the patient showed an expression of the wildest hostility, while otherwise his mimicry remained rather stiff, even when other affects broke through.) He is the husband [!] He still has the right to decide where he and his wife have to go in their marriage.[37]

How much Nijinsky told Kurt Binswanger at this point about his suspicions regarding Romola and Dr. Greiber is unclear, but in due time they surely talked about this difficult subject, since Kurt Binswanger was now assigned to be Nijinsky's therapist (replacing Ludwig Binswanger, who seems to have had enough of this complicated case). Persuading the patient to return to the hospital after this weekend in Heiden was not easy. "Three times he changed his mind," writes Kurt Binswanger. "After much back-and-forth disputation, he finally had the insight that it would really be best for him to return again to Bellevue." But before getting into the doctor's car to drive back, Nijinsky "demanded" to see Romola.

She was utterly carried away and broke into spasms of crying. The patient, with completely authentic affect and the deepest sensibility and expressiveness, declared his absolute love to her. He told her, with most intensely escalated affect, that only God can separate them. This scene made a theatrical impression. It required some effort to persuade both of them that a separation would be necessary. At the farewell, the patient was again catatonic. He no longer spoke with his wife, gazed upward in a stereotypic way. During the return trip he became increasingly accessible, was pleased by the beautiful landscape, laughed like a child whenever children threw snowballs at the car. On arrival at the *Parkhaus* he very cordially greeted the head nurse and attendants, was happy to see that flowers had been put in his room and new pictures on the wall. He thanked me for accompanying him. . . . [38]

A new era had begun for Nijinsky. The tearful farewell from Romola with "authentic affect" (her tears, his affect) marked their first true separation. No longer was there just talk about a threatened separation, now it felt like a real divorce. Romola had resigned herself (only temporarily, as we shall see) to leaving him in the hospital. He, not without great anger, realized that he was no longer "the husband." Dr. Greiber had come between them. It was a very significant event, a turning point in Nijinsky's relationship to the outside world, and the beginning of his leap into true madness.

Separation can be painful, but it is also a time for individuation of the personalities who have been separated. The loss of a love object may stimulate internal reorganization and growth. Remnants of the old relationship remain in memory, but are gradually transformed in accordance with the needs of the personality and reality. An individual hungry for companionship may form new relationships. Another individual, who prefers solitude, may eschew further relationships and remain forever divorced. Someone with a creative gift may use separation as a springboard for the imagination, to write a book, paint a picture, compose music, devise a theory, invent a machine, or design a ballet. Nijinsky had to face the challenge of separation from Romola in accordance with his personally accumulated wisdom about such events. Separation from his father had allowed him to develop into a great dancer and choreographer. The separation from Diaghilev had led to his marriage and becoming a father (a role that Diaghilev himself craved, but never achieved). By molding Kyra in his own image, Nijinsky had also re-created something of his own childhood, and in moments of happiness he laughed like a child. His final break with Romola had been coming for some time. There had been difficulties in understanding each other from the beginning. While touring the United States, Nijinsky had wanted to return to Russia, and Romola, more inclined to a "normal" life, left him briefly. Their separation had made progress in Switzerland, where Vaslav found God and Romola turned to Dr. Greiber. Bleuler's insistence on a divorce hastened the process, and a month of psychiatric hospitalization had furthered it. Their weekend in Heiden had forced Nijinsky and his wife to say goodbye to each other. Their separation was now both a psychological and a physical reality. That Nijinsky would choose to cope with it "catatonically" seems consistent with everything he had ever learned and done to maintain his personal integrity and stabilize his social existence. From early childhood on, it had always been primarily by moving his body or holding it still, by gesturing and posturing, by expressing himself nonverbally, that he had been able to show what it meant to "be in the world."

One of the people who watched him practice his art after returning to the Bellevue Sanatorium was the poet and novelist Robert Walser. "Nijinsky mocks the ground with his legs," wrote Walser. "He evokes compassion and sympathy by leaping like a good, well-trained little dog."

His dancing is like a fairy-tale from innocent, ancient times when people had enough health and energy to be like children, playing together in regal freedom.... It seems impossible for him ever to stop dancing and pendulating, as if he wants, as if he should, as if he must continue to dance interminably.... Seeing him means that one must love, honor, and admire him.[39]

NOTES

1. Elie Wiesel, *Twilight*, 71.
2. Karl L. Kahlbaum, *Die Katatonie oder das Spannungsirresein*.
3. Erwin H. Ackerknecht, *A Short History of Psychiatry*.
4. Kahlbaum, 41. Emphasis added.
5. Ibid., 53–56.
6. Eugen Bleuler, "Dementia Praecox," 211.
7. Adolf Meyer, "A Cooperative Study of Cases of Stupors and Particularly of Catatonic Developments."
8. Edward J. Kempf, "Affective-Respiratory Factors in Catatonia," 173.
9. Kay H. Blacker, "Obsessive-Compulsive Phenomena and Catatonic States—A Continuum."
10. Alan J. Gelenberg, "The Catatonic Syndrome."
11. Gaston Magrinat, Jeffrey A. Danziger, Isabel C. Lorenzo, and Abraham Flemenbaum, "A Reassessment of Catatonia"; James B. Lohr and Alexander A. Wisniewski, *Movement Disorders*.
12. Bellevue medical records, now in the University Archives, Tübingen, West Germany. Hereafter, cited as BMR.
13. RNN, 431.
14. Wolfgang Binswanger, M.D., private communication.
15. Ibid.
16. Ludwig Binswanger, *Zur Geschichte der Heilanstalt Bellevue in Kreuzlingen*, 10 and 14.
17. Ibid., 23.
18. Ludwig Binswanger, *Sigmund Freud*, 42.
19. Ibid.
20. Ludwig Binswanger, *Being-in-the-World*.
21. Ludwig Binswanger, "The Existential Analysis School of Thought."
22. Personal communication from Dr. N.E. (name withheld), who worked on the Bellevue staff, and from members of the Binswanger family.
23. Reese notes, BMR.
24. Ibid.
25. Personal communication from Wolfgang Binswanger, M.D.
26. Binswanger, *Sigmund Freud*, 11.
27. Binswanger notes, BMR. Emphasis in the original.
28. Ibid.
29. Henry-Louis de La Grange, *Mahler*, 424.
30. Bernard Taper, *Balanchine*, x.
31. Lydia Temoshok, Craig Van Dyke, and Leonard S. Zegans (editors), *Emotions in Health and Illness: Theoretical and Research Foundations*.
32. Binswanger notes, BMR.
33. Ibid. Emphasis added.
34. Ibid.
35. Ibid.
36. Ibid.
37. Ibid.
38. Ibid.
39. Robert Walser, "Der Tänzer."

Posterity is entitled to know
everything about the life of its great
ones—even the most intimate details.
If they are truly great, they must be
able to survive it.
                    Alfred Einstein[1]

Chapter 10

The Leap into Madness

In reviewing the course of Nijinsky's treatment at the Bellevue Sanatorium, one is struck by the repeated shifts between three dominant modes of behavior, each reflecting a dimension of his pre-illness personality style. As "the dancer," his core identity since early childhood, he continued to perform astonishing leaps, to invent new movements, and to think about creating further ballets. As "the lunatic," the role he had adopted since learning of his brother's death, Nijinsky elaborated ever more shocking, violent, moody, vengeful, and destructive aspects of his personality. Finally, as "the patient," a role he was destined to assume for many years, Nijinsky brought forward those qualities—passivity, dependency, obedience, and gentleness—that habitually had characterized his way of relating to people who loved and cared for him: first his mother, then Diaghilev, later Romola, and now his doctors and nurses.

The co-existence within a single individual of two or more well-defined personality styles suggests a pathological condition called multiple personality disorder. With this illness, contrastive dimensions of the personality seem to take over at various times, to assume independence, and to control speech and behavior so convincingly that onlookers cannot recognize them as belonging to the same individual.[2] With Nijinsky, however, the characteristics of "dancer," "lunatic," and "patient" were usually not sufficiently distinct from one another to warrant this diagnosis. It is true, of course, that artistic interests dominated the first half of his life, but they also made themselves felt later on, except that under the influence of his illness the results were much more eccentric and unrealistic than ever before. Even though madness was Nijinsky's overall adaptation during most of the second half of his life, streaks of lunacy had been there all along. Everyone who tried to relate to him or sought to understand him over the course of time was perplexed by the random fluctuations in his mood and behavior, vacillating unpredictably from meek dependence to violent rebelliousness, from abject conformism to daring originality, from cuddly passivity to destructive aggression. For Nijinsky, the process of going mad was hardly smooth or gradual. He did not slip or "descend" into madness, as was said of so many psychotic geniuses in the nineteenth century;[3] he leapt in and out of it with a ferocity that bewildered those who had to witness the resulting chaos.

After taking leave of Romola and Dr. and Mrs. Greiber at the end of their weekend outing to Heiden and returning to the hospital with Dr. Binswanger on 5 April 1919, Nijinsky was noted to be calm, composed, and behaving quite normally. "He went for a walk, played billiards, and slept well." But after breakfast the next morning, when his attendant left the room, he suddenly and without any warning "made a mess of his room, crushed all of his flowers and ripped the blossoms. Using a blue crayon, he painted rings, crosses, lines and other things all over the walls, as well as on the furniture, the rug, and the floor. He moved all the furniture and disorganized the wash-basin." Was he trying to convert his hospital room into a stage set and decorate it accordingly? When the attendant returned and discovered what Nijinsky had done, he received no explanation. "The patient merely left his room without speaking, went into the billiard-room, and pretended that nothing had happened."[4]

Following this maniacal outburst, Nijinsky was again noted to be "completely quiet all afternoon." The next two weeks alternated between "quiet days and those in which he clowns, threatens all kinds of things, makes faces, suddenly remains standing rigidly, rolling his eyes, giving the other patients dark looks, and completely failing to respond when one addresses him." It seemed that he was no longer willing to relate to the environment according to rules of ordinary politeness. He would behave boorishly in the company of other people, as if it no longer mattered what they thought of him. While appearing to be "distracted and out of sorts," he simply stopped conforming. For example, at the dinner table on 18 April 1919, "he fell asleep with his head in the potato-dish and his hands in the dessert-sauce." Later, when he displayed the behavior of an animal, he would grab food with his fingers, wolf it down, or throw it on the floor.

Another worrisome decline in Nijinsky's deportment had to do with sexual conduct. He was observed to lie on his bed, expose himself, and "masturbate a great deal." He also made inappropriate and quite outrageous approaches to some of the other patients. While walking through the park on 20 April, he went up to a woman, greeted her ostentatiously, and offered her his hand. She responded by reaching out to shake it, whereupon he abruptly pulled his hand back, and then "pounced on her, so that she fell to the ground in horror." He teased and provoked his male attendant by often "standing in his room, rigidly staring straight ahead, and refusing to go to bed ... then in one leap he would jump into the bed, tumble out again, and again stand around stiffly."

On 26 April, Romola, accompanied this time by Oscar Párdány, came to Bellevue to visit him. Nijinsky seemed "friendly and very happy" at first, spoke quietly with his father-in-law, and was noted to be "amorous toward his wife." But when they all sat down for lunch together, he began "making faces, became stuporous, sat completely stiff in his chair, stared ahead, and failed to respond" to anything that Romola or Oscar was saying. Finally, his attendant had to put him to bed. Later on, while Párdány was talking to him, Nijinsky suddenly "grabbed himself violently by the throat" as if he were having some kind of seizure, collapsed on a couch, and kept "blinking his eyes." When the attendant came into the room and asked Párdány to step outside, "the patient recovered completely." We do not know what Nijinsky and his father-in-law were discussing when he became so acutely upset, but information in the hospital chart suggests that it may have been the dancer's desire to live in Russia, and possibly his conflicts about returning to the stage. The chart shows the following entry written by Dr. Kurt Binswanger:

> Mr. Párdány tells us that in September–October 1918 the patient had an intimate friendship with the Russian Kostrowsky, who inspired his enthusiasm for Tolstoy. Since then the patient has changed himself, has wanted to live his life very simply, à la Tolstoy, to give everything away and move to the land.

This information could have come only from Nijinsky or from Romola. Binswanger also writes that Párdány told him about Nijinsky's homosexual relationship with Diaghilev:

> The Director of the Ballets Russes recognized Nijinsky's talent early on, took care of his education, and understood how to give him the right roles, with which he achieved enormous triumphs. But Diaghilev handled him terribly brutally, beat him, locked him in a room when he went away, allowed him to be with nobody else until his 18th. [sic] year, and abused him homosexually. There were good reasons for Nijinsky's suspicions of Diaghilev, because he had evoked the man's enmity by separating from him.

These disclosures, although one-sided, fragmentary, and partly incorrect, seem to have led to some progress in Nijinsky's psychotherapy. Dr. Binswanger reports that during their discussions over the ensuing weeks, the dancer became much "quieter." For the first time since coming to Bellevue he cried, talked about how "sad" he was feeling, and declared that he would rather "be with his wife and live with her" than stay in the Parkhaus. (Only later in the hospital chart is it mentioned that Nijinsky was trying to learn German; therefore I assume that his psychotherapy was conducted in French, a language he did not speak well.) No matter what Binswanger said or did, however, Nijinsky seemed unable to comprehend that his behavior was disturbing to others, and thus an obstacle to his being transferred to Haus Bellevue or one of the other pavilions, where he would have been able to mingle more freely with women. Transfer to an open unit, where supervision was less strict than in the Parkhaus, would have been the first step toward a visit back to St. Moritz and eventual release from the hospital.

Thus, by continuing to engage in what Kurt Binswanger characterized as outlandish "mannerisms," Nijinsky was in effect contradicting what he was saying, that is, "I want to live with my wife." He often seemed "lost in his thoughts." He would "grasp his billiard cue peculiarly" in the presence of other men (a phallic gesture of threat or defense, perhaps), which frightened them. He "twisted his body, rolled his eyes, and made oddly pompous and worrisome gestures." When asked why he did these things, Nijinsky merely answered "because I am an artist and I am sick." Every attempt at gaining insight into his abnormal childhood led either to absolute silence or to "conventionally polite" assertions that there was "really nothing the matter with him except for feeling slightly tired and perhaps nervous."

In terms of possibly enlarging the psychological understanding of Nijinsky's symptoms, it might have been helpful if the Bellevue psychiatrists had seen his notebooks from St. Moritz, since these provide not only a wealth of autobiographical data, but also copious fantasy material about "life," "death," and "feeling." Especially pertinent is Nijinsky's memory of his earlier hospitalization, at age twelve ("I was dying ... in the hospital I saw death with my own eyes"), because it suggests a close association between hospital confinement and death. Notable also is his persistent "pretending" to be a patient ("I will pretend to be dying, sick, etc. etc. so that I can enter a poor man's cottage"). The notebooks reveal what it meant for Nijinsky no longer to be dancing in public, to have lost the limelight and his "stardom." ("I want light, the light of twinkling stars. A twinkling star is life—and a star that does not twinkle is death.") And he suggests that some of his writing was done in a "trance," which might have given the Bellevue psychiatrists an incentive to urge him to write again, as part of his psychotherapy ("Everything I write is a spiritualistic trance. I should like everyone to be in such a trance, because Tolstoy, Dostoevsky, and Zola were also in such a trance").[5]

Unfortunately none of this information about Nijinsky's inner life came to the Binswangers' attention. The extracts from his notebooks which had been made in Zürich remained in Professor Bleuler's file, never to be consulted by any of his future therapists. Neither Romola nor Dr. Greiber saw fit to bring Nijinsky's original writings to Kreuzlingen, probably for the same reason that she later chose to censor them. They contain too many unflattering remarks. (For example, in editing the *Diary,* Romola removed the following passage: "I know the significance of stars that do not twinkle. My wife is an untwinkling star.")

Psychoanalytic studies of catatonic patients suggest that they suffer from a conflict between autonomy and giving in to the will of another person. An expert in this field, Dr. Edward Kempf, observed that under the influence of strong emotions, catatonics "vacillate between going into a stupor and staying out."

> To be or not to be does not depend upon caring at all to remain socially adaptable, but whether or not some beloved person will humor them sufficiently to entice the sulky affect to soften before it is too late. In this sense catatonically inclined persons are as helpless as nurselings, and entirely dependent upon someone's sympathetic transference and well-controlled understanding....[6]

Nijinsky's hospital records show that he repeatedly sought attention from people and tried to get them to respond to him, quite unlike the behavior of regressed schizophrenics, who abhor social contact and withdraw from others. Just as repeatedly, Nijinsky's efforts misfired, owing in part to the bewilderment he stimulated with his odd mannerisms. For example, when on 10 May a male patient invited him to play billiards, Nijinsky accepted, but then began "to manipulate his cue" in his usual provocative way until "it dropped on the other man's feet." An argument broke out, and Nijinsky challenged the patient to a fight. An attendant had to intervene and get Nijinsky to apologize, after which the two men were "reconciled."

Then, there was his ambiguous involvement with Herr Vogel (not his real name), a wealthy, unmarried patient, twelve years Nijinsky's senior, who not only looked like Diaghilev, but even claimed to have been "a dance-director for 5 years." Vogel played the violin, well enough so that Ludwig Binswanger, who was an amateur pianist, performed with him occasionally. Vogel also had a reputation for enticing other patients into his bedroom, which was strictly against the rules at Bellevue. (Vogel's diagnosis was "imbecility and hebephrenia.") At first Nijinsky seemed to be attracted to this man, "stared" at him a great deal, and tried to elicit his friendship, but when Vogel started to reciprocate, Nijinsky began complaining of "incomprehensible anxieties, and a vague feeling that he wanted to kill me." These are paranoid reactions. Nijinsky told the doctors that Vogel "has been

looking at me in a funny way. I know he's a good fellow, and yet I can't
get rid of the feeling that he wants to do something to me. I know this is
'sick.' It produces a dreadful feeling around my heart."⁷ (Dr. Greiber
had mentioned the "paranoid content" of Nijinsky's psychosis in St.
Moritz. Paranoid suspicions were also described during Nijinsky's last
year of touring with the Ballets Russes.)

Recognizing Nijinsky's susceptibility to paranoid thinking, especially
the frightful idea that certain men were out to do him harm, Kurt
Binswanger now established a policy of controlling his social contacts,
much as Diaghilev had done in the past, in order to minimize
encounters that might prove to be too stressful. In mixed company
Nijinsky tended to be much less disturbed. During a tea party at Dr.
and Mrs. Binswanger's house, for example, the dancer was noted to
"behave very nicely. He converses in a completely organized way about
art, and takes pleasure in looking at paintings and other art objects."
Soon, he was allowed to go on automobile rides through the neighboring
villages, became "very happy, expressed delight about the blossoming
trees, and talked animatedly about his home [in Russia], how the
peasants work there, etc."

Toward the end of May—Nijinsky had by now spent over two months
at Bellevue—he seemed sufficiently improved to go for walks without
an attendant. Around this time, he also formed an attachment to an
"English couple and a Swedish woman." The four would meet for tea at
the home of Kurt Binswanger and his wife, where Nijinsky was noted to
"converse happily [presumably in French], make childish jokes with the
doctor's little boy, and feel very much at ease." With the Englishman
(husband of one of the patients), he often "strolled in the park, talking
to him excitedly about art, and much about politics, and becoming very
lively." With the Swedish woman, a competent musician, Nijinsky even
felt inspired to do some dancing. Doctor Binswanger described it.

> When she began to play the piano, Nijinsky sank nonchalantly onto a
> lounging chair, the music gradually drew him into a semi-conscious state.
> Then he would start to *dance* again for the first time, no longer in the
> bizarre way he had done it before, but now with beautiful, artistic
> movements, mostly merry things based on Norwegian folksongs, after
> which he was a little unstrung but in a good mood.⁹

There still were moments of intense anxiety when Nijinsky deliberately avoided people and seemed unpredictably rude. "He walked stiffly

past his English friend, with eyes directed straight ahead, and failed to respond to his greetings." (Dr. Binswanger wondered if Nijinsky harbored "delusional ideas" toward this man.) By contrast, he seemed comfortable with the man's wife "and with other women and children, enjoyed talking, making all kinds of jokes, playing with his watch, pretending to have a monocle in his eye, and turning around in circles." It is difficult to know from Binswanger's notes whether such antics were considered normal or symptomatic of Nijinsky's illness.

This and other questions about his current progress came into focus when Romola, accompanied again by Dr. Greiber, visited the sanatorium on 22 May 1919, to find out how Nijinsky was doing. She wanted to know how soon he would be ready to come back to St. Moritz. It was a delicate question. Romola's mother and stepfather were still living at the Villa Guardamunt, and the summer tourist season was fast approaching. From confidential sources we know of another reason for Romola's concern. Dr. Greiber allegedly was still in love with her, and (over his wife's objections) had been asking Romola if she was planning to get a divorce. She said no. In his predicament, Greiber was beginning to develop a psychiatric illness of his own. He tried to control his symptoms by taking morphine, which led to a serious addiction.[10] One can only commiserate with these unhappy people: Romola's guilt over what was happening to her husband and Greiber's anxiety about his former patient and the patient's wife, whom he loved.

Kurt Binswanger told Romola that Nijinsky "must stay longer in the hospital; a change of environment at this point could only be damaging." This statement troubled her. The open-endedness of her husband's hospital stay, its considerable expense, the inconvenience of having him so far away from home, and the uncertainty about his future raised all sorts of questions in Romola's mind. Therefore, a conference was arranged with the hospital director, Dr. Ludwig Binswanger, who "explained to her in great detail that the patient has improved, and that a practical recovery is to be expected." What Binswanger meant by a "practical recovery" is not too clear. According to Nijinsky's chart, Romola was told that the dancer "will not be able to return home before fall, and a resumption of his work is not indicated before next spring [1920]." As will become apparent shortly, Romola wanted to know if Nijinsky would be able to resume having sexual intercourse. It is not unlikely that this question had also been discussed with Dr. Greiber. Dr. Binswanger indicated that he had some doubts about it.[11]

Ludwig Binswanger's prognosis about Nijinsky's future was cautious but optimistic. He knew that the dancer was far from recovered, but predicted that he would be able to "resume his work." He also knew that the outcome of catatonic disorders was not necessarily favorable. (In checking eleven randomly selected case records of Bellevue patients— eight men and three women—who were diagnosed to have catatonia during the time Nijinsky was hospitalized there, I found that nearly half of them, all men, were discharged as "unimproved." Only three men and one woman were considered "improved" when they left the hospital. Of the remaining two women, one was rediagnosed as a "chronic schizophrenic," and the other committed suicide three days after leaving the hospital.) Romola failed to be convinced by what the psychiatrists told her. She did not believe that Nijinsky was benefiting from hospital care. She thought that, if anything, he was getting worse, and that it would be better for him to come back to St. Moritz. But Dr. Greiber, with his medical training (and his own anxieties about what it would mean to have Nijinsky back at the Villa Guardamunt), saw things differently and urged Romola not to sign him out against the Binswangers' advice. Greiber also took the hapless dancer for "a walk through the park," and told Kurt Binswanger afterward that they had had a "good conversation." What was discussed we do not know, but after Romola's and Dr. Greiber's departure, Nijinsky was noted to be "somewhat worse again ... depressed at times, with his head sometimes held sideways, as if listening to something (voices?)." He "wagged his head" in a silly manner, "spread his fingers apart," "made grimaces," and again behaved in a rude and threatening way toward others.

Photographs of Nijinsky dancing _Till Eulenspiegel_ in 1916 show him spreading his fingers, wagging his head, making vile faces, and acting much as Kurt Binswanger described him at Bellevue in 1919. At the end of _Till Eulenspiegel_ the enraged townspeople condemn the troublesome mischief-maker to death, and he is duly executed. Already during his South America trip in 1917, the troubled Nijinsky had had difficulty dissociating himself from the roles he was dancing. He trembled with terror lest death overtake him during the ballet _Narcisse_, for example. It seems that this was exactly what Nijinsky feared might happen while dancing his heart out in front of the patients and staff at Bellevue. He complained that "his heart might stop." He told his attendant he felt certain that he "will be killed here. Herr Vogel and some other people say that his corpse will be stuffed into a suitcase." When Kurt Binswanger made his rounds on 25 May, he found Nijinsky in a state of panic, "pale, his entire body trembling, saying he knows he is 'sick' but he cannot rid himself of his terrifying ideas." He kept repeating, "I don't want to die here. I want to go on living. I am still young and have a loving wife and a child. I love everyone here and cannot understand why I have to be killed."[12]

Efforts to "reassure" Nijinsky gave only temporary relief. His fear of death was turning delusional, impervious to logic and reason. Therefore, Kurt Binswanger decided for the first time to use medication. He prescribed sodium bromide, a sedative given by mouth. (Today one would use a neuroleptic or antipsychotic drug.) The patient simmered down and fell asleep, but "in the middle of his sleep he suddenly woke up, startled, pleading, 'I don't want to die yet.'" Binswanger cautioned Nijinsky's attendant to be "extremely watchful" lest he become suicidal. It was suspected that his delusional fear of death might be the harbinger of a self-destructive impulse, an unconscious turning inward of the aggression and rage that Nijinsky had heretofore directed against others. Under constant supervision, he became even more agitated, and "increasingly mistrustful" of the attendant. For this reason, on 27 May, Binswanger assigned a more experienced and older man, Fritz Wieland, to watch over the patient.

Wieland had worked at Bellevue for five years and was considered one of the most self-assured and conscientious attendants there. In his way of relating to Nijinsky, Fritz Wieland seems to have combined the qualities of a Swiss-German overseer with those of the Russian Vasili Zuikov, who throughout his Ballets Russes years had helped keep the dancer under control. During the two months that Wieland looked after Nijinsky, some extremely dramatic changes were noted. First, he stopped obsessing about death, a move toward better mental health. Next, he became interested in choreographing two new ballets, a remarkable shift from delusional to creative thinking. Finally, he fell into a childlike stupor, followed again by a full-blown catatonic excitement.

Nijinsky's temporary move from madness to creativity was linked to an abrupt disavowal of everything connected with Diaghilev and the Franco-Russian culture. He "refused to speak French." He said, "I want to be German, the German culture attracts me, therein lies true passion, power, energy, monumentality." According to the medical record, which is the only source of information we have about the ballets Nijinsky planned to choreograph at the Bellevue Sanatorium, both were to be set to music by Richard Strauss. One was for *Elektra,* the opera Nijinsky had seen the night before Kyra's birth in Vienna, a story about the brutal destruction of a family. (Elektra seeks revenge on her mother Clytemnestra for the murder of her father Agamemnon. Consumed by brutality, she dances herself to death like a wild animal, after her brother Orestes has killed Clytemnestra. The other ballet Nijinsky had in mind was *Symphonia Domestica,* based on Strauss's great orchestral tribute to domestic tranquillity. (This symphony depicts twenty-four hours in the life of a happy family, with Strauss himself as the hardworking, devoted father, his wife Pauline as a quarrelsome but loyal wife, and their infant son Franz being bathed and put to bed, after which the parents engage in passionate love-making.)

Nijinsky's choice of these contrastive themes—a happy family versus one that is disintegrating—suggests not only the conflicts raging within him, but also a desire to resolve these conflicts creatively. *Elektra* probably alludes to his work with Diaghilev. Their plan had been to produce a ballet set to music by Strauss, to be called *Orestes and the Furies,* with Nijinsky dancing the role of Elektra's brother.[13] (Would his sister have played the role of Elektra? We know that she was to dance the Sacrificial Virgin in *Sacre.*) Nijinsky's intended *Symphonia Domestica* ballet most likely was meant to symbolize his marriage, the five troubled years with Romola, and his joy at being Kyra's father. While planning to work on these Strauss ballets in the hospital, Nijinsky often ranted (in imperfect German, the only language he now wanted to speak) against "the lax confusion of the Ballets Russes, where everyone did what he wished." He declared an interest in "seeing his good friend Richard Strauss in Berlin, and working in collaboration with Max Reinhardt, who can understand the organization of the big project he had in mind. This will require iron discipline." (Nijinsky told Dr. Binswanger that he had written to Reinhardt about his ideas, but I have been unable to find any letters to this effect.*) He talked incessantly and in a grandiose, exaggerated way about *Till Eulenspiegel:* "how despite the resistance of the company, which refused because of political motives, he had forced this ballet to be performed in New York.

---

*Nijinsky's sister did a musical film, *A Midsummer Night's Dream,* with Reinhardt in 1935, another example of how she carried out many of Nijinsky's dreams and expanded his work.

With these performances, he achieved his greatest success. For him, *Till Eulenspiegel* is the embodiment of Germanic existence." He also raved that "since the [Swiss] doctors can do nothing for me, I want to get away from here and go to Germany, to a clinic that is quieter!" He told Kurt Binswanger, "I have torn up all of my letters and drawings because an *invisible man* ordered me to do so [further signs of delusional thinking.]" He vilified Dr. Greiber: "He is an idiot. If I see him again I want to drag him to the ground and smash him."

In his excitement, Nijinsky kept asking for "German art-publications," to which Binswanger responded by giving him copies of the periodicals *Jugend* and *Simplicissimus*. Nijinsky found it difficult to concentrate on this material, which he did not seem to like or understand. He simply "flew through" the magazines, "nervously" turning the pages and glancing hurriedly at the pictures while ignoring the text. Binswanger had better luck with a book of paintings and engravings by Albrecht Dürer, whose exceptional skill in communicating the vitality of human form and expression seems to have fascinated Nijinsky. "This is my kind of art," he told Binswanger. One can see why: Dürer enriched the Gothic style of medieval German art with a glowing robustness. His inexhaustible vitality, transmitted through the important new medium of engraving, had taken Europe by storm, much as Nijinsky's revolutionary transformation of classical ballet into a highly personalized dance style electrified audiences around the time of World War I. In studying Dürer's work, Nijinsky undoubtedly came across his famous *Melancholia,* the image of a brooding genius surrounded by discarded instruments and useless symbols, and he may have recognized his own anguish in this engraving. "Nijinsky cares only for the mighty, monumental, and gigantic qualities embodied in the German classical style and the German soul," Dr. Binswanger wrote.

> Everything fanciful and over-ornamented, which is customary among the French, he hates. He adamantly refuses to speak French, but since his German is defective ... it is not always easy to converse with him. He practices German by reading from a newspaper, in a loud voice. Often he is excited while doing this, trembling with his whole body, most markedly with his legs.

Unfortunately, the dancer's overwrought condition precluded his making any progress either in learning German or in producing the Strauss ballets. He failed even to outline the stories, let alone sketch the choreography, scenery, or costumes. His only surviving artwork from the Bellevue Sanatorium consists of decorative drawings of intersecting circles and lines, the same abstract, semi-representational masks or faces Nijinsky had produced in St. Moritz. It was impossible for him to work on the musical selections for his ballets, to select appropriate segments from _Elektra_ and _Symphonia Domestica,_ or to organize these into danceable sequences. No orchestral scores were available at the Bellevue Sanatorium (although Ludwig Binswanger, as an amateur musician, should have been able to get hold of some), not even a piano reduction that might have been played for the dancer. Even if there had been scores, it seems doubtful that in his agitated state and without competent assistance, Nijinsky could have made much progress with Strauss's elaborate music. Thus, like many of the other ambitious projects conceived after the dancer's final break with Diaghilev, his new ballets never materialized.

Nijinsky's brief excursion into creative fantasy served at least to push his delusional fear of self-annihilation out of consciousness. "He was able to come out of himself," writes Kurt Binswanger; "it was easier to establish rapport with him than before." Only temporarily, however. On 31 May he was again noted to be "trembling, pale, looking mistrustful and paranoid." He refused to speak French and in response to questions about how he was feeling, "excitedly uttered broken words in German which had no connection." It was so difficult to understand what he was saying that Ludwig Binswanger, who again saw Nijinsky briefly in consultation, thought "surely he was hearing voices, although he denies it most strenuously." The next day he was speaking French again and told Dr. Binswanger about having "unbearable nightmares." Nijinsky could not explain what he was dreaming about, but "in a state of fear, he clasped the doctor's hand, begging that he should help him, because it was so horrible." He also described a number of uncanny daytime experiences. "Whenever he hears the noise of a locomotive in the distance," writes Binswanger, "he has the idea that he must go out and stop the whole train."

> Today he saw a picture of Christ in a magazine, and it seemed to him as though _he_ were Christ. He cannot explain such ideas to himself at all. He says that his thoughts are sick and that his poor head is sick. He also has the feeling that someone else may be inside his body. When he moves his arm, it feels as if this is someone else's arm, which does not belong to him.

Nijinsky repeatedly begged his doctors to do something about his disturbing obsessions, which he recognized were delusional (i.e., contrary to reality) and tried to negate by engaging in various behavioral stratagems (compulsive behavior, mannerisms, and rituals). "Why can't this get better?" he implored Kurt Binswanger in their mutual effort at trying to gain control over his runaway thoughts. "I would prefer to take a revolver and end it all. But I am still so young and don't want to die."

When Romola came for another visit, on 5 June 1919, she found him "worse than ever." At first Nijinsky refused to speak to her and "only communicated through signs and gestures." During dinner, "when she did not pour enough wine for him, he vehemently smashed the bottle on the table." When she tried to discuss plans for the future, he burst into a rage and "ranted" at her in German about "my monumental art, my projects with Strauss, etc." He said "I want to hear nothing at all about ever going back to France or America." He became "furious," writes Kurt Binswanger, "when his wife began to talk about her mother; he said that he also doesn't care a thing about his child. He no longer wanted to be bothered with such trivialities." During this visit, Nijinsky upbraided Romola for having taken control of his finances. He tried to make it clear to her that he "wants his savings to be transferred in his own name." He berated Romola for allowing Greiber to "treat her," and indicated in no uncertain terms that he "never wanted to hear anything more" about this man.

Although Nijinsky was going through the motions of asserting his independence, in reality he was merely shifting his allegiance from his wife to his doctors. "I gladly want to stay here now, so I can get healthy," he told her. "I am eager to do everything the doctors prescribe for me." Yet, the moment Romola left him, all his fears, obsessions, and delusions returned. "Why am I locked up," he would scream pitifully. "Why are the windows closed, why am I never left alone?" He seemed utterly without insight. "I am not a prisoner. My wife makes me nervous and sick. I have no work to do here. I belong to Richard Strauss and the grand opera."

Kurt Binswanger tried to stabilize Nijinsky's wretched mood by letting him stay in bed all day and sedating him heavily with bromides (1 gram three times a day), plus "hypnotica" (containing opium) at night. This was standard medical procedure, but it did little to help Nijinsky. If anything, he became more depressed than ever and tried to fight off his confusion by "entering ever more deeply into the problems of his artistic concepts." Binswanger gave him more art books, illustrations by Holbein and other painters, but Nijinsky finally rejected them all, grew truculent, and said, "This is English art, which no longer interests me." On 10 June, Binswanger made the ominous observation that the dancer was "knocking on his earlobes with both index fingers, getting very excited, and making a peculiar grinding noise [with his teeth].... He explains to his attendant that he always _hears_ someone talking in English. He can even _see_ this person. It is the man who is always playing tennis; he makes him terribly nervous."[14]

Tennis, we will remember, held a special meaning for Nijinsky: its movements had inspired him in 1913 to choreograph the ballet _Jeux_. He had quickly learned to play tennis during his vacation in New England in 1916. From his room in the Parkhaus, Nijinsky could see the Bellevue tennis court. It gave him pleasure to watch the other patients running, jumping, and hitting the ball, a reminder probably of certain ballet actions and his own athletic mastery. (In later years, during one of his rehospitalizations at Bellevue, he was often seen near the tennis court, not playing the game, but standing as if entranced and producing what one of the doctors remembered as "coarse, excessively loud" laughter.[15])

Nijinsky's remark about "hearing and seeing" someone play tennis was taken by the doctors to mean that he was definitely hallucinating. They had questioned him repeatedly about "hearing voices," but until now he had denied it. Nijinsky himself believed that his pressured thoughts about the English tennis player indicated a worsening of his illness. He became severely "depressed, cried a great deal, and said that one ought to operate on his head." When left alone, he often seemed to be "listening to voices, and giving them incomprehensible answers." On 15 June, a staff doctor he had never seen before made evening rounds, which made Nijinsky feel "excited" and "nervous." "Dr. H." seemed to be "entering his body." It was "like a knife being stuck into his heart." He felt his own face "taking on the features of Dr. H." and was "plagued enormously be the feeling that his own limbs no longer belong to him."

When Nijinsky raises his hand [writes Binswanger] it is someone else's hand. He wails that he will never get well.... He kept shouting angrily ... that he wants to get away from here and go to a hospital in Berlin ... nothing here does him any good. He hears too much music. The noise of the trains bothers him. He sees too many strange people.

There can no longer be any doubt that Nijinsky was having serious trouble with reality-testing, losing control over his perceptions, and experiencing awesome changes taking place within his body. The cause of these unfavorable developments is not entirely clear, however. In addition to psychosocial stresses and his psychotic illness (still being diagnosed as "catatonia"), one must consider the effects of medication at this time. Wieland and the nurses had been giving him substantial amounts of oral bromides and "hypnotica." The psychiatrists were also injecting two powerful drugs, scopolamine and morphine, which may have contributed to his confusion, as well as his frightening sense of being "entered into" and physically manipulated from the outside.

Scopolamine is a belladonna alkaloid, closely related to atropine. It produces fatigue, euphoria, drowsiness, and loss of memory. Scopolamine has strong anticholinergic effects. In small doses it slows the heart rate and inhibits the secretion of sweat and saliva, which results in dryness of the mouth and makes swallowing and speaking difficult. Scopolamine impedes the action of the lungs and intestines and interferes with the fine-tuning of small muscles in the eyes and ears, which can play havoc with perception. Larger doses lead to paralysis of the bladder and other vital organs. Scopolamine also has psychological effects: it increases the time needed for making decisions and slows down the thinking processes.[16] When given alone, especially in the presence of anxiety or physical pain, this drug can produce hallucinations and instigate uncontrollable behavior. For this reason it is usually combined with morphine, a potent tranquilizer, painkiller, and central nervous system depressant. Morphine-scopolamine mixtures were widely used for inducing anesthesia, assisting women in labor, and in psychiatry for the treatment of mania, delirium tremens, and other hyperactive states. Nijinsky usually received 1 milligram of scopolamine mixed with 100 milligrams of morphine sulfate, a standard dose. Whether this helped or hindered his recovery is hard to say, but at least by giving medication the doctors felt they were doing something positive.

How can one depict, coherently and in an orderly fashion, the sequence of events in a life that has become irrational? Kurt Binswanger's hospital notes show that for an entire month his strange, lonely, and befuddled dancer-patient suffered from uncontrollable mood swings. During the last week of June, for example, Nijinsky fluctuated wildly between "sadness and happiness." Often he showed a "gloomy facial expression," and when left alone would "keep himself very busy with newspapers and books." When he was with his attendant, Wieland, Nijinsky's behavior alternated between defiance and submission. He would "make trouble" for Wieland by excitedly running off in "different directions" while they were strolling in the park, or he would try to escape to Haus Bellevue, where the less disturbed patients lived (and where he had given his dance recital), instead of staying where he was supposed to, near the Parkhaus and the tennis court. The staff thought he was "hearing voices a lot." One time he said he heard "a young woman" talking to him; another time, "it was like a telephone." Occasionally, he "rapped his earlobes" to demonstrate where he thought the "voices" were coming from.

On 25 June, after a few "cheerful days," Nijinsky again became severely depressed, with "much crying" and "complaining that his head is very sick." He held his head in both hands like the puppet in *Petrushka,* "making upward movements while tensing his neck muscles to the utmost." He also made what the hospital staff described as "bizarre movements with his legs and thighs; pulling his feet up to his head." One is reminded of a ballet dancer's daily warm-up exercises, needed to keep muscles limber and joints stretched. Such maneuvers may indeed look "bizarre" to an untrained observer. While doing them, Nijinsky often "looked around suspiciously." Some of this "looking around" may have been his search for a reflection of himself, as dancers typically watch themselves in a mirror while exercising. (A posed photograph of Nijinsky gazing at himself in a mirror—it was taken by Stravinsky when the dancer was still with Diaghilev—shows a very striking attitude of haughty "suspiciousness.")

In a book called *Toys and Reasons,* Erik Erikson commented on the similarities between playfulness in childhood and the reasoning of adults. Children use toys and games to relate to each other (in addition to having fun) and to make deductions about what is going on around them. Adults do essentially the same thing (perhaps not quite as joyfully), with logic, rules, and theories that "create model situations in which aspects of the past are re-lived, the present is re-presented and renewed, and the future anticipated."[17] Nijinsky, too, seems to have been recapitulating roles from his past career, "re-presenting" fragments of ballets for people in his hospital, and rehearsing for an empty future. On 30 June it was noted that he "has been able to play for hours with his blanket, stereotypically making all kinds of figures with it, and looking at these for a long time." Such behavior is reminiscent of a lonesome child toying with a "security blanket" or other handy material (psychoanalyst Donald Winnicott called these things "transitional objects"—pieces of cloth, rag dolls, scraps of paper, etc.—to provide physical contact with something tangible and to symbolically replace a lost parent or longed-for companion).[18]

In his isolation, Nijinsky also made use of his body as a plaything. He would "hold his breath" for long periods of time, and then forcibly breathe in and out to the point of "turning blue-red." Dancers are experts in consciously manipulating their respiration. When warming up, they purge the body by expelling "bad air." They may deliberately exhale while practicing a difficult move. They "hold" the breath to gain better balance and control. Preparing for a difficult run or jump also requires controlled breathing. Nijinsky had experimented with his respiration since childhood in order to perfect his spectacular leaps. Undoubtedly, he also had discovered that deep breathing has an effect on consciousness. This principle is applied in many forms of meditation, tai chi chuan, for example (*chi* means breath in Chinese), as well as in hypnosis and "mind-expanding" experiences.

Altered respiration was quite common among "catatonics." Some clinicians compared it to the "stubborn rages" of children trying to "compel their parents to humor them. By taking great gasps and holding the breath, they seem able to work up such a marked degree of cerebral disturbance that muscular rigidity or epileptoid convulsions with loss of consciousness often follow."[19] Nijinsky may have been experimenting to find out how long he could be without oxygen before passing out. The memory of his childhood drowning accident, when he suddenly realized that "I could not breathe," probably was a factor—"I kept the little air I had, shutting my mouth, thinking that if God wishes, I shall be saved."[20] Breath-holding soon became part of his generally unruly conduct at Bellevue.

> 30 June—Patient refused for two days to let his bed be made; refused to let himself be washed; threatened his attendant, and wouldn't speak at all for long periods of time. Yesterday, severe excitement. He stood on his bed, forcibly breathing in-and-out with a hissing noise, like a rapacious animal, wild rolling of the eyes, throwing pillows around. He pounced on the attendant, and tripped while doing this.[21]

A give-and-take relationship seems by now to have been established between Nijinsky and Fritz Wieland, in which each played his predictable part, much as dancers in a pas de deux depend on each other for instantaneous response. Whenever the patient became more threatening, the attendant became more alert, paid more attention, stepped up the nursing care, or called the doctor to give another injection. The very fact that something was being done to help him seemed to relieve Nijinsky's agitation. For example, it was noted that "even before the injected medication could have taken effect, the patient was as if transformed, started to cry, became more approachable, grasped the doctor's hand, begged that one should help him, he is so terribly sick, it is awful with his head, he has so many fear-inducing thoughts, one should let his mother come to him. Then fell asleep." One day Nijinsky twisted his right ankle after "pouncing" on Wieland. There was pressure sensitivity over the lower part of the dancer's tibia, for which the attendant gave him "a bandage and moist compresses." While resting in bed, Nijinsky "always complained about his voices, someone is speaking in his ears. He believes to have seen Christ in his attendant [a reaction of gratitude, perhaps, for Wieland's sympathetic presence]. Then again, he expresses his deep yearning for his mother." Another time, Nijinsky developed "an irritation of the mucous membranes in the trachea, probably because of his forced breathing [or perhaps because of a lack of saliva secondary to scopolamine]. Inhalation therapy makes him feel very well."

These observations are consistent with the clinical observation that "catatonic patients seem to be able to pass into the catatonic state (even to stuporousness) almost as they please, *provided they have the mood which is inclined to make catatonic adaptations.* [When their] hurt feelings accumulate and run strongly into a heedless moroseness, it becomes too painful to stop.... It is decidedly more pleasureful to let go and let the mood run its course, punishing (in fantasy and actually) those who are more or less related to the causes of the inhibition and introversion."[22] Such behavior can be very trying and exhausting for a psychiatric nurse. Soon enough, Nijinsky had heaped so much abuse and punishment on his partner in catatonia that it became necessary to replace the conscientious Wieland with another male attendant. Unfortunately, Nijinsky's losing his "Christlike" Wieland precipitated a marked intensification of depression and anger: "3 July—Mostly he lies around, looks distracted and sunken into himself. Yesterday he banged his fist stereotypically against his thigh for more than an hour."

Several days later, Nijinsky "begged the doctor to give him something which will make him die." Passionately he cried, "I am afraid of going crazy. Give me some poison or something else." On 7 July, he had a "transient episode of excitement," complained of being "locked-up," and demanded to leave the hospital. "He walked around his room excitedly, and after his bath it was difficult to get him back into the room. But he remained courteous at all times, thanked the attendants amiably, and soon calmed down again." The next week he was "always more catatonic" and compulsively doing his breathing exercises:

> For hours he can inhale maximally and then expel the air rhythmically, while pressing the sides of his chest with both hands. Then again, the patient sits for a long time in the stiffest pose, his head pressed forward as far as possible, with the neck muscles tensed stiff as a board. He interrupts this posture with exaggerated movements of his head in all directions, resulting in muscular strain of the neck muscles, which have become very pressure-and-pain sensitive. He has severe pain, and constantly holds his neck. The corresponding muscles of the left side are not painful.

To reduce the pain, Nijinsky was given hot wet compresses. (Cold compresses might have been better; dancers and athletes prefer using ice and cold water to soothe the pain of strained muscles.)

By mid-July Nijinsky was giving full vent to his infantile rage. He pouted, "stared ahead soullessly," burst into tears, complained that he was "suffering as much as Jesus Christ." He "forcefully pushes people away when they try to touch him." (With Dr. Binswanger, however, he remained "friendly" and shook hands.) On his way to the toilet one day, he dramatically accosted a female patient, "glared at her, touched her provocatively, laughed stiffly in her face," and had to be restrained from making sexual advances. After that, "he sat rigidly in bed for a long time, holding the left hand cramped like a claw, with the thumb closed, index- and middle-fingers pressed in, and his eyes shut tightly."

There now began a pattern of wild, frenzied, sometimes violent, often self-destructive behavior which resembled nothing so much as the abhorrent practices of certain religious mystics described in Russian history. The thirteenth-century Hesychasts engaged in compulsive fasting and breath-holding. The "holy fools" of the fifteenth century would stand around in pillarlike immobility. The eighteenth-century Skoptsy flagellated and castrated themselves.[23] Several times Nijinsky tried to harm himself by "pressing his right index-finger into his right eye." He refused to eat and had to be fed. While walking in the park he "assumed bizarre postures and made tense movements." He would tear out his hair, try to mutilate himself with a knife, and jump around "like a crazed animal." Kurt Binswanger writes that Nijinsky "often holds his head supported by his hands while talking to himself, complaining that everything is mixed up in his head. Occasionally answers questions in Polish. Said yesterday 'Oh, my ideas don't have any direction, they change all the time, my existence is totally ruined.' Occasionally, he maximally contracts individual muscle groups, especially those of his neck and arms, and he can lie doing that for many hours, while breathing heavily and sweating so profusely that his mattress is soaked through." These symptoms resemble opium withdrawal and may have been produced, in part, by the morphine shots Nijinsky was getting.

On 16 July he began talking about "a man inside his head who does everything for him and speaks either German, Polish, or French." He felt this to be "horrible," and begged for relief, which Kurt Binswanger tried to provide by giving him more medication. Because of the severe agitation, especially at night, it was finally decided to reinstate Fritz Wieland as Nijinsky's attendant, to sleep in the same room and watch over him all day. But now the dancer no longer regarded Wieland as acceptable. He complained about him bitterly in a paranoid way: "The attendant strikes terror into me and wants to kill me." He called Wieland a "black man" (recalling the Blackamoor who slays Petrushka at the end of Stravinsky's ballet) and screamed, "I'm being killed here like a wild animal, it's awful to terrorize me like that." To avert what was recognized to be an incipient panic with homosexual overtones, on 21 July Binswanger assigned a female nurse as Nijinsky's roommate, with Wieland sleeping in an adjoining room. This arrangement resulted in immediate improvement: "The patient has become somewhat calmer at night, and sleeps quite well most of the time." A new symptom emerged, however. Nijinsky began to complain about his heart. It felt "like a piece of wood or a piece of paper," an oppressive, dehumanizing sensation in his chest, probably related to the anticholinergic effects of the scopolamine he was receiving, and to the woman in his room. (She may have reminded him of his estrangement from Romola, his heart gone cold, and her abandoning him for another man.) Now Nijinsky felt truly like a papier-mâché puppet, dead and waiting to be discarded, as in *Petrushka.*

As if to rid himself of this most ghastly fantasy and make himself feel alive again, Nijinsky instigated a whole series of animal imitations. He "jumped around like a monkey on the floor," started "eating like a monkey," and "sat on his attendant's lap" in order to be petted and fed. Nijinsky knew much about animals and how their behavior can evoke both love and fear from humans. Having worked in circuses, masturbated with dogs, created for Diaghilev the half-human, half-animal Faun, cuddled Kyra's pet rabbit, and recently (at the Suvretta House in St. Moritz) characterized himself as a "tired little horse," he now pulled out all the stops for Fritz Wieland, whose touching descriptions of the catatonic monkey business can best be appreciated verbatim.

21 July: Patient is reluctant to get into the bathtub. After half a minute in the water, he jumps out, quickly dries himself, runs into his room and leaps onto the lounging-chair, where he sits very tensely, crouching in the corner ... won't go to bed. Sits in the same spot for 1½ hours ... I try to put him to bed. He jumps on the floor and moves around on his hands and feet like an animal, an ape, and eats like one too, until he goes back to sit in the corner. Gets an injection. Sleeps from noon until 3 p.m. Quiet until after coffee, which he won't touch. Then sits at the back of his bed, until 8:30, pressed stiffly against the wall.

22 July: Can't get him to eat. In order for me to make his bed, patient has to be lifted out, and he then sits in his familiar corner rolled up like a hedgehog, so stiffly that he has to be lifted back into his bed.

23 July: In despair and great fear he tears his hair, and finally has to be stopped from doing this. Later on I was able to calm him by talking to him and petting him. From 7–8 p.m. he tried in all sorts of ways to harm himself: squeezes his throat shut by putting both hands around his neck; beats with his fists on his head, eyes, and neck; after eating, he tries to press the food out of his stomach by striking his abdomen [a response possibly to medication-induced constipation]; he tears his hair and tries to scratch his face [skin can itch because of dryness due to atropine or withdrawal from morphine]; he grabs a knife and tries unsuccessfully to stab himself in the chest. Patient is clear in his thinking, but only speaks German: "My existence is finished, I will never get well, it is better to die, my wife should come." For an hour he has been trying to hold his breath, until the doctor came to give him an injection. At 9 p.m. he fell asleep.

24 July: Lies in bed quietly. At 10 a.m. he suddenly leaps in the air, again tears his hair, whispers almost inaudibly in French "I'm being killed." Patient makes a fist, gets up and threatens to fight. This can only be

prevented by holding him firmly, and after I talk to him for a while, he calms down. Later he comes up to me and sits in my lap like a monkey, lets me feed him. Afterwards he is put to bed and stays there, lying quietly until 2 p.m., and eats a little. Then extremely excited again, pulling his hair just like this morning. Then he makes gymnastic movements, chatters with his lower jaw, and makes guttural sounds like a four-footed beast [he may have been trying to gargle, to produce saliva for his parched throat] ... drinks a cup of coffee [not the best thing for an agitated patient] and eats butter, but lets everything drool out of his mouth [another medication effect?]. After 4:30 he again holds his breath... gradually calms down after talking a little in German and French. Asks why there is no belt on his pyjama [a suicide precaution].

Where was Nijinsky's push into madness taking him in the summer of 1919? Can one detect a trajectory to the mental disorder that had broken out the previous year? First of all, it seems clear that his illness resembled very closely the catatonic or "tension-insanity" syndrome that Kahlbaum had described. Second, there can be little doubt that mood shifts, recurring swings from depression to mania, were catapulting Nijinsky into extremes of stupor and excitement. Third, he regularly dramatized his inner states through outward displays of aggressivity, passivity, hostility, and affection. Finally, he was confused about his identity, undirected in respect to his goals, and perplexed by the differences between fantasy and reality. Reliance on other people to make decisions for him, to do his thinking, and to give structure to his life were ingrained characteristics of Nijinsky's personality. Cut off from the artistic milieu that had nurtured his creativity and out of touch with his family, he was having to depend on the doctors, nurses, attendants, and patients of a psychiatric hospital for guidance in how to organize his daily activities. And now that his final effort at sublimation, his hoped-for ballets with Richard Strauss, had failed, Nijinsky was engaging in crazy animal scenes, violent choreographies, and other symbolic activities—behavior that resembled very closely the hair-pulling, masochistic orgies of a Russian religious fanatic. Perhaps Nijinsky's leap into madness would yet bring him where he had once dreamt of being, into a blissful state of oneness with nature, a Tolstoyan saintliness, a sexually abstinent detachment from the rest of the world.

NOTES

1. Alfred Einstein, *Greatness in Music*, 55.
2. Harold C. Sternlicht, James Payton, Gerhardt Werner, and Michael Rancurello, "Multiple Personality Disorder: A Neuroscience and Cognitive Psychology Perspective."

3. George Becker, *The Mad Genius Controversy.*
4. Dr. Kurt Binswanger, notes, BMR.
5. Notebooks on "Death," 25, and on "Feeling," 52, 70. See also *Diary,* 99.
6. Edward J. Kempf, "Affective-Respiratory Factors in Catatonia."
7. Dr. Kurt Binswanger, notes, BMR.
8. Theo C. Manschreck, "Delusional (Paranoid) Disorders."
9. Dr. Kurt Binswanger, notes, BMR. Emphasis in the original.
10. Personal communication from a close relative of Dr. "Greiber."
11. Correspondence between Romola Nijinsky and Dr. Ludwig Binswanger, BMR.
12. Dr. Kurt Binswanger, notes, BMR.
13. *Strauss-Hofmannsthal Briefwechsel,* 13.
14. Dr. Kurt Binswanger, notes, BMR. Emphasis in the original.
15. Personal communication from Dr. Wenger, Basel, Switzerland.
16. Enoch Callaway, Roy Halliday, Hilary Naylor, and Gail Schechter. "Effects of oral scopolamine on human stimulus evaluation."
17. Erik H. Erikson, *Toys and Reasons,* 44.
18. D. M. Winnicott, *Playing and Reality.*
19. Kempf, 176.
20. *Diary,* 42.
21. Dr. Kurt Binswanger, notes, BMR.
22. Kempf, 173–174. Emphasis in the original.
23. James H. Billington, *The Icon and the Axe.*

Chapter 11

In Search of a Cure

For nine years, from July 1919 to December 1928, Nijinsky was the object of numerous attempts to influence the course of his mental illness, which was threatening to become chronic. These efforts ranged all the way from having him father a second child to the innocuous process of bathing in the healing waters at Lourdes. Each intervention was well intended, but none had any lasting effects. Romola took the initiative on 26 July 1919, when she arrived at the Bellevue Sanatorium, accompanied by her stepfather, and "spent the entire day with the patient, fed him, and did not leave his bed." Dr. Kurt Binswanger saw this as an undesirable intrusion: "Nijinsky willingly lets everything be done to him, but is having intermittent anxiety attacks." In Binswanger's opinion, the dancer had actually been "improving somewhat" before Romola's arrival. He was "eating more," but "one seldom could get him to talk." Recently, while the attendant Wieland was feeding him, Nijinsky had remarked, cryptically, "Thank you, in another world then." Romola did not perceive any improvement; on the contrary, she felt that he had gotten worse. His silences seemed ominous, and he no longer showed any interest in her, for which she blamed the doctors. "It is impossible for my husband to stay here among the sick people at Bellevue," she told Binswanger. "I would surely become sick myself if I had to live among sick people all the time."[2]

It was at this point that Kurt Binswanger, echoing an earlier opinion of Dr. Greiber, began describing Romola as "severely psychopathic." (At that time the word "psychopathic" was used more often to describe difficult, neurotic personalities than hostile, antisocial individuals.) Romola was being disputatious and behaving in what the hospital staff thought was an irresponsible manner. She seemed to be putting her own needs before those of the patient. Binswanger reports her saying, "I can no longer tolerate being separated. I never want to leave my husband again. I want to nurse him myself, and make his life as agreeable as possible." She would not "obey certain rules about visiting-hours," had no "insight," and distrusted the doctors. "I always get an intolerable feeling of pressure around here," she told them. "Whenever I am away from my husband, I get the feeling that the doctors are trying to portray his condition better than it really is ... I don't believe he will ever be cured." Romola wanted Nijinsky out of the hospital "because if I fail to do anything now which might help him, I would never be able to forgive myself later on." Her stepfather, with whom the Binswangers felt they could "negotiate better," supported her position.

> Mr. Párdány confirms that the separation from her husband has evoked increasingly severe crises in the wife. Any further separation would be impossible. Out of consideration for the entire family, he asked us to give in to his daughter's demands.[3]

Párdány most likely knew about an immediate reason for her agitation. It was the deterioration in the relationship with Dr. Greiber, whose wife was putting pressure on him to stop seeing Romola. Greiber had become addicted to morphine. Despairing over Romola's unwillingness to get a divorce and marry him, he even attempted suicide at one point. (The details are fuzzy. According to confidential sources, Greiber "really loved his wife, and it was her intuition which saved him, because she discovered him, nearly dead, in a hiding place."[4]) Also deeply disturbing to Romola was that Nijinsky's life was again being managed in ways resembling his years with Diaghilev. Instead of the Russian impresario, it was now Dr. Binswanger who showed Nijinsky art books, monitored his friendships, gave advice on how to behave, and encouraged him to "dance," no matter how peculiarly. And the attendant Fritz Wieland, in Binswanger's employ, played a role curiously similar to Diaghilev's loyal valet Vasili Zuikov. Wieland's frequent feeding, holding, and comforting the dancer probably reminded Romola of the homosexuality she still consciously feared.

Most urgent was her need to preserve an image of herself as the good and loving wife of the "God of the Dance." She had fallen under his spell when her life seemed goalless, and by marrying him she found a direction for herself. Now, Nijinsky was mentally ill and acted as though he no longer wanted her. This gulf between them threatened Romola's sense of identity, indeed her very existence. She had to get him back. To undo the damage resulting from the collapse of his career was like a moral imperative; it meant that she would have to extricate him from what she saw as psychiatric oppression. The central mission of her life, as she later described it, was to keep Nijinsky from being "thrown into the hands of indifferent doctors who see only 'the case' and not the forlorn soul," and save him from "attendants who treat the patients like criminals."[5]

> I hardly realized at the time [writes Romola] that my decision meant a battle against the medical faculty, the authorities, and the whole world. The task before me was almost superhuman. I looked at Vaslav sitting helplessly mute before me. I clutched my hands in prayer; I shut my eyes and saw in a flash Nijinsky as he was—of another essence than ourselves—surrounded with an invisible magic halo.[6]

Clearly the Binswangers were put off by her antagonism and manipulation. Theirs was a private hospital catering to voluntary patients, not a state institution empowered to hold people against their own will or that of a relative. But to discharge someone as disturbed as Nijinsky, who had been threatening others and trying to mutilate himself, would have been morally unacceptable and legally irresponsible. (Money was not yet a major issue; Nijinsky's savings were far from depleted at this point.) The only solution was to seek consultation with the local medical administrator, a Bezirksarzt, who laid down the following conditions for Nijinsky's discharge from Bellevue Sanatorium:

"His relatives must arrange a special room in their St. Moritz villa, where anything that could be used for suicide has to be removed. They must hire two experienced attendants to watch over the patient day and night, and keep him under constant psychiatric supervision." Romola agreed, signed the necessary papers, and Nijinsky was discharged on 29 June 1919, "to his own family, unimproved, against medical advice."

> Accompanied by our head-nurse and the newly engaged private attendant Stigler [writes Kurt Binswanger], the patient and his relatives went by car to Rorschach [a railway stop], and from there by train. He had recurring severe anxiety attacks during the trip, behaved in a very conspicuous manner, made clownish gestures, didn't say a word, and communicated only with signs. Because the second attendant had not yet arrived, our head-nurse assumed the first night-watch and helped to arrange the room properly.[7]

For the next four months, the quality of care Nijinsky received was questionable at best and abominable at worst. Gone were the spacious grounds of the Bellevue Sanatorium, where he had been running and jumping, the tennis court where he watched his favorite game and laughed boisterously, the other patients whom he could frighten or entertain, Fritz Wieland's tolerant watchfulness, and the Binswangers' clinical expertise. In fact, there was no psychiatric supervision at Villa Guardamunt. Romola defied the agreement she had signed with the Binswangers. Medication was prescribed by Dr. Greiber and the two attendants were free to do whatever they felt was needed to keep Nijinsky under control. When in a cheerful mood, he would sit quietly, smiling or meditating, playing with his five-year-old daughter, or making drawings of houses and animals. (Compared with his earlier artwork, these look much more childlike, if not disorganized.) He seldom spoke. When depressed, he would cry, refuse to eat, and complain pitifully about his physical symptoms and mental confusion. There continued to be violent outbursts or rage, in which he threw things, screamed incoherently, and threatened to assault whoever came close to him. (In a television interview many years later, Romola reported that in his rages he feared hallucinatory demons were attacking him.[8]) Kyra remembers an incident when they were riding in an elevator: "My father suddenly started yelling and making angry faces. He was violent and refused to let me get out. It scared me to death. I've been afraid of elevators ever since."[9] It was a terrible environment for a young child.

In trying to maintain peace and quiet around the house, Romola would undertake to nurse him herself. She supervised his meals, kept him company, and helped dress and undress him, which led to conflicts with the two attendants, who felt responsible for these things and were accustomed to taking orders only from a doctor or nurse. Emilia Márkus was caught in the middle, wanting on the one hand to support her daughter, and on the other to bolster the attendants in making life endurable for her son-in-law. She took the position that it was undesirable for Romola to become too intimate with Vaslav, lest he again threaten her physically and possibly assault her the way he had before being hospitalized. Especially worrisome was Romola's desire for sexual intercourse, which always necessitated that the attendants be absent. There were many arguments about this with her mother. (What role Oscar Párdány played in the conflict is not known, but presumably his was a peacekeeping, stabilizing influence.) In September, two months after Nijinsky's return to St. Moritz, Romola became pregnant, probably not what she intended, since her wish was to cure him with love, not to have another child. Yet she knew that Vaslav wanted to have a son.

While the idea of reversing an illness through childbirth may sound naive, there were people then (and still are today) who believed that one of the "cures" for a failing marriage was to have another child. At least, Romola seems to have thought that, and medical influence could have played a role as well. Years later she told the dancer Anton Dolin (a great admirer of Nijinsky) that *"at the suggestion of one of the doctors at Kreuzlingen,* she had persistently attempted to persuade Vaslav to have sexual intercourse with her, with the thought that the birth of another child might have a salutary effect on his mental condition."[10] But was it really one of the Bellevue psychiatrists who had encouraged Romola to resume having intercourse with her husband, or Dr. Greiber? Or was this Romola's way of shifting the responsibility for what happened onto "one of the doctors"? "I agreed," she told Dolin, "although it was dangerous. I brought his second child into the world, a beautiful healthy baby."[11] (Questions have been raised in regard to this child's paternity. The birth certificate shows Nijinsky as her father, and Thomas Nijinsky and Eleonora Bereda as her paternal grandparents. We will return to the matter shortly.)

Details of the pregnancy are unavailable, but Romola apparently again developed some disabling symptoms and had to stay in bed, thus losing what little influence she had over Nijinsky's attendants. "They tried to keep his wife away from him," reports Kyra's governess, "because he was loud and mean and would jump on her the moment she entered his room." Also, "the attendants Hirt and Stigler would hit the patient." (Stigler had been with Nijinsky since leaving Bellevue; he quit in October and was replaced by Fritz Kühn, who gave notice on 15 November. Kühn's replacement stayed on the job for only two days, leaving Nijinsky with the single attendant Hirt.) After that, the situation deteriorated quickly. A new man from Zürich named Hammel tried to take charge on 29 November, but finding conditions at Villa Guardamunt "untenable," he went to the police and reported that Nijinsky was "not being supervised properly ... he throws his food on the floor, lets it lie there, and later eats it up with his fingers ... he is a danger to the community." Romola regarded Hammel's notification of the authorities as a personal betrayal and promptly fired him. When the police arrived, the dancer had "demolished his bed and was making threatening gestures." They decided to call a psychiatrist, Dr. Betzola, director of the Cantonal Insane Asylum in Chur, fifty kilometers from St. Moritz, to evaluate the situation and advise what to do.[12]

By the time Dr. Betzola came to the villa, Romola had "locked herself into her room," as was her custom at stressful moments, and refused to see anyone. From Betzola's report we learn that "two uniformed policemen were guarding the patient." He telephoned Dr. Binswanger, asking to have Nijinsky readmitted to the Bellevue Sanatorium, and two attendants (one was the trustworthy Fritz Wieland) were promptly sent from there. Betzola told them "the patient is extremely dangerous ... aggressive and destructive." While transporting him to the sanatorium, they would need to exercise "the greatest precaution because of suicide risk." Betzola also explained that "the patient's wife is without any insight and may even make trouble for us, in which case he is to be taken to the Cantonal Insane Asylum in Chur."[13]

On the train, Nijinsky was "excited most of the time, making peculiar noises, wanting to approach other people, and shoving the passengers. After changing trains in Rorschach, his excitement increased so much that he had to be held constantly by both attendants." The hospital admission, on 3 December 1919, was involuntary, "on orders of the police." Nijinsky "tried to hit" the admitting physician, then "went willingly to his room." When Kurt Binswanger arrived, Nijinsky "greeted him politely and pretended not to know him." After a while, however, he "became more accessible, acknowledged that the doctor and the attendants were familiar to him, and answered with short, abrupt sentences."

> On being asked how his wife is doing [writes Binswanger], he suddenly jumps up, emits a scream, makes a wild face as if he wants to scare somebody, then immediately is quiet again. The patient makes a severely catatonic impression, looks very "loaded" as if he might explode at any moment. Throws paranoid looks at the two attendants who are conversing in the room next door. Takes his dinner with good appetite. His room will be cleared; the patient will be guarded constantly (night-watch). Receives 20 drops of Scopolamine.[14]

For the first two weeks, Nijinsky was more nasty and belligerent than he had ever been before. "He wet his bed, stared at his attendant most of the night, jumped on him, urinated on the floor, refused to eat, threw bread into the attendant's face, then laughed suddenly, emitted screams, leapt out of his bed to the window, twisted his eyes, and made grimaces." When forced to eat, he "spat some of the food into the attendant's face, punched him violently in the stomach, and hurled the drinking-mug into his face." With Dr. Binswanger, he was "mistrustful but not unfriendly, shaking hands when asked to, smiling, but not allowing himself to enter a conversation. At most he answered yes or no."

Soon it was noted that Nijinsky was again "doing a lot of play-acting, assuming different postures, and staying rigidly in these poses for a long time." He played the provocateur, taunted his attendant, "threatened him with rolling eyes," laughed at him, and made "inviting gestures . . . the whole thing was like a pantomime." He also reverted to behaving "like an animal," "defecating on the rug," "lying around stiffly . . . with a watchful facial expression," and "slurping his meals after they had gotten cold." Binswanger thought Nijinsky was "listening to voices a lot," but could not "get him to talk" about the hallucinations. Dr. Greiber, perhaps because of some lingering concern for his former patient, came for a visit on 9 December, which had a negative effect. Nijinsky exploded with rage, began "hitting himself on the head and stomach with his fists," "repeatedly attacked his attendants," "flung chairs and tables at them." He had to be confined "for several hours to an isolation cell," where he "quickly calmed down." But four days later he had another "rage-attack."

> He bit himself in the hand, violently scratched his face, engaged in forced breathing, twisted his eyes, jerked his head up and let it flop back again, ground his teeth. After a continuous bath he was quieter again.[15]

Different from the dancer's first admission to Bellevue was his seeming absence of fear. Instead of the earlier dread that something awful might happen, that he might be put to death or die of a heart attack, this time he deliberately sought danger and assaulted others as well as himself with unbridled fury. Similarly absent this time was any inhibition of homosexuality. Nijinsky tried openly to seduce his male attendant, kissed his hands and feet, and said to him, "You are my wife." So insistent was he in trying to remove the attendant's wedding ring that the latter finally had to take his ring off and hide it. Nijinsky also chased one of the male doctors and tried to grab *his* wedding ring. When the doctor resisted, Nijinsky "hit him and then wept." He seemed more "confused" than ever before. The staff observed him "talking to himself, taking off his shirt and kneeling in front of his attendant with folded hands, eyes screwed-up, gnashing his teeth, ejaculating loud screams and spitting at the attendant." While in the bathtub, Nijinsky "made every possible sort of movement with his body," suggesting the religious ecstasies of saintly Russian catatonics, or an attempt at orgasm. Occasionally, he pointed to his navel, saying, "This is a woman or an idea." He may have been trying to express an attitude in regard to Romola's pregnancy, much as he did in 1913, while expecting their first child, or he may have wanted to give birth himself, perhaps to a new idea. He kept talking nonsense, "emitting words that did not hang together: planet, detective, airplane, medicine, art."

Christmas was approaching, Nijinsky's first in a hospital, away from his family. Dr. and Mrs. Binswanger brought "a lighted tree and various presents to his room" which "gave him pleasure, he laughed happily, shook hands with the doctor and his wife, and thanked them." But on Christmas Eve he began to "cry furiously" and "seemed to be afraid." He greeted the doctor like a guilty child, "often with pleading gestures and a frightened expression." A few days later he seemed "confused, apparently hallucinating constantly ... he gives no answers to any questions. Lies there absorbed with himself, a dark look on his face, and

listening. Repeatedly becomes aggressive." One episode is worth describing in detail, for it shows that these were not random or
disorganized attacks, but well-coordinated and goal-directed moves
against certain people, and therefore extremely dangerous.

> 28 *December*: He viciously attacked his attendant, who was busy dusting
> the room. The patient seized him by the neck, tripped him by putting his
> right foot behind his knee, and after he had fallen down, knelt on him
> and began choking him with both hands. Fortunately the attendant had
> been able to strike the alarm-bell with his hand while falling, so that help
> could be summoned in time. The patient had seized his attendant so
> cleverly that he was lying there completely helpless. As a result of this
> incident, a second attendant was ordered to be within calling distance at
> all times.[16]

After this brutal event, Nijinsky seemed contrite and tried to restrain
himself. In so doing, he became more agitated, "inwardly restless, often
scratching his head, shutting his ears with his index fingers, tearing
the hair around his ears, while making grimaces and sweating so
profusely that he had to be towelled dry." At night he "tossed and
turned in his bed," as if having constantly to dispel inner tension
through some form of physical activity. With the new year (1920), he
adopted a different approach to meals. Instead of refusing to eat, or
throwing his food on the floor or at his attendant, he now calmly "took
sufficient nourishment," but only "after his food had first gotten cold."
(What this meant is unclear; perhaps it was a way of expressing
ambivalence about accepting warmth, or the return of an earlier habit,
now exaggerated, when meals were served too hot and he had to wait
before eating.) A childlike simplicity was noted generally in Nijinsky's
behavior. "For no reason at all, he laughed and clapped his hands for two
hours," writes Kurt Binswanger in the first week of January. "When I
went to see him, he laughed amicably, gave me his hand, and said hello
with a roguish smile, but without allowing himself to enter into any
conversation."

Important information was conveyed to the dancer that day: his
mother and sister were "well, and hoping to come to Switzerland." They
had survived the revolution and were living in Kiev under the most
difficult conditions. "Earlier he had been very attached to his family,"
writes Dr. Binswanger, who expected that news of their survival might
lead to expressions of joy or relief. (According to Irina Nijinska Raetz,

Nijinsky thought that his mother and sister might have been killed during the war.[17]) His immediate reaction was noncommittal; he acted as if the news "did not affect him externally at all." But within a few days he was excited, "often talking to himself, doing much grimacing and tomfoolery, [and] wanting to play the role of 'a lunatic.'"

> He mimics every possible sort of emotion by making theatrical gestures. When the head-nurse tries to play chess with him, he brings everything into utter confusion. Talks about knives and blood. From time to time, he emits short screams. Yesterday he had an unprovoked temper tantrum, seized himself by the throat, knelt at his bed, then fell on his hands, thereby tearing his shirt. Carries out scratching movements on the sheets, while screaming loudly. Then calms down again.[18]

Again, one is left with the impression that in his despair and confusion Nijinsky was unconsciously enacting a fantasy of "madness," probably organized around memories of his brother and other observations of psychotic behavior. He would "pound the wall with all his might, and a furious expression on his face, because he apparently believes that he hears voices coming out of there.... Often he is in a bad mood, quietly crying to himself without saying why." He may have been dramatizing his wife's expected childbirth. All the "tomfoolery," as Binswanger called it, his preoccupation with "knives and blood," his kneeling and screaming, probably held meanings that the Bellevue psychiatrists had difficulty deciphering. With his birthday approaching, Nijinsky was obsessed with the fear of death. How many years was he expected to live? Was his illness progressing, and if so, would he ever dance again? While walking in the park, it was noted that he "fixed his gaze on everyone who went by, laughed very loudly, and always repeated the number 70." He made ceremonial gestures—"a long nose, pointing with his arm stretched out from his body"—reminiscent of *Till Eulenspiegel*, and delivered mock sermons, intoning words like "electricity," "Dominus vobiscum," "politics," "defense," "planets," "soldiers," "clock," "Dr. Greiber," "orthodox," and "Palestine," all vaguely related to themes described in Nijinsky's notebooks the year before. To Kurt Binswanger, unaware of these writings, the dancer's speech made no sense. Everything he did was impressively "theatrical.... When one reasons with him for a longer time, he laughs at you with an expression on his face that says: 'wouldn't you agree that I've been acting beautifully.'"[19]

Puzzling also was Nijinsky's response to being told, on 20 February, that "in a few days he will be transferred to a sanatorium in Vienna." Romola had made up her mind to leave Switzerland. Her parents had returned to Budapest, and she wanted to go to Vienna to deliver her baby in the same clinic where Kyra was born. Nijinsky seemed to "take the news with an expression of unconcern," as though it meant nothing to him. The next day, however, "he asked when he would be leaving, and spoke incomprehensibly about Dr. Greiber." The day after that, most remarkably, "he began doing various dance exercises by himself, for the first time" and "to talk to himself a lot about dancing." This shows that Nijinsky could still respond to external events and quickly switch from psychotic to balletic behavior.

When saying goodbye, several of the ladies gave him flowers, which he accepted with a majestic smile. On departing [24 February 1920] he looked around a bit suspiciously, but seemed to be happy about the upcoming trip.[20]

Romola was reunited with Nijinsky in Buchs, the border crossing from Switzerland to Austria. There he "kissed his wife, but in the automobile gave the attendant a punch in the ribs."[21] They went by train to Vienna, where he was admitted to the Steinhof, a psychiatric hospital founded in 1784 as a *Narrenturm* (tower of fools). Greatly enlarged in 1901 to serve the rapidly expanding population of the Austro-Hungarian Empire, the Steinhof Asylum came to house over 2,000 patients in thirty-four different pavilions, spread over 200 acres.[22] Clinical director of this massive institution was Dr. Julius Wagner-Jauregg, a professor at the University of Vienna who had pioneered the use of malaria-induced fever for treating patients with general paresis, a brain disease caused by tertiary syphilis. (For this, Wagner-Jauregg received the Nobel Prize in Physiology and Medicine in 1927.) Romola writes that "Professor Wagner-Jauregg assured me that as long as a schizophrenic patient has periods of agitation there is hope for improvement toward normalcy."[23] We do not know if Wagner-Jauregg ever examined Nijinsky personally—in so large a hospital it was clearly impossible for him to see every patient—or that "schizophrenia" was actually the diagnosis there, although that seems likely considering the symptoms and progress of his disease. (Steinhof medical records from the period of Nijinsky's confinement have been destroyed.) Romola undoubtedly consulted the professor in later years, as she did many Viennese specialists. *

Romola says she also consulted Sigmund Freud in Vienna about Nijinsky's illness. Again, we do not know if Freud actually examined the dancer. (Much of Freud's case material has been locked in confidential files at the Library of Congress.) Romola claims that he told her that "psychoanalytical treatment is utterly useless in cases of schizophrenia."[25] It seems unlikely that Freud would have spoken this way. "Schizophrenia" was a recent import from Switzerland, and not a congenial concept for psychoanalysts who preferred to talk about "narcissistic neurosis," a condition attributable to pathological investment of libido in oneself after it had been withdrawn from external love objects. While Freud usually was reluctant to psychoanalyze highly "narcissistic" individuals because of their difficulty in forming a stable transference, he actually did treat a number of psychotic or borderline patients, notably the Russian aristocrat Sergei Pankejeff, a man close to Nijinsky's age, later referred to as the "Wolf Man." (During their first interview, Pankejeff made sexual advances to Freud and then offered "to defecate on his head"![26]) We also know from his correspondence with Ludwig Binswanger that Freud strongly favored an analytic approach to the psychoses. But whether Freud or his Viennese colleagues would have been able to work with the generally inarticulate and "theatrical" Nijinsky and tolerate his "psychopathic" wife is another question.

"Most of the time I kept Vaslav with me at home," writes Romola. "Only when he was very agitated did I take him to the Sanatorium Steinhof."[27] This, too, could be misleading. In fact, they had no "home" in Vienna. Romola stayed either in hotels, where taking proper care of the sick dancer was always difficult, or with her sister, who was having marital problems of her own. Romola also stayed for a while at the sanatorium of Dr. Anton Loew, a private hospital in Vienna, where in June she went into labor and gave birth to Tamara Nijinsky. She returned to the Loew Sanatorium for several weeks in July and August, and received further treatment—bed rest, a nourishing diet, baths, compresses, and unspecified "medications"—for complaints that were not recorded in her medical chart.[28] (Perhaps Romola was having

* (Wagner-Jauregg, if we are to believe the memoirs of another artist's wife, Alma Mahler Werfel, gave generous attention to attractive women. "He stayed all night at my bedside, talking to me," writes Mahler's widow. "In the morning he got a good breakfast, took his leave, and said he had never spent so stimulating a night."[24]

difficulty facing the reality of her life in Vienna, with a sick husband, a young child, and an infant.)

Nijinsky's second child, born on 14 June 1920, was named Tamara after his former dance partner Tamara Karsavina. He held her in his arms for "a few hours [and] talked rationally," Romola told Anton Dolin many years later. Then he "slowly receded into his clouded mind and became silent."[29] (A charming photograph, taken a few years later, shows Nijinsky holding Tamara on his lap, with an animated expression on his face.) No doubt Romola was disappointed that, as far as reversing his mental illness was concerned, her labor had been in vain, one reason perhaps why she later, hoping to protect Tamara from the stigma of psychosis, tried to deny that Nijinsky was the father.

This brings us back to the question of Tamara's paternity. A striking physical resemblance can be seen between Tamara's daughter Kinga and photographs of Nijinsky—they have a very similar facial configuration. Kinga's son, Mark Gaspers, now a teen-ager in Phoenix, Arizona, also looks very much like Nijinsky in his student days. I have also been impressed with the resemblance of Tamara Nijinsky in profile and certain photographs of Nijinsky's sister, Bronislava Nijinska. To settle the question of paternity scientifically, however, would require genetic tests.

How rumors of Tamara Nijinsky's illegitimacy got started may be of some interest. She spent her formative years with Emilia Márkus and her husband in Budapest, and thus became estranged from her mother. ("Romola was that cold, sophisticated lady of whom I felt afraid and intimidated."[30]) During World War II, Emilia Márkus adopted Tamara, because as Nijinsky's daughter she was considered "stateless" and would have been at risk of deportation. The adoption infuriated Romola, since it meant she would now have to share the Pulszky estate not only with her sister Tessa, but also with Tamara. Romola also objected to the use of the "sacred name of Nijinsky" when Tamara began her career as an actress at the National Theater in Budapest, just as she had objected to her daughter Kyra's career as a dancer—"there can be only one Nijinsky!" Finally, when Tamara decided to get married, Romola attempted to remove her as an heir to the Nijinsky estate. She even went to the trouble of asking Dr. Ludwig Binswanger to prepare an affidavit stating that "marital relations were impossible with Nijinsky" at the time of Tamara's conception.[31] After the war, Romola tried a second time to disinherit Tamara. This time she wrote

Binswanger that "according to current views of medical science, it is impossible that in September 1919 the child Tamara could have been conceived by the mentally-ill Vaslav Nijinsky."[32] Romola never mentioned Tamara in any of her published writings, but after Nijinsky's death she began relating to her in a more friendly way.

In Vienna, after the birth of Tamara had failed to achieve its wished-for effect, Romola hoped that a "meeting between Vaslav and his mother might reestablish his normalcy."[33] Eleonora Bereda, then sixty-five, was still in Kiev with Nijinsky's sister, who wrote in her memoirs that "in the middle of 1920" a letter was "smuggled" to her by a pilot who had flown to Russia from Austria. "The letter was from Romola, written by another hand in Russian, telling us that Vaslav had been mentally ill for a year and a half and that it was essential for his recovery that Mother and I be with him."[34] Bronislava Nijinska had made a remarkable career for herself in postrevolutionary Russia, where she not only danced and designed her own "abstract" choreographic works, but had also established an École de Mouvement to teach the principles derived partly from her earlier work with her brother. Not until May 1921, however, was she able to leave Kiev, and it took six weeks—"a perilous journey, very emotional and traumatic, in a freight train"—before she arrived in Vienna with her mother and two small children.[35] (Bronislava Nijinska and her husband had been divorced.) Here is how she described her first visit to the Steinhof:

> When we entered his room Vaslav was sitting in an armchair; he did not get up to greet us. Mother rushed to embrace him, but Vaslav showed no emotional reaction on seeing his mother. He remained withdrawn into himself, also when I embraced him. Throughout our visit in his room, he had an absent look, staring into space and not uttering a word.[36]

Although the effects of medication cannot be ruled out, this description suggests that Nijinsky was again in a catatonic stupor, no longer maniacal as he had been much of the time during his recent Bellevue confinement. In spite of his depression, mutism, and withdrawal, he was alert to his surroundings, and it did not take long before his mother and sister were able to communicate with him. Bronislava talked about the dance and the theater, described her work in the École de Mouvement, and told him about her students, "who were now ready to take part in Nijinsky's choreography." These young Russians, although they had never seen him perform, had "great admiration" for Nijinsky. "I knew they would be devoted to him and would understand his dance." At first he pretended not to hear and "remained impassive," but while his sister was talking about two ballets that she and her students had "already devised," he suddenly came to life, "turned his head and looked straight into my eyes."

> He said very firmly, as if instructing me, "The *ballet* is never devised. The *ballet* must be created." Vaslav's beautiful eyes were sparkling, the sound of his dear voice rang in my ears, my heart brimmed over with hope.[37]

As mentioned earlier, sudden changes in behavior when a catatonic patient was confronted by a person he could trust were considered characteristic of this condition. Sufficiently supported by a loving friend, relative, or therapist, the helpless, dependent "catatonic" would temporarily relinquish his mutism, posturing, aggressiveness, or other compensatory defenses and lapse into seeming "normalcy." Bronislava had shared Vaslav's difficult childhood and his feverish early years with Diaghilev. She could address "that part of his consciousness that lived in his vision of Art," and she soon succeeded at mobilizing some of his old enthusiasm for ballet. "I knew that in this Vaslav was completely sane," she writes.[38] One wonders what might have happened if Nijinska had been able to devote herself entirely to her brother's rehabilitation. Would her belief in his "complete recovery" have been vindicated? It was impossible to find out. With two young children to care for, and exhausted after the long trip from Russia, she could not make the necessary sacrifice on behalf of Nijinsky. Instead, his mother took up residence in the Steinhof and stayed close to him, but the results apparently were unsatisfactory. According to Irina Nijinska—then eight years old, she probably heard this later from her mother—there were many conflicts with Romola, who as in the past rubbed Nijinsky's relatives the wrong way. "In Eleonora's mind," says Irina, "was the suspicion that Romola had been misappropriating Vaslav's funds. Romola was being very extravagant, and there were terrible scenes. At one point Romola even threatened to have Eleonora locked up in the Steinhof."[39] Further conflicts undoubtedly were stirred up when Romola found out that Bronislava wanted to rejoin the Ballets Russes. (Irina says that Romola "tore up the letter" Diaghilev had written

Bronislava about it.) On 25 July 1921, Bronislava wired Diaghilev, "I want to work with you. Please arrange my departure from Vienna immediately."[40]

Under these conditions of family strife, Nijinsky evidently resisted further dialogue with his family and withdrew once again into a state of catatonic inaccessibility. "The spark of consciousness suddenly died," Bronislava wrote. "Vaslav was again staring into the distance, indifferent to everything around him."[41] In September 1921, she left for London to begin the next phase of her own brilliant career, as Diaghilev's choreographer. Romola at this point began making plans of her own. She wanted to go to the United States, in hope of finding there work as an actress and an environment conducive to Nijinsky's recovery. To have him back as the "God of the Dance" was a dream she would pursue for years to come. But the rules about admitting mentally ill persons to the United States were very strict, and it was not until July 1922 that Nijinsky received permission to enter this country, and then only "for a temporary period of six months under medical bond of $1,000, for the purpose of medical treatment, on condition that he will be confined and treated in the New Jersey State Hospital, Trenton, New Jersey."[42]

Such an arrangement suited Romola not at all. Besides, she was running out of money. Her London bank account was down to $12,310 in December 1921.[43] With four mouths to feed, she decided to move back to Hungary, and stay in her mother's villa. A photograph of Nijinsky taken in Budapest in 1923 shows that he had gained weight. His face looks round and full. He sits neatly attired in a business suit, gently holding a grim-faced Kyra, now nine years old, between his knees. He is smiling and seems to be comfortably relaxed. But he was still uncommunicative, and there were recurring depressions and temper outbursts. Romola says that "during a short absence of mine from Hungary he was committed *by my parents* to the State Asylum near Budapest, where he was brutally treated."[44] The records of this institution, the state hospital in Budapest (Lipótmezö) do not show an admission for Nijinsky in those years and there is no documentation of a visit to Budapest's leading psychoanalyst, Dr. Sándor Ferenczi, who according to Romola was "consulted" at this time. Ferenczi was an urbane, cultivated man, and a member of Freud's inner circle. He may very well have been asked to advise a member of the prominent Pulszky family, which might explain Romola's determination at this point to alter her course of action and face certain realities. Nijinsky's earnings were being used up; she could no longer rely on him for financial support; it was unrealistic to expect doors to open in the United States; her talents as an actress were limited; she would have to think of other ways to generate income. Romola decided to ask her parents for a bank loan, and with three of their servants—a maid, a cook, a governess—plus a male nurse for Vaslav, she set out for Paris. Her plan was to go into business there and try to establish her independence.

First, Romola tried to start a taxicab company. "I am a bit frightened of what will happen," she wrote her stepfather. "An auto costs approximately 25,000 francs. If I buy only 4–5 autos, that will bring in only 400–500 francs a day. From that, at least 20–25 will go for repairs, etc. And if I earn only 8–9,000 francs a month, how will I live (make ends meet)?" Next, she tried to team up with "a French inventor" who wanted to manufacture toothache remedies and a bottled elixir, called "Bitter Water," that her mother used to drink. ("It has a terrible taste, and one has to drink it luke-warm slowly in the morning. It was a laxative ... brr.") Romola also wanted to open a pastry shop in Paris, on franchise from the well-known Gerbeaud bakery in Budapest. Altogether, she embarked on nine different business ventures, none of which succeeded. She was constantly on the verge of bankruptcy and sending telegrams home, twice a month, for additional loans. Finally, she was forced to send two of the servants, whose upkeep she could not afford, back to Budapest. A smaller apartment was found on the Champs de Mars, but Romola was afraid to move in. "One has to lease it for 3–6–9 years, and I do not dare do that since I do not know what will happen to us even until spring. Please help. I am very scared.... I have so many worries and problems."[45]

In her efforts to rehabilitate Nijinsky, Romola says she "consulted all the eminent French psychiatrists," but the only name she revealed was "Dr. Émile Coué of Nancy," a psychotherapist who believed strongly in the power of autosuggestion.[46] Whether Coué actually treated Nijinsky is not known. (During the 1920s, Coué achieved considerable popularity in England and the United States, promoting optimistic slogans like "Day by day, in every way, I'm getting better and better." Franklin Delano Roosevelt, after contracting poliomyelitis, was urged to see this man but refused to do so.) Romola also says she turned to "desperate means," faith healers, "fakirs, and Christian Science practitioners, but everything failed."[47] In the summer of 1923 she went with Nijinsky on a pilgrimage to Lourdes, the village near Spain where young Bernadette Soubirous, later canonized, had seen the Virgin Mary in a grotto. (Fresh mountain springs soon began to flow there, and their curative effects have become legendary. Millions of pilgrims are drawn to Lourdes every year, searching for miracles.) "I went with Vaslav to the grotto," writes Romola. "I washed his forehead in the spring and prayed. I hoped and hoped, but he was not cured.... Maybe my faith was not deep enough."[48]

Similarly ineffective were Diaghilev's several attempts, in Paris, to draw Nijinsky closer to the circle of the Ballets Russes, which was again enjoying great success thanks partly to the talent and new ideas his sister had brought with her from Russia. Serge Lifar, a young dancer trained in Kiev by Bronislava Nijinska, was now performing with the company and receiving favors from Diaghilev. Lifar wrote that Diaghilev "refused to reconcile himself to [Nijinsky's] misfortune, and never abandoned the hope that some shock might restore [him] to the world."[49] Lifar may have witnessed such a "shock" in 1923, when Diaghilev allegedly visited Nijinsky's apartment and told the sick dancer, "Vatsa, you are being lazy. Come, I need you. You must dance again for the Russian Ballet and for me." Nijinsky gave Diaghilev a "vacant stare," shook his head, and told him, "I cannot [dance] because I am mad."[50] Nijinsky surely was not being "lazy," and he probably resented Diaghilev's pretending to "need" him as a member of the company. It was obvious that Nijinsky's coveted position as premier danseur had long been taken by other men, and that his sister was now carrying out Nijinsky's dreams, expanding his work, and receiving more acclaim for her ballets than he ever had for his. Les Noces, Bronislava Nijinska's successful ballet-oratorio about a Russian wedding, was being performed successfully in Paris. (A decade earlier, her brother was supposed to have worked on it with Stravinsky.) Nijinska also was readying a new ballet called Les Biches, in which Diaghilev's wish for three men posing and dancing together finally was realized. Les Biches was a comment on ambisexuality, athleticism, and postwar "modernism." It made extensive use of certain arm gestures and body postures that Nijinsky had introduced ten years earlier with his ill-fated Jeux. Nijinska's ballet, also in modern dress, had three young men strutting about, flexing their muscles, and admiring each other. (One of them is seduced by a young girl dressed as a boy.) The choreography of Les Biches "delighted and astonished" Diaghilev, who wrote:

But then this good woman, intemperate and anti-social as she is, does belong to the Nijinsky family. Here and there her choreography is a bit too ordinary, a bit too *feminine,* but *on the whole* it is very good. The dance for the three men has come out extremely well, and they perform it with bravura—weightily, like three cannon.[31]

In 1924, Diaghilev again sought to make contact with Nijinsky, by inviting him to the rehearsals of his sister's ballets. One of these was *Les Facheux,* based on a story by Molière, with heavy, old-fashioned costumes designed by the painter Georges Braque, "unbecoming and difficult to dance in."[52] When Nijinsky entered the auditorium, his appearance, according to Lifar, "greatly distressed" the dancers. "He went on gazing intently over their heads, while a senseless half-smile played on his lips, the terrifying, unearthly half-smile of a human creature, *oblivious to all things.*"[53] How "oblivious" to his environment Nijinsky really was is debatable. Medical documents from Paris suggest just the opposite. But there can be little doubt that Diaghilev and the others who had known him since his charismatic early years were terribly unnerved by Nijinsky's pathetic smile, his lack of enthusiasm for his sister's ballets, and the absence of overt recognition of old friends. During rehearsals for *Le Train Bleu,* another Nijinska ballet in modern dress, set in a fashionable beach resort, the sick dancer just "sat and watched and didn't say anything." His sister started to cry. "I cannot go on, I just cannot go on," she said. "It is too terrible."[54] This ballet had been designed as a vehicle for Diaghilev's latest star, the Irish dancer Anton Dolin (whose real name was Patrick Kay). Dolin was working very closely with Nijinska and trying to learn from her "the secrets of her brother's legendary leaps, his soaring into the air, his slow descent."[55] In *Le Train Bleu,* Dolin wore a bathing suit designed by Coco Chanel and performed some extraordinary handstands, back flips, cartwheels, and other gymnastics. These would have fascinated Nijinsky earlier. Now, at age thirty-five, he showed "no response... eventually his wife led him away."[56]

Whether he consciously envied Dolin, was suppressing rivalrous feelings, or was quietly mourning the loss of his own athletic prowess we will never know. From medical documentation, however, it is clear that behind Nijinsky's placid exterior lay murderous rage, capable of exploding unpredictably, and that his inaccessibility contained elements of defense against hostile, vindictive impulses as well as a craving for love. The fact that his sister had now displaced him in the Ballets Russes could hardly have evoked satisfaction. (Lynn Garafola, a dance critic and historian, writes that Nijinska "had to possess Nijinsky physically to exorcise him creatively; she had literally to become him to become herself."[57]) For a revival of *L'Après-midi d'un Faune* in 1922, she had even assumed the role of the Faun, which they had created together. This and her other accomplishments may have symbolized a threat to Nijinsky's physical integrity. Having once been so close, they were now in different worlds.

Dolin's assessment of Nijinsky in 1924 adds another dimension. He asked Diaghilev for permission to meet "this god of the dance," whose shoes he was being asked to fill. Diaghilev at first said no, but then assented. (Dolin, Diaghilev's latest lover, says he got his way by refusing for three days "to speak to him.") Romola invited them both for tea. "I did not bother to consider," writes Dolin, "any possible embarrassment or distress such a meeting might cause Diaghilev or Nijinsky." He recalls the "suburban" look of the apartment, lace curtains, flowers in the windows, "portraits all around the room," photographs "everywhere," and a medical chart hanging conspicuously over a desk, "as if to remind us that we were visiting a sick man." Nijinsky resembled "a convalescent invalid."

> Diaghilev tried to make him speak, but he did not say a word. He just sat and laughed quietly. I asked him something and he replied, "*Je ne sais pas.*" Those four words expressed his whole tragedy and state of mind— he did not know.... During tea Nijinsky neither ate nor drank, and seemed powerless to do anything. He looked as healthy as any of us.[58]

Nijinsky was able to "comprehend a great deal," Dolin points out, but most of the time he communicated only nonverbally. For example, when Romola raised his hand to hold a cup of tea to his lips, he complied like an obedient child and drank. (This is typical of "catatonia" as described by Kahlbaum.) Before the visitors left, he let Diaghilev "embrace" him, indicating his willingness passively to accept affection. When Dolin put his arms on Nijinsky's shoulders, he "seemed to resent it" at first, then reciprocated by putting his own hand on the young Irishman, a sign of ambivalent trust. Later, he kissed Dolin three times, "as all Russians do in parting.... He came to the door with us, and said goodbye in Russian, and when Diaghilev asked if we might come again, he simply shook his head wistfully, as if to say, 'I am very tired.'"[59]

The year 1924 was very difficult for Romola, as we know from the letters she sent to her mother and stepfather in Budapest. There had been many illnesses all around, which may explain the medical atmosphere Dolin observed in their apartment. Kyra came down with "diphtheria for six weeks." Tamara had an "intestinal infection for four weeks." Romola herself "fell from a horse" onto her back. "I have big pains, I do not get treatment, it would be too expensive. My stomach hurts too, the doctor is sending me to Vichy." She tried to "place Vaslav for 2–3 months" with his sister, but Bronislava was far too busy with new ballets, not to mention having to look after her children and her aging mother, to assume this responsibility. ("Diaghilev and Bronia flee," wrote the frustrated Romola.) To make matters even more complicated, her sister Tessa fled her own marital problems and arrived in Paris. "I am sharing with Tessa my last piece of bread," Romola complained in a letter to Oscar Párdány.

> She is eating here since April. I am afraid she turned the head of the servants. I have to send them away anyway, since I have no money ... I am unable to pay this month's rent ... please try to convince the Wiener Bank Verein to wait until December [with a foreclosure]. If they sue, all they can do is auction off my lingerie.... I do not see a way out, since I do not have any valuables and am unable to find work.[60]

Nevertheless, Romola moved to an expensive apartment on the Avenue de la Bourdonnais, near the Louvre. She had sold a car "standing [unused] in the garage" and from that "could pay the rent for July, food, medication, and some very nervous creditors." She also discovered that "Vaslav had 1,000 francs in his Russian bank" and "after a lot of legwork finally got the money." It did not last long, however. Relying on her mother's influence with theatrical agents in Paris, she sought to "earn money *immediately*" by taking English-speaking roles on the stage or even "in the cinema," but nothing came of this either. Nor was Tessa able to find employment. So Romola borrowed funds from "an American friend" and made plans to send Kyra and Tamara back to Budapest. (Kyra had developed what Romola calls "an abnormality of character"; Professor Bleuler was asked for advice, and he recommended that the girl be "raised outside the family," presumably for Nijinsky's benefit as well as her own.) Romola's instructions to her family in Budapest show how she emphasized environmental, dietary, and linguistic factors in childrearing:

Please make certain that the children should always go to the *fresh air* . . .
watch what [Tamara] is eating . . . we cook with butter, and a change—
to eat meals cooked with lard (made from pig fat?)—can be harmful
unless the cook uses just very little. Both children have to be weighed
every week. . . . Kyra's stomach is very weak. She can have meat only
once a day. She should have a lot of vegetable and compote, and *alcohol
drinks*. She should not have tea, coffee, or bacon. Please allow the
children to take a bath every evening. They do not need too much
water. . . . For 6–8 weeks Kyra should learn only English and French,
nothing else.[61]

Tamara adjusted comfortably to her grandparents' home and remained in Budapest for many years, but Kyra, now ten years old, had to
be sent back to Paris after a few weeks. Romola enrolled her in ballet
classes at the Opéra, where she quickly made progress and soon was
performing on stage. This gave Romola the opportunity to renew an
acquaintance with Jacques Rouché, the director who a decade earlier
had tried to hire Nijinsky as his premier danseur. After Bronislava
Nijinska broke with Diaghilev and quit the Ballets Russes in 1925,
Romola tried to expliot this connection by presenting herself to Rouché
as her sister-in-law's business agent, "as I was for my husband."

I would like to know [writes Romola to Rouché] if you would like to have
my sister-in-law for a few performances at the Opéra. She would also be
able to produce new ballets, or to produce and dance in the works of my
husband, like Faune, Jeux, and Mephisto Waltz, a work still unknown in
Paris. Of these works, the copyrights are mine. I have also two [new]
ballets by my husband, but these will not be able to be produced until the
fall.[62]

Presumably, Romola was referring here to Nijinsky's unfinished
ballets from St. Moritz, which, needless to say, were never produced.
She did succeed, however, in obtaining an advance of five thousand
francs on a salary of sixty thousand francs that Bronislava was
requesting, as well as free tickets to the Paris Opéra Ballet. Later that
year, Romola, together with her sister Tessa, Vaslav, the cook Emma, and
the male nurse (a Viennese named Wolnersdorf) moved to a smaller
apartment in Neuilly, on the outskirts of Paris. Again in need of money,
Romola instigated a law suit against Diaghilev for unpaid debts from
Nijinsky's last performances in South America.   She wrote that

Nijinsky "always loved Paris [and] was at liberty and could enjoy long walks in the Bois de Boulogne, motor tours around Paris and the country, and enjoy the society of his mother and some of his former friends." She took him "to clubs where Cossacks danced, and when he saw these his expression changed, and for a few minutes he became his old self again."[63] This capacity to feel pleasure while watching native dances stayed with him always, a reminder of his childhood and his yearning for Mother Russia.

In 1926, Romola moved to the United States, in hope of finding work in Hollywood, and left Nijinsky with Tessa and the male nurse Wolnersdorf. Soon, he became unmanageable. According to a medical report, he was "violent toward certain persons in the street" and had "suddenly jumped out of the window." (Again, the memory of his famous leap in *Le Spectre de la Rose,* and his brother's fall.) Taken to a nursing home, he was examined on 11 June by a Dr. Heuyer, who describes "stereotypic gestures." Nijinsky "refused to open his mouth," "scratched his head and fingers to the point of drawing blood," gave "no precise or pertinent answers to questions," and produced "unmotivated laughter." Speech was "apparently incoherent, a word-salad, incomprehensible muttering." Heuyer found "no actual delirium," but thought there had been some "episodic hallucinations."

> At present he is calm. Eating and sleeping well. Good physical state, but leaning toward progressive weight gain. Paleness and beginning of obesity. No neurological signs.[64]

In making a diagnosis, Heuyer followed the Kraepelinian model: "A simple demential form of Dementia Praecox, presented by a catatonic phase and a preceding delirious phase." In spite of the "apparent chronicity" of Nijinsky's illness, one "could not affirm its incurability." Heuyer felt it desirable to "shield the patient as much as possible against memories of professional souvenirs or other things that might precipitate some dangerous, impulsive reactions." He also recommended that Nijinsky stay at "the health center" for "hydrotherapeutic treatment and the usual sedatives." There should be "minimal visits" and "no music." The doctor suggested "producing an abscess on the external aspect of the patient's thigh by injecting 2 cc. of terebenthine, to be opened after 5 days." Whether Nijinsky ever received this treatment is not known. It was based on an old clinical observation that psychological disturbances often seemed to remit when patients developed physical diseases. This led to the deliberate production of infections, "the first real progress in organic treatment of mental illness."[65] French psychiatrists were especially impressed with the benefits of sterile abscesses caused by turpentine oil. It was this principle of fighting psychosis with infection that Wagner-Jauregg had exploited when he first used malaria to treat general paresis. Romola, writing from Los Angeles in December 1927, mentions a Dr. Révay who had examined Nijinsky, "suggested blood and urine tests, and thought one could help with the Wagner-Jauregg malaria treatment, maybe."[66] Nijinsky did not have syphilis. This diagnosis was ruled out by the clinical findings, and the negative results of Wassermann tests done at various hospitals.

How long he remained in the Paris nursing home is not clear. We know from Romola's letters that she felt "homesick" in California, "not so much for Europe as for Vaslav.... I am very concerned that I am unable to care for him as I should, give him the clothes, take him to the fresh air, which would be imperative for him." She was also "very upset" because Max Reinhardt was not in Hollywood; she had expected he would help her to obtain appropriate roles in movies—"I heard he is in New York and he has great success." There were financial problems, as usual.

> Another creditor is after me and wants to repossess my stuff. They are trying to take my furniture and I am unable to find the money. Concerning the taxes, if Oscar does not answer immediately there will be big trouble. Yes, I would love to go back to Europe with a lot of money, to take care of the affairs there and rest a little bit, take radium baths ... the entire future is really unpredictable—if I will not be able to earn more money.[67]

In December 1928 Diaghilev tried for the last time to establish contact with Nijinsky. Diaghilev himself was in poor health, suffering from diabetes but not taking insulin, which had recently been introduced as the definitive treatment for this disease. (He died in Venice, on 19 August 1929, after a diabetic coma.) Diaghilev wanted to bring Nijinsky together with Tamara Karsavina, his former partner who had just rejoined the Ballets Russes and was scheduled to appear at the Paris Opéra, in *Petrushka,* one of Nijinsky's favorite works. These dancers had shared so much, their training in St. Petersburg and performing at the Maryinsky Theater, the wondrous early years with Diaghilev, Fokine's great ballets, Nijinsky's innovative *Jeux,* her objections to his choreographic style, and his fleeting infatuation with her. Diaghilev wondered if Karsavina might accomplish the miracle of "restoring him to his right mind."[68]

Always the impresario, he approached this goal more from the perspective of show business than psychotherapy. Instead of taking Karsavina to Nijinsky's apartment, where they might have become reacquainted, talked quietly, and gradually established some rapport, Diaghilev decided to transport the sick dancer to the Opéra and introduce them on the crowded stage, where she was already costumed as the Ballerina in *Petrushka.*[69] But first he introduced Nijinsky to Serge Lifar, who was dancing the part of the Blackamoor that evening. (Thus Diaghilev unwittingly structured the reunion between Nijinsky and Karsavina along the lines of the ballet, with poor Petrushka competing with a rival for the Ballerina's love.) Diaghilev brought Lifar to Nijinsky's apartment, stood the two men back to back and "measured" them—"Vaslav was half a head shorter" than Lifar. Diaghilev bragged about the way Lifar could jump—"Yes, yes, Vatsa, he can leap, he leaps very well, you'll see."[70] Lifar, fifteen years younger than Nijinsky, felt awed and disturbed in his presence. He noted that Nijinsky was lying "half-naked on a low divan.... His nervousness showed only by the movements of his hands. At one moment he would scratch them until they bled while at another moment he would make affected gestures with them." He had the "furtive look of a hunted beast" but seemed "quite sane" while speaking. "He smiled at me, so frankly, so childlike, that I fell immediately under the spell of his charm."[71]*

At first, Nijinsky seemed to ignore what Diaghilev was saying, but then he began to listen "with attention and even with some sign of good

---

*Lifar's several different descriptions of the same event leave some doubt as to whether he actually met Nijinsky in his Paris apartment or may have seen him at the nursing home. In his biography of Diaghilev, Lifar wrote that "we journeyed to the mental home in Passy" and found Nijinsky not in "a room, but a prison cell."[72] In his autobiography, Lifar wrote that "we entered his apartment... his sister-in-law was not there. A servant went in to 'announce' us to Nijinsky, but it was obvious what he was really doing was to make sure the unfortunate man was in a fit state to see us. A door opened. The door of Nijinsky's room. It was like a dungeon."[73] (Nicolas Nabokov's ornate and partly apocryphal version of this visit has Nijinsky picked up from "a sanatorium compound, which was closed in by a quadrangle of high stone walls."[74])

sense." Lifar was struck by the dancer's flabbiness and the "strange" way he got out of bed:

> First of all he went on all-fours from his divan, then crawled around the room, and only then stood upright. I noted that, in a general way, he seemed to be attracted by the floor, to feel a need to be as low down as possible (his divan in fact was almost on a level with the floor) and to grab hold of something. As he walked he leaned forward and felt at his ease only when lying down.[75]

This description suggests a man who is massively depressed; it also suggests a patient with a back injury or herniated disc. One wonders if Nijinsky might have learned this behavior from Romola, who several years earlier had been in "big pain" after her fall off the horse.

After getting Nijinsky to the Paris Opéra, Diaghilev had him brought to the stage for a posed photograph. Karsavina took his right arm, Diaghilev held his left shoulder, and Lifar supported him from the rear. While the camera was clicking, everyone managed a smile, and Nijinsky's gracious expression suggests that he was alert to his surroundings and trying to comply with Diaghilev's wish for everyone to put up a good front. Karsavina wrote afterward that Nijinsky's contact with her had been quite genuine: "His eyes looked straight into mine. I thought he knew me, and I was afraid to speak lest it might interrupt a slow-forming thought. He kept silent. I then called him by his pet name, 'Vatsa!'... on meeting my eyes he turned his head like a child that wants to hide tears."[76]

After the performance, Nijinsky kept saying that he did not want to leave. The stage had been his home, and Paris was the scene of his greatest triumphs. Now, it had become the setting for a grievous humiliation, the public demonstration to colleagues, audience, and the world at large that a great star had been snuffed out. Nijinsky was no longer twinkling. He had become a chronic invalid.

NOTES

1. BNM, 515.
2. Kurt Binswanger, notes, BMR, 26–28 July 1919.
3. Ibid.
4. Personal communication from Dr. "Greiber's" family.
5. Romola Nijinsky, *The Last Years of Nijinsky*, 24.
6. Ibid.
7. BMR, 29 July 1919.

8. Interview with Romola Nijinsky, videotape of *Et liv*.
9. Personal communication from Kyra Nijinsky Markevitch.
10. Elizabeth J. Brunowski, *A Psychobiographical Study of Vaslav Nijinsky*, 191. Emphasis added.
11. Anton Dolin, *Last Words*, 56.
12. All quotations are from the summary of events prior to Nijinsky's readmission to the Bellevue Sanatorium in December 1919, see BMR.
13. Notes of J. Sprengler, psychiatric attendant, Binswanger Archives, Tübingen University.
14. Dr. Kurt Binswanger, admission note, 3 December 1919, BMR.
15. Dr. Kurt Binswanger, notes, 13 December 1919.
16. Ibid., 30 December 1919.
17. Irina Nijinska Raetz, personal communication.
18. Dr. Kurt Binswanger, notes, 12 January 1920.
19. Ibid., 30 January 1920.
20. Ibid., 24 February 1920.
21. BMR, 27 February 1920.
22. Peter Haiko, Harald Leupold-Löwenthal, and Mara Reissberger, "'Die Weisse Stadt.'"
23. Romola Nijinsky, unpublished notes. Nijinsky Archives.
24. Alma Mahler Werfel, *And the Bridge Is Love*, 87.
25. Romola Nijinsky, unpublished notes. Nijinsky Archives.
26. Peter Buckley, "Fifty Years After Freud: Dora, the Rat Man, and the Wolf-Man."
27. Romola Nijinsky, unpublished notes. Nijinsky Archives.
28. Medical records from the Wiener Sanatorium Dr. Anton Loew. Nijinsky Archives.
29. Dolin, 56–57.
30. Tamara Nijinsky, personal communication.
31. Letter from Romola Nijinsky to Dr. Ludwig Binswanger, 27 July 1942. Binswanger Archives, Tübingen.
32. Letter from Romola Nijinsky to Dr. Ludwig Binswanger, 26 September 1946. Binswanger Archives, Tübingen.
33. Romola Nijinsky, unpublished notes. Nijinsky Archives.
34. BNM, 514.
35. Irina Nijinska Raetz, personal communication.
36. BNM, 514.
37. Ibid. Emphasis in the original.
38. Ibid., 515.
39. Irina Nijinska Raetz, personal communication.
40. Telegram from Bronislava Nijinska to Sergei Diaghilev, 25 June 1921, Bibliothèque de l'Opéra, Paris, Kochno Fond, 65.
41. BNM, 515.
42. Letter from U.S. Department of Labor, Bureau of Immigration, Washington, D.C., to Dr. Henry A. Cotton, Superintendent of the New Jersey State Hospital, 1 July 1922.
43. Affidavit, 6 December 1921, from Bankers Trust Company, New York. Nijinsky Archives.
44. Romola Nijinsky, unpublished notes. Emphasis added.
45. Romola Nijinsky, unpublished correspondence, 7 December 1923. Nijinsky Archives.
46. Romola Nijinsky, unpublished notes. Nijinsky Archives.
47. RNN, 432.
48. Romola Nijinsky, unpublished notes.
49. Serge Lifar, *Serge Diaghilev*, 206.
50. RBN, 503.
51. Richard Buckle, *Diaghilev*, 418. Emphasis in original.
52. Garafola, 120.
53. Lifar, 207. Emphasis in the original.
54. Interview with Anton Dolin, from Bronislava Nijinska, documentary shown on PBS-TV, 1989.
55. Dolin, 43.
56. RBN, 505–506.
57. Garafola, 132.

58. Dolin, 51–52.
59. Ibid.
60. Romola Nijinsky, unpublished letter, 15 July 1924.
61. Romola Nijinsky, unpublished letter, 9 August 1924. Emphasis in the original.
62. Romola Nijinsky to Jacques Rouché, unpublished letter, 6 March 1925, Bibliothèque de l'Opéra, Paris.
63. Romola Nijinsky, unpublished notes. Nijinsky Archives; RNN, 432.
64. Medical report, 11 June 1926. Property of David Leonard, London.
65. Lothar R. Kalinowsky, and Paul H. Hoch (editors), *Shock Treatments*, 2–3.
66. Letter from Romola Nijinsky to Emilia Márkus, 9 December 1927. Nijinsky Archives.
67. Ibid.
68. RBN, 508.
69. Tamara Karsavina, *Theatre Street*, 292.
70. Serge Lifar, *Ma Vie*, 62–63.
71. Lifar, *Ma Vie*, 61–62.
72. Lifar, *Diaghilev*, 485.
73. Lifar, *Ma Vie*, 61.
74. Nicolas Nabokov, *Old Friends and New Music*, 137.
75. Lifar, *Ma Vie*, 63.
76. Karsavina, 295.

The condition of the patient is only
an accident in the history of the
disease.

J.-M. Charcot[1]

Chapter 12

Invalidism

Chronic disability all too often is the sad outcome of illnesses that fail
to remit. With an impaired organ system—cardiovascular, pulmonary,
gastrointestinal, urogenital, cerebrospinal, or the immune system itself—patients wait for months, years, or decades for an effective
treatment to be applied or, if there is not one, to be discovered. As inner
resources for fighting disease gradually diminish, the environmental
support structure of friends, family, and finances often weakens as
well. Patients grow older, more dependent, disheartened, and crippled
in mind and body. The painful story of Nijinsky's invalidism from age
thirty-nine to forty-eight emerges from medical records and from
correspondence among those who could not forget him.

A letter from Romola to the Bellevue Sanatorium, written on 22 April
1929, brings us up-to-date. She is currently staying at the fashionable
Savoy Hotel in London, has not seen her husband for three years, is
"very, very, busy," and wants the Binswangers to accept him again as a
patient. She feels upset with the way her sister is mismanaging things

in Paris. Tessa has not found a job and has run out of money. Romola blames her for neglecting Nijinsky's care. He has been confined to a small apartment, 10 rue du Conseiller-Collignon, near the Ranelagh Gardens, and seems to be slowly deteriorating. "I am so sorry," Romola writes the Binswangers, "that twice already in the last year you arranged a trip for him and it did not work out, but I was in America and my sister wrote me each time that he was too excited to travel."[2] This time, Romola wanted to make sure to get the dancer to Switzerland. .

> A passport in my husband's name will be issued on the 25th. of this month by the French authorities ... and he could come to you at the latest by Sunday the 28th, in the evening. I think Sunday would be the best, the quietest day to travel. I only want to know whether you will send one or two attendants...please let them serve him breakfast in the sleeping car [and] send someone who is kind, since my husband is very fearful, and this will be his first trip without a member of the family. ... Please give my husband a friendly, sunny room, and a very forbearing attendant. He needs to have a lot of good warm people around him. Then he will be more obedient and easier to manage.[3]

Dr. Binswanger dispatched two of his men to Paris, "Herr Butz and the attendant Köningsdorfer." They found Nijinsky in Tessa's apartment "in a cell, where he was often raving and smearing feces. He looked fairly neglected and had not been in the fresh air at all for a long time." Returning him to Bellevue Sanatorium was not easy. "It was necessary to hold him down at all times, despite the two Scopolamine injections he was given." Once Nijinsky was settled into his confortable room in the Parkhaus, he became more tractable and was noted to be "completely quiet, smiling amiably." An interview on 3 May 1929 describes him as "silly and answering questions senselessly. He looks pale, strongly mongoloid facial features. Condition of his musculature is good. But the patient does not let us conduct a regular examination." Soon, his behavior fluctuated between sullen, stiff passivity and states of excitement when he would be "aggressive in a very clever and malicious way." Nearly every day he was taken for walks in the park. "There he mostly lies down [on a chaise-longue], and with a tense facial expression withdraws quietly into himself. This morning he threw the breakfast dishes against the wall."[4]

After four weeks of observation, it was decided to assign Nijinsky to a female therapist, Dr. Marta Wenger, a "robust, clear-thinking and intelligent Swiss woman," who was married to one of the other staff psychiatrists.[5] She would take care of Nijinsky for the next three years. Dr. Wenger's notes describe his "good physical recovery" and considerable weight gain, not unusual among the long-term patients at Bellevue, where an outstanding *pâtissier,* Max Straub, reigned in the kitchen. Nijinsky was very fond of rich, cream-laden pastries and "got rounder all the time." It was also noted that when he was allowed to stuff himself, he would be noticeably "less aggressive." (Nijinsky's high-calorie, high-fat diet probably contributed to his progressive arteriosclerosis.) He also became very "lazy." It was almost impossible to get him to participate in the "work-therapy" program. When asked to "join one of the attendants cutting wood in the carpentry shop," Nijinsky would agree, but then just stand around and "for the most part remain completely passive." Another expedient form of occupational therapy was work in the garden. Dr. Wenger tried to keep Nijinsky "busy picking flowers, but he would just hold the stalks stiffly in his hands." Calisthenics were attempted. Again, he usually remained inert and "exercised only a little bit." Mostly, Nijinsky wanted to be left alone. If someone tried to approach him, he would say, quite coherently, "Ne me touchez pas" (Don't touch me).[6]

He no longer seemed interested in any spontaneous dancing, a sad change from his stay at Bellevue Sanatorium ten years earlier. For nearly a month, Frau Mai, described as "a rather unsophisticated piano teacher,"[7] tried to work with him: "She made an effort to cure the sick man by playing musical pieces from his successful ballets." His response was minimal. Nijinsky's life in the ballet had definitely become a thing of the past. "When a book of pictures about him as a dancer was shown to the patient, he looked at it rather solemnly, then with one finger thrust the book away and said 'fini.'" As Dr. Wenger put it, he remained "unchanged," "passive," "out of contact with the environment," and "catatonically mute." He "smiled and laughed" a lot, "silly" emotional responses usually felt to be signs of "indifference." Yet at times he was able to display warmth and genuine pleasure. For example, one day when he was "playing with a kitten that had been running after him, a charming smile radiated across his entire face." Deep sadness also became apparent while Nijinsky was "watching the construction of a stage-set for our Christmas play—his eyes filled with tears." There were also moments of "irritability when he was always ready to slap you in the face."[8]

Nijinsky continued to have only sporadic contact with his wife. Six months after his admission, she began "sending him cards every few weeks from her trips," and just before Christmas 1929, she came to see him briefly. If was their first contact in more than three years. "He was in quite a good mood during the visit of his very nice wife," writes Dr. Wenger. "Often he is unclean, smearing urine all over the floor." Romola left him again for almost a year, not returning until September 1930, which was the last time they would see each other for the next four years. She was surprised to find him "quite well." There had been some medical problems, beginning with a "pharyngitis" in May 1930. "During the inspection of his throat, Nijinsky became extremely negativistic, pressed his tongue to his gums in such a way that it could not be pushed down, and struggled so much that he became very pale and started to sweat. For several days he had a fever, but recovered very rapidly." In November he complained of "severe toothache," became "loud and excited," and "had to have an injection." The dentist found "no bad teeth," and there were no further complaints.[9] The dentist's opinion of "no bad teeth" seems surprising, considering photographs taken of Nijinsky at this time, which suggest poor dental hygiene and very bad-looking teeth. The most likely explanation is that the pathological process was in his gums—recession of gum tissue and enlarged spaces between the teeth—rather than in the teeth (dental caries). When a periodontal abscess forms, it produces pain, relieved once the abscess points and drains, which may explain why Nijinsky had no further complaints, for a while at least.

His "mutism" always frustrated Dr. Wenger in her efforts to find out what ailed him. There were days when he would just "stand around in the snow, murmuring irritably to himself whenever one tried to draw him out." (The content of his "murmuring"—if indeed this was speech—is not described, but some of the other doctors felt that Nijinsky was "hallucinating."[10]) On 1 May 1931, Dr. Wenger found him in a state of "fairly great confusion, the reasons for which could not be definitely ascertained." Two months later, he was "physically well, saying very little, but in a good disposition." Throughout the summer, he communicated mainly nonverbally: "[He is] usually in a good mood, quietly happy, withdrawn, occasionally somewhat irritated, which one can detect immediately in his face." On 17 November, "he used gestures to make [Dr. Wenger] understand that he was having pain in his abdomen."

> This was followed by diarrhea and a slight collapse. The patient looked very pale, sweated profusely, and had a weak pulse. Was given Cardiozol [heart medication], after which he recovered, but continued to have tachycardia [fast pulse] for several days. Psychically unchanged.[11]

What caused these abdominal and cardiac crises, which were to affect Nijinsky for years to come? Recurring gastrointestinal symptoms may have been a physiological manifestation of his intense mood disturbance. Anxiety, fear, and depression can lead to slowing (hypomotility) of the gut, while aggressive feelings, hostility, and resentment tend to produce hypermotility and spasms. Changes in the pulse and blood pressure are also associated with intense emotion. It is thought that the limbic system of the brain and a center called the *locus ceruleus* mediate between emotions, thoughts, and physical feelings. Other, less likely possibilities would be "abdominal epilepsy"—a seizurelike attack hitting the abdominal organs—or a slowly growing tumor of the adrenal gland, called a pheochromocytoma, which by secreting spurts of adrenalin can suddenly raise the blood pressure and speed the heart.

The week before Christmas 1931, Nijinsky experienced his "second mild state of collapse." Dr. Wenger examined him as best she could and found that his temperature had risen to 38 degrees Centigrade, suggesting an infectious process. There was "definite tenderness in the left chest, low in the back." Auscultation revealed no abnormal breath sounds. After a few days, the symptoms had "faded away," and he was his usual self, "sometimes aggressive and then ready to slap people vigorously in the face." Seven weeks later, on 2 February 1932, his physical condition was judged to be "improved, his heart holds up quite well under temporary treatment with Digitalis." But on 22 March "he again briefly lost his good color; the pulse continues to be regular but not very strong." His blood pressure was not recorded. Romola had gone back to the United States, and "for months" did not communicate with the Bellevue staff. Only after hearing about Nijinsky's medical problems did she begin sending "frequent letters" to the doctors, giving them "advice for treatment" and enclosing "money for clothes and laundry" for Nijinsky.[12] To her mother in Budapest, Romola wrote that "Vaslav is not well, he had two heart attacks, I am very worried, although the doctors have reassured me."[13]

From Romola's letters to Emilia Márkus and her husband as well as other sources, we learn that Nijinsky's wife had gotten herself involved in a tempestuous love-hate relationship with an actress, Lya de Putti, the daughter of a Hungarian, Count Hoyos. They had gone to Hollywood, allegedly to make films, and according to Romola, Lya "wanted to take me to Hawaii and California." She is described as possessive and manipulative, borrowing money from Romola, never repaying it, and generally making her life miserable by saying things like "Romus, if you stay with me and stop worrying about Vaslav . . . we will live like kings for three years and then commit suicide. If not, then go and starve to death with your husband. You are mine or nobody's." Romola's answer, as she describes it, was "Thank you, Lya, I will stay as your friend, but for 13 years I have fought for Vaslav, who is a saint for me. I will not abandon him in the 14th year."[14] This relationship came to an end when Lya "in her anger swallowed a [chicken] bone, which in her system, poisoned by alcohol, caused a terrible gas poisoning . . . and as a result of the surgery she caught pneumonia and died." To Oscar Párdány Romola wrote:

> I do not wish to go into details. Lya could not accept that she had lost . . . me, and could not torture us any longer. . . . Who nursed her, who called Walter [Lya's friend] to her deathbed! Who supported the servants that had been plotting against me all summer, who called the 8 best doctors, who called the priest, who nursed her day and night. . . the good stupid Romola.[15]

Her next passionate attachment was to Frederica Dezentje, a married woman from Holland, described by Romola as "my only true friend." Frederica encouraged Romola's various projects in Nijinsky's behalf, and probably gave her financial support. Romola had been writing articles, collecting photographs and memorabilia, contacting wealthy ballet patrons, organizing exhibits, and trying to raise money. "Frederica did not let me despair, she stays at my side through thick and thin," Romola wrote to Emila Márkus. "She begs me to stand on my own two feet, to get rid of every bad influence. If I ever become somebody, that will be thanks to Frederica."[16] Plans were made for an exhibition of Nijinsky's drawings in the Leggett Gallery of the new Waldorf-Astoria Hotel. "Mrs. Vanderbilt will be one of the hostesses," writes Romola, "and I will be giving lectures about 'The Art of the Dance' ... illustrated by Vaslav's friend Gavrilov who will dance in full costume. In this way we hope that we will be hired by some artistic academy or university, on a full-time basis, from which Vaslav's dream may develop: the Bayreuth of dance."[17]

Romola also hoped to obtain financial assistance from two wealthy patrons of the arts, the Princess Edmond de Polignac in Paris and Lord Harold Sidney Rothermere in London. "I think if we could collect $10,000 that would keep Vaslav in Kreuzlingen for the rest of his life, or another good Swiss institution."[18] Failing in that effort, she made plans for writing a book about Nijinsky, which she hoped to publish and thus augment her income. (As can be surmised from Mme Nijinsky usually staying in the best and most expensive hotels, she was not as destitute as she often claimed. However, she was notably negligent in paying her bills.) "Frederica quietly accepted all the hardships with me," Romola wrote her mother in 1932. "Frederica always had a consoling word, encouraging words for me to keep fighting. She tried everything to help me secure Vatsa's existence, and that we should be able to create a little home for ourselves. Without her, I would have given up a long time ago."[19]

Frederica herself was chronically ill, suffering from pulmonary tuberculosis. During one of her acute attacks, she had to stay in an oxygen tent for seventeen·days. "I am unable to live without her," writes Romola. "If I have to leave for even half an hour, we call to each other, and she says 'Schatzi, Liebling, komm' schon zurück, ich langweile mich furchtbar ohne Dich' (Darling, beloved, come back, I'm terribly bored without you)." Frederica Dezentje's illness, coming on the heals of Lya de Putti's traumatic death and the news of Nijinsky's medical problems, plunged Romola into an existential crisis. "Do you really believe in an afterworld?" she asked in a letter to her mother. "I will pray ... that my bitter life should end, so that Vatsa, Frederica, and I can be together soon."[20]

The next year, Romola's first book about Nijinsky was published, thanks to editorial guidance, ghostwriting, and other significant help from the distinguished ballet scholar Lincoln Kirstein. Her (and his) book is dedicated "to the memory of Frederica Dezentje, without whose affection and friendship this book could not have been written." A letter from Lincoln Kirstein to Romola Nijinsky (3 April 1933) shows the strength of his affection for her, and how he was guiding her work. He urged her to write about "Carnaval, Petrushka, Everything and Everything." He told her to read "the Bible and the Outcast."[21] Kirstein was indebted to Mme Nijinsky for having introduced him to the young Russian dancer George Balanchine, who was a member of the Ballets Russes and one of Diaghilev's choreographers. (Balanchine's subsequent collaboration with Kirstein led to the formation of a ballet school in New York, and later the New York City Ballet.[22])

Frederica died in 1932, leaving Romola bereft and mournful. "I will say goodbye for good to the new world. I have to find the money for Frederica's and my grave." In a moving letter to Emilia Márkus, she confessed that Frederica and Vaslav were the only people who ever "meant anything" to her. "They both had that unselfish goodness, and innocent nobility."

> When Frederica stopped breathing so did I.... I am unable to live alone.... Do you remember how angry I was against fate, against the entire world when I lost Vaslav, how I committed one stupidity after another, in order to forget the void?... My friendship with Lya was nothing more than a narcotic, to be able to forget.... I do not want to make the same mistakes, I do not want to become an alcoholic or take morphine [shades of Dr. Greiber!] just as I could never have married again.[23]

What kept Romola going was the confidence she felt in her ability to vanquish adversity at other people's expense, not to mention the generous (and anonymous) support she received from people like Lincoln Kirstein. In her loneliness after Frederica's death, she pined for her two daughters. "I would like to see Kyra and Tamara," but am unable to go back to places where I was with Frederica."[24] The next year Romola did go back to London, however. Kyra, then nineteen years old, visited her there in a hotel. She was working as a dancer, and needed a place to stay. At that time, Kyra was romantically involved with Igor Markevitch, the brilliant Russian musician and Diaghilev's last boyfriend, whom she later married. Romola was not at all pleased with Kyra's career—there was to be only one dancer named Nijinsky, and that was Vaslav, the "God of the Dance."

My mother was living with a lesbian who liked to dress like a man [Kyra recalls]. I remember very well the funny little man's hat she would wear. Once I found them in bed together. Mother told me she had given up on men. "The only man in this world I will ever love is Vaslav." I asked if I could stay with her. "Impossible," she told me. Fortunately I received an invitation to go to Sweden and went there instead. I danced in cabaret and was a great success.[25]

Nijinsky, now forty-four years old, had become "big, and fat and stereotypic," a chronic invalid. "He only lives in his laughter," writes Dr. Wenger, who after three years of trying to work with him psychotherapeutically had been replaced by a Russian-speaking psychiatrist, Dr. Kroll.[26] Kroll is described as a "well-educated man, musical, who played the violin, had travelled widely, and was psychoanalytically trained."[27] But in ten weeks of daily contact, he "did not succeed in getting the patient to say one word in his mother-tongue." (Nijinsky's mother-tongue was actually Polish.) "At good times he is mutistic, [but] on days when he is excited he speaks exclusively French." What Nijinsky said is not recorded. Kroll mentions no hallucinations, but describes him "exploding whenever one tries to make contact with him." One day while "pounding the wall with his hand" (was he hearing voices or simply acting out his anger?) he fractured a bone, the second metacarpal of the right hand, resulting in "severe pain." It was bandaged, and "healed without the necessity of a plaster cast." For the next two or three months he seemed to obtain pleasure from "looking at his finger, stroking it, and plucking the tips of his ears."[28]

As the years passed, Nijinsky spoke less and less. He became "disinclined to engage in any movement." His habits deteriorated, and he occasionally soiled himself. No longer did he dance spontaneously, but if someone showed interest in him and asked him to dance, he complied willingly. The hospital had an "athletic instructor, an energetic Swedish woman," who invited him occasionally to join her in waltzes. "He leads well, more or less rhythmically. His entire face lights up with a smile... several times he danced waltzes and other dances with visible pleasure."[29] Otherwise, he remained generally listless.

Nijinsky's social isolation resulted partly from Romola's possessive self-interest. She had given orders that he should have no visitors. In March 1933, when Igor Markevitch, at Kyra's request, tried to visit him, the young musician was not allowed to see his future father-in-law because "written permission would have to come from the patient's wife." A few days later, "on the recommendation of a personal acquaintance of Dr. Ludwig Binswanger," Markevitch tried once more to gain access to the sick dancer, but received "the same negative reply."[30] Thus, Nijinsky remained disconnected from anyone in the artistic community who might have been motivated to spend time with him or to be companionable. Without family or friends from outside the hospital, he just "continued to sit around inertly, occasionally incensed, then again smiling, but wholly without interest in the events of his environment.... He screws his finger into his ear a little bit and murmurs to himself.... Once he gave a short but adequate answer in Russian and smiled in a friendly way."[31]

A crisis arose when Nijinsky's hospital bill did not get paid in 1933. Who, in the absence of Romola, would assume financial responsibility? Her stepfather Oscar Párdány came from Budapest in August to discuss the question with the Binswangers, and an attempt was made to appoint a conservator. Nijinsky "smiled amiably and gave brief but adequate answers in the Russian language" when his therapist brought this to his attention, but with Párdány, Nijinsky "showed no reaction and would not speak to him at all." A Swiss attorney was consulted. He ruled that "it would be difficult to name anyone other than his wife as guardian." A visit from Romola "seemed imminent" in September, but still she failed to show up. The hospital staff grew optimistic when they heard that "she has written a book about him and after all is doing a lot of advertising, which ought to bring in money." She kept her distance. Just before Christmas, Nijinsky developed "a cold with coughing" and spiked a high fever (39.1° C). Aspirin was prescribed. "There was a very copious, greenish nasal discharge, which the patient smeared on his pants leg." He "stayed in bed for several days," had a "noticeably weak pulse," and was given coramin.[32]

Nijinsky's mood tended to improve after a bout of physical illness and the attention he received for it. For example, following his midwinter upper-respiratory infection he became more outgoing and "well-disposed." A relationship of sorts even developed between him and one of the other men, a "manic patient who invites him to his room occasionally, and talks to him in a friendly way. Nijinsky repays this patient's trust and 'flattery' with affectionate smiles." Two further medical crises occurred in 1934. The first was a bout of "indigestion." Nijinsky "threw up two of his meals" and was found to be constipated, a not uncommon problem among hospitalized patients who are physically inactive and receiving medication. His pulse was found to be "a little weak," and he was again given coramin. A medical consultant, Dr. Sträuli, found "a considerable amount of blood in his hard stools, due to hemorrhoids." Later that year Nijinsky had "an attack of severe pallor and pulse-weakness," which recurred after "an attempt to get him to do calisthenics." His blood pressure was taken: "Before applying the apparatus, his pulse on palpation had been very weak, but while recording it, his [systolic] blood pressure became markedly stronger, 144 mm."[33]*

"*A visit from his wife!*" reports his psychiatrist, Dr. Kroll, on 4 April 1934. Having been away for four years, Romola created quite a stir at Bellevue. "Generous as always," writes Dr. Kroll sarcastically, "she brings with her many presents, for which the hospital is expected to pay customs duty and freight charges. But at least she buys some clothes and laundry for the patient, who smiles at everything." Romola's displeasure with the way Nijinsky was being treated surfaced immediately. She wrote a letter to Dr. Boeckli, an outside medical consultant, complaining that he was "being kept in an attendant's room on the first floor, where no other patients are living." Regarding the nonpayment of his hospital bill, Romola explained that her daughter Kyra is "extraordinarily gifted and will be ready to contribute to her father's support in just a few years." But there was no point in sending Kyra the bill. "It would be too heavy a burden for a young person," the Binswangers were told. Romola also demanded that "a specialist in Zürich be consulted in regard to Nijinsky's heart. This she would pay for 'immediately.' In addition, the patient's foot ought to be photographed."[34]

After her whirlwind visit, Romola disappeared again, only to return in October, accompanied by "a woman friend" and "Professor Adler from Vienna," with whom she wanted Nijinsky to consult. Dr. Alfred Adler (1870–1937) was an early follower of Freud. He had developed his own brand of psychoanalysis called "individual psychology," based on

---

*None of Nijinsky's blood-pressure readings at the Bellevue Sanatorium would be considered significantly elevated today. But his blood pressure was checked so infrequently that it is impossible to say when the hypertension that was one of his major symptoms later in life actually became manifest. His diet at the sanatorium was very rich. This, plus lack of exercise, smoking, and his thickened "athlete's (dancer's) heart" probably contributed to the slowly progressive arteriosclerosis that later interfered with Nijinsky's circulation, heart action, and kidney function.

the concept that every human being has "a feeling of inferiority which constantly presses towards its own conquest."[35] Those who are physically or mentally handicapped tend to "overcompensate" for their inferiority. As a result, they develop a "superiority complex" which can have beneficial as well as pathological consequences. An example Adler liked to cite was the musician Ludwig van Beethoven, who was severely hard of hearing. In struggling to adapt to this "organ inferiority," he not only produced beautiful compositions but became isolative and paranoid. (We now know that Beethoven had a great many other problems as well, so Adler's theory seems simplistic.)[36] Unlike Freud, who explored personal conflicts primarily, Adler tended to address the environmental factors limiting people's struggle for power and self-realization. He had a knack for imparting hopefulness to patients and was considered a therapeutic optimist. Romola had talked him into coming to Bellevue and was urging him to assume responsibility for Nijinsky's psychiatric care.

> A wealthy American, together with other benefactors were prepared to finance the treatment [writes Dr. Kroll]. Adler explained that his plan was to take the patient to Vienna, and to establish a residence for him there with a physician trained by him. He also wants to give Nijinsky piano lessons.[37]

The central issue of course was whether the ailing dancer would cooperate with this approach. Nijinsky was told that for Adler to treat him, he would have to "go voluntarily" to Vienna. "During their consultation the patient smiled once in a while, but otherwise maintained his usual stiff attitude," says Kroll. Finally Nijinsky indicated that "he would not go," and Romola departed with her entourage.

Dr. Adler's optimism may nevertheless have had a positive effect. Four weeks after their consultation, Nijinsky was seen "listening to the playing of Händel's *Largo* and clearly reacting to the rhythm by making some desirable movements, and smiling with delight." For the next twelve months he remained generally "in a good mood," was "very seldom incensed," and "never became aggressive." Dr. Kroll mentions that the dancer "fairly frequently received letters from female admirers who ask for his autograph," but rarely "took notice" of these tokens of esteem, and "remained exceedingly passive whenever one tried to get him to do any work."[38]

During the following year Romola kept herself busy editing and translating (with Jennifer Mattingly's help) the famous *Diary of Vaslav Nijinsky,* as it came to be called, based on selections from his St. Moritz notebooks. Romola claimed to have forgotten that these important documents still existed. They were accidentally found one day in a trunk full of old things belonging to Kyra. She invited Alfred Adler to contribute a preface for the *Diary,* and he accepted. "Nijinsky's spiritual death has aroused the sympathy of a great portion of the civilized world," wrote Adler.

> When I visited him two years ago in a sanatorium, he was quiet, well-nourished, and interested in his guests. But he did not speak and only occasionally broke into a friendly laugh. The attending physician informed me that this patient was always quiet and could not be forced to speak. At the time, even his wife was unable to draw him into conversation.[39]

Adler's preface (which Romola never published) describes Nijinsky as a "great unhappy artist, the recipient of much admiration which yet fell far below his expectations...."

> He wishes to prove his singularity, the expression of which has been frustrated by the objectionable activities of people who hindered him.... [He] is driven by what I have called an "inferiority complex."

Adler was speculating; he had not been able to interview Nijinsky. Whatever knowledge he had must have come from Romola.

> Our poor hero, badly prepared for life, burdened from childhood by highly strained expectations, lacking the ordinary course of education, and put automatically in a class of people whose better schooling and background made him feel slighted, tried in vain to save his striving for superiority by despising rational thinking.[40]

Adler wanted to demonstrate what he calls Nijinsky's "irrationalism." "You can read it in this book.... He is God, inventor, poet, writer, but constantly limited by the trickery and failures of other individuals." Regarding the matter of his treatability by the methods of Individual Psychology, Adler said that he "could not answer ... everything hinges on the establishment of a creative contact between doctor and patient. The possibility of establishing such a contact must first be ascertained, since treatment is a task for two individuals; the abilities of both should be taken into consideration, as this is a cooperative activity which is not only of a scientific but also of an artistic nature."[41]

Romola decided against publishing Adler's comments on Nijinsky—they were released only after her death—because she felt that "the argument that Nijinsky suffered from an inferiority complex is entirely erroneous."[42] Instead, she wrote her own preface, describing Nijinsky as "a humanitarian, a seeker of truth, whose only aim in life was to help, to share, to love."[43] In her opinion his illness was caused by "an uncanny, invisible power ... a ghastly force." She later asked another famous psychiatrist, Carl Gustav Jung, to write a preface for the *Diary*. But Jung, unlike Adler, had never met Nijinsky. He answered Romola's letters, commented on a question she had raised about "colors, specifically the absence of color in dreams," but then politely excused himself from complying with her request.[44]

On 20 April 1936, Kyra Nijinsky was married to Igor Markevitch. It was a high-society event in Budapest's beautiful Matthias Church, with Tamara Karsavina and the Hungarian composer Ernst von Dohnányi as their witnesses. Emilia Márkus had finally put down her foot on the couple's living together openly without benefit of clergy. Markevitch gives a marvelous description of Romola's mother:

> Emilia Márkus lived each moment conscious of being a national institution. If certain people classified her as the Hungarian Sarah Bernhardt, others would swear that in her greatest era she surpassed the Duse. Everyone admitted that she should have had a more universal language than Hungarian, so that her real dimensions might be recognized.... She held under her power a second husband, Oscar Párdány, an angel of patience and elegance who apparently only served as her chauffeur.... Despite her advanced age, Emilia Márkus continued to "act," but it was now in her daily life that she was the actress and stage director.... There was something heroic and moving in this perpetual manner of constantly being in a performance.[45]

Romola stopped briefly at the Bellevue Sanatorium before flying to Budapest for the wedding. Nijinsky "smiled at her sweetly," let her "guide his hand in signing autographs, and even went on an automobile-ride with her." After the wedding she sent a reporter from the French journal *Paris du Soir* to the hospital, and a photographer to take pictures of Nijinsky, a way of creating publicity for his forthcoming *Diary*. In July there was another medical crisis. Nijinsky suddenly began to "look unwell; his pulse was irregular; he was put to bed and given fifteen drops of Digalen, fifteen drops of Coramine, and two cc. of Coramine by injection. He recovered more slowly than usual, and very inadequately. "His extremities remained cold, and he looked so ominous that the head nurse feared death. At about 6 o'clock in the evening he vomited up his mid-day meal." After that, his condition improved. Fifteen minutes later the consultant, Dr. Sträuli, arrived and "expressed the suspicion of a coronary sclerosis. He believes that such attacks can sometimes have a fatal outcome." Sträuli advised giving theophylline, a drug that relaxes smooth muscles in the coronary arteries, bronchial tubes, and pulmonary blood vessels. (Theophylline also directly stimulates the heart, kidneys, brain, and skeletal muscles.) After receiving his first dose—amount unspecified—Nijinsky began to "look much better but remained in bed. Systolic blood pressure is 130 mm."[46]

"At the request of his wife," Nijinsky had a second consultation one month later, this time with a medical specialist from nearby Constance, Dr. Hassenkamp, who took a chest X-ray and did an electrocardiogram. "The tests show clear signs of arteriosclerosis, especially widespread in the aorta," reports Hassenkamp. "Blood pressure 160. His attacks should be regarded as a result of arteriosclerosis, with the possibility of death any time during an attack." (Today, internists believe the diastolic blood pressure is more important to follow than the systolic in diagnosing hypertension or the risk of arteriosclerosis.) The alarming pronouncement about Nijinsky's heart seems to have had a paradoxical effect. Twenty years earlier, when he was in excellent physical shape, he had experienced states of panic, usually associated with a fear of sudden death due to heart failure. Now, in his late forties, obese, inactive, and diagnosed to have arteriosclerotic cardiovascular disease, Nijinsky seemed unworried, unconcerned, and "friendlier than before." He was observed to be laughing a lot, and showing no appreciable fear.[47] One might call this "inappropriate affect," one of the cardinal signs of schizophrenia. On the other hand, it may have been reassuring for Nijinsky to see his heart in an X-ray picture and beating on the electrocardiograph machine, and to be validated in his belief that he could die of his heart problems.*

In October 1936, seven weeks after the "heart attack," Nijinsky's mental status was thoroughly reevaluated by one of the staff psychiatrists, who reported that the dancer was able to give "very short but sensible answers to questions put to him in Russian."[48]

> *Doctor:* Do you have memories of Moscow?
> *Patient:* It was very beautiful in Moscow.
> *Doctor:* Wouldn't you like to eat a Russian pastry sometime?
> *Patient:* (Much laughter) Russian pastries are delicious.
> *Doctor:* Wouldn't you like to eat Russian caviar with me?
> *Patient:* First it will be necessary to have some delivered here (followed by uncontrollable laughter).

It may be argued that the patient's replies were actually more "sensible" than the doctor's questions. Moscow was not a city Nijinsky was very familiar with. Asking him about Leningrad (St. Petersburg) would have been far more appropriate. One also wonders about the doctor's preoccupation with Russian cuisine. Nijinsky's joking response, that caviar would have to be "delivered here" before they could eat it, seems very much to the point. Surely none of his answers can be considered typically "schizophrenic"—i.e., bizarre, tangential, or autistic. But when sensitive issues related to Nijinsky's career as a dancer were touched on, he would clam up and say nothing, which suggests severe thought-blocking; for example:

> *Doctor:* Can you remember dancing with Pavlova?
> *Patient:* (No reaction)
> *Doctor:* What about Karsavina?
> *Patient:* (No reaction)
> *Doctor:* Do you have memories of Diaghilev?
> *Patient:* (No reaction)

---

*A modern interpretation of Nijinsky's first electrocardiogram, taken on 19 September 1936, is difficult because only two standard leads were used, as was customary at that time, and the paper speed is not specified. Nevertheless, there appears to be a borderline intraventricular conduction defect. This and other ECG findings were nonspecific, and one cannot make the diagnosis of an organic heart lesion in 1936. (See Appendix A for a full discussion of Nijinsky's electrocardiograms and their significance.)

In January 1937 he had "another heart attack" and recovered completely within a few hours. Romola stopped to see him briefly. She requested yet another medical consultation, this time with a cardiologist from Zürich, Dr. Haemmerli-Schindler, who found "nothing more serious" than what he called "dancer's heart," a not uncommon problem among athletic individuals who have stopped exercising and become flabby and obese. In view of Nijinsky's reluctance to work or engage in physical activity, it was recommended that he be given "general body massage, lose weight, receive 15 drops of Coramine each time he goes for a walk, and eliminate fried foods and roast-sauces from his menu." With this regime he lost three kilograms (nearly seven pounds) in nineteen days. It had a good effect on his physical condition, but bad effects on his disposition. When dieting, Nijinsky became "irritable and often threatening." He indicated his displeasure "by making special ceremonies with his filled-up chamber-pot," placing it in front of the bed, for his attendant to trip over. When told to stop this obnoxious behavior, he would put the potty "on the dining-table or an elegant cabinet" instead.[49]

A new Russian-speaking therapist was assigned that summer, "Dr. O.R." (otherwise unidentifiable), who found Nijinsky "somewhat thinner, but psychologically without any change.... he stays in bed until 11 in the morning and is usually in an irritable, grumbling mood. Better in the evening .... He insults the attendant with coarse Russian expressions. But when one diverts him, he immediately starts laughing." Dr. O.R. recorded one of their typical conversations, which demonstrates very nicely the dancer's mischievous sense of humor.

Doctor: Why are you so unfriendly?
Patient: Because I'm a little dog.
Doctor: But not a nice one!
Patient: Oh yes, I'm a dear, adorable one.
Doctor: Why are you so nasty today?
Patient: Because I'm a thief.[50]

That year (1937) Nijinsky received more visitors than ever before. Romola came to see him five times between February and August. In July she brought along her parents and Tamara, now seventeen, who was living with Emilia Márkus and Oscar Párdány in Budapest. Nijinsky had not seen either of his children for over a decade. According to Dr. Wenger, who was again spending some time with the patient, "his condition has in no way changed; the stepfather often drives him out and goes walking with him." Kyra visited in August, and used this occasion to dance for Nijinsky. "According to his attendant, the patient looked on with interest." We have no description of what Kyra actually danced, but it is known that she had appropriated some of her father's old roles, notably Spectre, and enjoyed performing these as solo improvisations, consistent with her personal need "to dance alone."[51] "The daughter made an effort," writes Dr. O.R., "to explain the new dance movements, and in her opinion the patient perceived and followed these with interest."[52]

Five months later, when Kyra visited him a second time, she was accompanied by her husband, "a very emotional occasion," as Mark-evitch recalls it.[53] Nijinsky "smiled in a very friendly way at his daughter and son-in-law." Kyra was convinced that she could "under-stand him exceptionally well." She believed that his mood swings were caused by environmental events, rather than internal disease. For example, when Nijinsky fell into an "irritable mood," Kyra believed this was due to her having arrived too late for her visit.[54] Ludwig Binswanger doubted that Kyra actually had much rapport with her father. One day he stayed in Nijinsky's room to see for himself how the two got along: before Kyra's arrival, Binswanger observed that "today the patient digs a finger stereotypically into his ear, always a sign that he is having a bad day. He was rejective and morose." After Kyra entered his room "his demeanor brightened a little. He allowed her to kiss him, and answered her questions sporadically, as he usually does."

> But his answers completely miss the point. His daughter believes they make sense, in that she can interpret most of his answers as meaningful responses to her questions. During her visit, which lasted about 10–15 minutes, the patient's mood became increasingly unrestrained. At times he laughed loudly for no apparent reason. After she left the room, he again fell into his morose mood.[55]

Nijinsky was not the only patient to undergo careful diagnostic reappraisal that year. In 1937 psychiatry was in the throes of a revolution, brought on by the use of "somatic" treatments that were starting to replace the timeworn custodial management of severely disabled patients. This revolution had begun with the discovery of barbiturates and the invention of "deep sleep therapy" in the 1920s, leading to carbon-dioxide narcosis in the 1930s. Now, a number of so-called "shock treatments" were being introduced, including convulsions produced by injection (and later with electricity), and insulin shock. The results looked promising, and psychiatrists throughout the world were reexamining their patients to find out which ones might be eligible for these new procedures.[56]

Very important for any well-managed psychiatric hospital was the identification of patients afflicted with schizophrenia. Many experts considered this to be primarily a metabolic disease caused by abnormal chemical reactions within certain brain cells. That theory was especially attractive to Dr. Manfred Sakel, a Viennese specialist in the use of insulin to treat physiological excitements. Insulin, a pancreatic hormone, had a calming effect, presumably because it lowered the patient's blood sugar (hypoglycemia). Romola, as she puts it, had been "relentlessly visiting clinics, research laboratories, and mental institutions" throughout the world.[57] That is how she met Dr. Sakel. Now, she wanted this physician to come to the Bellevue Sanatorium and treat Nijinsky.

Since its isolation in 1922, insulin had been used in small doses to help patients with alcoholism, delirium tremens, anorexia, and other debilitating diseases. Sakel's method, called "insulin-shock," was more drastic and risky. (Prolonged hypoglycemia can lead to death, and even a single insulin coma may produce permanent localized damage in certain parts of the brain.) He compared its importance to the discoveries of Jenner, Pasteur, and Koch.[58] Sakel believed that the destruction of brain tissue was essential for treating schizophrenics. "Sick and defective cells" were thereby killed off, allowing healthy ones to function better. This theory seemed consistent with the idea that schizophrenia was caused by improperly functioning brain connections, what Bleuler had called "loose associations." (But Bleuler used this term in a psychological sense; others tended to concretize it, for example, the neuropsychiatrist Stransky, who proposed "intrapsychic ataxia" as an explanation for schizophrenia.[59]) Moreover, Sakel believed that to cure the disease, one had to "destroy pathological connections again and again."[60]* That was why he established a very rigorous treatment

---

*An enthusiatic advocate of Sakel's method wrote that "the objective of insulin-shock treatment is the destruction of brain cells, in other words, the production of a controlled brain lesion."[61] This assumption, that brain lesions can be therapeutic, was not only shared by the influential Professor Otto Pötzl in Vienna, who wrote an introduction to Sakel's book on insulin-shock, but soon also led to neurosurgical procedures in which parts of the brain were removed (lobectomy) or the connections between thalamus and frontal cortex were severed (lobotomy).

regime. For two to three months the patient had to be kept in bed every morning (except on Sunday). Breakfast was withheld, and a dose of insulin injected. The patient would begin to sweat, drool, become sleepy, lose consciousness, and then go into a coma. Sometimes there was a convulsive seizure. After several hours the patient was revived with a sugar solution, given through a stomach tube or by injection.

Ludwig Binswanger was extremely reluctant to sanction the use of this costly, time-consuming, and dangerous procedure at the Bellevue Sanatorium, but the pressure to use insulin-shock was enormous. In 1935, Sakel's book about "the new method of treating schizophrenia" was published, and he went to the United States to train the staff of Rockland State Hospital.[62] The next year he visited Worcester State Hospital in Massachusetts, Bellevue Hospital in New York, and other psychiatric centers. In Switzerland he was welcomed to the large State Hospital in Münsingen by Dr. Binswanger's colleague Dr. Max Müller, who gave insulin to hundreds of "schizophrenics." The results were mind-boggling. By combining the statistics from eleven Swiss hospitals, Müller claimed a "full or good" remission for ninety percent of the patients who had received insulin within the first six months of illness. (Although Müller's figures dropped significantly, to forty-five percent for patients who had been ill longer than eighteen months, he reported only one fatality.[63]) Similarly impressive results were reported elsewhere.[64]

Nevertheless, Binswanger remained skeptical. To this philosopher-psychiatrist, mental illness was "a life-historical phenomenon" and not something to be treated chemically. "The norm of behavior is by no means fixed once and for all, but varies according to an individual's education and culture," he wrote. "What appears abnormal—or a deviation from the norm—to one person may look to another quite normal, *or even like the supreme expression of a norm.*"[65] Schizophrenia especially was a slippery concept. There was no objective way to make the diagnosis, nothing like the sputum test for tuberculosis or the blood-serology (Wassermann) test for syphilis. It was a matter of clinical judgment, and the diagnostic parameters varied widely. For example, schizophrenia was being diagnosed much more frequently in Phila-delphia than in Baltimore, two cities of comparable population. How could a brain-destructive procedure like insulin-shock or lobotomy be justified under these circumstances?

Binswanger was not alone in raising objections to the widespread use of insulin-shock. "It is too easy," wrote Dr. Adolf Meyer, professor of psychiatry at Johns Hopkins University, "for non-psychiatrists [like Dr. Sakel] to assume a dominant position and to become more or less antipsychiatric in the field." Somatic therapies were inadmissible unless their success "justifies the always disturbing disruption and usurpation [of patient care] by some narrow technician." In spite of glowing worldwide statistics proving the efficacy of insulin-shock, the American Psychiatric Association warned that "its exact value has yet to be determined, and it can be stated definitely that it is not a specific, nor by any means a cure for all cases of dementia praecox."[66]

In August 1937, Dr. Sakel arrived at Bellevue to see Nijinsky, and Binswanger felt duty-bound to get his opinion "because the patient's wife had raised questions about an insulin cure." Sakel noted that "despite the long duration of the patient's illness, his motility is remarkably good."[67] This emphasis on motility is important. The results of insulin-shock were generally better with catatonic and paranoid patients than the more deteriorated ones called "hebephrenic." All along, Nijinsky had been called "catatonic" and sometimes "paranoid." What the underlying disease process was had been left open. Bleuler was not sure whether it was primarily a disturbance of thought process (schizophrenia) or of mood (manic-depressive—today called "bi-polar affective disorder"). Binswanger had at first thought that Nijinsky's alternating stupors and excitements were "psychogenic." It was usually the course of a psychosis and its outcome that determined the final diagnosis. Patients who repeatedly broke down but ultimately recovered were more likely to be called manic-depressive than those who became chronically disabled and failed to return to their pre-illness level of functioning. That is why experienced clinicians like Adolf Meyer and Ludwig Binswanger were so skeptical about Sakel's statistics; the patients who did best with insulin-shock had not been psychotic long enough for the diagnosis of schizophrenia to be confirmed.

Now that Sakel had come up with a "cure" for schizophrenia, the urge to diagnose it grew stronger. More and more patients with unclear or borderline conditions were being called schizophrenic, thus making them eligible for insulin-shock. That is exactly what happened to Nijinsky. On 13 August 1937, the doctors held a conference.

> *Dr. Sakel:* I'm not altogether pessimistic. While I wouldn't promise the patient's wife a complete cure, there is the greatest probability that his condition will at least improve.

Dr. Binswanger: I'm not at all enthusiastic. What about Nijinsky's heart? [While acute cardiac failures did not occur "very commonly," there had been many reports of arrhythmias and fibrillation as well as "more serious cardiovascular disturbances," including vasomotor collapse.[68]]

Dr. Haemmerli-Schindler (the internist from Zürich): In my opinion the patient's collapse-states are the result of a disturbance in central, neurophysiological regulation, rather than actual heart disease.

Dr. Sakel: That is of great theoretical interest to me, since it confirms my theory that the seat of schizophrenic disturbance is in the vegetative centers of the brain.

Dr. Haemmerli: Myocardial damage would be impossible in Nijinsky's case.

Dr. Sakel: That again is reassuring. Experience shows that the administration of glucose immediately stops all centrally induced conduction disturbances of the heart.

Dr. O.R. (who had immediate responsibility for Nijinsky's care): What exactly is the risk factor?

Dr. Haemmerli: Ten to twenty percent.

Dr. O.R.: In that case, if we should ever carry out the treatment here, for which Dr. Binswanger has no enthusiasm whatsoever, I must insist that the patient's wife certify in writing that she has been made aware of the ten to twenty percent danger of death. I also want both of you, Dr. Sakel and Dr. Haemmerli, to come here to Bellevue several times while Nijinsky is being treated.[69]

Romola had set the wheels in motion by bringing Sakel to Bellevue, but now she seemed in no hurry to proceed with the treatment. She had her own agenda, as usual. "The question of insulin-shock is not realistic at this time, because the wife will be going to America this fall," writes Dr. O.R. "Nothing can be started before she returns." Before leaving Nijinsky again, Romola spent "almost every afternoon walking with him in the park, and even going for a boat-ride. On good days he is friendly and smiles, but barely talks. Between times he often is irritable." On 12 October 1937 she left for the United States.

Eight months later, Romola returned. "Nijinsky has just as little contact with her as with any of us," Dr. O.R. commented. Another six weeks were to elapse before she finally signed the necessary papers, and then, on 18 July 1938, "the insulin cure was finally started."[70]

NOTES

1. Jean-Marie Charcot, *De l'expectation en médecine*, 1857.
2. Letter from Romola Nijinsky to Dr. Kurt Binswanger, 22 April 1929, BMR.
3. Ibid.
4. BMR, 29 April and 3 May 1929.
5. Personal communication from Dr. Wolfgang Binswanger.
6. Dr. Wenger, notes, BMR, 1 June 1929–1 March 1930.
7. Personal communication from Dr. Wolfgang Binswanger.
8. Dr. Wenger, notes, BMR, 30 November 1929–5 November 1930.
9. Ibid., 1 November and 20 December 1929, 5 June and 5 November 1930.
10. Dr. O.R., notes, BMR, 5 August 1930.
11. Ibid., 17 November 1931.
12. Dr. Wenger, notes, BMR, 2 February, 22 March, and 29 April 1932.
13. Letter from Romola Nijinsky to Emilia Márkus, 30 December 1931. Nijinsky Archives.
14. Ibid.
15. Letter from Romola Nijinsky to Oscar Párdány, 11 December 1931. Nijinsky Archives.
16. Letters from Romola Nijinsky to Emilia Márkus, 30 December 1931 and 14 February 1932. Nijinsky Archives.
17. Letter from Romola Nijinsky to Oscar Párdány, 11 December 1931. Nijinsky Archives.
18. Letter from Romola Nijinsky to Emilia Márkus, 30 December 1931. Nijinsky Archives.
19. Letter from Romola Nijinsky to Emilia Márkus, 5 October 1932. Nijinsky Archives.
20. Letter from Romola Nijinsky to Emilia Márkus, 30 December 1931. Nijinsky Archives.
21. Letter from Lincoln Kirstein to Romola Nijinsky, 3 April 1933. Nijinsky Archives.
22. Bernard Taper, *Balanchine*, 151.
23. Letter from Romola Nijinsky to Emilia Márkus, 5 October 1932. Nijinsky Archives.
24. Ibid.
25. Personal communication from Kyra Nijinsky.
26. BMR, 1 February 1933.
27. Personal communication from Dr. Wolfgang Binswanger.
28. BMR, 12 August, 5 July, 15–27 October, and 29 November 1932.
29. Ibid., 29 November–3 December 1932. Description of the "energetic Swedish woman" from discussions with Dr. Wolfgang Binswanger.
30. BMR, 9 March 1933.
31. Ibid., 7 April, 8 June, and 12 August 1933.
32. Ibid., 12 August, 5 September, 2 October, 1 and 31 December 1933.
33. Ibid., 3 February–18 August 1934.
34. Ibid., 4 April and 1 May 1934. Emphasis in the original.
35. Alfred Adler, *The Individual Psychology of Alfred Adler*, 116.
36. For a much deeper analysis of Beethoven, including the influence on his life and work of delusions about his father, see Maynard Solomon, *Beethoven*.
37. BMR, 2 October 1934.
38. Ibid., 2 October and 8 November 1934; 2 April, 3 July, and 7 November 1935.
39. Alfred Adler, "The Preface to *The Diary of Vaslav Nijinsky*."
40. Ibid.
41. Ibid.
42. From a letter by Eric Glass, Romola Nijinsky's literary agent, quoted in Heinz L. Ansbacher, "Discussion of Alfred Adler's Preface to *The Diary of Vaslav Nijinsky*."
43. Romola Nijinsky, Preface to *The Diary of Vaslav Nijinsky*, xii.
44. Letters from C. G. Jung to Romola Nijinsky, 24 May 1956 and 2 September 1960.
45. Igor Markevitch, *Être et avoir été; memoires*, 342–343.
46. BMR, 7 March, 6 July, 20 August 1936.
47. Ibid., 19 September 1936.
48. Ibid., 7 October 1936.

49. Ibid., 5 January, 15 February, 24 April, 7 June, and 13 August 1937.
50. Ibid., 6 November 1937.
51. See Kyra Nijinsky, *She Dances Alone.*
52. BMR, 13 August 1937.
53. Igor Markevitch taped interview, 6 August 1972. The New York Public Library, Dance Collection.
54. BMR, 17 January 1938.
55. Dr. Ludwig Binswanger, notes, BMR, 21 January 1938.
56. Lothar B. Kalinowsky and Paul H. Hoch (editors), *Shock Treatments.*
57. Romola Nijinsky, unpublished notes.
58. Manfred Sakel, "Address at the University of Vienna ..."
59. Hans Hoff, "History of the organic treatment of schizophrenia," 5.
60. Ibid., 11.
61. O. H. Arnold, "Results and Efficacy of Insulin Shock Therapy," 215.
62. Manfred Sakel, *Neue Behandlungsmethode der Schizophrenie.*
63. Joseph Wortis, "The history of insulin shock treatment," 25–26.
64. New York State Department of Mental Health, *Insulin Shock Therapy, Study by the Temporary Commission on State Hospital Problems,* New York, 1944.
65. Ludwig Binswanger, "Insanity as Life-Historical Phenomenon and as Mental Disease," 237. Emphasis added.
66. Letter from Adolf Meyer to Joseph Wortis, and statement by the Public Education Committee of the American Psychiatric Association, in Wortis, 30–31.
67. BMR, 13 August 1937.
68. Kalinowsky and Hoch, 38.
69. BMR, 13 August 1937.
70. Ibid., 20 September and 12 October 1937; 2 June and 18 July 1938.

It has so happened that we by chance
hit upon the wrong end of the right
path ...

                    Manfred Sakel[1]

Chapter 13

Moving Again

D_{r.} Manfred Sakel, the inventor of insulin-shock treatment, was, along with a Hungarian, Meduna (metrazol-shock), two Italians, Bini and Cerletti (electro-shock), and a Portuguese, Moniz (lobotomy), among that handful of Europeans who in the 1930s pioneered what later came to be known as biological psychiatry. Born in Poland, and educated in Czechoslovakia, Sakel went to medical school in Vienna, and then specialized in internal medicine in Berlin, where he conducted in his kitchen some crude animal experiments to prove that large doses of insulin were not necessarily fatal. Applying his findings to humans, Sakel became an expert in using insulin to reduce the drastic motor agitation associated with drug withdrawal from morphine, and in treating schizophrenia, which he reasoned was caused by "a disruption of the basic intercellular pathways and constellations of the primary particles in the nerve cells."[2]

Few of his colleagues in Vienna supported Sakel. Most thought him unscientific. He seemed vain and isolative, his theories one-sided and untenable. As his contemporary L. von Meduna put it, "Shock treatment in those days was like trying to fix a Swiss watch with a hammer."[3] Yet Sakel anticipated some of today's chemical approaches to the treatment of mental disease. (It has recently been discovered that the brain produces its own insulin-like substances, and that insulin could be a naturally occurring regulatory peptide within the central nervous system.[4]) "Whatever may be the verdict," wrote neurologist Foster Kennedy, "in reference to Manfred Sakel's contribution to the treatment of so-called 'schizophrenia,' we shall not again be content to minister to a diseased mind merely by philosophy and words."[5] Patients with "so-called schizophrenia" reacted strongly to the massive disruption of brain function produced by Sakel's "treatment," but they were not "cured" the way he claimed. Nevertheless, his method became extremely popular for a while and made a good deal of money for the hospitals using it. Sakel never accepted an academic appointment. He preferred private practice and gave generously to charitable causes. His writings are a hodgepodge of pseudoscience and rhetoric. After the introduction of modern psychopharmacotherapy in the 1950s, insulin-shock treatment completely disappeared, except in eastern Europe, where its use continued for another decade.

Romola Nijinsky swore by Dr. Sakel. At her request, and against the stubborn opposition of Dr. Ludwig Binswanger, he personally supervised her husband's insulin-shock treatment at Bellevue Sanatorium. On the first day, 18 July 1938, Nijinsky received twenty units of insulin. This had no appreciable effect, so the dosage was doubled the next day, making the dancer sleepy, and after that increased to sixty units, and then to eighty units. On 25 July 1938, he for the first time had "strong myoclonic twitchings," definite evidence of a brain effect, and went into a "fairly deep sleep." With 100 units, Nijinsky showed "very marked muscular contractions throughout his entire body," and to Dr. O.R.'s amazement "made a movement with his arms and body as though he would dance, or wanted to." Then he began drooling, "perspired heavily," and became comatose, totally unresponsive to any stimuli, including pain. (This was what Sakel called "wet shock," as opposed to "dry shock," when patients had epileptic seizures.) After four hours, Nijinsky was given a glucose solution, injected into a vein of his arm. He woke up ten minutes later, groggy, confused, and grimacing. Later that day his facial expressions seemed "somewhat more attentive than usual," and he became "surprisingly friendly." But there was an ominous worsening in his ability to communicate. Speech, we must remember, was never Nijinsky's strong point; before his illness he was often tongue-tied and with his catatonia had come long spells of silence, but he had never completely lost the capacity to form sentences. There were even times when he engaged in brief conversations. After Nijinsky's first prolonged insulin-coma, however, he "no longer answered any questions, but simply parroted back (echolalia), in German or French, anything one said to him."[6]

Sakel was undismayed. He had often observed pathological speech— "aphasic phenomena," "primitive sounds," and "inarticulate babbling"—after giving patients large doses of insulin.[7] But that did not deter him. On the contrary, because he felt that one had to find "the right dose to produce the stranglehold effect of insulin on the individual cells," he recommended pushing ahead despite any aphasia or other neurological signs.[8] On 5 August, Nijinsky's dose was increased to 120 units, producing an even deeper coma. (By now, Dr. Binswanger had gotten so upset with what Sakel was doing that he instructed the lawyer Dr. Böckli, who held power of attorney for Nijinsky, to contact Dr. Max Müller, Switzerland's most experienced insulin-therapist, asking Müller to "take over the insulin-cure as soon as the treatment Dr. Sakel has gotten started will be finished, in about 2–3 weeks."[9])

After the seventeenth insulin treatment, however, some favorable changes were observed. While walking in the park, Nijinsky now "held his body much more erect," and his mood seemed "generally much improved." He was less irritable, no longer grumbled so much, and "gave the impression that he has lost his hallucinations." There also were positive changes in his physical condition. After the twenty-fifth treatment, it was noted that "his veins, which at the beginning were very brittle, so that a hematoma formed with every intravenous injection, have become much more resistant, and his general body turgor is improved." He also had gained weight, three kilograms, and his electrocardiogram now looked completely normal when compared to the pre-insulin tracings.[10] "Physically he tolerates the treatment very well," wrote Dr. O.R., but his speech functions remained grossly impaired: "Always the same echolalia. Only very rarely does he produce a sentence that hangs together. With a Russian-speaking woman doctor, he doesn't say anything coherent at all."[11]

These findings suggest that Nijinsky either had moved from a mute to an echoing catatonic syndrome or had developed a transcortical aphasia.* In view of his probable earlier brain injury at age twelve, the repeated prolonged insulin-comas may have caused further impairment of speech. But remarkably, just as Nijinsky had developed superior athletic skills during adolescence, he now seemed to compensate for the loss of linguistic ability by improving his muscle power and coordination. "Although he continues to produce a word salad [i.e., grossly incoherent speech]," writes Dr. Clare Haas, who assumed responsibility for Nijinsky's insulin treatments after Sakel left in September,† "he now shows adequate mimicry and body movements in response to music." After the thirty-ninth coma, he even "spontaneously, although shyly, made some dance movements." Dr. Haas was especially impressed that Romola, "who used to compare him to a teddybear," found Nijinsky's gait and movements to be "definitely more elegant and graceful ... generally freer, more open, and often spontaneous.... A few days ago he embraced and kissed his wife with spontaneous affectivity, while earlier he would only present his cheek like an automaton, to be kissed."[14]

Dr. Haas was trained as a dermatologist. (A refugee from Nazi Germany, she underwent psychiatric training only after emigrating to the United States, and worked for many years on the staff of Rhode Island State Hospital.) Her notes on Nijinsky show that he regularly became "very excited" when given insulin and came close to having "epileptic fits." Because of his habit of picking pieces of skin from his fingers, she gave him some plastic dough to play with, but without success. After a while, he gave up "this ugly habit; his hands have healed, compared to before when they were full of self-inflicted wounds."[15] Dr. O.R., who had observed Nijinsky for a much longer period of time, was less impressed than Dr. Haas with the benefits of insulin. One week after the first course of treatment had ended (forty-eight shocks altogether), Dr. O.R. found "the patient completely unchanged. The same word salad, the same inconsequential speech,

---

*The latter is a language disorder produced when the neural circuiting of the language-dominant cerebral hemisphere (usually the left) is disconnected from either the surrounding sensory association cortex or the motor areas of the brain. A hallmark of transcortical aphasia is relative preservation of repetition or "echoing" in the face of impaired comprehension and/or fluency.[12]

†With the German takeover of Austria, Dr. Sakel could not return to Vienna. He had already established residence in New York, and in 1938 moved there permanently. Romola Nijinsky hoped to follow him, so that her husband's shock treatments could be continued, a plan with which Sakel concurred.[13]

echolalia. Mornings in a dissatisfied and irritable mood. Evenings better, friendly."[16] Romola on the other hand thought she could perceive true "improvement."

> My husband (thank God, knock on wood) has been walking very well. . . . He is affectionate, happy, accessible at all times . . . goes to the bank and shopping with me, greets people, lifts his hat, plays the radio and phonograph, yesterday tried to use the telephone . . . went to church with me, crossed himself, got down on his knees, and for the first time in 19 years said "*Aide deux fois.*" Isn't that flabbergasting?[17]

She broadcast the good news to friends and ballet fans throughout the world: Nijinsky was dancing again. Romola wanted him to have a second course of treatment, with the hope that he would soon return to a normal life. But the cost of insulin-shock worried her. In addition to a patient's customary sanatorium fees, insulin treatment meant having to pay for private nurses and ongoing medical consultation. Hoping to defray the considerable expense involved, Romola asked her friends in London to establish a "Nijinsky Foundation." Tamara Karsavina was the chairman, Lady Juliet Duff the vice-chairman, and Mr. Philip Morrell the honorary secretary and treasurer.[18] Acquaintances and wealthy admirers were asked to contribute funds. "Please be so kind," Romola wrote to Dr. Haas, "and certify in English—I need this for the Foundation—that after Dr. Sakel's departure you completed his first cure, and that you can detect a significant improvement (that's true, isn't it?) and that you expect even greater progress with further treatment."[19]

This sort of proselytizing on behalf of an experimental treatment made Ludwig Binswanger very unhappy, and he finally put his foot down. There was to be no more insulin-shock for Nijinsky at Bellevue, he told his staff. "I don't understand their reasons," wrote the disappointed Dr. Haas to Dr. Sakel. "The skepticism of Dr. Binswanger, his assistants, the nursing personnel, and the resulting atmosphere is a long chapter that I hope one day to *talk* to you about."[20] Dr. Haas also spoke with Romola about Binswanger's edict. It made no sense to her, and she recommended that Dr. Max Müller be consulted. (Binswanger had already given Müller the green light, if he wished, to take over the Nijinsky case.)

Dr. Max Müller was the director of a large state hospital at Münsingen, near Bern. In his autobiography, he described how he felt about "stemming the flood of patients coming from Binswanger's luxury sanatorium" in the late 1930s. Because Münsingen was a publicly funded institution, designed to serve mentally ill patients from the most densely populated canton of Switzerland, Müller had found it irksome at first to admit private patients from the outside to his already crowded asylum. He soon realized, however, that this could be lucrative. By offering insulin, metrazol, and other forms of shock treatment to private patients, he was able to collect "80,000 Swiss Francs each year" for the hospital. He also managed to enrich "the various Münsingen establishments, especially the Hotel Löwen, where relatives of patients often stayed for months, and spent much money." Müller claims, however, to have had "great misgivings" about admitting Nijinsky. He had heard that Romola "bothered herself very little about him, lived mostly in America, sometimes did not see him for two years, and when she did visit, mostly complained about everything." Müller also feared "Romola's constant striving, through propaganda and sensationalism in the world-press, to make sure that her husband would not be forgotten." She was promoting the idea that insulin treatment would restore him to normalcy. In Müller's opinion, it was unlikely that "anything therapeutic could be promised" for Nijinsky. Only after Romola "assured" him there would be no further "publicity" did Müller agree to proceed, but not before December 1938.[21]

On Tuesday, 27 September, Romola, Vaslav, and a male nurse left Kreuzlingen for a month's vacation. They headed for Vevey, on the Lake of Geneva, to visit Kyra and Igor Markevitch and their nine-month-old son, named Vaslav in Nijinsky's honor, whom the dancer had not yet seen. Romola described the trip to Dr. Haas: "It went marvellously well (knock on wood). My husband ate in the Restaurant Wagon, like a prince.... Since our arrival here, he has been continually in a good mood, greets and plays with his grandson, carries him around, kisses him, etc."[22] The male nurse tells a somewhat different story. Although during the first week Nijinsky was generally "in a good mood," "enjoyed his walks at the lake," and "showed great interest in everything, especially music played on his phonograph, and watching the dancers at a theater in Montreux," he was consistently "nervous" and sometimes "very tired" in the evening. On 3 October, he had a "mild cough," and stayed in bed. After spending a day with his relatives, he was in a notably "bad mood" and seemed to "hallucinate momentarily." Asked by the nurse what was the matter, Nijinsky responded (in French), "I don't know; I'm too sick." Whenever he had to stay "alone with the ladies" (i.e., Kyra, Romola, and her sister Tessa, who was also visiting Vevey), Nijinsky would become more "demanding." The nurse noted that he seemed to prefer being with Tessa rather than Romola. He made "menacing gestures," which made Romola "immediately leave the room." Once he "picked up a chair and threw it on the ground." Another time he "threatened the nurse with a knife." These "crises" tended to be short-lived, however. A tailor came to measure him for some new clothes on 12 October; that made him "very nervous." Generally, Nijinsky felt more "calm" and "agreeable" when left alone with his male nurse, who helped him get dressed and undressed, took care of his hygienic needs, and occasionally gave him a "colonic irrigation to aid with digestion."

> One afternoon Madame Nijinsky graciously offered him a glass of water and received the contents on herself. This happened in the garden of the hotel. We went for a light meal. Messieur [sic] Nijinsky sat down at the table without saying a word, threw his bread on the floor, and instantly started laughing.[23]

After returning to Kreuzlingen at the end of October, Nijinsky was noted to be "more sad" and "eating much less." A diet of fresh fruits seemed to reduce his constipation, however, and he quickly gained back two kilograms. "His digestion is OK," writes Romola to Dr. Haas. "Your prescription has helped him ... my husband goes walking by himself every morning. Hurrah! Bravo! I will give you the Nobel Prize."[24] In November, Romola and Tessa consulted a dentist, Dr. E. Mischol, whose bill came to 319 Swiss francs. It was never paid.[25] Romola could barely contain her anger at the Bellevue staff for having failed, after so many years of hospitalization, to restore Nijinsky to his former self. "Not everything seems to have gone according to the wife's wishes," says Dr. O.R. "She often scolds us: everyone is against her."[26] To try to make peace, Dr. Binswanger had invited Romola, Vaslav, and Tessa for tea on Friday afternoon, 2 December. Nijinsky's behavior did not seem "particularly mannerly."

> He licks his fingers and helps himself to copious amounts of the cake being served. But in general he is quite orderly, even if his only interest is in the pastries. According to his wife, the beautifully set table gave him special pleasure.[27]

On Saturday, 10 December 1938, he was transferred to Dr. Müller's hospital in Münsingen. The Nijinsky Foundation agreed to pay 500 Swiss francs for professional fees, Fr. 300 a month for insulin treatment, Fr. 12 a day for a private nurse, and Fr. 20 a day for "first class room and board."[28] (Romola had insisted that "my husband receive the best room."[29]) On admission, he was noted to have an "indolent expression." "He barely pays attention to what is going on around him." His way of greeting Dr. Müller seemed very mannered and inappropriate: "He offers the fingertips of his left hand, and without answering any questions, quietly lets himself be led to his room."[30] A special nurse, Karl Kämpf, was assigned. Three days later, "the catatonic patient, without offering any resistance, came to the insulin ward for treatment." He "showed some fear" before receiving his first injection (sixteen units), then fell asleep, and after the treatment showed his usual "echolalia," "barely comprehensible sounds," and "unmotivated laughter." A week later, with incrementally higher doses of insulin, he seemed "somewhat changed."

> While walking he often makes "gestures" with his hands and feet ... enjoys the freshly fallen snow as well as the children tumbling in the snow outside. In the evening he twice jumped high up, while excited and laughing.[31]

With 120 units of insulin, Nijinsky went into very deep "shock," became "cyanotic" (blue in the face due to loss of oxygen), had "violent myoclonic convulsions," a "very fast pulse," and "wet himself." Because of his severe twitching and "fighting against the injection like a wild beast," it took "some juggling" to get the sugar solution into him so that the hypoglycemia could be stopped. After that, Dr. Müller decided to bring the dose of insulin down to eighty units, and to premedicate Nijinsky with barbiturates in order to reduce the violence of his convulsions. With the beginning of the new year, he showed improvement, saying to his nurse "in an affectionate mood, *Vous êtes très gentil et très joli.*" His ability to form sentences had apparently returned. Reports were duly sent to the Nijinsky Foundation, which forwarded another sum (1,459.50 Swiss francs) at the end of January 1939, and 1,262.80 in May.[32] There seemed to be some progress for a while: "He dances with his wife for the first time in 20 years," and "sometimes makes single dance-movements, but only when he is especially well-disposed, and never for more than about 10 minutes."[33] But in general his mood remained depressed, and his behavior "negativistic." February 1939 was a discouraging month. He "puts powder into his jam, spits on the floor a great deal, and also into his hand, which he then wipes on his coat." While playing the phonograph, he "became furious, banged on it violently until it was turned off."

> It often appears that the presence of his wife upsets the patient. His mood is better when she is not around. He chatters a lot to himself, but one can't understand what he says, only that it is incoherent.[34]

Day after day "he received more shock." (Philip Morrell in London wrote Dr. Müller in May 1939: "My Committee will be glad to know whether you consider that Nijinsky will be able to live a normal life."[35]) He now began to experience "after-shocks," as they were called, spontaneous episodes of hypoglycemia in the afternoon, when he would complain about headaches and abdominal pain, turn pale, sweat profusely, have a weak pulse, and maintain a blood-sugar level of only 30 mg. percent. Intravenous glucose had to be administered on an emergency basis. "The patient has now had 5 1/2 months of insulin treatment," writes Dr. Müller on 2 June 1939.

> During this time almost nothing has changed in his psychological state. He is mostly dull and without initiative; although on walks he goes along, he takes no notice of the environment, and is quietly happy when one leaves him in peace. He sometimes reacts to the presence of his wife by producing the most terrible obscenities, but at other times with a certain friendliness. There is no real contact between him and his wife.[36]

Romola as usual wanted to see things differently, and "again made ambitious plans for the future." She "insisted" that a dance barre be installed next to the insulin ward, where she tried "with indefatigable patience" to get Nijinsky to do some exercises every day. In Dr. Müller's opinion, "nothing came of this."[37] Romola nevertheless informed their friends in London, Paris, and New York that the dancer was making significant progress. "News spread through the world that he was on the way to recovery," writes Serge Lifar, who was organizing a gala performance to raise money for the Nijinsky Foundation in Paris.[38] On 9 June, "a great many cars with French license plates" arrived in Münsingen, unannounced. Romola had invited Lifar and the press to the hospital, and wanted to demonstrate the "miracle" of Nijinsky's recovery. Dr. Müller found this invasion of privacy deplorable: "I had no idea what had been going on behind my back."[39]

> For propaganda purposes, photographs of the patient were made. Lifar danced for him. Nijinsky is supposed to have jumped high several times, but in contrast to his healthy times, he let himself fall down with a thud. He also jumped away from the others a number of times. The applause gave him pleasure, and he participated briskly.[40]

As the press photographs show, Nijinsky watched with apparent interest while Lifar, wearing dance slippers, rose on his toes to demonstrate some classical steps. Nijinsky bowed to Lifar, smiled at him, and mirrored his gestures. Their interaction resembles something from a ballet. When Lifar rolled up a trouser leg to show his nicely developed calf muscles, Nijinsky touched him with obvious pleasure, and danced a little. Whether his *entrechats-six* and "perfect *cabrioles, pas de bourrée*" were "absolutely faultless," as Lifar says they were, seems debatable. Nothing of the sort can be seen in the photographs. But his description of Nijinsky's symptoms is telling. The sick man's unceasing, restless "playing with his hands" reminded Lifar of the "plastique of Siamese dancers." Lifar also noted Nijinsky's love for "pastry more than anything else," and the "exquisite ... smooth rounded gesture[s] of his outstretched fingers" while eating strawberries. But he was dismayed by Nijinsky's apparent neurological defects, his "contortions," "hysterical jerking," "hoarse, terrifying laughter," and disturbed speech. "He does not know what he has said the moment before and there is no logical sequence either in his ideas or words, no *continuity*. He lives only by momentary reflexes."[41]

Müller was so angry at Romola for her betrayal in bringing photographers to the hospital—the snapshots of Nijinsky and Lifar were publicized in *Paris Match*—that he "threatened to discharge the patient."[42] But Nijinsky's behavior seemed surprisingly better after Lifar's visit, an improvement the doctors attributed to the effects of insulin-shock. (More likely, the changes were related to all the coaxing, admiration, mirroring, body contact, "dance therapy," and applause that Lifar's visit entailed, and the unexpected interruption of Nijinsky's hospital routines.) Until the end of June 1939, he seemed more "affectionate" with his wife, and even produced "something like sentences" for a few days. (One day he asked the nurse, "May I take this pastry?" "Which color do you like, green?" And to Romola he said: "All this costs too much money; everything is really very expensive.") Thus, it was decided to "continue to shock him every day." Soon, however, the improvement in his speech functions disappeared; he was producing "a pure word salad," and "defecating into his pyjamas."[43] He also complained of "neuralgic back-pain," probably related to his many convulsions, and required some "massage." At the end of July, after a total of 180 insulin-shocks, it was decided to terminate the treatment. Romola thought that Nijinsky was now "walking much better," compared to the way he walked after his insulin comas in Kreuzlingen. (She usually told people that there had been 270 treatments altogether. The true figure is 228: 48 at Bellevue Sanatorium and 180 in the Münsingen Hospital.) After it was all over, Dr. Müller acknowledged that he also had observed Nijinsky making some "dance movements, and a few rather stiff turns around his own axis."[44]

In August 1939 Romola was prevailed upon to take him out of the hospital, a move she had been resisting for some time. With a male nurse, they moved to Adelboden, a mountain resort in the Bernese Oberland, twenty-five miles south of Münsingen, and stayed in a small hotel, the Pension Huldi. It reminded Romola of St. Moritz. "The place was similar but not the same. Everything went better than we had hoped, and we seriously began to consider making a home for ourselves in Switzerland."[45] She claims that Nijinsky was "taking great interest" in radio broadcasts, especially the news of Hitler's invasion of Poland in September and the Franco-British declaration of war on Germany. He even seemed to remember a few things from the past. For example, when Romola showed him a book of paintings from the Prado Museum in Madrid, he "not only recognized the pictures, but named them correctly, Titian, Goya, Rubens, etc." She says that he "asked questions about our family and his colleagues." His "talent for play-acting came back very clearly," and he "reacquired many social habits." On the whole, however, Nijinsky seemed unduly shy and very childlike, behaving toward Romola more "like a son to his mother."[46] The nurse, Albert Loewer, reports that "his mood is very changeable, especially between 4 and 5 in the afternoon. After these moments of nervousness, he easily becomes irritable ... in the morning he often masturbates."[47] The sexual activity disturbed Romola—as we shall see, she later accused one of Nijinsky's male nurses of stimulating him—and Mr. Loewer was promptly replaced by a woman.

In her nursing notes, Franciska Widmer reports that the patient "let himself be washed and bathed [but] threatened to become aggressive toward me." He "absolutely" refused to let her serve him his meals, and he "made gestures with his shoes" as if to kick her. Miss Widmer thought Nijinsky was "hallucinating," but because she spoke only German she could not "really describe the content" of his hallucinations.[48] Romola took issue with the nurse: Nijinsky was *not* hallucinating. To Dr. Müller she wrote, "He is completely clear ... all his questions and answers are correct ... Kämpf [his nurse in Münsingen] always denied that there had been hallucinations."[49] Indeed, no hallucinations were reported during Nijinsky's seven months' hospital stay earlier that year, while he was receiving insulin.*

Nijinsky's behavior in the hotel clearly was peculiar and offensive. On walks with his nurse, he would "play with rocks like a child," "tear the buds off flowers," "pick up bunches of grass and throw them away while laughing loudly." One time he "had great fun repeatedly lighting matches and then blowing them out," so that the nurse, fearing he might set fire to his room, had to hide them.[51] Romola hoped that all these pranks would disappear if only "dear Dr. Müller, you would think about another insulin cure in the spring. I can't help having the feeling that much more could be accomplished with my husband." She wanted to "rent a Chalet" in Vevey in order to be closer to Kyra and Igor Markevitch, but that plan never materialized.[52] Nijinsky's intractability was disturbing: "He refused to obey the nurse at all, didn't want to get dressed in the evening, and ran stark naked around his room."[53]

On 20 September, Romola had to take him back to the hospital, where he immediately "recognized" his old room, seemed "to feel happy in his environment," and "laughed" a lot. The good nurse Kämpf was again assigned to take care of the dancer, and they apparently got along splendidly. ("Mr. Nijinsky was always kind and good to me," writes

---

*Auditory hallucinations—persistent entry into consciousness of unreal voices and conversations—are thought to be among the cardinal signs of schizophrenia. But Eugen Bleuler felt that schizophrenia can also occur without hallucinations or the other so-called accessory symptoms. He called such cases "simple" schizophrenia, to distinguish them from "catatonic," "paranoid," and "hebephrenic" forms of the disease. Today, some psychiatrists speak of "negative symptoms" (apathy, inertia, mutism, and asociability) when schizophrenic patients do not demonstrate any hallucinations, delusions, incoherence, bizarre behavior, or other "positive symptoms." It is debatable, however, whether one can diagnose an illness when its cardinal symptoms are absent. Perhaps "positive" and "negative" schizophrenia are two different diseases.[50]

Kämpf. "I always found him to be a very affectionate man.") On their daily promenades, Nijinsky was usually calm and "orderly."[54] "I remember perfectly Mr. Nijinsky at that period," writes Christian Müller (Dr. Müller's son), now a professor at the Medical School of Lausanne:

> I would see him walking in the gardens and on the roads surrounding the hospital. Small, squat, obese, totally mute, accompanied by a male nurse, dressed in a long coat and wearing a fur hat, he really presented the image of an autistic schizophrenic, buried in sand.[55]

When left alone, Nijinsky had moments of "excitement," during which he "talked to himself" or ran "angrily" around his room. (Nowadays, such excitements would most likely be controlled with appropriate neuroleptic medication, given orally or by injection.) Romola pressed for more insulin treatment. To be effective this time, Müller told her, each coma would have to be systematically interrupted by a chemically induced convulsion, Sakel's so-called "dry shock" technique. It consisted of injecting the drug metrazol during the second or third hour of coma. That way, the seizures could be "more precisely timed in relation to the insulin injection" and produce longer periods of amnesia.[56] Romola decided not to go ahead with it because she had been warned (by the Zürich cardiologist Dr. Haemmerli) that metrazol-induced convulsions can make "a much stronger demand on your husband's circulatory system than insulin."[57] Instead, she talked Dr. Müller into letting the nurse, Mr. Kämpf, do private duty outside the hospital. Nijinsky, Kämpf, and Romola moved into the nearby Hotel Löwen. The dancer improved sufficiently to visit "public places like restaurants, concerts, and the theater...."[58]

In October they were back in Adelboden, but not with the faithful Kämpf, who was needed for work in Münsingen. (Due to the threat of German invasion in 1939, the Swiss army had to be mobilized, and some of the male nurses were being called up for military duty. "I think you are letting yourself get too alarmed over your nurse Kämpf," Dr. Müller wrote to Romola. "Should Switzerland enter the war, one can still see whether he might be deferred, unless you want to return your husband to the Institution, which I think would be the better thing to do."[59]) The nurse now working for them was a man Romola suspected of getting sexually involved with Nijinsky. "I can't prove it absolutely," she wrote Dr. Müller, "but one day I came into the room unexpectedly, and found a very peculiar situation." Twice the nurse had been "left alone with my husband, and his homosexual appearance became apparent to others as well." Nijinsky was now "practicing this habit [masturbation] every day, after lunch. Then he is relaxed. Couldn't this damage his heart?"[60] (Romola need not have worried: orgasms are a healthier way to release tension than convulsions produced with "dry shock.") She writes that after she confronted the nurse with her concerns about homosexuality, the man "quit immediately and then made as much trouble for me as he could,"[61] meaning that he reported to Dr. Müller his own version of what was going on in the hotel.

Kyra, who was having marital problems at this time, had been staying with her parents. With her was a "small wild boy" (her son Vaslav) who kept getting Nijinsky very "excited" and "angry." Nijinsky would then try to "scare the ladies" by making threatening gestures suggesting he "wanted to hit Kyra and her son." One night he "threw his table lamp on the floor and everything he could get his hands on." Romola had a "real nervous breakdown, cried terribly in the adjoining room, and said she did not want to eat any more. She complained to the chambermaid about all the tricks being played on her, and about the moods of the nurse."[62] After Kyra and her son moved out of the hotel, Romola calmed down somewhat. Kyra then rented a house in the village, where her husband, Igor Markevitch, occasionally came to visit her. Markevitch also spent time with Nijinsky. "I had to do everything for him," he recalls. "I fed him, I dressed him, I shaved him."[63] Young Vaslav sometimes "stood there watching," says Nijinsky's nurse, and Romola "took it badly" when the nurse asked the boy to leave, or closed the door on him. One day she accused him of "locking Mr. Nijinsky in his room," when in fact "no door was locked."

The nurse tried to impress on Dr. Müller that no proper "occupational therapy" was available for Nijinsky in Adelboden. The patient would get "bored," while his wife "over-reacted to everything... she is extremely nervous and writes letter upon letter, apparently related to her bad financial situation."[64] Müller was not surprised. Nijinsky's bills for treatment from May to August had "unfortunately" never been paid, as the psychiatrist had to remind Romola in January 1940: "The balance comes to 1,957 Swiss Francs."[65] Due to the war, the flow of money from London to Münsingen had dried up. The Nijinsky Foundation wrote that nothing could be sent, "whether in the form of sterling or a draft."[66] In her panic, Romola was hoping to escape to the United States, hence her many letters. "At the end of this month [January 1940] I am going to America, and taking my husband with me," Romola wrote Dr. Müller. She was desperately trying to reach Dr. Sakel, to arrange for further insulin treatment in New York. But Sakel did not answer her, nor was "a word about Nijinsky" mentioned in his letters to Müller—another plausible reason for Romola's anxiety.[67]

In April 1940, she took Nijinsky to Zürich for another consultation with Dr. Haemmerli-Schindler. An electrocardiogram shows the same pattern of heart block reported in the earlier pre-insulin tracings (see Appendix A). But in trying to help Romola obtain medical clearance for Nijinsky's emigration to the United States, Dr. Haemmerli minimized the findings. "There is no conduction disturbance," he wrote Dr. Sakel. "The same happy picture also shows up in the chest x-ray, where the heart-silhouette seems to be intact.... The heart sounds are clean, only the diastolic blood-pressure is somewhat high, which surely is attributable to the raised position of his diaphragm." Nijinsky had gained weight again, but "it makes no sense," thought Dr. Haemmerli, . to put him on a diet. "As soon as he is comfortably settled in the United States, these extra-cardiac problems can of course easily be remedied."[68]

"All bills will be paid," the optimistic Romola wrote Dr. Müller from Zürich. "My husband, thank God, is marvelous ... we get many invitations, his behavior is faultless."[69] She had hired the good nurse Kämpf to come along. Her plan was to take a train to Italy, and there get a boat to New York. Kämpf was supposed to go with them to Genoa, before returning to Münsingen. But on 4 May, Dr. Müller cabled Romola, requesting that Kämpf be sent back immediately. "We can no longer do without him. His stay in Zürich has turned out to be much longer than we anticipated."[70] Worse yet, with Germany threatening all of western Europe (Holland, Denmark, Norway, Belgium, and Luxembourg had already fallen, and France was under siege), Romola had not succeeded in obtaining the necessary travel papers for her husband. Being stateless, Nijinsky had only a passport, valid for going to neutral countries, and being mentally ill excluded him from immigration to the United States. Frantically, Romola sent telegrams to President Roosevelt, Secretary of State Cordell Hull, and various American women's organizations, all to no avail. "FORMER NOTED MALE DANCER DENIED PRIVILEGE OF VISITING THIS COUNTRY," headlined the *Boston Daily Globe* on 9 May 1940. The *New York Times* said:

Despite a Labor Department Ruling that the dancer should not be barred
because of insanity ... the consulate refused Nijinsky a six-month
visitor's visa on the ground that spread of the war might prevent his
return to Europe. "Vaslav's life depends on America," Mme. Nijinsky
said. "Why does America give me hope and then dash it?" ... Nijinsky
himself, a sunburned, healthy looking, middle-aged man, sat beside his
weeping wife with a bewildered expression.[71]

A week later, they were back in Münsingen. Dr. Müller generously
agreed to readmit Nijinsky to the State Hospital and shelter him there
for the duration of the war, at no cost to Romola. She, with her
Hungarian passport and valid visa, would then have been free to go to
the United States. But Romola refused to accept this arrangement.
Why? According to Dr. Müller, it was because "Kämpf was reluctant
once more to undertake Nijinsky's nursing care" (not surprising, since
Romola had stopped paying him a salary for private duty).[72] There was
some kind of argument. "Mrs. Nijinsky accused us of taking her
husband's customary nurse away from him ... and of replacing him
with someone else," say the hospital records. "Without telling us why,
she removed the patient from our hospital [on 17 July 1940]."[73] The
reason Romola later gave for signing Nijinsky out against Dr. Müller's
advice is that she did not want to "abandon" him, not a very convincing
explanation, considering that many times before she had gone to the
United States without him, and left him under medical supervision.
Her other explanation is that an "old friend" of her mother had urged
her to go to Budapest and emigrate to the United States from there. "In
Hungary they know who you are—Francis de Pulszky's granddaughter.
Your husband will be received with open arms."[74]

Romola had in fact been in touch with her mother and stepfather in
Budapest, requesting permission to stay in their home. Emilia was now
in her eighties, and in failing health. Both she and Oscar Párdány
(himself afflicted with heart disease, and taking daily insulin injections
for his diabetes) felt reluctant to have Romola and her sick husband
under the same roof with them once more. Therefore, they tried to
discourage her from coming. The war made traveling across Europe
very dangerous; it would be safer to remain in Switzerland. If she
insisted, they proposed that Romola and Vaslav stay in an apartment on
the upper floor of a small building Emilia owned on Castle Hill, the old
royal enclave of Buda (where the Hilton Hotel is now located). "This
house is at your disposal," Párdány wrote Romola, "and if you decide to
come, Tamara can help you, because she knows how to drive a car."[75]

Traveling across Germany by train, on a transit visa and without an attendant, turned out to be less difficult than Romola had expected. "The trip went well," she wrote Dr. Müller later, from Budapest. "We spent a day in Salzburg, and one in Vienna. My husband and I visited the Mozarteum and the sights of Salzburg. He behaved perfectly.... In Vienna in the Hotel Bristol where he hadn't been for twenty years, he recognized the old employees and greeted them in a friendly way."[76] Their arrival in Budapest, on a "sweltering day," was less agreeable, however. Romola felt put out because no one was at the station to meet them. She writes that her mother and stepfather had "deliberately" left town.[77] So she booked rooms in the Ritz Hotel, and told newspaper reporters that she planned to go "to the United States and give lectures, beginning in October [1940] ... then I will write two books, one about the world's most famous dancers from antiquity to *Taglioni* in the 19th. century, the other a novel ... then every year we will organize dance-festivals in America."[78]

From Tamara Nijinsky's diary we learn about some of the bitter realities that year. Romola quickly ran out of money, was forced to leave the hotel, and became dependent on Emilia Márkus. Instead of accepting her mother's invitation to live in the apartment on Castle Hill, Romola demanded to have rooms in the spacious, ornately decorated, museumlike "mansion." That was where she and Vaslav had stayed in the past, in the "tower" apartment, which now was empty. Why could they not stay there again? After a tense discussion, Emilia relented, had furniture brought up to the tower rooms, and engaged a male nurse, Ferenc Kovács, to take care of Nijinsky. After moving in, there were further clashes with the family. Romola wanted money. She kept asking Oscar Párdány, and he had to tell her there was no money for her. Emilia tried to stay out of the bickering; Tamara had to serve as a go-between while Romola played the role of a hurt, neglected child. "I decided to keep away from my family as much as possible," she writes in her second book, *The Last Years of Nijinsky*. "From now on we lived alone, hardly seeing anybody, taking our meals in our rooms, high above the intriguing, misapprehending members of my family."[79] Tamara recalls bringing sandwiches and coffee upstairs to her parents.

Tatacaboy [Kyra and Tamara's nickname for their father] generally is calm, speaks very little, I would say almost nothing. He sits for long periods of time in the salon or on the terrace without saying a word. Memme [Romola] says he likes music and listens to the radio. But sometimes he is in a bad mood and does not let himself be washed, or does not eat anything. One day Granny got frightened, and this is not a good situation for her. They were sitting in the car, and Granny offered Tatacaboy some fruit. He grabbed it out of Granny's hand and threw it away. Sometimes he laughs real loud (pleasantly). One day Granny was laughing about something; he began to laugh as well, jumped from the couch in the salon, he jumped a few centimeters up from the floor.[80]

Food was rationed, but Oscar and Emilia purchased what they could get on the black market. "The atmosphere was extremely tense," writes Tamara. Once Nijinsky threw "a can of soda-bicarbonate" at Emilia. "It was like a mischievous game." Another time he stepped up to the table where Emilia was playing solitaire, "placed his two palms on the table, bent down a bit, and watched Granny's game." Then, suddenly, "with a little laugh, he mixed up Granny's cards." But there were also moments of anger: Nijinsky tossed dishes from the table (after that, the maid took to serving food on paper plates); he threw a heavy iron ashtray; he smashed a huge round vase in the foyer; he broke the tail of a Renaissance horse. There was talk about putting Nijinsky in the state hospital at Lipótmezö, but Romola said she "wouldn't send her dog there." Tamara, most likely repeating what she heard from her grandmother, wrote "one ought to place Tatacaboy in a sanatorium, and Memme should go to America to work. It is a pity that he was removed from the Binswangers."[81]

On Sunday evening, 22 September 1940, Tessa arrived in Budapest. Romola thought her sister's presence might reduce some of the tension between herself and her mother because "now Tessa will be scolded instead of me," but just the opposite happened. Nijinsky became more excited, perhaps sexually. He ran after his male nurse, "attacked him four times," and succeeded in "cutting him." After that, Romola refused to sleep in the upstairs apartment. A few weeks later, while on a stroll with her and Mr. Kovács (the male nurse), Nijinsky suddenly leapt away, made for a group of pedestrians, "assaulted a poor man's child, and hit him in the mouth so that the child spat blood." According to Kovács's report, Nijinsky "then attacked his wife. She ran away from him, and then he again attacked me, and kicked me hard, and then here at home he tore off his clothes." Four days later, while getting dressed, he "kicked over a table," picked up a knife, and "cut" Romola and the nurse.[82] (None of these violent episodes are mentioned in Romola's book about the "last years." She also failed to acknowledge her own disruptiveness in Budapest, the vicious quarrels with her stepfather, and the custody fight, mentioned earlier, over Tamara.)

Germany invaded Russia in 1941, and Hungary sided with the aggressor. German troops were stationed in Budapest. Part of Emilia Márkus's villa was requisitioned for military occupancy. Jews had to wear a yellow star (Párdány also was forced to do so, even though he had converted to Catholicism in 1903!). Emilia hid several of her Jewish friends in the villa. Her cook and maid quit because they did not want to work in a "Jewish" home. Foreigners were threatened with deportation. Nijinsky, being stateless, required a legal guardian (Romola). She made the rounds of foreign consulates and embassies, those that were still open, hoping somehow to escape. To Dr. Müller in Münsingen she wrote about Nijinsky's "recent worsening due to the bad influence of my mother and stepfather [as usual, Romola had to blame others] .... I want to bring him back to Switzerland.... Professor Benedek [a well-known psychiatrist in Budapest] strongly recommends a course of metrazol shock.... I only want it to be done by you, dear Mr. Hospital Director."[83] Müller was sympathetic, but there was nothing he could do. Romola had missed her chance to receive further psychiatric care for her husband in Switzerland. (Incredible as it sounds, Dr. Müller had just been contacted by a dancer from the Bavarian Opera in Munich, Sigfrid Jobst, who was choreographing Beethoven's *The Creatures of Prometheus.* "All the time I was working on this ballet, I thought that the difficult but magnificent role of 'Prometheus' could and should only be embodied by Vaslav Nijinsky."[84])

While waiting to take his bath on Wednesday, 13 August 1941, the agitated dancer picked up the heavy wooden stove used for heating the water and threw it into the bathtub. This must have required enormous strength. Romola's elderly mother became terrified. Oscar Párdány called the nearby state hospital, Lipótmezö, and asked that Nijinsky be admitted there. He arrived in a straightjacket. Romola gave a brief history: his brother had been "mentally ill (feeble-minded?)" and his sister is a "very eccentric individual." "Two children were born to us, both living and well.... I had one abortion from my husband .... When his illness began he was taken to Kreuzlingen.... Sakel himself treated him with insulin.... Since his stay here [in Budapest] his condition has gradually gotten worse." The examining doctor described Nijinsky as having "well-developed bones and muscles." But his teeth looked "neglected," and there were many "wounds and scabs" on his skin. His heart was enlarged by "two finger-breadths on the left and one on the right." Neurological examination showed no abnormal reflexes. Psychologically, he was "totally indifferent, deeply inhibited, and unreachable."

> He does not answer any questions ... but smiles in a dull, awkward manner and mumbles unintelligibly in a very low voice. Observing his behavior, one gets the impression that he is constantly under a multitude of emotions, and he is anxious.[85]

Lipótmezö, founded in the nineteenth century as Hungary's first and biggest state mental institution, housed hundreds of patients in large, old-fashioned wards, with little privacy. During the war it was even more understaffed than usual. After three days, during which Nijinsky received adequate care, Romola signed him out, and, with a new male nurse named Brindus, moved into a rented cottage near Lake Balaton, sixty miles southwest of Budapest. These arrangements had been made for them by Paul Bohus Világosi, a man who from now on was to play a major role in Romola's life. (In her book she refers to him as "Pavel Vihus.") They were distantly related on the Pulszky side of the family and had first met at a party given in 1913 by Romola's aunt Polyxena in honor of her marriage to Nijinsky. Paul was six years Romola's junior. He always said he was "in love" with her, and he seems to have been equally in love with Nijinsky.

> My understanding [says Tamara Nijinsky] was that Paul loved Vaslav just as a friend (no sex; Romola would not have allowed that). He admired him very much as an artist, could handle him very well, and was a good nurse-companion. He was short, like Nijinsky, but very effeminate. In later years, he wore a toupee, used makeup, and always had gold bracelets on his wrists. He was a superb cook, kind, polite, ready to help, run errands, etc. I have the feeling that Romola had no problem whatsoever leaving Vaslav with Paul. He spoke a lot, and always had stories to tell, generally about the aristocracy of the Austro-Hungarian Empire. One had to sort out, from what he said, how much really happened and how much was his fantasy."[86]

Very important were Paul's social connections and money. (Romola often introduced him as "Baron.") He owned land and properties, which led to trouble when Horthy's dictatorship collapsed and Hungary fell first to Nazi Germany and then to the Soviet Union.

The winter of 1941–1942 was very harsh. Having alienated herself from her mother, Romola was now penniless. To raise some cash, she tried selling translations of Nijinsky's *Diary*, until a friend, Mr. Quand, the general manager of Hungary's national bank, gave her enough money to put the dancer into a private sanatorium, in the summer of 1942. "Without a doubt," wrote the examining physician, "he needs complete isolation because strangers who happen to be in his environment have an agitating effect on him."[87] Tamara visited her father there: "I went with my fiancé and brought Tatacaboy some pastries. He eats with great delight. It seems that during this entire ordeal, he is the only one 'at peace' . . . at least he acts the most normal and decent."[88] (It was in 1942 that Romola tried legally to disown Tamara.) In 1943, the German invasion of Russia was halted at Stalingrad, and with the tide turning against them, Nazi barbarity escalated. Romola first learned from visiting musicians (conductors Wilhelm Furtwängler and Ernest Ansermet) about the ruthless extermination of "inmates of mental homes,"[89] a policy that had been in force in Germany for nearly a decade. Jews, gypsies, homosexuals, and other "undesirables" were rounded up throughout Hungary, with little resistance from the rest of the population. Nijinsky was obviously at great risk. In May he was taken to the St. John Community Hospital in Budapest because of a bladder infection and bleeding hemorrhoids. Professor Kluge, a psychiatrist from the medical school, saw him there on behalf of the District Court.

> The patient looks around day-dreamingly, his attention cannot be fixed, does not give adequate answers, at times he murmurs unintelligibly, at other times he hits anyone who approaches him unexpectedly and is usually irritated. He has not worked for years. He is suffering from late-stage schizophrenia, in other words he is mentally ill, therefore his placement in a mental hospital is necessary for the sake of safety.[90]

How safe it was for him to stay in the hospital is questionable, but he remained for over a year, receiving custodial care, "airing out" (i.e., going for walks), sodium nitrate for his skin lesions, and anal suppositories for the hemorrhoids. In 1944 Budapest came under bombardment, and Paul Bohus found someone who was willing, at a price, to hide refugees in the hills near Sopron, close to the Austrian border. In July, Romola took Nijinsky there. "Don't be frightened," she told him. "You are coming with me and we will stay together and I will look after you alone." He apparently did quite well; Romola says that he "enjoyed every flower, every stream, every butterfly," and even began speaking a little again. She felt, overoptimistically, that he would soon be "well enough to advise and supervise ... dancers and choreographers from all over the world." But he still could not cope on his own, and whenever Paul and Romola returned to Budapest (to pawn their jewelry and "heirlooms"), Nijinsky stayed in the psychiatric ward of a county hospital.

The Red Army was now entering Hungary from the east, causing a frantic exodus of German troops and refugees to the west. Romola heard the "crying and screaming of people," saw Jews rounded up for extermination camps and corpses thrown into mass graves. There were daily air raids. With Paul's help she gained access to some underground passages near a Carmelite convent, where they managed to hide. After one of the bombardments, she found Nijinsky "covered with dust" among the broken furniture of their roofless hideout and took him back to the hospital. No medical records of this period are available, but Romola writes that Nijinsky "allowed me to make all decisions, and followed me wherever I took him."[91]

On Monday evening, 12 March 1945, she and Paul Bohus were having supper in their partially destroyed dwelling. All day there had been earth-shaking noises from the bombing of Vienna, forty miles to the west. Suddenly, they heard a knock at the door. "There stood Vaslav in his old gray winter coat, wearing his little tyrolean hat and carrying a bundle in which his clothing and belongings were wrapped." His Polish attendant, Stan, had taken him out of the hospital because orders were received to exterminate all psychiatric patients within twenty-four hours. Paul, Vaslav, Stan, and Romola ran away to hide in nearby caves, where she says Nijinsky was the "calmest, the most obedient" of all the refugees.[92] When the Russian troops finally arrived, he virtually came back to life.* The language of his childhood, the victorious soldiers, the folk songs, the playing of balalaikas, music by Tchaikovsky and other Russian composers on the radio, all kinds of familiar sights and sounds seemed to cause an "awakening from a long and deep sleep." He felt

---

*Rumors that Nijinsky had actually been killed were to circulate for some time. The Associated Press reported in April 1945 that "the world-famous dancer was executed by the Nazis in Budapest before the Russians captured it." From London, Mrs. Martin Wangh wrote to Dr. Ludwig Binswanger, inquiring about "Vaslav Nijinsky, whose death from starvation we have read about. I am most distressed to think that Mrs. Nijinsky is wandering about destitute."[93]

comfortable among the men, "approached" them, and joined in their laughter and singing. Romola felt that "some inward barrier" had broken down; "he seemed melted towards the outside world." It was as though "the primitive Russian soldiers had a better method of treating him than we had, with all the doctors and nurses of the last twenty-six years."[94]

The soldiers were astonished when the legendary "Nijinsky," a household word in Russia, suddenly turned up among the tattered refugees. They wanted to see him, to talk to him, and to dance for him—"peasant dances, trepak, Cossack, and the Cherkess dances." At first Nijinsky only clapped his hands encouragingly. Then, one evening he stood up, "jumped" into the animated crowd, and began "to whirl and dance."[95] It was an astounding and most unexpected performance. According to Romola, "he became quite sociable, spoke Russian without inhibition, and very rarely seemed irritable, only when he failed to understand something, or when he had fear."[96] These observations suggest that the fifty-six-year-old dancer, in spite of his physical deterioration and by now chronic psychosis, still had the capacity to perform some of the motor patterns acquired in childhood. In a congenial environment, he could relax and behave quite "normally."

With the cessation of hostilities, Romola and Paul sought permission to go to Vienna. They did not want to return to Budapest and risk getting stuck in Soviet-held territory. On 12 June 1945 Colonel de Meyer, head of the International Red Cross delegation, issued a letter requesting "all military and civil authorities to help and assist Mrs. Nijinsky and her companions."[97] Under military protection, they were allowed to live in the Sacher Hotel, then an official residence for allied personnel, and during the ensuing months, as life gradually returned to Vienna, they walked in the war-torn parks, went to mass at St. Stephen's Cathedral, attended a threadbare performance of *Lohengrin*, and looked at paintings in unheated palaces. It "surprised" Romola that her husband could still "recognize almost every picture" and even comment on the paintings: "Oh, a Velásquez, the Madonna with the Cherries, a Raphael, and so on." If true, these observations suggest that Nijinsky had retained some of the knowledge instilled in him when Diaghilev, as was his custom with young dancers, would take him to museums and sensitize him to the different artists and their work.

A less favorable report comes from Dr. Alfred Auersperg, the psychiatrist who examined Nijinsky in Vienna after the war and found him "unable to give fitting answers to questions."[98] Margaret Power, a ballet enthusiast from London then working in Austria, also said that the dancer was incapable of any conversation. "I used to chatter to him in French or English, but he never answered."[99] (Not only was Nijinsky's preferred language Russian, but he always was at his best in nonverbal communication.) "He would kiss my cheek," adds Margaret Power, "always quite unexpectedly—not in greeting or farewell, but just out of affection."[100] While listening to the Vienna Choir Boys, he sat with an expression of "ecstasy" on his face. And when the former Imperial Ballet, his old company, came from Leningrad to Vienna, Nijinsky "followed each step" of the classical ballets he knew so well and accompanied their dancing "with a perceptible movement of his body." Afterward, the dancers "crowded around" him, and he accepted their flowers and compliments, but said nothing.[101]Also, in the daily routine of getting out of bed, bathing, shaving, brushing his teeth, putting on his clothes, tying his shoelaces, having meals, taking his medication, going to the bathroom, and keeping occupied, Nijinsky remained inert or helpless. Paul and Romola, assisted when possible by a nurse or attendant, inevitably had to do these things for him.

They wanted to move on. Kyra was in Italy. Anton Dolin was collecting money for the Nijinskys in the United States, and trying to have Margaret Power forward the funds to them. On 25 April 1946 a military pass was issued by Colonel W. P. Yarborough, the American provost marshal, for "Mrs. Romola Nijinsky, the well known authoress, and wife of the world famous ballet dancer Vaslav Nijinsky" to leave Vienna.[102] Since Russian-speaking persons were usually detained by the American military police, his mutism seemed advantageous at the various checkpoints. Asked who he was, Nijinsky always kept his mouth shut. "The man in the car is insane," explained the driver. "We are taking him to an asylum."[103] (Colonel Yarborough's letter surely helped in crossing the borders: "There is nothing political or irregular involved," it reads. "Mr. Nijinsky is insane as you know. This paper will merely serve to keep uninformed officials from unnecessarily molesting him."[104])

After a few days in Salzburg, Romola, Paul, and Vaslav moved into an abandoned castle, Schloss Mittersill, in the mountains between Kitzbühl and Zell-am-See. This castle had been requisitioned by the U.S. Army. "It was medieval and romantic," writes Romola, "with its drawbridge, dungeons, towers and ramparts, private chapel, banquet hall, and torture chamber, in which in past centuries witches and prisoners were held."[105] An elderly White Russian and ex-army officer named Feodor was engaged as Nijinsky's "valet." There were occasional visitors: Margaret Power and Tamara Nijinsky ("Mother kept father under control by treating him like a small child, cutting his meat at the table, watching his every step, and letting the attendant [Feodor] take over when there was trouble").[106]

Always agile and mischievous, Nijinsky played an excellent game of table tennis, and was "quite proud" whenever he beat an opponent. Romola describes him as gregarious, happily mingling with guests, and helping "in the preparation of festivities."[107] She went so far as to write Cyril Beaumont, in London, that his dancing "is quite as marvellous as it used to be... as graceful and light as ever [but] he only dances when he is in the mood." Romola wanted Beaumont to know that "we intend to go to Paris in the autum and from there to the States... where Mr. Nijinsky will undergo one more insulin shock treatment from his physician Dr. Sakel [who] feels my husband will be able to appear again.... Both Mr. Nijinsky and myself would be grateful to you if you would inform the public of the truth about us."[108]

Photographs show Nijinsky at age fifty-seven looking strong and alert. A documentary film shows him walking with grace and dignity. People who visited Mittersill often commented on his excellent physical condition, his sweet smile, and his childlike demeanor. Intellectually, however, Nijinsky remained a wreck, unable to think or plan for himself, and mumbling "words" that seemed to make sense only to Romola. By watching his facial expressions and anticipating his immediate needs, she usually understood what he "wanted or did not want." And with the constant assistance of Paul Bohus and a handful of servants—a cook, a housekeeper, Feodor, and some "peasant women" who volunteered their services—it was possible for him to live reasonably comfortably in the sheltered environment of Schloss Mittersill.

NOTES

1. Quotation from a statement Dr. Sakel made soon after his arrival in the United States; see Joseph Wortis, "In Memoriam—Manfred Sakel."
2. Manfred Sakel, *Schizophrenia*, 35.
3. Personal communication from F. C. Redlich, M.D., former professor and chairman of psychiatry, Yale Medical School.

4. Denis G. Baskin, Barbara J. Wilcox, Dianne P. Figlewicz, and Daniel Dorsa, "Insulin and insulin-like growth factors in the CNS."
5. Foster Kennedy, "Preface" to Sakel, xv.
6. Dr. O.R., notes, BMR, 18–29 July 1938.
7. Manfred Sakel, *Pharmacological Shock Treatment*, 121–125.
8. Max Rinkel and Harold E. Himwich, *Insulin Treatment in Psychiatry*, 215.
9. Letter from Dr. Böckli to Dr. Müller, 20 July 1938. Archives of the Psychiatric Clinic Münsingen.
10. See Appendix A for a complete description of Nijinsky's electrocardiograms.
11. BMR, 15 August 1938.
12. David F. Benson, *Aphasia, Alexia, and Agraphia.*
13. Letter from Dr. Manfred Sakel to the American Consul General in Zürich, 3 September 1938. Property of David Leonard, London.
14. Draft of an undated letter, from Dr. Haas to Dr. Sakel. Property of Marguerite Dorian Taussig, New Bedford, Massachusetts, (now in the New York Public Library, Dance Collection).
15. Dr. Haas, notes, BMR, 3–16 September 1938.
16. Dr. O.R., notes, BMR, 23 September 1938.
17. Letter from Romola Nijinsky to Dr. Haas, 26 September 1938. Property of Marguerite Dorian Taussig, New Bedford, Massachusetts (now in the New York Public Library, Dance Collection).
18. See letterheads of the Nijinsky Foundation, 10 Gower Street, London W.C. 1 (1938).
19. Romola Nijinsky to Dr. Haas, 26 September 1938.
20. Draft of an undated letter from Dr. Haas to Dr. Sakel. Property of Marguerite Dorian Taussig, New Bedford, Massachusetts, (now in the New York Public Library, Dance Collection).
21. Max Müller, *Errinnerungen*, 178.
22. Letter from Romola Nijinsky to Dr. Haas, 1 October 1938. Property of Marguerite Dorian Taussig, New Bedford, Massachusetts, (now in the New York Public Library, Dance Collection).
23. Nursing notes from the trip to Vevey. Münsingen Archives.
24. Letter from Romola Nijinsky to Dr. Haas, 13 November 1938. Property of Marguerite Dorian Taussig, New Bedford, Massachusetts, (now in the New York Public Library, Dance Collection).
25. See correspondence between bill collector E. Fischer and the administration of Münsingen Hospital, 14 and 15 February 1940. The bill came to "Fr. 181 for Mrs. R. Nyinsky [sic] and Fr. 138 for Madame de Julszky [sic]." Münsingen Archives.
26. BMR, 10 December 1938.
27. Ibid., 2 December 1938.
28. Letter from Dr. Böckli, 6 December 1938. Münsingen Archives.
29. Letter from Romola Nijinsky to Dr. Müller, 28 November 1938. Münsingen Archives.
30. Münsingen medical records (hereafter, cited as MMR), 10 December 1938.
31. MMR, 20 December 1938.
32. Dr. Müller to Philip Morrell, 12 January 1939, and Philip Morrell to Dr. Müller, 27 January and 22 May 1939. Münsingen Archives.
33. MMR, 8 January to 4 February 1939.
34. Ibid., 14 February 1939.
35. Letter from Philip Morrell to Dr. Müller, 22 May 1939.
36. Ibid., 12 March, 24 May, and 2 June 1939.
37. Müller, 178.
38. Serge Lifar, *Serge Diaghilev*, 529.
39. Müller, 178.
40. MMR, 9 June 1939.
41. Lifar, 530–532. Emphasis in orignal.
42. Müller, 179.
43. MMR, 7 July 1939.

44. Ibid., 31 July 1939.
45. Romola Nijinsky, _The Last Years of Nijinsky_, 31. (Hereafter, cited as _Last Years_.)
46. Letter from Romola Nijinsky to Dr. Müller, 14 September 1939. Münsingen Archives.
47. Letter from Albert Loewer to Dr. Müller, 22 August 1939. Münsingen Archives.
48. Letter from Franciska Widmer to Dr. Müller, 14 September 1939. Münsingen Archives.
49. Letter from Romola Nijinsky to Dr. Müller, 14 September 1939. Münsingen Archives.
50. Nancy C. Andreasen, "Negative symptoms in schizophrenia ..."
51. Letter from Franciska Widmer to Dr. Müller, 14 September 1939. Münsingen Archives.
52. Letter from Romola Nijinsky to Dr. Müller, 14 September 1939. Münsingen Archives.
53. MMR, 20 September 1939.
54. Letter from Karl Kämpf to Romola Nijinsky, 18 February 1963. Nijinsky Archives; Kämpf, notes, 20–24 September 1939. Münsingen Archives.
55. Letter from Professor Christian Müller to the author, 15 June 1988.
56. Sakel, _Pharmacological Shock Treatment_, 43.
57. Letter from Dr. Haemmerli-Schindler to Romola Nijinsky, 14 August 1939. Property of David Leonard, London.
58. _Last Years_, 31.
59. Letter from Dr. Müller to Romola Nijinsky, 6 October 1939. Münsingen Archives.
60. Letter from Romola Nijinsky to Dr. Müller, 3 November 1939. Münsingen Archives.
61. Ibid.
62. Letter from the nurse (J.K.) to Dr. Müller, 5 October 1939. Münsingen Archives.
63. Taped interview, Igor Markevitch, 6 August 1972. The New York Public Library, Dance Collection.
64. Letter from nurse J.K. to Dr. Müller. Munsingen Archives.
65. Letter from Dr. Müller to Romola Nijinsky, 5 January 1940. Münsingen Archives.
66. Letter from Philip Morrell's secretary to Dr. Müller. 19 February 1940. Münsingen Archives.
67. Romola Nijinsky to Dr. Müller, 4 January 1940; Dr. Müller to Romola Nijinsky, 6 November 1939. Münsingen Archives.
68. Letter from Dr. Haemmerli-Schindler to Dr. Sakel, 23 April 1940. Property of David Leonard, London.
69. Romola Nijinsky to Dr. Müller, 29 April 1940. Münsingen Archives.
70. Letter and telegram from Dr. Müller to Romola Nijinsky, 4 May 1940. Münsingen Archives.
71. _New York Times_, 9 May 1940.
72. Müller, 179.
73. MMR, 17 July 1940.
74. _Last Years_, 53.
75. Personal communication from Tamara Nijinsky.
76. Letter from Romola Nijinsky to Dr. Müller, 8 June 1941. Münsingen Archives.
77. _Last Years_, 56–57.
78. Clara M. Lasker, interview with Romola Nijinsky, published in Budapest on 2 August 1940. Emphasis in the original.
79. _Last Years_, 60–61.
80. Tamara Nijinsky, diary, August 1940. Nijinsky Archives.
81. Ibid., 15 August–14 September 1940.
82. Ferenc Kovács, Summary Report, 23 October 1940, to the Budapest Orphans Court, File Number 18440/17, 1941.
83. Letter from Romola Nijinsky to Dr. Müller, 8 June 1941. Münsingen Archives.
84. Letter from Sigfrid Jobst to Dr. Müller, 22 March 1941. Münsingen Archives.
85. Report from Budapest-lipótmezö Hospital, 14 August 1941.
86. Tamara Nijinsky, personal communication.
87. Dr. Gábor Major, reporting from Dr. Batizfalvy's Sanatorium, Budapest, 16 July 1942.
88. Tamara Nijinsky, diary.
89. _Last Years_, 90.
90. St. John Community Hospital, report, 6 July 1944.
91. _Last Years_, 116–134.
92. Ibid., 136–145.

93. Newspaper clippings, and letter from Mrs. Martin Wangh to Dr. Ludwig Binswanger, 6 April 1945. Tübingen Archives.
94. *Last Years*, 159–160.
95. Ibid., 161.
96. Letter from Romola Nijinsky to Dr. Ludwig Binswanger, 26 September 1946. Tübingen Archives.
97. Military documents, Nijinsky Archives.
98. Professor Alfred Auersperg, "Medical Statement," 3 July 1945. Property of David Leonard, London.
99. RBN, 529.
100. Ibid., 530.
101. *Last Years*, 196–205.
102. Letter from the Office of the American Provost Marshal Headquarters, U.S. Forces in Austria, 25 April 1946.
103. Romola Nijinsky, *Last Years*, 212.
104. Memo from Colonel W. P. Yarborough to General Lewis, 17 September 1946. Nijinsky Archives.
105. *Last Years*, 210.
106. Power's comment, RBN, 530; Tamara's comment, personal communication.
107. *Last Years*, 217–221.
108. Richard Buckle, *In the Wake of Diaghilev*, 84–85.

*Don't dance with your toes pointing
skyways. They will do that when
you are dead.*
                    Irish Folk Song

Chapter 14

The Dance of Death, and Immortality

Hoping to move back into the mainstream of society, Romola visited
Paris during the winter of 1946. The war had made it a "depressing
place," and she did not think someone like Nijinsky, who needed "care
and peace," should live there.[1] The following summer she went to
London. She looked up old friends. (A note from Tamara Karsavina:
"Could you possibly meet me for lunch at the Hungarian Club.... I am
so looking forward to hearing all your news.") She spoke with booking
agents about a lecture tour of the United States. She borrowed money
from Barclays Bank on an insurance policy. ("It was a considerable
disappointment to us," writes the bank manager, "to learn that you had
gone [back to Austria] without making any arrangement for the
repayment of our advance.") Her plan was to remove Nijinsky from
Schloss Mittersill, take him to England, and perhaps go with him to
New York.[2]

With a "very competent male nurse" and Paul Bohus, who "attended to everything," they left Austria in November 1947. Nijinsky seemed "frightened" by a noisy military band at the railway station, but soon, according to Romola, "regained his composure." She wanted him to be seen by the Zürich internist Dr. Karl Rohr, so two weeks were spent in Switzerland. (Romola says Nijinsky stayed at the "Hirschlanden Clinic," but it was the Brunner Sanatorium, a small psychiatric hospital in Küsnacht, on the Lake of Zürich.[3]) His physical examination revealed high blood pressure. The readings are missing, but ten months later, in London, Nijinsky's blood pressure was reported to be 174/110. (That, with a diastolic level at 110, is significantly above normal.) Dr. Rohr suspected kidney disease and prescribed a special diet, vitamin supplements, a barbiturate sedative (luminal), and medication (quinidine) to stabilize the heart rhythm and help reduce the blood pressure.[4] An electrocardiogram taken on 18 February 1948 shows that Nijinsky still had an irregular pulse (owing to "fairly frequent premature ventricular beats") and signs of cardiac abnormality ("a persistent axis deviation"[5]).

In London he seemed "thrilled" to be back in the city of his "many triumphs," but unaware that "two decades" (actually, it was over thirty years) had passed since his last visit. Romola described some other memory defects: Nijinsky could not recall Diaghilev's death in 1929 or his mother's in 1932. She attributed the blanks in his mind to the effort she had made, for many years, to keep him "in ignorance" of important events, lest these upset him. (Romola was good at making up stories, for example, that Nijinsky's mother, long dead, had called to ask "how are you." "She can't come to see you because she is too old, but we will go and visit her one day.") Romola was happy about the courtesy of people with whom Nijinsky had contact in England. The fact that they treated him with kindness explained why he "responded with normal behavior." In her book, Romola claims that Nijinsky "never became excited or upset" during the last three years of his life.[6] But daily reports written in 1948 and 1949 by his male nurse show this to be untrue: Nijinsky is described as alternating between "very angry," "changeable," "bad," and "very restless" moods.[7] Two physicians came to see him from time to time, Dr. Wilson, who lived in the neighborhood, and a Hungarian practitioner named Dr. Csato. I have not been able to find out who Dr. Wilson was. The other doctor Romola mentions, Dr. Tibor Csato, had been trained in Vienna and Munich and had published papers about gastrointestinal diseases. Information about him is limited. Dr. Csato was neither a member of the Royal Society of Medicine, with traceable hospital connections in London, nor does he seem to have been a specialist in the three fields in which Nijinsky might have benefited most from professional intervention: psychiatry, cardiology, and nephrology.[8] (It is of more than passing interest that, despite the very high level of expertise in London, Nijinsky seems never to have been examined or treated by a psychiatrist during the years he lived in England.)

At the beginning of their stay, he and his wife, with their constant companion Paul and Nijinsky's male nurse, lived in an elegant old hotel, Great Fosters, close to where London's Heathrow Airport is located today. Four rooms had been found for them there by Romola's friend Alexander Korda, a film director from Budapest. On earlier occasions, when Romola was traveling alone or with another woman, she had greatly enjoyed staying in this "well-known shooting lodge, built in the time of Queen Elizabeth." This time, however, she felt very uncomfortable at Great Fosters. The food was "unsuitable," "strangers" kept crossing her path; she yearned for the comfort of a "private home." The "dreary winter" of 1947–1948 was spent playing chess and card games. She and the three men also went to the movies quite often. Nijinsky was especially impressed the first time he saw a film in Technicolor. Twice they went to see Korda's *An Ideal Husband* (!), based on Oscar Wilde's play. Nadine Legat, the widow of Nijinsky's St. Petersburg ballet teacher, came to visit them at Great Fosters. (With her Russian speech and sympathetic manner, she probably was a mother figure for Nijinsky—Eleonora Bereda would have been ninety-two in 1948.) Mme Legat "admired his wonderful thighs and feet" and asked him to dance for her. "Oh, I have lost the habit," Romola reports him saying, while laughing. (It was not true—a lie, or a delusion? Nijinsky had recently danced for the Russian troops in Hungary.) But Romola writes that Mme Legat "sized up his feelings, his timidity, and knew very well how to handle him. For Nadia, Vaslav had never been ill. She felt that he was a genius, far ahead of us, on a different level of mentality, and that there was fundamentally nothing wrong with him. I am sure that she was right."[9]

In the spring of 1948, they moved into a "charming English country house" called Whinmead, near Sunningdale in Windsor Great Park, Surrey. In this relaxed and beautiful setting, Nijinsky and his male nurse went for walks in the forest or sat quietly in the garden, while Romola worked on her correspondence. (She wrote to Eleanor Roosevelt, who replied: "I am afraid it will not be possible for me to see you as you suggest. Also, there is no way in which I can help Mr. Nijinsky gain entry into the United States."[10]) Twice that year they motored into London and went to the theater. A newspaper reporter interviewed Nijinsky.

> His round face with the high, balding forehead and cheeks puckered in a fixed, querulous smile gives him the air of a benevolent, elderly, quizzical doll. His bright, brown eyes dance into and away from you, while his fingers rapidly open and close in a series of nervous, spasmodic movements. His voice seldom rises above a mutter and rarely says more than "Oui" or "Non." But even age and the prosaic, uneasily-fitting sports jacket and grey flannels, have failed to hide the essential grace and litheness of the short, slim body of . . . the greatest dancer the world has seen.[11]

There were a number of "misfortunes" that year. Romola, whose father had been born in London, had applied for British citizenship. This was not granted for some time. She injured herself falling down the stairs, and for eight months "was crippled and unable to walk." There was a financial setback: Alexander Korda decided not to produce the movie based on her writings he had promised Romola, and took her off his payroll. (Romola saw this as a conspiracy: "a little group of Diaghilev's former friends" had been criticizing her "literary activities," and making it "their business to belittle Vaslav as an artist."[12]) His male nurse gave notice, forcing her briefly to be Nijinsky's "constant attendant." (In fact, Paul Bohus was always around to keep an eye on the dancer, do the shopping and cooking, and take care of household chores.) The nurse returned in August 1948 and described Nijinsky as "hallucinating from time to time," but giving "clear answers" and being "very attentive."[13]

On 19 September, after walking along the lakeshore of Virginia Water, Nijinsky complained of "rheumatic pains," and seemed to be "hindered while walking." Romola describes him "holding his hand over the back of his hip."[14] He was put to bed for four days, after which a doctor diagnosed "neuritis." (Who made this diagnosis is not known, but it is possible that Nijinsky was already having symptoms related to the kidney disease that was to prove fatal within less than two years.) Headaches also became more of a problem in 1948. An "abscessed tooth" was pulled on 4 October, after which he felt "better" and went to a "Beethoven concert." A "young Polish sculptor" (Romola does not give the name) visited him that autumn to make a bust, and "a cast of his feet." For the rest of the year, Nijinsky remained generally in a "very good" mood, and only occasionally was "bad" or "angry," usually in the evening. Christmas was uneventful. In January 1949 he again had dental problems, but all of February was a "good" month.[15]

The biggest event that year was an exhibition of Nijinsky's drawings at the Harold Rubin Art Gallery in London, from 15 March to 8 April 1949. Romola invited the most important people she could think of, including Queen Mary. A secretary politely acknowledged the invitation, but Her Majesty had to decline.[16] (There were several other replies from Queen Mary's private secretary over the years, in response to Romola's letters calling attention to herself and her well-known husband, or asking favors, such as her request to become a British subject. One has the impression that she was not very popular or successful politically in England. Whether that had to do with Romola's self-aggrandizing personality or the old Pulszky scandal, or her husband's former homosexuality, or his "madness," or a combination of these and other factors, is difficult to say. In a letter written after Nijinsky's reburial in Paris, Margaret Power told Romola, "I think you are right— Paris appreciates her artists much more than London, and I think it is therefore better that the body of Vaslav should rest there."[17])

After attending the opening of his art show at the Rubin Gallery, Nijinsky "showed great interest" in going to the theater.[18] Whether he did, and what he may have seen, is not known. The daily notes written by his male nurse stop in May 1949, but Romola describes her husband, after a party, dancing "a little minuet or a czardas" (again, presumptive evidence that he had not "lost the habit"). She still wanted to move to the United States, and kept sending letters to musicians, artists, socialites, and people with political connections. One of Romola's American friends even tried to find out if Nijinsky might be accepted for treatment at Chestnut Lodge, an excellent private psychiatric hospital in Rockville, Maryland. There was a discussion with Dr. Frieda Fromm-Reichmann, a psychoanalyst especially gifted in working with highly disturbed artistic patients like Nijinsky. But it was decided (was it a matter of money?) not to encourage his admission to the Lodge.[19]

One morning in "the late sunny autumn," Nijinsky suddenly began hiccupping, became alarmed, and ran to Romola, who tried in vain to stop the attack by giving him gulps of water.[20] The intractable hiccups recurred for several days, and Romola telephoned Dr. Rohr in Zürich for advice. He told her to get in touch with Dr. János Plesch, a Hungarian physician, formerly a professor of medicine in Berlin, who had escaped the Nazis and moved to London. Plesch was an authority on cardiovascular disease. He had been doing research on blood flow for many years, had invented a blood-pressure measuring apparatus that required no mercury, and (in 1937) had published an influential monograph, Physiology and Pathology of the Heart and Blood Vessels, dedicated to his friend Albert Einstein. The choice of Professor Plesch as a consultant for Nijinsky was fortunate. He was fond of artists, and (before his death, in California in 1957) wrote a book about Rembrandt.[21] Plesch asked that the dancer be brought to London, and examined him very carefully. It was clear that he had generalized arteriosclerosis and was suffering from high blood pressure. Plesch was an expert in this condition; he considered hypertension a symptom and not a disease, and explained this to Romola. Laboratory tests were ordered, which disclosed that Nijinsky had some impairment in kidney function. (Romola says she was told his kidneys were not "quite in order.") Whether this was the result or the cause of his elevated blood pressure is not known—no autopsy was done—but Nijinsky's medical history suggests that there had been cardiovascular instability long before any definite evidence of kidney dysfunction was detected. Persistent hypertension can produce renal impairment, and so can insulin-shock. (Severely reduced blood-oxygen levels during repeated insulin-coma may have damaged not only Nijinsky's brain, but also his kidneys and heart.)

Plesch's approach to the treatment of high blood pressure was to recommend a strict diet of "low nitrogen, common salt, and alcohol content," and a change of climate.[22] Romola writes that he also prescribed some "Swiss medication" for Nijinsky (presumably an antihypertensive drug), and agreed to see him again "after six weeks." During that interval they went to Switzerland, so that Nijinsky could benefit from the "change of climate as well as a more varied diet." After returning to London, Romola received disquieting news from Budapest, which temporarily pushed his illness into the background. The eighty-nine-year-old Emilia Márkus had fallen down the steps; in November, she became very ill with jaundice; on 24 December she was dead. Romola had very mixed feelings about her mother. She writes that she "hesitated" about flying to Budapest to see her dying mother and decided not to because "nobody was able to guarantee my exit from Hungary," which is understandable in view of the Communist takeover there. Emilia's death came as a "dreadful shock." Although there had been much strife between the two women, including the struggle over Tamara Nijinsky's adoption and inheritance, Romola finally realized that Emilia "was my mother, and I simply could not grasp the fact that she who had always been, had suddenly ceased to exist."[23]

The new year (1950) brought further "complications." The lease on their home in Surrey was due to expire. Romola and Paul went looking for new places "as far as Sussex and Kent" without finding anything suitable, or affordable. So they decided to move back to the Great Fosters Hotel. While packing to leave the house to which he had gotten quite attached—"Dom, nash dom" (home, our home) he used to say—Nijinsky observed "melancholically" that they were having to live "like gypsies" again. His male nurse went along to the hotel. Luckily, after only a few days there, "a perfect stranger, Major Wright," called Romola to say he had a house near Arundel, fifty miles south of London, and "would be glad to lend it to Mr. Nijinsky." The offer was gratefully accepted. "We motored down in a dreadful gale," writes Romola. "It was an atrocious drive. When we moved, as always, Vaslav was puzzled and nervous." After a few days, she noticed that his face looked unusually "flushed." The nurse thought it was due to sunburn, but there were other worrisome symptoms. Nijinsky seemed not to enjoy his walks as much as before, and was more "quiet and silent" than usual.[24]

His progressive lethargy (probably a sign of impending uremic coma due to kidney failure) was interrupted one day when Serge Lifar called from Paris, inviting Nijinsky to a gala performance he was planning at the Opéra, in June, to honor the memory of Auguste Vestris (1760–1842), the illustrious dancer with whom Nijinsky was often compared. (In telegrams, when Diaghilev wanted to disguise Nijinsky's identity, he would refer to him as "Vestris."[25]) Romola gladly accepted Lifar's invitation, and made plans to go to Paris in May. She felt Nijinsky had been "neglected" by the dance world in England and that he would be treated "differently" in France. She also wanted to spend another vacation in the mountains of Switzerland. Soon there was a second telephone call from Lifar, this time to say that he had been invited to do a television program about ballet for the British Broadcasting Company and would be flying to London early in April with the Paris dancers. Romola agreed to pick him up at the airport.[26]

The last week of March she spent in London, visiting friends and attending to "some business." (After much finagling, which included letters to Buckingham Palace and contacts with high officials in the Home Office, Romola had at last been granted British citizenship.[27]) Was Nijinsky going to be able to join her in London? He had a "slight indisposition," so she could not be sure. The nurse said it was not necessary to call a doctor. On Sunday afternoon, 2 April, Nijinsky and the nurse arrived in London, where Romola, having met Lifar at the airport earlier that day, picked them up at Waterloo Station and took them to the Welbeck Hotel. Nijinsky seemed in a good mood. "I am so amazed at how fit Vaslav looks," commented Mr. Beau, a friend of Lifar. "He is quite a young man, and so sociable." (A photograph taken of Nijinsky by the BBC confirms his "fit" appearance.)

On Monday morning he complained of a headache, but went with Romola to see pictures at the Wallace Collection and to sign autographs for admirers in a restaurant. (In the past, when he was "catatonic," Romola had found it necessary to "guide his hand" while signing autographs.[28]) The entire afternoon was spent at the Alexandra Palace, watching Lifar and the dancers rehearse for their television program. Nijinsky seemed "enchanted" by the ballerina Nina Vyroubova, and was fascinated to see her dance simultaneously on the stage and in the TV monitor. That evening, with his eyes closed, he suddenly "clutched his hands," and while tapping the fingers of one hand on the other, made "some dancing movements as he used to many years ago when he was composing and concentrating on a new bit of choreography." "How strange," Romola thought. "Then suddenly with his left arm he began to make *port de bras* around his head as he used to do while dancing *Le Spectre de la Rose*."[29] It was the beginning of the dance of death.

The following day he "lay limply on his bed." His pulse was "slightly faster" than usual and he refused to eat. Romola was alarmed and called "a very good Hungarian doctor," recommended to her by some "acquaintances." (We do not know his name; Romola says he "had been practicing in Germany and London lately." But it could not have been Professor Plesch because in 1950 Plesch was living in Montreux,

Switzerland.) After examining Nijinsky, the new doctor told Romola he was concerned about the high blood pressure. He ordered some blood tests, talked to her about possible treatments, and warned her that if there were renal complications, they would be facing "a difficult task." Romola says that at this point she "began to lose faith in all these doctors" and called Zürich hoping that Professor Rohr, who was familiar with Nijinsky's long medical history, might provide a better prognosis. Rohr was on vacation, and Romola tried to page him over the Swiss broadcasting stations, but to no avail.[30]

On Wednesday afternoon, 5 April 1950, Nijinsky's blood test showed that he was in renal failure. His clinical condition had deteriorated markedly. His face was "pinched and flushed"; he seemed "dazed"; he could no longer answer any questions. It was clear that he would have to be hospitalized. "It still did not penetrate into my brain," writes Romola, "that Vaslav's life might be in danger." On Thursday morning, he was in a coma. An ambulance took him to the London Clinic, Devonshire Place, where intravenous fluids and an antibiotic (streptomycin) were administered immediately. (The London Clinic is a small private hospital near Harley Street, reserved for well-to-do patients. No permanent records are maintained there, and since the "very good Hungarian doctor" who treated the dying Nijinsky cannot be identified, we only know about these terminal events from Romola.)

Most of the day the dancer remained unconscious. Romola was told that he was "beyond human help," his "kidneys were gone." During the night, a priest came to administer the last rites. The next morning—it was Good Friday—he was somewhat better, more alert, and able to breathe without panting. Nijinsky again made movements with his arms as if he were dancing "in *Spectre de la Rose*." He said something that sounded like the Russian word "Mamasha," diminutive for mother. Romola could not tell "whether he was calling his mother or me." He stretched out his hand, and she kissed it. Saturday, 8 April, he seemed a little better and was able to eat some breakfast. Romola thought "all was now well." She went into another room.

Suddenly, she was called back. There had been a crisis. Whether it was acute respiratory failure, a brain catastrophe, or cardiac arrest we do not know. Romola says that the doctors had left the hospital. Nijinsky was "sitting up" in the arms of his male nurse, who shouted, "Look, look!" Evidently he had stopped breathing and was turning blue. Oxygen was given, and some "injections" (probably adrenalin or aminophylline). He "sighed once." The nurse laid him back. "His eyes, his mouth closed. He seemed to stretch."[31] Nijinsky was dead. The cause, according to his official certificate, was "uremia with chronic nephritis."[32]

A funeral Mass was held the next week. "Five hundred people from all over the world packed the stately church of St. James's, in Spanish-place, Marylebone," reports the *Evening News*.

> A dozen extra police had been drafted to the church to keep the crowds in check, but it was about 100 people who gathered outside. Some arrived at the church with floral tributes. One elderly woman in black came with a simple bouquet of fresh-picked primroses. Nijinsky's widow, Mme. Romola Nijinsky, arrived at the church a few minutes before the service began, supported by two friends. Their 30-year-old daughter Kyra, an interpreter in a Rome fashion house, was not able to attend. [Actually, Kyra was nearly 36; it was Tamara who would have been 30, but she was trapped in Communist Hungary.] The pallbearers included Frederick Ashton and Michael Soames [sic], of the Sadler's Wells Ballet, Serge Lifar, from France, and Anton Dolin.[33]

Richard Buckle tells us that he and Cyril Beaumont were also among the pallbearers. "Only Beaumont had seen Nijinsky in his glory. He confessed afterwards that he had found the weight of the coffin almost intolerable." Also in attendance were Tamara Karsavina, Marie Rambert, Lydia Sokolova, and Margaret Power. Nijinsky was laid to rest in St. Marylebone Cemetery in the Finchley Road. "Afterwards, as the mourners moved away, Beaumont looked back to see a new figure standing by the grave. It was the Hindu dancer, Ram Gopal."[34] Thus the "God of the Dance" joined the Immortals. His once powerful, lithe, enchanting body had finally capitulated to disease—the ravages of physical and mental decay.

But Nijinsky's spirit would not die. Like Petrushka and Till Eulenspiegel, he kept coming back to life. His first resurrection took place in 1953, when Serge Lifar arranged to have him taken to Paris, so that he should be close to another "God," Auguste Vestris, and to Lifar himself, after he died. Nijinsky's remains were disinterred, examined, and put into a lead-lined wooden coffin. Before it was sealed, his admirers took a final look at the face. Its fantastic expressions had entranced a generation of ballet lovers; its bizarre mimicry had puzzled many a psychiatrist. "I saw him in his new coffin of light oak," writes

Nadia Legat. She brought a group of her dance students to Victoria Station to wish him bon voyage. "The girls went and bought flowers themselves ... white, red and purple rhododendrons ... roses, carnations, and all sorts of beautiful things."[35] Before entering his new grave in the Montmartre Cemetery, Nijinsky was blessed by a Russian Orthodox priest. His sister was there, a most fitting presence at this second burial. "I was amazed," writes Margaret Power, "to see Bronia looking so old and worn. Surely she is younger than Vaslav? Her hair is quite white, and she really looked very ill and pale."[36]

> The service at the Russian Church was very impressive, and the church was packed with people, and there were many flowers ... "everybody" was there, all the Ballet people—Kchessinska, Preobrajenska and many of the old emigré Russians, and also many of the young dancers from the Opéra and the Ballet Schools. The Archbishop spoke in Russian of course. He spoke of the beauty in Vaslav's life, of the talent given him by God, and of the wonderful beauty and pleasure he was able to give to the people who saw him. He said that this joy which Vaslav gave to us was still with us, held in precious memory in our hearts.... The sun was shining and the birds were singing, and somehow there was no sorrow, only the memory of a beautiful life which showed only joy and light.... I remember the simple, affectionate childlike man whom I loved.[37]

All that is true. Nijinsky will never be forgotten because of his impact on ballet. He was the inventor of male dancing in our time, with its synthesis of power, elegance, virility, and expressiveness. Without him there would have been no Lifar, no Dolin, no Eglevsky, no Nureyev, no Baryshnikov, none of the magnificent men who followed in his footsteps and have enriched our lives. The joy, the wonder, the excitement Nijinsky gave to ballet have made him immortal. His place in history is secure. Books have been written about him. Films and ballets based on his life have appeared (notably Béjart's *Nijinsky, Clown of God;* a BBC documentary *God of the Dance;* and a full-length motion picture, *Nijinsky,* by Herbert Ross). There is a Nijinsky Prize for exceptional male dancers. There has even been a racehorse, ironically named "Nijinsky, the Horse of the Century."[38]

But there is another side to Nijinsky's immortality, a tragic one. This man will never die because he never lived. From infancy on, his life was hemmed in by impediments. Some of these he tried to leap over—his father's abandonment, his mother's poverty, the exploitation of talent that is so often found in institutions, schools, and companies where artists work. When he was young and supple, he had a phenomenal track record. He danced all the great roles and created new ones. He achieved stardom in only a few years. He found love in the arms of men and women. He became world famous. Yet certain barriers Nijinsky could never surmount—the depressiveness in his family, the isolative, malignant qualities in his own personality, and the psychosis that he shared with his brother. As long as he was in the theater and pretending to be a slave, clown, lover, specter, puppet, half-animal, or whatever role he was dancing, the inner disturbances of mood could be kept under control. Offstage, however, he remained childlike, helpless, and insecure, with but a single interest—the art of ballet—to give any meaning to his life.

Most of his relationships with people were grossly impaired by an irritable, tempestuous explosiveness. Outbursts of rage would disrupt his sweet, affectionate, and childlike appeal. Lovers could tolerate him only when there was a definite payoff—sexual favors for Prince Lvov, dancing for Diaghilev, self-aggrandizement for Romola. Handicapped by his utter perfectionism and a tendency to want to do everything in his own way, he finally became completely unsociable, an eccentric recluse. Most of his ballets remained unfinished—what a terrible loss. Think of the marvelous things Nijinsky might have done with *Mephisto Waltz*, the Bach ballet, *Papillons de la Nuit,* or the improvisatory *Dance of Life Against Death*. If only he had been able to work well with others and win the kind of support a man of genius needs. The behavior of an artist may seem eccentric at times, but to succeed in the theater it is necessary to maintain a certain amount of sociability and be conciliatory. A certain craftiness may also help, if one hopes to be a leader, to run a company, to form a school. One must be able to bend to the will of others, and also know how to manipulate them. These were qualities that Diaghilev and Romola Pulszky possessed. But not Nijinsky.

Only a handful of people knew him intimately: his adoring little mother ("Mamasha"); his sister (a playmate and model in experimental choreography); his sexual partners. His sister perhaps understood him better than any other woman. They shared a desire for artistic perfection, and perhaps a secret, unspoken wish for incestuous union. She was gynandrous and played transvestite roles. He was androgynous and accepted male lovers. His nervousness became more noticeable after Bronislava's marriage, and his first breakdown coincided with the collapse of the ballet company they had tried to form together. World War I and the Russian revolution drove them further apart; by the time they saw each other again, Vaslav was psychotic and Bronislava had established herself as an independent choreographer.

Sexuality seems to have been a huge problem for Nijinsky, matched only by his wife's homophobia, although she overcame that, to a certain degree, by accepting female lovers. Romola lived for another twenty-eight years. She traveled widely, usually with Paul Bohus, visited Russia—where she had an amusing interview with Krushchev—and Japan, where she fell in love with a transvestite actress who remarkably resembled the young Nijinsky. Romola died in 1978, in Paul Bohus's arms in a Paris hotel. She, too, lies in the Montmartre Cemetery, but not close to her husband. Their hasty marriage, when Nijinsky was at the height of his fame and Romola sought his reflected glory, probably made too great a demand. It forced him to curtail his polymorphous perversity, his self-loving interest in masturbation, homosexuality, and prostitution. He felt that she lacked the "soul" of a dancer. The language barrier hindered communication even further, isolated them, and led to a sort of paranoid *folie à deux*. But another wife (or male lover) would probably have been equally unsatisfactory in the long run. Sex and physical intimacy were always a problem for Nijinsky. He tried both homosexuality and heterosexuality, but abandoned both. The ballet, almost more than any other artistic enterprise, demands an openness toward the human body, a willingness to worship sensuality, and a capacity for experiencing physical pleasure with others. Nijinsky rebelled against closeness. He danced singular roles. He was incredibly narcissistic. But with illness he turned against his own body and neglected it. He stopped exercising, stuffed himself with rich food, attacked his head and abdomen with his fists, tore his hair, and tried to damage his eyes.

What was this terrible illness that crippled so great an artist? His doctors called it neurasthenia, catatonia, mania, depression, schizophrenia, paranoia, and dementia praecox, all perfectly legitimate technical descriptions of mental disorder. (A modern diagnosis of Nijinsky's psychosis or "madness" can be found in Appendix B.) But none of these terms have any explanatory power. What causes these diseases is still unclear, just as we are in the dark about the basic causes of malignant cancers. The real value of a diagnosis is that it guides treatment and stimulates research, but there was precious little to be

done in either of these directions when Nijinsky was a patient. He had
the very best treatment that money could buy at the time. He received
private psychiatric care in one of the world's finest mental hospitals. He
was seen in consultation by some of the most knowledgeable psychiatrists of Europe. Skilled psychoanalysts like Ludwig Binswanger tried to
work with him. Manfred Sakel himself gave him insulin-shock. But
nothing really helped Nijinsky, which tells us as much about the
treatment as about the disease. Compared to the amount of time and
effort devoted to research in cancer, cardiovascular disease, bacterial
and viral infections, and other major medical-social problems, psychiatric research then, as today, was relatively neglected.

I can think we can do more to help someone like Nijinsky today than
was possible when he became so disturbed. The training of dancers has
changed, with greater emphasis on nutrition, stress reduction, preven-
tion of disability, and improved self-care. Antibiotics are available to
combat the sorts of infections Nijinsky had, including gonorrhea,
upper-respiratory diseases, and typhoid fever. There has been considerable improvement in the diagnosis and treatment of arteriosclerosis,
heart disease, and kidney impairment. Much better medication can
now be prescribed for the control of disabling anxiety, fear, and
depression. Cyclic mood disorders can be regulated. Confusion, rage,
mania, hallucinations, and disabling mental states can be managed more
effectively. Interpersonal techniques, psychotherapy, and marriage
counseling have become more sophisticated. "Catatonia" has almost
disappeared, and the incidence of "schizophrenia" is declining. Genetic, environmental, and social sources of mental disturbance are now
much better understood. Special programs for the rehabilitation of
dancers and other performing artists are available in many major cities.
Long-term hospitalization of psychiatric patients is almost unheard of
nowadays.

Nijinsky looms as a magnificent example of a man who achieved
greatness and suffered miserably. Self-sacrificing, creative, destructive, and victimized by misfortune, he inspired an entire generation of
dancers, not to mention the musicians, painters, designers, sculptors,
writers, poets, and psychiatrists whose lives he profoundly affected.
Movement was his métier. It freed him from the confines of a small
environment in St. Petersburg, and propelled him into the heady world
of the Ballets Russes. He danced his way around the globe, and he leapt
into that mysterious universe called madness. He was a saint, a genius,

a martyr, and a madman. One can see him still, arcing in space, jumping and flapping, cavorting and flailing, shooting into the sky, suspended, laughing, crying, grimacing, screaming. He remains a myth, an apparition, an emblem, a creature of fantasy, a biological creation, a fleeting image of God. Nijinsky, the God of the Dance.

NOTES

1. Romola Nijinsky, *Last Years* 220.
2. Letter from Tamara Karsavina to Romola Nijinsky, 19 June 1947; letters from Curtis Brown Ltd., 7 July, 15 July, and 7 October 1947; letters from Barclays Bank Ltd., 15 July, 28 August, and 3 September 1947. Nijinsky Archives.
3. Brunner Sanatorium roster of admissions for 1947 reads "Vaslav Nijinsky, arrived from Mittersill, left for London."
4. Letter from Dr. Karl Rohr to Romola Nijinsky, 15 June 1950. Nijinsky Archives.
5. See Appendix A.
6. *Last Years*, 227, 230.
7. Nurse's notes, 3 August 1948–17 March 1949. Property of David Leonard, London.
8. I am grateful to Dr. Martin Bax for helping to track down Nijinsky's physicians in London.
9. *Last Years*, 228–229.
10. Letter from Eleanor Roosevelt to Romola Nijinsky, 7 April 1947. Nijinsky Archives.
11. Milton Shulman, "The Mists Are Dispersing for Nijinsky," *Evening Dispatch* (Edinburgh), 31 March 1948.
12. Letter from the Under Secretary of State to Romola Nijinsky, 24 June 1948; *Last Years*, 232–234.
13. Nurse's notes, 19–28 August 1948.
14. Ibid., 19 September 1948; *Last Years*, 236.
15. Nurse's notes, 26 September 1948–28 February 1949; *Last Years*, 236.
16. Letter of thanks from Queen Mary's private secretary to Romola Nijinsky, 21 March 1949. Nijinsky Archives.
17. Letter from Margaret Power to Romola Nijinsky, 17 June 1953. Nijinsky Archives.
18. Nurse's notes, 15–16 March 1949.
19. Personal communication from Otto Will, M.D., former clinical director of Chestnut Lodge.
20. *Last Years*, 239.
21. J. Kenéz, "János Plesch."
22. Ibid.
23. *Last Years*, 238–241.
24. Ibid., 243.
25. Richard Buckle, *Diaghilev*, 187.
26. *Last Years*, 243–244.
27. Letters to Romola Nijinsky from H. Montgomery Hyde, 10 January 1949, and from Queen Mary's private secretary, 25 October 1949. Nijinsky Archives.
28. BMR.
29. *Last Years*, 246.
30. Ibid., 247–248.
31. Ibid., 251.
32. Death Certificate D8-611194. Nijinsky Archives.
33. Newspaper clipping, "Nijinsky: They Pay Last Tribute," *Evening News*, 14 April 1950.
34. RBN, 537–538.
35. Letter from Nadia Legat to Romola Nijinsky, 14 June 1953. Nijinsky Archives.
36. Letter from Margaret Power to Romola Nijinsky, 17 June 1953. Nijinsky Archives.
37. Ibid.
38. Rolf Palm, *Nijinsky, Das Pferd des Jahrhunderts*.

Appendix A

NIJINSKY'S ELECTROCARDIOGRAMS

Let me first offer my interpretations of each of the tracings in chronologic order, and then I shall make some general comments. The first one is dated 9/19/36 and consists of just Standard Leads I and II. I cannot determine the heart rate or time intervals with any precision because there is no indication of the paper speed. Although some kind of a marker is present beneath each strip, the oscillation period between corresponding peak points is not given. However, on rough inspection, there may be a borderline first degree AV block, meaning simply a PR interval of about 0.20 seconds. A more striking finding, which is less equivocal, is the rather marked left axis of −30 degrees. This would signify at least a borderline left anterior fascicular block (also known as a left hemiblock). Because of the rather wide terminal S-wave in both leads I and II, the question of a possible right bundle branch block is also raised, but again one cannot be certain in the absence of true time measurement and the configuration of the precordial leads which, of course, were not included in cardiograms of this vintage.

The next tracing is dated 7/06/38 and appears to have been taken with the earlier type of instrument, which was a string galvanometer describing its graph on a moving photographic plate or strip. Again, there is no indication of the paper speed, but if it is the usual standard of 25 mm/second, then this strip shows a sinus bradycardia, again with a left anterior fascicular block and a possible right-sided intraventricular conduction delay. This tracing gives us the three standard bipolar leads and again suggests a slightly prolonged PR interval, consistent with a first degree AV block. Comparison with the previous tracing shows perhaps a slightly more marked left axis deviation, but otherwise no significant change.

A little more than a month later, on 8/16/38, a direct writing instrument was used to obtain a tracing under presumably standardized paper speed of 25 mm/second. This shows a sinus arrhythmia with normal intervals, including a PR measuring 0.18 and a QRS measuring 0.08, both intervals well within normal limits, and more strikingly a shift in axis rightward to −15 degrees, which no longer satisfies criteria for an intraventricular conduction defect. At least as far as can be judged from the three standard bipolar leads, this record is now entirely within normal limits.

On 4/19/40, another tracing consisting of the three standard bipolar leads was obtained, this time showing a reversion to left axis deviation of −35 degrees, thereby returning to the pattern of a left anterior fascicular block. The other intervals, including the PR and QRS, remain within normal limits.

The final tracing in this series is dated 2/18/48, and consists of the three standard bipolar leads and an approximation of a unipolar lead that was really a bipolar lead measuring the difference in potential between the back and a point on the anterior chest, which gives a graph that would be roughly comparable to the precordial V4 lead of today's customary 12-lead tracing. This shows a slightly prolonged PR interval of 0.21 seconds and moderately frequent premature ventricular contractions of unifocal origin. The left axis deviation is now much more marked with an axis of −45 degrees. According to current criteria, this is an abnormal record showing first degree AV block and left anterior fascicular block. The premature ventricular beats are probably benign in type and simply represent a somewhat irritable myocardium.

I doubt that any of these electrocardiograms would have been considered abnormal at the times they were taken. The concept of left anterior hemiblock, or more precisely left anterior fascicular block, to my knowledge was not a widely recognized abnormality at least until the early or possibly mid-1950s. By today's criteria, however, the presence of left axis deviation beyond −30 degrees in the anterior plane makes the tracing abnormal. When simultaneous precordial leads are examined in such cases, the marked left axis deviation is often associated with evidence of small anterior or anteroseptal myocardial infarctions, but certainly not always so. The curious reversion to normal in the above tracing of 8/16/38 suggests rather that a localized inflammatory process or perhaps a change in drugs with myocardial side-effects might have accounted for this change, rather than permanent scarring of the intraventricular conducting system that would have resulted from infarction. Moreover, in terms of subjective symptoms or cardiac function, it is very unlikely that this electrocardiographic finding would have had any recognized consequences. With respect to the first degree AV block, the prolongation of

PR interval is minimal and would have had no effect on cardiac function or rhythmicity. Thus, while most of the above tracings are abnormal, particularly the latest one of 2/18/48, it would be my guess that whatever the cause, little if any impairment of cardiac functional capacity resulted.

—Raphael B. Reider, M.D.*

*Dr. Reider is a consultant in internal medicine to the Health Program for Performing Artists and Assistant Clinical Professor of Medicine, University of California, San Francisco.

Appendix B

A FORMAL DIAGNOSIS OF NIJINSKY'S PSYCHOSIS

As has been emphasized throughout this book, diagnostic criteria change in the course of history, according to new scientific knowledge and theories about disease. A diagnosis can serve a purpose if it leads to an effective treatment or gives a good prediction about the patient's eventual outcome. Until the discovery in the fifties of drugs that could diminish the severity of the more blatant symptoms of psychotic patients, interest in the diagnostic classification of these patients was slight. A study published in 1970 showed that when lithium was introduced as a treatment for manic-depressive psychosis at the Johns Hopkins Hospital, the diagnosis of manic-depressive illness greatly increased while the diagnosis of schizophrenia decreased. It is unlikely that there was any real difference in the patient populations before and after the introduction of lithium treatment. A 1972 study compared hospital diagnoses in London and New York and found schizophrenia diagnosed nine times more frequently than mood disorders (depression and mania) in New York. In London the two diagnoses were used with about the same frequency. Studies of the patients showed no significant differences in their clinical states.

Ten years ago the American Psychiatric Association published its third revision of their *Diagnostic and Statistical Manual of Mental Disorders* (DSM III) in an effort to bring order to the problem of lack of standardization in diagnostic usage. Discrete diagnostic entities were described, while rigid, and to some, arbitrary criteria were listed. Psychotic disorders without known physical causes were almost all neatly put into two mutually exclusive categories: schizophrenia and mood disorders. Many critics thought this was no great advance from the diagnostic system Emil Kraepelin proposed one hundred years ago. Some skeptics suggested it would be more useful to classify the classifiers.

Eugen Bleuler, who examined and diagnosed Nijinsky in 1919 as schizophrenic in a manic excitement, coined the word schizophrenia in 1911 as a substitute for Kraepelin's dementia praecox. Neither Kraepelin nor Bleuler thought that they were describing a single disease, but a syndrome of probably heterogeneous etiology. Bleuler called it "the group of schizophrenias." The syndrome was described as "a specific type of alteration of thinking, feeling and relation to the external world which appears nowhere else in this particular fashion." Among characteristic symptoms were "weakening of judgment, of mental activity and of creative ability, the dulling of emotional interest and the loss of energy, loosening of the inner unity of intellect, emotion and volition in themselves and among one another." They also described disorders of association, incoherence or blocking of thought and speech, impoverishment of affect, inappropriate affect, inability to establish affective relationships with others, a tendency to divorce oneself from reality, bizarre and tangential thinking, stereotypy, mannerisms, and tics of various sorts.

According to these criteria, Nijinsky would have to be considered schizophrenic. But he also showed many of the characteristics of manic-depressive psychosis, or, as we call it today, bi-polar affective disorder: recurring, severe fluctuations in mood from mania to depression, psychomotor agitation or retardation, loss of energy, marked disturbances of sleep and appetite, delusional feelings of worthlessness and self-reproach, excessive and inappropriate guilt, diminished ability to think and concentrate, thoughts of death, death-wishes, and suicide.

The current use of DSM III as the bible of diagnosis has led to a decrease in the diagnosis of schizophrenia and an increase in the diagnosis of mood or affect disorders. Research has uniformly shown that mood disorders have a better outcome than schizophrenia, and there has been an understandable reluctance to make the diagnosis of schizophrenia. Bleuler himself, if we are to believe Romola Nijinsky, was astonished by the dancer's favorable response to insulin when he visited the Binswanger hospital in 1938, and brief remissions (without insulin) seem to have occurred in 1945 (when Nijinsky was reunited with Russians) and during his final years, in England.

DSM III, which uses a sort of Chinese menu to make a diagnosis, lists nine symptoms of "major depression" and requires the presence of five of them to make the diagnosis. Nijinsky exhibited all nine at one time or another. To make a diagnosis of "manic syndrome," DSM III lists seven symptoms and requires the presence of at least three of them. Once again, Nijinsky exhibited all seven symptoms on more than one occasion.

What then do we do in diagnosing someone who exhibits symptoms of both schizophrenia and a mood disorder? DSM III provides the answer: we make a diagnosis of Schizoaffective Disorder. DSM III requires that the patient has at one time have had symptoms of both a schizophrenic and a mood disturbance and at other times with psychotic symptoms but without mood symptoms. The relationship of Schizoaffective Disorder to schizophrenia is at the present time unclear. The prognosis is thought to be somewhat better than for schizophrenia, but not nearly as good as that for a mood disorder.

The current use of DSM III has also led to an increase in the diagnosis of personality disorders. One of these, called Narcissistic Personality, is defined in terms of the following criteria: grandiose sense of self-importance and uniqueness; preoccupation with fantasies of unlimited success, power, brilliance, beauty, or ideal love; exhibitionism, requiring constant attention and admiration; cool indifference or marked feelings of rage, inferiority, shame, humiliation, or emptiness in response to criticism; disturbances of interpersonal relationships, i.e., entitlement, exploitativeness, alternation between extremes of overidealization and devaluation of others, and lack of empathy. Nijinsky appears to have exhibited every one of these criteria.

DSM III gives little attention to catatonic symptoms and states that although common several decades ago they are now rare in Europe and North America. Nijinsky without question suffered from catatonic symptoms, but we include these as part of the schizoaffective diagnosis.

Thus, our final diagnosis according to DSM III of the tragic genius Vaslav Nijinsky must be Schizoaffective Disorder in a Narcissistic Personality.

—Joseph H. Stephens, M.D., and Peter Ostwald, M.D.*

*Dr. Stephens is Associate Professor of Psychiatry, Johns Hopkins University School of Medicine.

Bibliography

Abenheimer, Karl M. "The Diary of Vaslav Nijinsky," *The Psychoanalytic Review*, vol. 33 (1946), 257–284.

Ackerknecht, Erwin H. *A Short History of Psychiatry*, 2nd edition. New York: Hafner, 1968.

Adler, Alfred. *The Individual Psychology of Alfred Adler*, edited by H. L. Ansbacher and R. R. Ansbacher. New York: Basic Books, 1956.

Adler, Alfred. "The Preface to *The Diary of Vaslav Nijinsky*," *Archives of General Psychiatry*, vol. 38 (1981), 834–835.

Andreasen, Nancy C. "Negative symptoms in schizophrenia: Definition and reliability," *Archives of General Psychiatry*, vol. 39 (1982), 784–788.

Ansbacher, Heinz L. "Discussion of Alfred Adler's Preface to *The Diary of Vaslav Nijinsky*," *Archives of General Psychiatry*, vol. 38 (1981), 836–841.

Arnold O. H. "Results and Efficacy of Insulin Shock Therapy," in *Insulin Treatment in Psychiatry*, edited by Max Rinkel and Harold E. Himwich. New York: Philosophical Library, 1959.

Baer, Nancy Van Norman. *Bronislava Nijinska: A Dancer's Legacy*. San Francisco: The Fine Arts Museum, 1986.

Baskin, Denis G., Barbara J. Wilcox, Dianne P. Figlewicz, and Daniel Dorsa. "Insulin and insulin-like growth factors in the CNS," *TINS*, vol. 11 (1988), 107–111.

Beaumont, Cyril. *Bookseller at the Ballet: Memoirs 1891 to 1929: Incorporating The Diaghilev Ballet in London; A Record of Bookselling, Ballet Going, Publishing, and Writing*. London: Beaumont, 1975.

Beaumont, Cyril W. *Vaslav Nijinsky*. London: C.W. Beaumont, 1932.

Beaumont, Cyril. "The Wedding of Nijinsky," *Dancing Times*, vol. 44 (1964), 523–524.

Becker, George. *The Mad Genius Controversy: A Study in the Sociology of Deviance*. Beverly Hills, Calif.: Sage Publications, 1978.

Benois, Alexandre. *Reminiscences of the Russian Ballet*, translated by Mary Britnieva. London: Putnam, 1941.

Benson, David F. *Aphasia, Alexia, and Agraphia*. New York: Churchill and Livingstone, 1979.

Bernstein, Jeremy. "The Sporting Scene: Raking," *The New Yorker* (March 28, 1988), 88–98.

Billington, James H. *The Icon and the Axe: An Interpretive History of Russian Culture.* New York: Knopf, 1966.

Binswanger, Ludwig. *Zur Geschichte der Heilanstalt Bellevue in Kreuzlingen.* Privately published, 1957.

Binswanger, Ludwig. *Sigmund Freud: Reminiscences of a Friendship,* translated by Norbert Guterman. New York and London: Grune & Stratton, 1957.

Binswanger, Ludwig. "Insanity as Life-Historical Phenomenon and as Mental Disease: The Case of Ilse," in *Existence: A New Dimension in Psychiatry and Psychology,* edited by Rollo May, Ernest Angel, and Henri F. Ellenberger. New York: Basic Books, 1958.

Binswanger, Ludwig. "The Existential Analysis School of Thought," translated by Ernest Angel, pp. 191–213 in *Existence: A New Dimension in Psychiatry and Psychology,* edited by Rollo May, Ernest Angel, and Henri F. Ellenberger. New York: Basic Books, 1958.

Binswanger, Ludwig. *Being-in-the-World: Selected Papers of Ludwig Binswanger,* translation and critical introduction by Jacob Needleman. New York: Basic Books, 1963.

Blacker, Kay H. "Obsessive-Compulsive Phenomena and Catatonic States—A Continuum," *Psychiatry,* vol. 29 (1966), 185–194.

Bleuler, Eugen. "Dementia Praecox, oder die Gruppe der Schizophrenien," in *Handbuch der Psychiatrie,* edited by G. Aschaffenburg. Leipzig: Deuticke, 1911. (Translated into English by Joseph Zinkin and published by International Universities Press, New York, 1950.)

Bleuler, Eugen. *Lehrbuch der Psychiatrie.* Berlin: Springer, 1916. (First edition.)

Bleuler, Eugen. *Autistic Undisciplined Thinking in Medicine and How to Overcome It,* translated and edited by Dr. Ernest Harms. Darien, Conn.: Hafner Publishing Co., 1970.

Blum, David. "Profile" on violoncellist Yo Yo Ma, *The New Yorker* (May 1, 1989).

Bourman, Anatole, in collaboration with D. Lyman. *The Tragedy of Nijinsky.* Westport, Conn.: Greenwood, 1970. (Reprint).

Brunowski, Elizabeth J. A Psychobiographical Study of Vaslav Nijinsky. Ann Arbor, Mich.: University Microfilms International, 1984.

Buckle, Richard. *Diaghilev.* New York: Atheneum, 1979.

Buckle, Richard. *In the Wake of Diaghilev.* New York: Holt, Rinehart and Winston, 1983.

Buckle, Richard. *Nijinsky.* New York: Simon and Schuster, 1971. (Reprinted, with revisions, by Penguin Books, New York, 1980.)

Buckley, Peter. "Fifty Years After Freud: Dora, the Rat Man, and the Wolf-Man," *American Journal of Psychiatry,* vol. 146 (1989), 1394–1403.

Callaway, Enoch, Roy Halliday, Hilary Naylor, and Gail Schechter. "Effects of oral scopolamine on human stimulus evaluation," *Psychopharmacology,* vol. 85 (1985), 133–138.

Chaplin, Charlie. *My Autobiography.* New York: Simon and Schuster, 1964.

Charcot, Jean-Marie. *De l'expectation en médecine.* 1857.

Cocteau, Jean. *The Difficulty of Being,* translated by Elizabeth Sprigge, with an introduction by Ned Rorem. New York: Coward-McCann, 1957.

Comini, Alessandra. "Mother Russia at the Dawn of the Twentieth Century: From Mysticism to Mathematics," in *Unofficial Russian Art: Politics and Culture in the Soviet Union.* Las Vegas, Nev.: Reed Whipple Cultural Center, 1981.

Cope, Ralph. *To Be an Invalid: The Illness of Charles Darwin*. Chicago and London: University of Chicago Press, 1977.

Croce, Arlene. *Going to the Dance*. New York: Knopf, 1982.

Croce, Arlene. "Footnotes in the Sands of Time," *The New Yorker* (November 23, 1987), 140–148.

Croce, Arlene. "The Tiresias Factor" ("Profile" of Peter Anastos), *The New Yorker* (28 May 1990).

Darroch, Sandra Jobson. *Ottoline: The Life of Lady Ottoline Morrell*. London: Book Club Associates, 1976.

de La Grange, Henry-Louis. *Mahler*. Garden City, N.Y.: Doubleday, 1973.

Denby, Edwin. *Dance Writings,* edited by Robert Cornfield and William Mackay. New York: Knopf, 1986.

Dolin, Anton. *Pas de Deux: The Art of Partnering*. New York: Dover, 1967.

Dolin, Anton. *Last Words: A Final Autobiography*. London: Century, 1985.

Doran, Allen R., Alan Breier, and Alec Roy. "Differential Diagnosis and Diagnostic Systems in Schizophrenia," *Psychiatric Clinics of North America,* vol. 9 (1986), 17–33.

Dunning, Jennifer. "Essay on 'L'Après-midi d'un Faune,'"in *L'Après-midi d'un Faune; Vaslav Nijinsky 1912*. London: Dance Books, 1983.

Edel, Leon. "The Madness of Art," *American Journal of Psychiatry,* vol. 132 (1975), 1005–1012.

Ehrler, Paul. *Heliotherapie*. Rorschach: Nebelspalter-Verlag, 1985.

Einstein, Alfred. *Greatness in Music,* translated by César Saerchinger. New York: Oxford University Press, 1941.

Eksteins, Modris. *Rites of Spring: The Great War and the Birth of the Modern Age*. Boston: Houghton Mifflin, 1989.

Ellenberger, Henri F. *The Discovery of the Unconscious: The History and Evolution of Dynamic Psychiatry*. New York: Basic Books, 1970.

Erikson, Erik H. *Toys and Reasons: States in the Ritualization of Experience*. New York: Norton, 1977.

Feldman, David Henry, with Lynn T. Goldman. *Nature's Gambit: Child Prodigies and the Development of Human Potential*. New York: Basic Books, 1986.

Ferguson, Ian. "Nijinsky's Birthday?" *Dancing Times,* vol. LXXII, # 875 (August 1983), 862–864.

Fisher, H.A.L. *A History of Europe*. Boston: Houghton Mifflin, 1939.

Flach, Frederic (editor). *Affective Disorders*. New York: Norton, 1988.

Fokine, Michel. *Memoirs of a Ballet Master,* translated by Vitale Fokine and edited by Anatole Chujoy. Boston: Little, Brown & Company, 1961.

Fraser, John. "The Diaghilev Ballet in South America," *Dance Chronicle,* vol. 5 (1982), 11–23.

Freud, Sigmund. "Mourning and Melancholia [1917]," vol. 14, pp. 243–258, in *Standard Edition of the Complete Psychological Works of Sigmund Freud,* edited by J. Strachey. London: Hogarth Press, 1973.

Garafola, Lynn. *Diaghilev's Ballets Russes*. New York: Oxford University Press, 1989.

Gardner, Howard. *Frames of Mind*. New York: Basic Books, 1983.

Gelenberg, Alan J. "The Catatonic Syndrome," *The Lancet* (June 19, 1976), 1339–1341.

Georgotas, Anastasios and Robert Cancro (editors). *Depression and Mania*. New York: Elsevier, 1988.

Gold, Arthur and Robert Fiztdale. *Misia—The Life of Misia Sert*. New York: Knopf, 1980.

Gosling, F.G. *Before Freud: Neurasthenia and the American Medical Community*. Urbana and Chicago: University of Illinois Press, 1988.

Green, William A. et al. "Psychosocial Factors and Immunity," *Preliminary Report of the Meeting of the American Psychosomatic Society,* March 31, 1987.

Grigoriev, Serge L. *The Diaghilev Ballet 1909–1929*, translated and edited by Vera Bowen. London: Constable, 1953.

Gross, Valentine. *Nijinsky on Stage*, with a Chronology by Jean Hugo and an introduction and notes by Richard Buckle. London: Studio Hill, 1971.

Guest, Ann Hutchinson. "Nijinsky's Dance Notation," in *L'Après-midi d'un Faune, Vaslav Nijinsky*. London: Dance Books, 1983.

Haiko, Peter, Harald Leupold-Löwenthal, and Mara Reissberger. "'Die Weisse Stadt'— Der 'Steinhof' in Wien, Architektur als Reflex der Einstellung zur Geisteskrankheit," *Kritische Berichte,* vol. 9 (1981), 3–37.

Hanna, Judith Lynne. *Dance, Sex and Gender: Signs of Identity, Dominance, Defiance, and Desire*. Chicago and London: University of Chicago Press, 1988.

Hargrave, Susan Lee. "The Choreographic Innovations of Vaslav Nijinsky: Towards a Dance-Theatre," Ph.D. dissertation, Cornell University, 1980.

Hartley, Marsden. "The Drawings of Nijinsky," *Nijinsky, an Illustrated Monograph*, edited by Paul Magriel. New York: Henry Holt, 1946.

Haskell, Arnold, in collaboration with Walter Nouvel. *Diaghileff: His Artistic and Private Life*. New York: Da Capo Press, 1978. (Reprint.)

Heilbrun, Carolyn G. *Toward a Recognition of Androgyny*. New York: Knopf, 1973.

Hoff, Hans. "History of the organic treatment of schizophrenia," in *Insulin Treatment in Psychiatry,* edited by Max Rinkel and Harold E. Himwich. New York: Philosophical Library, 1959.

Holroyd, Michael. *Lytton Strachey: A Critical Biography*. New York: Holt, Rinehart and Winston, 1968. 2 vols.

Horowitz, Mardi J. *Stress Response Syndromes*. Northvale, N.J.: Aronson, 1986.

Hughes, H. Stuart. *Consciousness and Society: The Reorientation of European Social Thought 1890–1930*. New York: Knopf, 1961.

Humphrey, Doris. *The Art of Making Dances*. New York: Grove, 1959.

James, William. *Collected Essays and Reviews*. New York: Longmans, Green, 1920.

Jones, Robert Edmond. "Nijinsky and Til Eulenspiegel," in *Nijinsky, An Illustrated Monograph*, edited by Paul Magriel. New York: Henry Holt, 1946.

Jung, Carl Gustav. "Die Schizophrenie," in *Beiträge zur Schizophrenielehre der Zürcher Psychiatrischen Universitätsklinik Burghölzli (1902–1971),* edited by Manfred Bleuler. Darmstadt: Wissenschaftliche Buchgesellschaft, 1979.

Kahlbaum, Karl L. *Die Katatonie oder das Spannungsirresein* [1874], translated into English by Y. Levij, M.D., and T. Pridan, M.D., and published as *Catatonia*, with an introduction by George Mora, M.D. Baltimore, Md.: Johns Hopkins University Press, 1973.

Kalinowsky, Lothar R. and Paul H. Hoch (editors). *Shock Treatments, Psychosurgery, and Other Somatic Methods in Psychiatry,* 2nd edition. New York: Grune and Stratton, 1952.

Karlinsky, Simon. "Sergei Diaghilev; Public & Private," *Christopher Street* (March 1980), 50.

Karsavina, Tamara. *Theatre Street*. London: Dance Books, 1981. (Reprint.)

Kempf, Edward J. "Affective-Respiratory Factors in Catatonia," in *Selected Papers,* edited by Dorothy Clark Kempf, M.D., and John C. Burnham, Ph.D. Bloomington: Indiana University Press, 1974.

Kendall, R. E. *The Role of Diagnosis in Psychiatry.* Oxford: Blackwell, 1975.

Kenéz, J. "János Plesch (1878–1957): A Hungarian Doctor's Successful Life in Europe," *Therapia Hungarica,* vol. 26 (1978), 90–91.

Kennedy, Foster. "Preface" to Manfred Sakel, *The Pharmacological Shock Treatment of Schizophrenia,* translated by Joseph Wortis. New York: Nervous and Mental Disease Publishing Company, 1938.

Kirstein, Lincoln. *Nijinsky Dancing.* New York: Knopf, 1975.

Kirstein, Lincoln. *Four Centuries of Ballet: Fifty Masterworks.* New York: Dover, 1984.

Kirstein, Lincoln. *Dance—A Short History of Classic Theatrical Dancing.* Princeton, N.J.: Princeton Book Company, 1987. (Reprint.)

Krasovskaya, Vera. *Nijinsky,* translated by John E. Bowlt. New York: Schirmers, 1979.

Lange-Eichbaum, Wilhelm. *Genie, Irrsinn, und Ruhm: Eine Pathographie des Genies,* edited by W. Kurth. Munich: Reinhardt, 1961.

Laufer, Maurice W. and Eric Denhoff. "Hyperkinetic Behavior Syndrome in Children," *Journal of Pediatrics,* vol. 50 (1957), 463–474.

Legat, Nicolas. "Pages from the Memoirs of Nicolas Legat," translated by Sir Paul Dukes, *The Dancing Times* (May 1931), 125.

Lieven, Prince Peter. *The Birth of Ballets-Russes,* translated by L. Zarine. New York: Dover, 1973. (Reprint.)

Lifar, Serge. *Serge Diaghilev: His Life His Work His Legend, An Intimate Biography.* London: Putnam, 1940.

Lifar, Serge. *Ma Vie, from Kiev to Kiev,* translated into English by James Holman Mason. London: Hutchinson, 1970.

Lipowski, Z. J. "Somatization: The Concept and Its Clinical Application," *American Journal of Psychiatry,* vol. 145 (1988), 1358–68.

Loewenberg, Peter. "A Creative Epoch in Modern Science; Psychiatry at the Burghölsli, 1902–1912," *The American College of Psychoanalysis Newsletter,* vol. 16 (1985), 1–2.

Lohr, James B. and Alexander A. Wisniewski. *Movement Disorders: A Neuropsychiatric Approach.* New York and London: Guilford Press, 1987.

Macdonald, Nesta. *Diaghilev Observed: By Critics in England and the United States 1911–1929.* New York: Dance Horizons, 1975.

Magriel, Paul (editor). *Nijinsky, an Illustrated Monograph.* New York: Henry Holt, 1946.

Magrinat, Gaston, Jeffrey A. Danziger, Isabel C. Lorenzo, and Abraham Flemenbaum. "A Reassessment of Catatonia," *Comprehensive Psychiatry,* vol. 24 (1983), 218–228.

Mahler, Margaret S., Fred Pine, and Anni Bergman. *The Psychological Birth of the Infant.* New York: Basic Books, 1975.

Mahler Werfel, Alma. *And the Bridge Is Love.* New York: Harcourt, Brace, Jovanovich, 1958.

Mann, Thomas. *Pro and Contra Wagner,* translated by Allan Blunden. Chicago: University of Chicago Press, 1985.

Manschreck, Theo C. "Delusional (Paranoid) Disorders," pp. 816–829 in *Comprehensive Textbook of Psychiatry,* 5th edition, edited by Harold I. Kaplan and Benjamin J. Sadock. Baltimore: Williams and Wilkins, 1989.

Markevitch, Igor. *Être et avoir été; memoires.* Paris: Gallimard, 1980.

Massine, Léonide. *My Life in Ballet,* edited by Phyllis Hartnoll and Robert Rubens. London: Macmillan, 1968.

McNeal, Ann P., Andrea Watkins, Priscilla M. Clarkson, and Isabel Tremblay. "Lower Extremity Alignment and Injury in Young, Preprofessional, College and Professional Ballet Dancers," *Medical Problems of Performing Artists,* vol. 5 (1990), 83–88.

Meyer, Adolf. "A Cooperative Study of Cases of Stupors and Particularly of Catatonic Developments," unpublished paper given in 1926 to the American Psychiatric Association, now in *McCormick Collection, The State Historical Society of Wisconsin,* IE 499, 4 — 12/26, A. Meyer Folder.

Mirsky, D. S. *A History of Russian Literature,* edited and abridged by Francis J. Whitfield. New York: Knopf, 1966.

Money, Keith. *Anna Pavlova: Her Life and Art.* New York: Knopf, 1982.

Müller, Max. *Errinnerungen: Erlebte Psychiatriegeschichte 1920–1960.* Berlin: Springer, 1982.

Nabokov, Nicolas. *Old Friends and New Music.* Boston: Little Brown & Co., 1951.

Nectoux, Jean-Michel. *L'Après-midi d'un Faune: Mallarmé, Debussy, Nijinsky.* Paris: Les Dossiers du Musée D'Orsay, 1989.

Newman, Barbara. *Striking a Balance: Dancers Talk About Dancing.* Boston: Houghton Mifflin, 1982.

New York State Department of Mental Health. *Insulin Shock Therapy, Study by the Temporary Commission on State Hospital Problems.* New York, 1944.

Nijinska, Bronislava. *Early Memoirs,* translated and edited by Irina Nijinska and Jean Rawlinson. New York: Holt, Rinehart and Winston, 1981.

Nijinsky, Kyra. *She Dances Alone,* a film starring Kyra Nijinsky; Robert Dornhelm, director; produced by Frederico DeLaurentiis and Earl Mack.

Nijinsky, Romola. *Nijinsky.* New York: Simon and Schuster, 1934.

Nijinsky, Romola (editor). *The Diary of Vaslav Nijinsky.* New York: Simon and Schuster, 1936. (Reprinted by University of California Press, Berkeley, 1971.)

Nijinsky, Romola. *The Last Years of Nijinsky.* New York: Simon and Schuster, 1952.

Nijinsky, Romola. Videotape of *Et liv,* a documentary by Donya Feuer (J. Andersen, producer), Norwegian television, 1975. (Available in The New York Public Library, Dance Collection, Lincoln Center.)

North, Carol, and Remi Cadort. "Diagnostic Discrepancy in Personal Accounts of Patients with 'Schizophrenia,'" *Archives of General Psychiatry,* vol. 38 (1981), 133–137.

Ostwald, Peter. "Psychotherapeutic Approaches in the Treatment of Performing Artists, *Medical Problems of Performing Artists,* vol. 2 (1988), 131–136.

Palm, Rolf. *Nijinsky: Das Pferd des Jahrhunderts.* Munich: Bertelsmann, 1973.

Parker, Derek. *Nijinsky, God of the Dance.* Wellingborough, Eng.: Equation, 1988.

Pickering, Sir George. *Creative Malady.* London: Oxford University Press, 1974.

Porter, Roy. *A Social History of Madness: The World Seen Through the Eyes of the Insane.* New York: Weidenfeld & Nicolson, 1988.

Rambert, Marie. *Quicksilver: An Autobiography.* London: Macmillan, 1972.

Reiss, Françoise. *Nijinsky, A Biography,* translated by Helen and Stephen Haskell. London: Adam and Black, 1960.

Rinkel, Max, and Harold E., Himwich. eds. *Insulin Treatment in Psychiatry.* New York: Philosophical Library, 1959.

Romanovsky-Krassinsky, Princess. *Dancing in Petersburg, The Memoirs of Kschessinska,* translated by Arnold Haskell. London: Gollancz, 1960.

Rubinstein, Arthur. *My Young Years.* New York: Knopf, 1973.

Rubinstein, Arthur. *My Many Years.* New York: Knopf, 1980.

Rush, John and Kenneth Z. Altshuler (editors). *Depression: Basic Mechanisms, Diagnosis, and Treatment.* New York: Guilford Press, 1986.

Sakel, Manfred. *Neue Behandlungsmethode der Schizophrenie.* Vienna: Moritz Perles, 1935.

Sakel, Manfred. *The Pharmacological Shock Treatment of Schizophrenia,* translated by Joseph Wortis. New York: Nervous and Mental Disease Publishing Company, 1938.

Sakel, Manfred. *Schizophrenia.* New York: Philosophical Library, 1958.

Sakel, Manfred. "Address at the University of Vienna at the 30-year Celebration of His Discovery," pp. 375–380 in *Insulin Treatment in Psychiatry,* edited by Max Rinkel and Harold E. Himwich. New York: Philosophical Library, 1959.

Sandoz, Maurice. *Diaghilev-Nijinsky and Other Vignettes.* New York: Kamin, 1956.

Sataloff, Robert, Alice Brandfonbrener, and Richard Lederman (editors). *Textbook of Performing-Arts Medicine.* New York: Raven Press, 1990.

Sert, Misia. *Misia and the Muses: The Memoirs of Misia Sert.* New York: John Day, 1953.

Sokolova, Lydia. *Dancing for Diaghilev,* edited by Richard Buckle. London: John Murray, 1960.

Solomon, Maynard. *Beethoven.* New York: Schirmer, 1978.

Stern, Daniel. *The Interpersonal World of the Infant.* New York: Basic Books, 1985.

Sternlicht, Harold C., James Payton, Gerhardt Werner, and Michael Rancurello. "Multiple Personality Disorder: A Neuroscience and Cognitive Psychology Perspective." *Psychiatric Annals,* vol. 19 (1989), 448–455.

Strauss, Richard and Hugo von Hofmannsthal. *The Correspondence Between Richard Strauss and Hugo von Hofmannsthal,* translated by Hanns Hammelmann and Ewald Osers. Cambridge: Cambridge University Press, 1980.

Strauss-Hofmannstahl Briefwechsel. Zürich: Atlantis, 1950.

Stravinsky, Igor and Robert Craft. *Memoirs and Commentaries.* Garden City, N.Y.: Doubleday, 1960.

Stravinsky, Vera and Robert Craft. *Stravinsky in Pictures and Documents.* New York: Simon and Schuster, 1978.

Sullivan, Mark D. "Organic or Functional? Why Psychiatry Needs a Philosophy of Mind," *Psychiatric Annals,* vol. 20 (1990), 271–277.

Taper, Bernard. *Balanchine: A Biography.* New York: Times Books, 1984.

Taylor, Paul, *Private Domain.* New York: Knopf, 1987.

Temoshok, Lydia, Craig Van Dyke, and Leonard S. Zegans (editors). *Emotions in Health and Illness: Theoretical and Research Foundations.* New York: Grune & Stratton, 1983.

Terr, Lenore C. "Terror Writing by the Formerly Terrified; a Look at Stephen King," in *The Psychoanalytic Study of the Child,* vol. 44 (1989), 369–390.

Thompson, Oscar. *Debussy: Man and Artist.* New York: Tudor, 1940.

Van Vechten, Carl. "The Russian Ballet and Nijinsky," in *Nijinsky, An Illustrated Monograph,* edited by Paul Magriel. New York: Henry Holt, 1946.

Walser, Robert. "Der Tänzer," pp. 61–62 in *Deutschland Erzählt,* edited by Bruno von Wiese. Frankfurt: Fischer, 1962.

Waugh, Anne Wilson. "Vaslav Nijinsky: Genius and Schizophrenia," *American Imago,* Vol. 35 (1978), 221–37.

Wender, Paul. *The Hyperactive Child, Adolescent and Adult: Attention Deficit Disorder Through the Lifespan.* New York: Oxford University Press, 1987.

West, Louis J. "Dissociative Reaction," pp. 885–899 in *Comprehensive Textbook of Psychiatry,* edited by A. M. Freedman and H. I. Kaplan. Baltimore: Williams and Wilkins, 1967.

Whitworth, Geoffrey. *The Art of Nijinsky.* London: Chatto and Windus, 1913.

Wiesel, Elie. *Twilight.* New York: Summit Books, 1988.

Wiley, Roland John. "About Nijinsky's Dismissal," *Dancing Times* (December 1979), 176.

Wiley, Roland John. *Tchaikovsky's Ballets.* Oxford: Clarendon, 1985.

Wilson, Colin. *The Outsider.* New York: Delta, 1956. (Eleventh printing.)

Wilson, S. A. Kinnier. *Neurology,* edited by A. Ninian Bruce. London: Edward Arnold & Co., 1940.

Winnicott, Donald. *Playing and Reality.* London: Tavistock, 1971.

Wortis, Joseph. "The History of Insulin Shock Treatment," in *Insulin Treatment in Psychiatry,* edited by Max Rinkel and Harold E. Himwich. New York: Philosophical Library, 1959.

Wortis, Joseph. "In Memoriam—Manfred Sakel, M.D., 1900–1957," *American Journal of Psychiatry,* vol. 115 (1958), 288.

Zlobin, Vladimir. *A Difficult Soul; Zinaida Gippius,* edited, annotated, and with an introductory essay by Simon Karlinsky. Berkeley: University of California Press, 1980.

Index